D0210088

# Kyoto

"All you've got to do is decide to go
and the hardest part is over.

## So go!"

TONY WHEELER, COFOUNDER – LONELY PLANET

WITHDRAWN

THIS EDITION WRITTEN AND RESEARCHED BY
Chris Rowthorn

# Contents

(Left) **Ponto-chō p56**
Spot geisha on this
atmospheric street.

(Above) **Tea ceremony
p173** Take part in an
age-old ritual.

(Right) **Nishiki Market
p55** See an amazing
array of local delicacies.

# Welcome to Kyoto

*Kyoto is old Japan writ large: quiet temples, sublime gardens, colourful shrines and geisha scurrying to secret liaisons.*

## Temples, Shrines & Gardens

There are said to be over 1000 Buddhist temples in Kyoto. You'll find true masterpieces of religious architecture, such as the retina-burning splendour of Kinkaku-ji (the famed Golden Pavilion) and the cavernous expanse of Higashi Hongan-ji. Within the temple precincts are some of the world's most sublime gardens, from the Zen masterpiece at Ryōan-ji to the riotous paradise of moss and blossoms at Saihō-ji. And then there are the Shintō shrines, monuments to Japan's indigenous faith. The mother of all shrines, Fushimi Inari-Taisha, has mesmerising arcades of vermillion *torii* (shrine gates) spread across a mountainside.

## Cuisine

Few cities of this size offer such a range of excellent restaurants. Work your way through the entire spectrum of Japanese food, from impossibly refined cuisine known as *kaiseki* to hearty plebeian fare such as *rāmen*. There's also a wide range of French, Italian and Chinese restaurants, where the famed Japanese attention to detail is paired with local ingredients to yield fantastic results. Best of all, many of Kyoto's restaurants are in traditional wooden buildings, where you can gaze over intimate private gardens while you eat.

## The Japanese Way of Life

While the rest of Japan has adopted modernity with abandon, the old ways are hanging on in Kyoto. Take a morning stroll through the textile district of Nishijin and watch the old Kyoto ladies emerge from their *machiya* (traditional townhouses) to ladle water onto their stoops. Visit an old *shōtengai* (market street) and admire the ancient speciality shops: tofu sellers, fishmongers, pickle vendors and tea merchants. Then join the locals at a local *sentō* (public bath) to soak away the cares of the day.

## The Changing Seasons

No educated Kyotoite would dare send a letter without making a reference to the season. The city's geisha change their hair ornaments 12 times a year to celebrate the natural world. And Kyoto's confectioners create seasonal sweets that reflect whatever is in bloom. Starting in February and lasting through the summer, a series of blossoms burst open like a string of firecrackers: plums, daphnes, cherries, camellias, azaleas and wisteria, among many others. And don't forget the *shinryoku* (the new green of April) and the brilliant autumn foliage of November.

## Why I Love Kyoto

By Chris Rowthorn, Author

I love Kyoto because it's rich, deep and incredibly liveable. I've spent over 20 years in the city and I still make new discoveries every day. If I vary my daily walking route just a bit, I am bound to find something new: a secret temple, an interesting shop or a great place to eat. The city is surrounded by mountains on three sides and the hiking is excellent. It's also one of the most bike-friendly cities on earth. I love the people and the dialect they speak. Finally, it's just the right size: not too big and not too small.

**For more about our author, see p224.**

Top: Daigo-ji (p74)

# Kyoto's
# Top 10

## Fushimi Inari-Taisha *(p70)*

**1** This sprawling Shintō shrine is arguably Japan's most arresting visual spectacle. Thousands of vermillion *torii* (entrance gates to a Shintō shrine) line paths that criss-cross this mountain in southeast Kyoto. Visit the main hall and then head up the hill towards the summit. Be prepared to be utterly mesmerised – it's quite unlike anything else on earth. If you have time, do the circular pilgrimage route around the top of the mountain. And don't be afraid to get lost – that's part of the fun at Fushimi.

◉ *Central Kyoto*

## Gion District *(p82)*

**2** Gion, Kyoto's traditional entertainment district, is the best place in the city to catch a glimpse of 'old Japan'. With no fewer than three geisha districts scattered about, you stand a good chance of spotting a geisha scurrying to an appointment. But geisha are only part of the story here: Gion also contains some of the most picturesque lanes in Kyoto, including Shimbashi, which may be the single most attractive street in all of Asia. And don't forget Minami-za Theatre, the city's traditional kabuki theatre.

☆ *Southern Higashiyama*

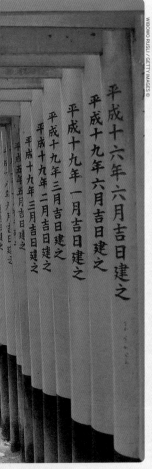

### Arashiyama Bamboo Grove
*(p110)*

**3** Western Kyoto is home to one of the most magical places in all Japan: the famed bamboo grove in Arashiyama. The visual effect of the seemingly infinite stalks of bamboo is quite different from any forest we've ever encountered – there's a palpable presence to the place that is utterly impossible to capture in pictures, but don't let that stop you from trying. If you've seen *Crouching Tiger, Hidden Dragon,* you have some idea of what this place is about.

⊙ *Arashiyama & Sagano*

### Kyoto Imperial Palace Park *(p71)*

**4** Home to the Kyoto Gosho (Imperial Palace), this vast swathe of green in the city centre is a true sanctuary. Often overlooked by tourists, who rush to see the city's temples and shrines, the Kyoto Imperial Palace Park is the perfect place to spend a lazy afternoon reading a book, napping, playing with the kids or picnicking. The variety of trees here is amazing, and there's usually something in bloom. In spring, don't miss the fantastic *shidare-zakura* (weeping cherry trees) at the north end of the park.

⊙ *Central Kyoto*

### Kinkaku-ji *(p103)*

**5** Talk about eye candy: the gold-plated main hall of this immensely popular temple in northwest Kyoto is one of the most impressive sights in all Kyoto – especially if your tastes run to the grand and gaudy. The main hall rises above its reflecting pond like an apparition. If you are lucky enough to be here on a bright sunny day, you almost need sunglasses to look at it. Go early on a weekday morning to avoid the crush of people that descend on the temple each day.

⊙ *Northwest Kyoto*

## Ginkaku-ji (p94)

**6** A paradise tucked at the base of the Higashiyama mountains, Kyoto's famed Silver Pavilion is everything a Buddhist temple ought to be. The eponymous pavilion looks over a tranquil pond, and the expansive stroll garden is sublime. Make your way past the unique sand mounds (used to reflect moonlight into the main hall for moon-viewing ceremonies), then climb the pathway to a lookout that offers panoramic views over the entire city. The autumn foliage here is among the best in the city.

◉ *Northern Higashiyama*

## Chion-in (p81)

**7** Called by some 'the Vatican of Pure Land Buddhism', this temple complex in the Southern Higashiyama district is a thriving hub of religious activity. The main hall is one of the largest temple structures in Japan. Take off your shoes, go inside, take a seat on the floor and allow yourself to be transported to blissful realms by the chanting of the monks. Then head up the hill to admire the enormous 70-tonne temple bell. This is truly the best place in Kyoto to see how the Japanese practise Buddhism. RIGHT: MONKS IN TRADITIONAL CLOTHING

◉ *Southern Higashiyama*

6

## Blossoms & Foliage (p71)

**8** Starting with daphnes and plums in February and ending with crimson maple leaves in December, the year in Kyoto is a delightful progression of colourful blossoms and foliage. Sure, everyone wants to see the cherries of early April, but don't despair if you can't make it then: even in winter there are blossoms of some sort to be found. For the widest variety of blossoms and foliage in the city, head to the Kyoto Imperial Palace Park.

⊙ *Central Kyoto*

## Nishiki Market *(p55)*

**9** There's something strangely enjoyable about touring a food market where over half of the goods on display are utterly baffling (is it a food, a spice or some sort of Christmas tree decoration?). Even after years in Japan, we're not sure about some of the things on sale here, but we love wandering Kyoto's Nishiki Market. The place positively oozes 'old Japan' atmosphere and you can imagine what it was like here before someone decided to attach the word 'super' to the word 'market'.

🏠 *Downtown Kyoto*

## Kurama-dera *(p120)*

**10** This mountain temple in the hills north of Kyoto (a mere 30 minutes away by direct train) is easily the most pleasant half-day trip out of the city. New-Agey Kyotoites claim that UFOs regularly land here. We're not sure about that, but we can certainly understand why visitors from near and far love this place: the walk through the soaring cedar trees to the main hall near the summit is pure magic. If you have time, hike over the top to the village of Kibune.

💮 *Kitayama Area & North Kyoto*

# What's New

### Hokuriku Shinkansen

The Hokuriku Shinkansen cuts travel time between Tokyo and Kanazawa to just over two hours. Kanazawa, only 2½ hours northeast of Kyoto by comfortable express train, is a brilliant add-on to any Kyoto trip. The new Hokuriku Shinkansen makes it extremely easy and comfortable to do the Tokyo–Kyoto–Kanazawa loop, which is one of the top one-week Japan travel itineraries.

### Cheap Yen

The Japanese yen is cheaper than it's been in years, meaning that Kyoto is more affordable than ever. It's now among the cheapest tourist cities in the developed world.

### The Heisei Chishinkan Wing of Kyoto National Museum

A superb new wing of the Kyoto National Museum was opened to the public in September of 2014. (p82)

### Ritz-Carlton Kyoto

The Ritz-Carlton Kyoto was unveiled in 2014. The hotel occupies a superb position in Downtown Kyoto, overlooking the Kamo-gawa river and the Higashiyama mountains. (p139)

### Ryokan Helpline

Kyoto city government recently created a multilingual helpline to make it easier for ryokan owners to communicate with foreign guests.

### Free Public Wi-fi

Kyoto City recently installed wi-fi hotspots across the city specifically for tourists to use. (p184)

### Wider Sidewalks

Kyoto City is expected to start work soon on a plan to widen the sidewalks (footpaths) along Shijo-dōri, Kyoto's main downtown thoroughfare.

### Better Bus Passes

Kyoto's one- and two-day bus passes now cover city buses all the way out to Arashiyama, one of Kyoto's main sightseeing districts.

### Machiya Boom

Kyoto's traditional townhouses, known as *machiya*, are being given a new lease of life as restaurants, shops, bars and even accommodation for travellers.

### Expanded Nonsmoking Areas

Kyoto has banned outdoor smoking downtown, around Kyoto Station and in the Kiyomizu/Sannen-zaka/Ninen-zaka sightseeing areas.

### Giant New Shopping Outlets

Kyoto has been undergoing a retail renaissance in the past few years. New offerings include Æon Mall Kyoto (p52), which is home to most major Japanese retailers, and Tokyu Hands (p66), a gadget and gift paradise.

For more recommendations and reviews, see **lonelyplanet. com/kyoto**

# Need to Know

**For more information, see Survival Guide (p175)**

## Currency
Yen (¥)

## Language
Japanese

## Visas
Visas are issued on arrival for most nationalities for stays of up to 90 days.

## Money
ATMs that accept foreign cards are available in post offices and some convenience stores. Credit cards are accepted in most hotels and department stores, but only some restaurants and ryokan.

## Mobile Phones
Only 3G phones work in Japan. SIM cards are very hard to find. Mobile phone rental is common and easy.

## Time
Japan Standard Time (GMT/UTC plus nine hours)

## Tourist Information
Kyoto City Tourist Information Center (TIC; Map p213; ☎343-0548; ☺8.30am-7pm), located in the main concourse on the 2nd floor of the Kyoto Station building, runs between the *shinkansen* (bullet train) station and the front of the station.

## Daily Costs

### Budget:
### Less than ¥10,000

➡ Guesthouse accommodation: ¥3000

➡ Two simple restaurant meals: ¥2200

➡ Train/bus transport: ¥1500

➡ One temple/museum admission: ¥500

➡ Snacks, drinks, sundries: ¥1000

### Midrange:
### ¥10,000–20,000

➡ Business hotel accommodation: ¥9000

➡ Two midrange restaurant meals: ¥4000

➡ Train/bus transport: ¥1500

➡ Two temple/museum admissions: ¥1000

➡ Snacks, drinks, sundries: ¥2000

### Top End:
### More than ¥20,000

➡ First-class hotel accommodation: ¥20,000

➡ Two good restaurant meals: ¥6000

➡ Train/bus transport: ¥1500

➡ Two taxi rides: ¥3500

➡ Two average temple/museum admissions: ¥1000

## Advance Planning

**Several months before** Make accommodation reservations several months in advance if you are travelling in cherry-blossom season (March and April) and the autumn-foliage season (October and November).

**One month before** Buy a Japan Rail Pass. This pass can save you a lot of money if you are planning to travel extensively by rail within Japan after visiting Kyoto.

**A few days before** Buy a pair of comfortable slip-on walking shoes (you'll be taking your shoes off a lot in Kyoto).

## Useful Websites

**Lonely Planet** (www.lonelyplanet.com/kyoto) Up-to-date info on every aspect of Kyoto.

**Kyoto Visitor's Guide** (www.kyotoguide.com) Great all-around Kyoto info.

**HyperDia** (www.hyperdia.com/en/) Train schedules in English.

**Inside Kyoto** (www.insidekyoto.com) Monthly event information and much more.

## WHEN TO GO

Kyoto is crowded in the cherry-blossom (late March to early April) and autumn-foliage (November) seasons; be sure to advance book your accommodation.

## Arriving in Kyoto

**Kansai International Airport**
JR Haruka Airport trains to Kyoto Station (¥2850, 1¼ hours); Osaka Airport Transport buses to Kyoto Station (¥2550, 1½ hours); shared MK taxi vans to hotels, inns and houses in Kyoto (¥3600, around 1½ hours).

**Osaka International Airport**
Osaka Airport Transport buses to Kyoto Station (¥1310, 55 minutes); shared MK taxi vans to hotels, inns and houses in Kyoto (¥2400, around one hour).

**Kyoto Station** *Shinkansen* (bullet trains) from Tokyo to Kyoto Station take about 2½ hours and cost ¥13,080 for an unreserved seat. There are also *shinkansen* from cities such as Hiroshima, Osaka, Nagoya and Yokohama.

For much more on **arrival,** see p176.

## Getting Around

Kyoto is a compact city with an excellent public transport system.

➡ **Taxi** The best way to get from Kyoto Station to your hotel or ryokan unless you're on a tight budget (in which case the bus or subway is a good choice).

➡ **Subway** Gets you quickly between north and south (the Karasuma subway line stops at Kyoto Station) or east and west (the Tōzai subway line runs between Higashiyama and the west side of the city).

➡ **Bus** For destinations not well served by the subway lines (including sights in the northwest of the city such as Kinkaku-ji).

➡ **Bicycle** A brilliant way to explore Kyoto (the city is mostly flat).

➡ **Walking** Kyoto is a walker's paradise.

For much more on **getting around,** see p179.

## Sleeping

Kyoto has a wide range of foreigner-friendly accommodation, with some of the best ryokan (traditional Japanese inns) in Japan. First-class hotels are also well represented, along with cheaper business hotels and even a few capsule hotels. You'll also find plenty of guesthouses and the odd youth hostel scattered about.

### Useful Websites

➡ **Lonely Planet** (www. lonelyplanet.com/japan/ kansai/kyoto/hotels) A wide range of hotels, ryokan and guesthouses.

➡ **Japanese Guesthouses** (www.japaneseguesthouses. com) A site that specialises in ryokan bookings.

For much more on **sleeping,** see p133.

# Top Itineraries

## Day One

### Southern Higashiyama (p78)

 Start your Kyoto experience by heading to the city's most important (and popular) sightseeing district: Southern Higashiyama. This area contains the thickest concentration of worthwhile sights in Kyoto.

>  **Lunch** Sobadokoro Shibazaki (p87); filling noodles and a lacquerware gallery.

### Northern Higashiyama (p91)

If you have the energy after lunch, continue heading north along the base of the Higashiyama mountains. Start at **Nanzen-ji** and follow the **Path of Philosophy (Tetsugaku-no-Michi)** all the way to **Ginkaku-ji**, stopping at **Hōnen-in** along the way.

> **Dinner** Omen (p99); brilliant udon and more within minutes of Ginkaku-ji.

### Downtown Kyoto (p53)

After dinner, head back to your lodgings (which may very well be located in Downtown Kyoto). You'll probably be pretty walked out if you've done both Southern and Northern Higashiyama in one day, so a short amble around the streets of Downtown Kyoto will probably be sufficient to round out this day.

## Day Two

### Arashiyama & Sagano (p108)

 After exploring the Higashiyama area, you'll want to head west to the Arashiyama and Sagano district, which has a dense concentration of first-rate sights. Start at **Tenryū-ji** and work your way north to **Giō-ji** or **Adashino Nembutsu-ji**.

>  **Lunch** Buddhist vegetarian fare at Shigetsu (p115).

### Northwest Kyoto (p101)

It makes sense to stay on the west side of town in the afternoon of this day. Take a taxi from the end of the morning's route to **Kinkaku-ji** and/or **Ryōan-ji**. If you still have energy to burn, you can check out **Myōshin-ji** late in the afternoon.

> **Dinner** Delicious eel in retro surroundings at Kyōgoku Kane-yo (p60).

### Downtown Kyoto (p53)

This is a pretty big day, with a fair bit of transport, so you probably won't feel like doing too much walking on this evening. We recommend some strolling around Downtown Kyoto. The atmospheric lane of **Ponto-chō** is a great place to wander, as is **Kiyamachi-dōri**, particularly the stretch between Shijō-dōri and Gojō-dōri.

WIBOWO RUSLI / GETTY IMAGES ©

Ponto-chō (p56)

# Day Three

## Southeast Kyoto (p75)

 You'll probably be feeling like a break from the crowds about now. For this reason we suggest heading to Southeast Kyoto. Here, you'll find two absolutely stunning attractions: **Tōfuku-ji** (don't forget to enter the Hōjō Garden) and **Fushimi Inari-Taisha**, Kyoto's mind-blowing Shintō sanctuary.

> **Lunch** Sushi at Tsukiji Sushisei (p60) downtown after the morning's touring.

## Downtown Kyoto (p53)

After exploring Southeast Kyoto in the morning and eating lunch downtown, it makes sense to spend the afternoon exploring Downtown Kyoto and perhaps doing some shopping. Be sure to take a pass through the wonderful **Nishiki Market**, then visit one of the awesome *depachika* (department store food floors) at nearby **Daimaru** or **Takashimaya** department stores. Then, walk through the **Teramachi Shopping Arcade**. When the covered section runs out, keep following Teramachi as far as **Marutamachi-dōri** (the last few blocks contain some of Kyoto's best traditional shops).

> **Dinner** Sublime tempura at Yoshikawa (p62).

## Gion (p82)

 This day involves less walking than the preceding two, so it's ideal for an evening walk through Gion district's **Shimbashi** and **Hanami-kōji** areas.

# Day Four

## Kitayama Area (p116)

 Today's the day to step off the beaten track and immerse yourself in some greenery. Heading north into the Kitayama (Northern Mountains) is the perfect way to relax after three days of urban sightseeing. Heading to **Kurama** and hiking over the hill and down to **Kibune** is our favourite day trip out of the city. Other options include **Ōhara** or **Takao**.

> **Lunch** Noodles by the temple steps at Yōshūji (p123) in Kurama.

## Central Kyoto (p68)

If you spend the morning in the Kitayama, you will probably return to Kyoto city in the early afternoon. If this is your last day in the city, you might want to spend the remainder of the day shopping for souvenirs in Downtown Kyoto. But, if you still have the energy for sightseeing, you might consider visiting the enclosed Zen world of **Daitoku-ji**. Other options include **Nijō-jō** or a stroll in the **Kyoto Imperial Palace Park**.

> **Dinner** Try *kaiseki* (Japanese haute cuisine) at Kiyamachi Sakuragawa (62).

## Downtown Kyoto or Gion (p82)

 If you haven't done it yet, take a stroll through the Gion district and consider a stop in **Bar Main Higashiyama**. If you have, consider instead a stroll through **Ponto-chō** where you might stop for a drink in a bar such as **Atlantis**.

# If You Like...

## Temples & Shrines

**Nanzen-ji** A world of Zen temples and subtemples scattered amid the trees. (p93)

**Ginkaku-ji** The famed 'Silver Pavilion' boasts one of Kyoto's finest gardens. (p94)

**Hōnen-in** A secluded retreat a short walk from the perpetually crowded Ginkaku-ji. (p96)

**Kinkaku-ji** A golden apparition rises above a tranquil reflecting pond – arguably Kyoto's most impressive single sight. (p103)

**Tenryū-ji** This temple takes *shakkei* (borrowed scenery) to a new level – it borrows the entire sweep of Arashiyama's beautiful mountains. (p110)

**Daitoku-ji** Each subtemple at this Zen complex has a sublime garden: a must for garden lovers with an aversion to crowds. (p72)

**Myōshin-ji** This is a walled complex containing many fine subtemples and one of Kyoto's most famous gardens, Taizō-in. (p106)

**Kurama-dera** Climb a path lined with towering cedar trees to this mountain temple in the hills north of the city. (p120)

**Chion-in** A vast Pure Land Buddhist temple – the Vatican of Japanese Buddhism. (p81)

**Shōren-in** The crowds usually give this Southern Higashiyama temple a miss – don't make that mistake. (p85)

## Museums

**Kyoto National Museum** The special exhibits here are often spectacular and the permanent

CLAIRE TAKACS / GETTY IMAGES ©

Kyoto Botanical Gardens (p73)

collection is a good introduction to Japanese art. (p82)

**Kyoto Municipal Museum of Art** Holds two of Kyoto's best yearly art shows: the Kyoten and the Niten. Other special exhibits are often worth a look. (p98)

**National Museum of Modern Art** The permanent collection here is small but interesting and the special exhibits are usually excellent. (p98)

**Kyoto International Manga Museum** If you are a fan of Japanese manga (comics), you simply must make a pilgrimage to this fine downtown museum. (p56)

## Japanese Performance Arts

**Minami-za** Kabuki (stylised Japanese theatre) is a visual spectacle like none other, and Minami-za, Kyoto's main kabuki theatre, is the place to see it. (p88)

**Miyako Odori** Held in April, this is the grandest of all Kyoto geisha dances. If you are in town, ensure you *do not miss it*. (p88)

**Kamogawa Odori** Held in May by the Ponto-chō geisha district, this is a small-scale but charming geisha dance. (p64)

**Kyō Odori** The Miyagawa-chō geisha district holds its dance in April and it's a must-see affair. (p88)

**Kitano Odori** Held up north in the Kamishichiken geisha district every April, this is a quaint and touching dance. (p39)

**Gion Odori** The only major geisha dance held in autumn (November), this is put on by the Gion Higashi geisha district. (p90)

## Food & Drink

**Omen** Noodles are only the beginning of the offerings at this comfortable and welcoming restaurant in Northern Higashiyama. (p99)

**Roan Kikunoi** The perfect place to enter the temple of *kaiseki* (Japanese haute cuisine). (p62)

**Kyōgoku Kane-yo** Sit at the tables downstairs or on the tatami mats upstairs at this popular downtown *unagi* (eel) specialist with 'Old Japan' atmosphere. (p60)

**Yoshikawa** We don't know which is more impressive here: the sublime tempura or the perfect Japanese garden. (p62)

**Ippūdō** Just the thought of the noodles and *gyōza* (dumplings) makes us want to dash downtown to this bustling *rāmen* (noodle soup) joint. (p57)

**Nishiki Market** Head to this downtown food market to see the wild and wonderful ingredients that go into Kyoto cuisine preparation. (p55)

**Sake Bar Yoramu** Work your way through a sampling set of the good stuff at this tiny downtown sake specialist. (p63)

**Tsukiji Sushisei** This sushi specialist is the perfect place for a sushi fix while exploring Downtown Kyoto. (p60)

## Gardens

**Ryōan-ji** Ponder the meaning of the 15 magical rocks at Japan's most famous Zen garden. Head here early to avoid the crowds. (p105)

**Tōfuku-ji** This abstract expressionist garden is like no other in Kyoto – and it's also one of the city's most beautiful. (p75)

**For more top Kyoto spots, see the following:**

➡ Eating (p29)
➡ Drinking & Nightlife (p36)
➡ Entertainment (p38)
➡ Shopping (p40)
➡ Temples & Shrines (p42)

**Heian-jingū** The stroll gardens behind the main hall of this Shintō shrine are worth the trip when the cherries bloom in April. (p98)

**Kyoto Botanical Gardens** The cherries in these stunning and expansive gardens are superb and the greenhouse contains some exquisite orchid species. (p73)

**Ginkaku-ji** The gardens at the 'Silver Pavilion' have it all: luxuriant moss, a bamboo forest, waterfalls, ponds and maples that turn crimson in November. (p94)

**Sentō Gosho** This walled garden in the heart of the city is often overlooked by visitors – don't make that mistake. (p71)

**Katsura Rikyū** The garden at this detached imperial villa is sublime. For fans of Japanese gardens, a pilgrimage here is a must. (p112)

**Murin-an** Blink and you'll miss this tiny pocket garden. That would be a shame as it's a charming little sanctuary in an elegant villa. (p95)

**Ōkōchi Sansō** Wander the paths and admire the views over the city, the maple leaves and the wonderful hidden contemplative corners of this Arashiyama villa. (p110)

**Saihō-ji** The nickname for this temple is Koke-dera (Moss Temple) and this place more than lives up to its name. (p112)

## Shopping & Markets

**Tenjin-san Market** Held on the 25th of each month at Kitano Tenman-gū, there are always treasures hidden among the bric-a-brac here. (p107)

**Kōbō-san Market** Held on the 21st of each month at Tō-ji, this is a good market for used kimonos and antiques. (p77)

**Nishiki Market** Kyoto's main downtown food market is a must-see attraction. There are also plenty of souvenir shops scattered among the food shops. (p55)

**Zōhiko** A treasure trove of sumptuous Japanese lacquerware. (p65)

**Chion-ji Tezukuri-ichi** *Tezukuri* means 'handmade' and that's what you'll find at this market held on the 15th of every month. (p100)

**Tōzandō** A paradise for the practitioner of Japanese martial arts, with some great samurai armor on display. (p100)

**Wagami no Mise** This Japanese paper *(washi)* specialist is a dreamland for creative types. (p65)

**Ippōdō Tea** Kyoto's finest tea shop is worth a visit for the ambience and aroma alone. (p65)

## Scenic Strolls

**Daimonji-yama (**p96) There is no finer walk in the city than the 30-minute climb to the viewpoint above Ginkaku-ji in Northern Higashiyama. (p96)

**Kurama** (p120) The climb to the mountain temple of Kurama-dera is a classic (continue to Kibune if possible). (p120)

**Fushimi Inari-Taisha** Paths lined with *torii* (Shintō shrine gates) criss-cross this mountain shrine in Southeast Kyoto. The walking here is great. (p70)

**Kyoto Imperial Palace Park** If you prefer your strolling on the flat, the broad arcades of Kyoto's Central Park are just the ticket. (p71)

**Kamo-gawa riverbank** Make like a local and take your morning or evening constitutional on the banks of Kyoto's main river.

**Path of Philosophy (Tetsugaku-no-Michi)** The stroll along this canal in Northern Higashiyama is beautiful in any season. (p96)

## Traditional Architecture

**Katsura Rikyū** Connoisseurs often rank this imperial villa as the finest example of Japanese traditional architecture. Join a tour and judge for yourself. (p112)

**Ōkōchi Sansō** Perched on a hillside overlooking Arashiyama and Kyoto, this traditional villa is the stuff of dreams. The gardens are spectacular. (p110)

**Byōdō-in** One of the few extant examples of Heian-era architecture, Byōdō-in will make you wish that a lot more survived. (p132)

**Gion** (p82) Head to the preserved streets of this entertainment district: Hanami-kōji and Shimbashi. Both are lined with lovely traditional wooden buildings. (p82)

**Nishijin** Kyoto's weaving district, Nishijin is home to the thickest concentration of *machiya* (traditional townhouses) in the city. (p105)

# Month by Month

## January

**Kyoto comes to life after the lull of the New Year holiday (things open on 2 or 3 January). It's cold, but not too cold for travelling and the city is uncrowded.**

### 🎎 Hatsu-mōde

The first three days of the New Year (1 to 3 January) are when Kyotoites make the all-important first Shintō shrine visit of the year. Kyoto's three most popular shrines for this are Yasaka-jinja, Heian-jingū and Fushimi Inari-Taisha. Transport will be crowded.

### 🏃 Tōshiya (Archery Contest)

Held at Sanjūsangen-dō from 8am to 4pm on the Sunday closest to 15 January (check with the Tourist Information Center; TIC). Hundreds of kimono-clad archers gather for a competition of accuracy and strength.

## February

**It's still cold in February and snow is possible in the city (but usually melts by noon). The mountains north of the city may be covered in snow all month.**

### 🎎 Setsubun Matsuri at Yoshida-jinja

Held on the day of *setsubun* (2, 3 or 4 February; check with the TIC), this festival marks the last day of winter. People climb up to Yoshida-jinja in the Northern Higashiyama area to watch a huge bonfire in which old good-luck charms are burned. The action starts at dusk.

## March

**By March it's starting to warm up. Plums usually bloom in mid-March and the cherry blossoms usually start to emerge by month's end. It's a pleasant, uncrowded time.**

## April

**Spring is in full swing by April, although mornings and evenings can still be chilly. The cherry blossoms usually peak in early April, which means thick crowds in the sightseeing districts.**

### 🎎 Cherry-Blossom Viewing

*Hanami* (cherry-blossom viewing parties) take place all over town when the cherries blossom in early April. Top spots include Maruyama-kōen, Kyoto Imperial Palace Park and the Kamo-gawa riverbanks. In the evening, join the crowds on Gion's Shimbashi.

## May

**May is one of the best months to visit Kyoto. It's warm and sunny, and the blossoms are out wherever you go. Note the dates of the Golden Week holidays (29 April to 5 May) and book well in advance.**

### 🏃 Yabusame at Shimogamo-jinja

The annual *yabusame* (horseback archery) event

on 3 May is one of the most exciting spectacles in Kyoto. Held on Tadasu-no-mori, the tree-lined approach to Shimogamo-jinja, the action runs from 1pm to 3.30pm.

### ☆ Aoi Matsuri (Hollyhock Festival)

One of Kyoto's leading festivals involves a procession of imperial messengers in ox carts and 600 people dressed in traditional costume; hollyhock leaves are carried or used as decoration. The procession begins around 10am on 15 May from the Kyoto Imperial Palace and heads for Shimogamo-jinja where ceremonies take place. It sets out again at 2pm and arrives at Kamigamo-jinja at 3.30pm.

## June

**June is generally a lovely time to travel in Kyoto – it's warm but not sweltering and the new green on the trees is beautiful. However, it is also the month of the rainy season, so expect humidity and occasional downpours.**

### ☆ Takigi Nō

Held at Heian-jingū on 1 to 2 June, this is a festival of *nō* (stylised dance-drama) held by flaming torchlight in the outdoor courtyard.

## July

**When the rainy season ends in late June or early July, the heat cranks up and it can be very hot and humid. Still, if you don't**

**mind sweating a bit, travel is perfectly possible.**

### ☆ Gion Matsuri

Gion Matsuri is one of Japan's biggest festivals and it's the peak event of the Kyoto year. The main event is held on the morning of 17 July, when huge festival floats are hauled through Downtown Kyoto starting at around 9am and continuing until just before noon. On the three evenings leading up to the 17th, huge crowds of people, many dressed in light cotton robes called *yukata*, flock to the Shijō-Karasuma area to inspect the floats parked in waiting along the streets (and, more importantly, to eat and drink). A slightly smaller parade of floats is held from 9am to noon on 24 July. Exact routes and details on smaller events related to the festival can be found online.

## August

**August is hot and humid in Kyoto, but the skies are usually sunny and most tourist sites are uncrowded, except during the O-Bon holiday in mid-August – book ahead.**

### ☆ Daimon-ji Gozan Okuribi

Mistakenly referred to by many as Daimon-ji-yaki (literally, burning of Daimon-ji), this impressive event on 16 August is held to bid farewell to the souls of ancestors. Enormous fires are lit in the form of Chinese characters or other shapes on five mountains. The main fire is the character for *dai* (great),

on Daimonji-yama, behind Ginkaku-ji, which is lit at 8pm. The other fires are lit at 10-minute intervals thereafter, working anticlockwise (east to west). Watch this event from the banks of the Kamo-gawa, Yoshida-yama or pay for a rooftop view from a hotel.

### ☆ Tōki Matsuri

Kyoto's largest ceramics fair, held from 7 to 10 August, is a good place to snap up some bargains, especially late on the last day. The market runs along Gojō-dōri, between Kawabata and Higashiōji. It's a 10-minute walk from Gojō Station on the Keihan line.

## September

**Sometime in early to mid-September, the heat breaks and temperatures become very pleasant in Kyoto. Skies are generally clear, making it a great time to travel.**

## October

**October is one of the best months to visit Kyoto: the weather can be warm or cool and it's usually sunny. The leaves start changing colour at the end of the month, particularly in the hills.**

### ☆ Jidai Matsuri (Festival of the Ages)

One of Kyoto's big three festivals features more than 2000 people dressed in costumes ranging from the 8th to the 19th centuries parading from the Kyoto Imperial Palace to Heian-jingū on 22 October.

(Top) Men in traditional costumes at Jidai Matsuri
(Bottom) Gion Matsuri parade

## 🎏 Kurama Hi Matsuri (Kurama Fire Festival)

*Mikoshi* (portable shrines) are carried through the streets of this mountain hamlet, accompanied by young men in loincloths bearing giant flaming torches. The festival climaxes at 10pm on 22 October at Yuki-jinja in Kurama. Trains to and from Kurama will be packed (we suggest going early and returning late).

# November

**November rivals October and April/May as the best months to visit. Skies are clear and temperatures are pleasantly cool. Foliage usually peaks late in the month.**

# December

**December is cool to cold in Kyoto. The autumn foliage may still be good early in the month. Most shops, museums and restaurants shut down from 29 or 30 December, but transport runs and accommodation is open. Almost all temples and shrines stay open throughout.**

## 🎏 Ōmisoka (New Year's Eve)

People gather in their homes on 31 December to feast then visit local temples to ring temple bells before heading to their local shrine to pray for a lucky year. Bell ringing happens around midnight and shrine visiting happens all evening on New Year's Eve and for the first few days of the New Year. Yasaka-jinja and Heian-jingū are great places to enjoy the action.

# With Kids

*Kyoto is great for kids. The usual worries aren't an issue in ultra-safe and spotless Japan. Your biggest challenge will be keeping your children entertained. The very things that many adults come to Japan to see (temples, gardens and shrines) can be a bit boring for kids.*

WIBOWO RUSLI / GETTY IMAGES ©

Kiyomizu-dera (p80)

## Keeping Kids Happy

The best way to keep your kids happy in Kyoto is to mix your diet of traditional Japanese culture with things kids are more likely to enjoy. Fortunately, there is no shortage of child-friendly attractions in Kyoto, from game centres to parks and a steam locomotive museum. If your kids are older, you have lots of options: go on a hike in the mountains around the city, rent a bicycle and explore, or take them to youth-oriented shopping areas downtown such as Shingyōgoku shopping arcade and the Shijō-Kawaramachi shopping district.

## Where Do the Children Play?

On a sunny day in Kyoto, local parents of young children tend to congregate in the Okazaki-kōen area. This region of Northern Higashiyama features a park, playing fields, a playground, and two museums. Best of all, the area is completely flat and has wide pavements, perfect for those with strollers. It can also be accessed by subway (take the Tōzai subway line to Higashiyama Station and walk north along Shira-kawa Canal). Tip: the pond behind the Kyoto Municipal Museum of Art (p98) is perfect for picnics. The Kamo-gawa riverbank is also great for kids and on hot days they can wade in the river. The area around Demachiyanagi is one of the most popular spots for parents and children to play.

## Getting Around with a Stroller

Kyoto is pretty easy to navigate with a stroller. Most train stations have elevators, as do large department stores and museums. The major streets downtown have wide pavements, but once you get into the narrower streets, pavements may not exist at all. Fortunately, Kyoto drivers are relatively sane. While taxis do not have child seats, most drivers will leap out and help you get your stroller into the trunk. You can usually get your stroller into restaurants – but you'll find that some fancy places are not willing to accommodate a stroller and/or fussy children. Go for larger 'family restaurants'. As for sightseeing, most areas of Kyoto are relatively easily negotiated with strollers, but the Southern Higashiyama area has some hills and stairs. Most temples in Kyoto do not have access ramps – you have to carry your child inside (it's usually safe to leave the stroller outside).

## Kid-Friendly Attractions

### Fushimi Inari-Taisha

Your kids will be entranced by the hypnotic arcades of *torii* (entrance gates) at this sprawling Shintō shrine (p70). There's plenty of room to run and play here.

### Arashiyama Monkey Park Iwatayama

Both kids and adults will find the antics of the monkeys at this park (p113) fascinating, and it's easy to combine this with a trip to the sights of Arashiyama.

### Kyoto Imperial Palace Park

The Central Park of Kyoto, this sprawling expanse (p71) of fields, trails, ponds and woods is perfect for a picnic, walk or bicycle ride with the kids.

### Umekōji Steam Locomotive Museum

With 18 vintage steam locomotives, one of which you can ride, this museum (p74) is a must for train-crazy boys and girls.

### Kyoto Botanical Gardens

For a picnic, a stroll or a frisbee toss, these gardens (p73) are just the ticket. And the cherry blossoms last longer here than almost anywhere in town.

### Kaleidoscope Museum of Kyoto

This charming little museum (p56) will delight curious and creative young ones. It's an ideal rainy day activity and it's close to both subway lines.

### Kiyomizu-dera

With fortunes to take, holy water to drink and an incredible underground sanctuary, this temple (p80) will keep even the most hyper kids happy for an hour or two.

### Shinkyōgoku Shopping Arcade

This is where Japanese kids come on their school excursions (after they've seen the obligatory temples). If it's tacky, cheap and gaudy, you'll find it here.

## Eating with Kids

Food can be an issue in Japan if your child is a picky eater. Let's face it: even adults can be put off by some of the things found in Japanese cuisine – asking a kid to eat sea urchin might simply be too much.

With this in mind, choose your restaurants carefully. If you're going to a *kaiseki* (Japanese haute cuisine) restaurant, have your lodgings call ahead to see if they can rustle up some kid-friendly dishes. Ditto if you'll be dining at your ryokan.

There are quite a few so-called 'family restaurants' in Kyoto and these usually serve something finicky kids can stomach (pizza, fried chicken, French fries etc). These places often serve special children's meals.

You'll also find all the usual Western fast-food chains represented in Kyoto. And there are supermarkets and convenience stores everywhere, so you can self-cater for kids who simply won't eat what's on offer in restaurants.

### NEED TO KNOW

➡ **Changing facilities** Department stores, some train stations and public buildings.

➡ **Cots** Available in hotels (book in advance) but not ryokan.

➡ **Health** Diseases are not a big problem.

➡ **Highchairs** Available in some restaurants.

➡ **Kids' menus** Usually only in 'family restaurants'.

➡ **Nappies (diapers)** Widely available.

➡ **Strollers** Available, but consider bringing your own.

➡ **Transport** Comfortable and safe; child seats available in rental cars but not taxis.

# For Free

*You may think that the cost of sightseeing in Kyoto is going to require taking a second mortgage on your home. Luckily there's plenty you can do for free. Indeed, you could fill at least a week with activities that are absolutely free. Here are just a few.*

Kyoto Station

## Temples

The general rule is that you can tour most of the grounds for free, but you pay to enter the gardens and the main hall. There are exceptions to this, so if you see a temple, don't hesitate to march in and check it out. If the main hall is open, remove your shoes and enter. If you have to pay, someone will let you know. Following are some temples with spacious grounds that can be toured free of charge.

### Nanzen-ji

The sprawling grounds of this superb Northern Higashiyama temple (p93) make it our favourite temple for a stroll.

### Chion-in

You can tour the grounds *and* enter the main hall at this temple (p81) for free.

### Tōfuku-ji

At the south end of the Higashiyama mountains, this fine Zen temple (p75) has expansive grounds.

### Hōnen-in

This tiny Pure Land paradise (p96) is a must-see. There is a gallery in one of the halls that often has free art exhibits.

## Shrines

Like temples, you can usually tour the grounds of Shintō shrines completely free of charge. Of course, some faithful believers pay a special fee to enter the *haiden* (prayer hall) to be blessed, but this is unlikely to concern the tourist. If there is a treasure hall or garden, you may have to pay to enter, but otherwise, shrines are free.

### Fushimi Inari-Taisha

One of Kyoto's top sights (p70), the only money you're likely to drop here is to buy a drink after climbing the mountain.

### Heian-jingū

This vast popular Northern Higashiyama shrine (p98) has a huge gravel-strewn courtyard that you can explore for free. Note that you must pay a fee to enter the gardens.

DAVID CLAPP / GETTY IMAGES ©

### Shimogamo-jinja

Take a stroll through the magnificent Tadasu-no-Mori (Forest of Truth) that leads to the main hall at this shrine (p73).

### Yasaka-jinja

Overlooking Gion both physically and spiritually, this popular shrine (p85) is highly recommended in both the daytime and evening, when the lanterns make it magical.

## Parks

Kyoto is studded with parks, ranging from the huge Imperial Palace Park to tiny pockets in residential neighbourhoods where local kids gather to play. All of Kyoto's parks are free.

### Kyoto Imperial Palace Park

Kyoto's Central Park (p71) is a treasure that many visitors to the city overlook. It has everything from baseball diamonds to carp ponds.

### Maruyama-kōen

Above Yasaka-jinja and smack on the main Southern Higashiyama sightseeing route, this lovely park (p84) is a great spot for a picnic. It's also Kyoto's most popular *hanami* (cherry-blossom viewing) spot.

## Imperial Properties

All of Kyoto's imperial properties can be toured for free – Kyoto Imperial Palace, Sentō Gosho, Shūgaku-in Rikyū Imperial villa and Katsura Rikyū imperial villa. Keep in mind, however, that only the main one, the Kyoto Imperial Palace, allows children (as long as they are accompanied by adults). Children below the age of 20 are not permitted at the other three.

## Other Attractions

### Kamo-gawa

Like the Kyoto Imperial Palace Park, this is a great place to spend a relaxing afternoon strolling and picnicking. In summer you'll be treated to free fireworks shows as local youths hold impromptu *hanabi taikai* (fireworks festivals).

### Nishiki Market

It costs nothing to wander through this wonderful market (p55). Of course, you might find something that you just *have* to buy...

### Department Stores

Have a look at the fabulous variety of goods for sale in Kyoto's department stores. While you're there, stop by the food floor and snag some free food samples.

### Kyoto Station

Kyoto's new station building is pretty impressive and the view from the rooftop observatory is the best you'll get – short of paying to ascend Kyoto Tower or expending the energy to climb Daimonji-yama.

### Festivals

There's nothing like a colourful Kyoto festival, and they're always free. If you're lucky, you might even be asked to participate.

### Hikes

It doesn't cost anything to enjoy Kyoto's natural beauty. There are myriad hikes in the mountains that surround the city. The best of these is the Daimonji-yama (p96) climb.

## Saving Money

Here are some tips that will really help you stretch your hard-earned yen:

**Sleep cheap** You can find private rooms in business hotels, guesthouses and budget ryokan for as low as ¥4000 per person if you look around. If you're willing to share rooms in guesthouses or hostels, you can find beds for as low as ¥2000 per person.

**Fine dine in the daytime** Many of Kyoto's finest restaurants serve pared-down versions of their dinnertime fare at lunch. A *kaiseki* (Japanese haute cuisine) restaurant that can charge ¥20,000 a head at dinner might serve a lunchtime set for as little as ¥2500.

**Rent a cycle** Kyoto is largely flat and drivers are generally safe and courteous, making Kyoto a great city to explore on bicycle.

**Buy a bus, train or subway pass** Some great ticket deals (p179) are available for Kyoto and the surrounding areas.

# Like a Local

*Kyoto is a relatively small city, but its population is well educated and up on the latest trends from Tokyo and the rest of the world. It's fun to leap right in and enjoy some of the finer things in life with the discerning locals of this surprisingly cosmopolitan city.*

## Eating & Drinking Like a Local

If you want to eat like a local, head downtown to the streets surrounding Kiyamachi-dōri and into that tight warren of lanes that lie between Oike-dōri and Shijō-dōri (north–south, respectively) and Kawaramachi-dōri and Karasuma-dōri (east–west, respectively). Here you'll find hundreds of restaurants packed cheek by jowl, and hungry Kyotoites out prowling among them, searching for the new, the tasty and the innovative.

Rather than heading to a particular restaurant, fashionable Kyotoites are just as likely to stroll the area looking for something that catches their eye. Knowing this, restaurants tend to display pictures of their food or actual meals out the front to lure them. Only high-end traditional Japanese restaurants maintain the reserve of an almost blank facade (it's worth noting that some of the best meals can be found behind such imposing fronts).

These days European restaurants are all the rage, and you'll find a huge variety of French, Italian and Spanish restaurants competing with traditional Japanese eateries. In addition, there is an almost endless supply of intimate unique shops that serve meals, along with the usual international coffee chains.

Japanese sweets and tea are having something of a renaissance and you can find chic teahouses popping up all over town. These tend to attract well-to-do Japanese women with plenty of free time and disposable income. They're a nice break from well-known international coffee chains and they're less crowded and more comfortable.

## Shopping Like a Local

On weekends Kyotoites pour into Downtown Kyoto to browse the myriad shops, arcades, department stores and malls. Well-heeled shoppers tend to favour Daimaru and Takashimaya department stores (both on Shijō-dōri), while pretty young things and those of more moderate means gravitate towards Fuji Daimaru Department Store (Shijō-dōri) and malls such as Mina and OPA (both on Kawaramachi-dōri). Those with more eclectic taste prefer the independents that fill the streets west of Kawaramachi-dōri and north of Shijō-dōri.

Meanwhile, those in search of bargains on electronics, cameras and household goods head to the giant retailers such as Yodobashi Camera and Bic Camera, both near Kyoto Station. More options can be found nearby in the Æon Mall Kyoto, just south of Kyoto Station.

## Kyoto Dos & Don'ts

➡ Do dress neatly, but not formally, when going into nice shops, department stores, museums and restaurants.

➡ Don't speak with an 'outdoor voice' in restaurants and other public places.

➡ Don't wear sleeveless T-shirts, flip-flops (thongs), cut-off shorts or track suits (sweats) when out exploring.

➡ Don't smoke while walking around – it's considered bad form and it's illegal on the streets of Downtown Kyoto.

Kaiseki (haute cuisine) dishes

# Eating

*Kyoto is famous the world over for its temples and gardens. What few people outside Japan realise is that Kyoto is also one of the world's great food cities. In fact, when you consider atmosphere, service and quality, it's hard to think of a city where you get more bang for your dining buck.*

## Kyoto's Restaurant Scene

Kyoto punches way above its weight in the culinary arena. Among the reasons for this is that Kyoto was the centre of the country for most of its history, and its chefs had to please the most demanding palates in the realm: the imperial court, the nobility and the heads of the main religious sects.

Even after losing the imperial court to Tokyo, Kyoto remained a major sightseeing destination for both domestic and international visitors, meaning a continual stream of demanding diners passing through. In addition, Kyoto sits atop excellent groundwater (essential for making good tofu, sake and tea), and has very fertile soil for growing vegetables in the city and surrounding areas. In fact, you can still find several distinct subspecies of vegetables in the city's markets known as *kyō-yasai* (Kyoto vegetables). The result is a relatively small city packed with fine restaurants.

Naturally, Kyoto is full of restaurants that specialise in local cuisine. In addition, you'll find all the other major types of Japanese

## NEED TO KNOW

### Price Ranges

In our listings, we've used the following price codes to represent the cost of a meal for one person, not including a drink:

| ¥ | under ¥1000 |
|---|---|
| ¥¥ | ¥1000 to ¥5000 |
| ¥¥¥ | over ¥5000 |

### Opening Hours

Most restaurants are open 11am to 2pm for lunch and 6pm to around 11pm for dinner, although some places (especially cafes) stay open all afternoon as well. Most places close one day a week (Monday or Tuesday being the most common for a day off).

### Tipping

There is no tipping in restaurants or cafes.

### Credit Cards

Credit cards can be used at some mid-range and high-end places, especially those in department stores. Credit cards cannot be used in most small local eateries. To be safe, *never* count on being able to use a credit card at a restaurant in Kyoto.

### Reservations

You won't need a reservation at most of the restaurants we recommend. However, at traditional high-end restaurants (*kaiseki* etc), a reservation is a good idea. If you don't speak Japanese, the easiest thing to do is simply ask someone at the place you're staying to call and make the reservation for you.

### Dress Code

For casual restaurants, you can wear whatever is comfortable. For nicer places, smart casual is usually fine (note that you'll feel very out of place in shorts at a high-end restaurant in Kyoto).

cuisine and regional specialities represented in Kyoto: sushi, *rāmen* (noodle soup), tempura, *okonomiyaki* (savoury Japanese cabbage pancakes) and a lot of dishes you may not have heard of.

In addition to Japanese cuisine, Kyoto is packed with good international restaurants, particularly French, Italian, Chinese and Thai, as well as the usual international chains that you'll find elsewhere.

Even if you're travelling on a tight budget, you shouldn't worry about going broke to eat well in Kyoto. There are scores of restaurants offering full meals in the ¥600 to ¥800 range, especially at lunchtime. And some of the city's esteemed high-end eateries have been forced to slash their prices and offer various specials in the hope of luring cost-cutting clientele.

## Kyoto Specialities

*Kyō-ryōri* (Kyoto cuisine) is a style of cooking that evolved out of Kyoto's land-locked location and age-old customs of the imperial court. The preparation of dishes makes ingenious use of fresh seasonal vegetables and emphasises subtle flavours, revealing the natural taste of the ingredients. *Kyō-ryōri* is selected according to the mood and hues of the ever-changing seasons, and the presentation and atmosphere in which it's enjoyed are as important as the flavour.

### KAISEKI

*Kaiseki* (Japanese haute cuisine) is the pinnacle of refined dining, where ingredients, preparation, setting and presentation come together to create a dining experience quite unlike any other. Born as an adjunct to the tea ceremony, *kaiseki* is a largely vegetarian affair (though fish is often served).

One usually eats *kaiseki* in the private room of a *ryōtei* (traditional, high-class Japanese restaurant) or ryokan. The meal is served in several small courses, giving one the opportunity to admire the plates and bowls, which are carefully chosen to complement the food and seasons. Rice is eaten last (usually with an assortment of pickles) and the drink of choice is sake or beer. The Kyoto version of *kaiseki* is known as *kyō-kaiseki* and it features a variety of *kyō-yasai* (Kyoto vegetables).

A good *kaiseki* dinner costs upwards of ¥10,000 per person. A cheaper way to sample the delights of *kaiseki* is to visit a *kaiseki* restaurant for lunch. Most places offer a boxed lunch containing a sampling of their dinner fare for around ¥2500. An easy way to sample *kaiseki* is by booking a night in a 1st-class Kyoto ryokan and asking for the breakfast/dinner option.

### TOFU-RYŌRI

Kyoto is famed for its tofu (soybean curd), a result of the city's excellent water and large population of (theoretically) vegetarian Buddhist monks. There are numerous *tofu-ya-san* (tofu makers) scattered throughout the city and a legion of exquisite *yudōfu* (tofu cooked in an iron pot) restaurants – many are concentrated in Northern Higashiyama along the roads around Nanzen-ji and in the Arashiyama area. One typical Kyoto tofu by-product is called *yuba*, sheets of the chewy, thin film that settles on the surface of vats of simmering soy milk. This turns up in many ryokan meals and *kaiseki* restaurants.

## Eating in a Japanese Restaurant

When you enter a restaurant, you'll be greeted with a hearty *'irasshaimase'* (Welcome!). In all but the most casual places the waiter will next ask you *'nan-mei sama'* (How many people?). Answer with your fingers, which is what the Japanese do. You will then be led to a table, a place at the counter or a tatami room.

At this point you will be given an *o shibori* (a hot towel), a cup of tea and a menu. The *o shibori* is for wiping your hands and face. When you're done with it, roll it up and leave it next to your place. Now comes the hard part: ordering. If you don't read Japanese, you can use the romanised translations we provide to help you, or direct the waiter's attention to the Japanese script. If this doesn't work, there are two phrases that may help: *'o-susume wa nan desu ka'* (What do you recommend?) and *'o-makase shimasu'* (Please decide for me).

When you've finished eating, you can signal for the bill by crossing one index finger over the other to form the sign of an 'x'. This is the standard sign for 'bill please'. You can also say *'o-kanjō kudasai'*. Remember there is no tipping in Japan and tea is free of charge. Usually you will be given a bill to take to the cashier at the front of the restaurant, but some places allow you to pay while seated at your table. Only the bigger and more international places take credit cards, so cash is always the surer option.

When leaving, it is polite to say to the restaurant staff, *'gochisō-sama deshita'*, which means 'It was a real feast'. Note that if you are invited to dine in a private home, it's also polite to use this expression when finishing the meal and some people repeat the phrase when leaving the house.

### EATING ETIQUETTE

When it comes to eating in Japan, there are quite a number of implicit rules, but they're fairly easy to remember. If you're worried about putting your foot in it, relax – the Japanese don't expect you to know what to do, and they are unlikely to be offended as long as you follow the standard rules of politeness from your own country. Here are a few major points to keep in mind:

**Chopsticks in rice** Do not stick your *hashi* (chopsticks) upright in a bowl of rice. This is how rice is offered to the dead in Buddhist rituals. Similarly, do not pass food from your chopsticks to someone else's. This is another funeral ritual.

**Polite expressions** When eating with other people, especially when you're a guest, it is polite to say *'itadakimasu'* (literally 'I will receive') before digging in. This is as close as the Japanese come to saying grace. Similarly, at the end of the meal, you should thank your host by saying *'gochisō-sama deshita'*, which means, 'It was a real feast'.

**Kampai** It is bad form to fill your own glass. You should fill the glass of the person next to you and wait for them to reciprocate. Raise your glass a little off the table while it is being filled. Once everyone's glass has been filled, the usual starting signal is a chorus of *kampai,* which means 'cheers'.

**Slurp** When you eat noodles in Japan, it's perfectly OK, even expected, to slurp them. In fact, one of the best ways to find *rāmen* (egg noodle) restaurants in Japan is to listen for the loud slurping sound that comes out of them!

## Major Cuisine/Restaurant Types

With the exception of *shokudō* (all-round restaurants) and *izakaya* (Japanese pubeateries), most Japanese restaurants concentrate on a speciality cuisine. Following we discuss the main types of restaurants you are likely to encounter and we provide sample menus for each type. If you familiarise yourself with the main types of restaurants and what they serve, you'll be able to get the most out of Kyoto's incredible culinary scene.

### SHOKUDŌ

A *shokudō* is the most common type of restaurant in Japan, and is found near train stations, tourist spots and just about any other place where people congregate. Easily distinguished by the presence of plastic food displays in the window, these inexpensive places usually serve a variety of *washoku* (Japanese dishes) and *yōshoku* (Western dishes).

At lunch, and sometimes dinner, the easiest meal to order at a *shokudō* is a *teishoku* (set-course meal). This usually includes a main dish of meat or fish, a bowl of rice, *misoshiru* (miso soup), shredded cabbage and some *tsukemono* (Japanese pickles). In addition, most *shokudō* serve a fairly standard selection of *donburi-mono* (rice dishes) and *menrui* (noodle dishes). When you order noodles, you can choose between *soba* (thin brown buckwheat noodles) and udon (thick white wheat noodles), both of which are served with a variety of toppings. Expect to spend ¥600 to ¥1000 for a meal at a *shokudō*.

### SUSHI & SASHIMI

There are two main types of sushi: *nigiri-zushi* (served on a small bed of rice – the most common variety) and *maki-zushi* (served in a seaweed roll). Sushi without rice is known as sashimi or *tsukuri* (or, politely, *o-tsukuri*).

Sushi is not difficult to order. If you sit at the counter of a sushi restaurant you can simply point at what you want, as most of the selections are visible in a refrigerated glass case between you and the sushi chef. You can also order à la carte from the menu. When ordering, you usually order *ichi-nin mae* (one portion), which usually means two pieces of sushi. Be careful, since the price on the menu will be for only one piece.

If ordering à la carte is too daunting, you can take care of your whole order with just one or two words by ordering *mori-awase,* an assortment plate of *nigiri-zushi*. These usually come in three grades: *futsū nigiri* (regular *nigiri*), *jō nigiri* (special *nigiri*) and *toku-jō nigiri* (extra-special *nigiri*). The difference is in the type of fish used. Most *mori-awase* contain six or seven pieces of sushi.

Before popping the sushi into your mouth, dip it very lightly in *shōyu* (soy sauce), which you pour from a small decanter into a low dish specially provided for the purpose. If you're not good at using *hashi* (chopsticks), don't worry – sushi is one of the few foods in Japan that it's perfectly acceptable to eat with your hands. Slices of *gari* (pickled ginger) will also be served to help refresh the palate. The beverage of choice with sushi is beer or sake (hot in winter and cold in summer), with a cup of green tea at the end of the meal.

### RĀMEN

The Japanese imported this dish from China and put their own spin on it to make what is one of the world's most delicious fast foods. *Rāmen* dishes are big bowls of noodles in a meat broth, served with a variety of toppings, such as sliced pork, bean sprouts and leeks.

In some restaurants you may be asked if you'd prefer *kotteri* (thick and fatty) or

---

### CHEAP EATS IN KYOTO

It's easy to get the impression that eating well in Kyoto will cost an arm and a leg. In fact, you can eat cheaper in Kyoto than in almost any other major city in the developed world, especially if you follow certain guidelines. Here are some tips to help you save money and still eat well.

**Luxury lunches** Many of Kyoto's elite *kaiseki* (Japanese haute cuisine) and international restaurants serve a delicious lunch set or *bentō* (boxed meal, usually of rice, with a main dish and pickles or salad) that cost a fraction of their normal dinner offerings.

**Eat on your feet** If you really want to save money, try eating in the *tachi-kui* (stand-and-eat) noodle restaurants found around train stations in the downtown shopping areas. You can get bowls of noodles at these places for as little as ¥250. They usually serve *onigiri* (rice balls) as well.

**Take it away** You can get really good prepared dishes, including sushi, tempura, salads, *yakitori* and pastries for reasonable prices in the *depa-chika* (department store food floors) of all of Kyoto's major department stores. The best selections can be found at Takashimaya and Daimaru.

**Eat Japanese food** As a rule, Japanese food is cheaper than foreign food in Kyoto. This holds true for restaurants, supermarkets and speciality import stores.

*assari* (thin and light) soup. Other than this, ordering is simple: just sidle up to the counter and say *rāmen*, or ask for any of the other choices usually on offer. Expect to pay ¥500 to ¥900 for a bowl. Since *rāmen* is derived from Chinese cuisine, some *rāmen* restaurants also serve *chāhan* or *yaki-meshi* (both dishes are fried rice), *gyōza* (dumplings) and *kara-age* (deep-fried chicken pieces).

*Rāmen* restaurants are easily distinguished by their long counters lined with customers hunched over steaming bowls. You can sometimes *hear* a *rāmen* shop as you wander by – it's considered polite to slurp the noodles and aficionados claim that slurping brings out the full flavour of the broth.

### SOBA & UDON

*Soba* (thin, brown buckwheat noodles) and udon (thick, white wheat noodles) are Japan's answer to Chinese-style *rāmen*. Most Japanese noodle shops serve both *soba* and udon in a variety of ways.

Noodles are usually served in a bowl containing a light, bonito–flavoured broth (bonito is a tuna-like fish), but you can also order them served cold and piled on a bamboo mat with a cold broth for dipping (this is called *zaru soba*). If you order *zaru soba*, you'll receive a small plate of wasabi and sliced spring onions – put these into the cup of broth and eat the noodles by dipping them in this mixture. At the end of your meal, the waiter will give you some hot broth to mix with the leftover sauce, which you drink like a kind of tea. As with *rāmen*, feel free to slurp as loudly as you please.

*Soba* and udon places are usually quite cheap (about ¥800 a dish), but some fancy places can be significantly more expensive (the decor is a good indication of the price).

### OKONOMIYAKI

Sometimes described as Japanese pizza or pancake, the resemblance is in form only. Actually, *okonomiyaki* are various forms of batter and cabbage cakes cooked on a griddle.

At an *okonomiyaki* restaurant you sit around a *teppan* (iron hotplate), armed with a spatula and chopsticks to cook your choice of meat, seafood and vegetables in a cabbage and vegetable batter.

Some restaurants will do most of the cooking and bring the nearly finished product over to your hotplate for you to season with *katsuo bushi* (bonito flakes), *shōyu* (soy sauce), *ao-nori* (an ingredient similar to parsley), Japanese Worcestershire-style sauce and mayonnaise. Cheaper places, however, will simply hand you a bowl filled with the ingredients and expect you to cook it for yourself. If this happens, don't panic. First, mix the batter and filling thoroughly, then place it on the hotplate, flattening it into a pancake shape. After five minutes or so, use the spatula to flip it and cook for another five minutes. Then dig in.

Most *okonomiyaki* places also serve *yaki-soba* (fried noodles with meat and vegetables) and *yasai-itame* (stir-fried vegetables). All of this is washed down with mugs of draught beer.

One final word: don't worry too much about the preparation of the food – as a foreigner you will be expected to be awkward, and the waiter will keep a sharp eye on you to make sure no real disasters occur.

## Vegetarians & Vegans

Travellers who eat fish should have almost no trouble dining in Kyoto: almost all *shokudō, izakaya* and other common restaurants offer a set meal with fish as the main dish. Vegans and vegetarians who don't eat fish will have to get their protein from tofu and other bean products. Note that most *misoshiru* (miso soup) is made with *dashi* (stock) that contains fish, so if you want to avoid fish, you'll also have to avoid *misoshiru*.

Kyoto has several vegetarian and/or organic restaurants that serve dishes suitable for vegetarians and vegans. Reviews that include the vegetarian icon (🌱) indicate places that have a good vegetarian selection.

Following is a list of restaurants that specialise in vegetarian or vegan cuisine:

**Biotei** (p57) High-quality veggie food in Downtown Kyoto.

**mumokuteki cafe** (p61) Casual vegan and vegetarian food in a cafe atmosphere downtown.

**Hakko Shokudo Kamoshika** (p114) Great sets of fermented foods, mostly vegetarian, in Arashiyama.

**Kerala** (p58) The best Indian restaurant in Kyoto – try the veggie lunch set. Located on Kawaramachi-dōri downtown.

**Earth Kitchen Company** (p99) Wonderful vegetarian and seafood *bentō* to take away on Marutamachi-dōri, near the river.

## Cooking Courses

If you want to learn how to cook some of the delightful foods you've tried in Kyoto, we recommend **Uzuki** (www.kyotouzuki.com; 3hr class per person ¥4000), a small cooking class conducted in a Japanese home for groups of two to four people. You will learn how to cook a variety of dishes and then sit down and enjoy the fruits of your labour. You can consult beforehand if you have particular dishes you'd like to cook. The fee includes all ingredients. Reserve via the website.

Another great cooking school in Kyoto is **Haru Cooking Class** (料理教室はる; Map p211; http://www.kyoto-cooking-class.com/index.html; Shimogamo Miyazaki-chō 166-32, Sakyō-ku; per person from ¥5900; ⊙classes from 2pm daily, reservation required), a friendly one-man operation located a little bit north of Demachi-yanagi. Haru speaks great English and can teach both vegetarian and nonvegetarian cooking. He also offers tours of Nishiki Market. Reserve by email.

## Department Store Dining

Yes, we know: the idea of dining in a department store sounds as appetising as dining in a petrol station. However, Japanese department stores, especially those in a large city such as Kyoto, are loaded with good dining options. And, unlike many street-level shops, they're usually fairly comfortable with foreign diners (if there's any communication trouble, they can always call down to the bilingual ladies at the information counter).

On their basement floors, you'll find *depa-chika* (from the English word 'department' and the Japanese word *chika,* which means 'underground'). A good *depa-chika* is like an Aladdin's cave of gustatory delights that rivals the best gourmet shops in any Western city. On their upper floors, you'll usually find a *resutoran-gai* (restaurant city) that includes restaurants serving all the Japanese standards – sushi, noodles, *tonkatsu* (deep-fried breaded pork cutlet), tempura – along with a few international restaurants, usually French, Italian and Chinese.

If you find yourself feeling peckish in Downtown Kyoto, here are two good department dining options:

**Takashimaya** (p65) At the corner of Shijō and Kawaramachi streets, this elegant department store has an incredible food floor (on the B1 level) and the best department store *resutoran-gai* in the city (on the 7th floor).

**Daimaru** (p65) On the north side of Shijō, between Kawaramachi and Karasuma streets, Daimaru has a world-class food floor (note the awesome Japanese sweet section) and a solid *resutoran-gai* on the 8th floor.

## Eating by Neighbourhood

➡ **Kyoto Station Area** There are eateries scattered all around the station building, ranging from plebeian to posh. (p51)

➡ **Downtown Kyoto** The centre of Kyoto's dining scene, it has the thickest concentration of restaurants in the city. (p57)

➡ **Southern Higashiyama** Offerings here fall into two categories: tourist eateries near the temples and refined places in Gion. (p86)

➡ **Northern Higashiyama** Not a dining centre, but plenty of eateries are scattered about, including cheap places near Kyoto University. (p98)

➡ **Arashiyama & Sagano** Cheap eateries for tourists cram the main drag, with a few high-end spots further out. (p114)

## Lonely Planet's Top Choices

**Omen** (p99) Brilliant noodles and great atmosphere near Ginkaku-ji.

**Kyōgoku Kane-yo** (p60) Perfect *unagi* (eel) in classic 'old Kyoto' surroundings.

**Yoshikawa** (p62) Great tempura and a breathtaking garden.

**Kiyamachi Sakuragawa** (p62) A superb introduction to *kaiseki*.

**Café Bibliotec Hello!** (p57) A cafe with style to spare.

## Best by Budget

### ¥

**Musashi Sushi** (p58) Conveyor-belt sushi at its best.

**Goya** (p98) Great Okinawan near Ginkaku-ji.

**Ippūdō** (p57) Delectable *rāmen* in the heart of Downtown Kyoto.

### ¥¥

**Tōsuirō** (p60) Artisanal tofu in traditional surroundings.

**Tsukiji Sushisei** (p60) Really good Tokyo-style sushi at reasonable rates.

**Shunsai Tempura Arima** (p62) Friendly and approachable tempura in a family-run restaurant.

### ¥¥¥

**Gion Karyō** (p87) Classic *kaiseki* in the heart of Kyoto's main geisha district.

**Roan Kikunoi** (p62) Adventurous and experimental *kaiseki* downtown.

**Hyōtei** (p100) Refined *kaiseki* in a superb setting.

## Best Rāmen

**Ippūdō** (p57) Toothsome Kyushu-style *rāmen* and crispy *gyōza*.

**Karako** (p98) Delicious thick meaty soup and tender pork slices.

**Rāmen Santōka** (p86) Hokkaidō-style *rāmen* at its best.

## Best Sushi

**Den Shichi** (p77) Out of the way, but excellent.

**Tsukiji Sushisei** (p60) High-quality sushi in an approachable setting.

**Ganko** (p61) Big, touristy and bright, but very good à la carte sushi.

## Best Noodles (Soba/Udon)

**Honke Tagoto** (p60) Simple and satisfying *soba* and udon in the shopping district.

**Hinode Udon** (p99) Cramped and delicious noodles near Nanzen-ji.

**Omen Kodai-ji** (p87) Wonderful noodles in a smart setting in Southern Higashiyama.

## Best Kaiseki

**Kiyamachi Sakuragawa** (p62) Smart creative *kaiseki* in intimate surroundings.

**Gion Karyō** (p87) Wonderful *kaiseki* in a classic setting.

**Kitcho Arashiyama** (p115) No-holds-barred *kaiseki* served in superb private rooms.

## Best for Kids

**Ganko** (p61) Bustling eatery with children's set meals and plenty for adults to like.

**Capricciosa** (p59) Simple Italian eatery with noise levels suitable for the loudest children.

**Nishiki Warai** (p57) Entertaining fare *(okonomiyaki)* good for slightly older children (hot griddles not safe for young ones).

## Best Cafes

**Prinz** (p76) A long way from anywhere, but worth the trip.

**Café Bibliotec Hello!** (p57) *Machiya* (traditional Japanese townhouse) cafe with style to spare.

**Saryo Zen Cafe** (p59) Modern Japanese-style teahouse with delicious Kyoto sweets.

## Best for a Break from Japanese

**Kerala** (p58) Reliable Indian downtown.

**Liberte** (p59) Simple but tasty French with a bakery attached.

**Din Tai Fung** (p60) Mouth-watering dim sum and tasty Chinese noodle and rice dishes in Takashimaya.

# Drinking & Nightlife

*Take a stroll down Kyoto's main nightlife strip, Kiyamachi-dōri, and you might think that there's one bar for every resident of Kyoto. Sure, some can only seat three patrons at a squeeze, but there's no shortage of watering holes. And the variety is astonishing – everything from rough-and-ready student hangouts to impossibly chic spots where you just might spot a geisha.*

## Kyoto Nightlife

Like its restaurant scene, Kyoto has a deeper nightlife scene than most cities of its size, Japanese or foreign. Indeed, visitors from much bigger cities often remark on the sophistication and scope of the nightlife here in the Old Capital. One reason must surely be the number of visitors the city keeps happy after sightseeing hours are over. Another must be the sheer variety of influences the city absorbs from all these visitors.

Of course, there's more to Kyoto nightlife than just bars and clubs. For starters, there are *izakaya*, which are Japanese-style pub eateries that serve a variety of sake and beer (or sake and beer joints that happen to serve a variety of Japanese food – sometimes it's hard to tell).

## What to Drink in Kyoto

While beer is the overwhelming favourite as the drink to have with dinner, sake (*Nihonshu*) is making a comeback here in the Old Capital. It's especially popular with sushi, *kaiseki* (Japanese haute cuisine) and at *izakaya*. Sake is usually consumed cold in Japan, especially the good stuff, but at down-market places such as *izakaya* and *yakitori* (meat grilled on skewers) restaurants, some people order it hot (the Japanese word for this is *atsukan*). Nondrinkers usually order *oolong-cha* (a smoky brown Chinese-style tea) at restaurants and almost every place stocks this. At some high-end Japanese restaurants and almost all Western ones, wine will be on the menu, the variety increasing with the quality of the restaurant. Finally, after dinner, in addition to beer, wine and sake, you'll find the full range of cocktails and spirits served in Kyoto's myriad bars.

## Drinking & Nightlife by Neighbourhood

→ **Southern Higashiyama** A mix of high-end (hard to enter) traditional spots, hostess bars and approachable nightspots. (p88)

→ **Downtown Kyoto** Home to plebeian and raucous Kiyamachi and refined and traditional Pontochō. (p62)

→ **Kyoto Station Area** Not much of a nightlife destination, but plenty of bars and *izakaya* about if you need them.

## Lonely Planet's Top Choices

**World Peace Love** (p64) Kyoto's coolest club.

**Bar K6** (p63) A slick spot for a civilised drink near the river.

**Sake Bar Yoramu** (p63) A sake lover's paradise.

**Bar Main Higashiyama** (p88) A stylish haunt in Southern Higashiyama.

**Bar Bunkyu** (p64) Tiny whisky bar with a knowledgeable owner.

**Sama Sama** (p64) A cosy cave on Kiyamachi.

## Best Cheap Bars

**A Bar** (p63) Raucous student *izakaya* with cheap food and communal tables.

**Rocking Bar ING** (p63) Dark hole-in-the-wall bar with a legendary owner and dedicated local clientele.

## Best for Meeting Locals

**Tadg's Gastro Pub** (p63) Both expats and Japanese frequent this welcoming spot near Downtown Kyoto.

**Rub-a-Dub** (p64) Late in the evening on weekends, this place pulls in a crowd of local reggae fans.

**Gael Irish Pub** (p88) The convivial atmosphere here makes it very easy to meet people.

## Best Upmarket Bars

**Bar K6** (p63) Single malts and expertly mixed cocktails are the draw at this smart local gathering spot.

**Tōzan Bar** (p88) The basement bar at the Hyatt Regency Kyoto

is worth a trip for the design alone.

**Atlantis** (p64) A great spot for a drink on exclusive Pontochō lane.

## Best Foreign-Themed Bars

**Tadg's Gastro Pub** (p63) A friendly Irish-run spot with great craft beers and satisfying pub fare.

**Pig & Whistle** (p88) An old-school English-style pub that offers all the usual draws: pints, fish and chips, and darts.

## Best Romantic Bars

**Bar Main Higashiyama** (p88) Perfect for a nightcap after a stroll in Gion.

**Bar Bunkyu** (p64) A quiet nook for some serious quality time.

**Tōzan Bar** (p88) Dark and dignified with lots of cozy spaces.

## Best for Sake

**Sake Bar Yoramu** (p63) Carefully curated sake expertly explained.

**Tōzan Bar** (p88) Not a sake specialist, but a great collection and an English menu.

### NEED TO KNOW

#### Opening Hours

➡ *Izakaya*: around 6pm to midnight

➡ Bars and clubs: around 7pm to 2am or later

➡ Karaoke boxes: afternoon to midnight or later

#### Get the Scoop

**Kansai Scene** (www.kansaiscene.com) This magazine has listings of foreigner-friendly bars as well as detailed event listings. It's available at major bookshops and foreigner-friendly businesses. See the website for stockists.

**Deep Kyoto** (www.deep-kyoto.com) This website has listings on little-known Kyoto bars, cafes and restaurants, as well as some event information.

#### Door Policy

Most bars have no door policy per se, but some places may be uncomfortable if you just walk in (it's not necessarily discrimination – Kyoto bars are famous for requiring guests to be introduced by an established patron). Clubs usually admit all comers, as long as you aren't obviously addled or inappropriately dressed.

#### Dress Code

➡ Bars: whatever you happen to be wearing is fine at most places. Go smart casual at hotel bars and upmarket places in Gion and Pontochō.

➡ Clubs: casual and comfortable or absolutely fabulous.

PLAN YOUR TRIP DRINKING & NIGHTLIFE

# Entertainment

*If you've never seen the otherworldly spectacle of kabuki (stylised Japanese theatre) or the colourful extravagance of a geisha dance, then you've come to the right place: Kyoto is the best city in Japan to enjoy traditional Japanese performing arts. In addition, you'll find a lively music scene, plenty of cinemas and modern performances of all sorts.*

## Traditional Performing Arts

### KABUKI

Performances of kabuki, Japan's most colourful and popular traditional form of performance art, are regularly held at the Minami-za theatre. It's easiest to get tickets to the year-end Kao-mise (Face Showing) performances, but you can also get tickets to other events throughout the year. The best place to check for upcoming events is in the *Kyoto Visitor's Guide,* available at bookshops and foreigner-friendly accommodation around town. Tour companies can also help with tickets.

### GEISHA DANCE

Each year Kyoto's geisha (or, properly speaking, *geiko* and *maiko* – fully fledged and trainee geisha respectively) perform fantastic dances (known as *odori*), usually on seasonal themes. Three of the geisha districts perform their dance in April, to coincide with the cherry blossoms, one performs in May, and the final one performs its dance in November, to coincide with the autumn foliage. For a small additional fee, you can participate in a brief tea ceremony before the show. We *highly* recommend seeing one of these dances if you are in town when they are being held. Ask at the Kyoto Tourist Information Center (TIC) or at your lodgings for help with ticket purchase. Tour companies can also help with tickets.

### GEISHA ENTERTAINMENT

In addition to geisha dances, it's possible to arrange private geisha entertainment. While it's not cheap – expect to pay around ¥70,000 for two hours with two geisha, excluding dinner and drinks – it can be the memory of a lifetime, and if you're part of a group you can share the costs. Various Kyoto tour companies arrange geisha entertainment, including **Kyoto Culture.org** (www.kyotoculture.org).

Another way to experience geisha entertainment is to join a regularly scheduled geisha event. One of the best is put on by Gion Hatanaka, a Gion ryokan.

## Music

Kyoto's large music venues usually specialise in classical music or touring Japanese acts (for big international acts, it's necessary to travel to Osaka). Smaller venues host a wide variety of Japanese acts, both traditional and modern, as well as independent international acts. Small specialised live-music halls in Japan are known as 'live houses' and we list great ones. For information on upcoming traditional music events, check the *Kyoto Visitor's Guide* or *Deep Kyoto* (www.deepkyoto.com). For modern acts, check *Kansai Scene* magazine or *Deep Kyoto.*

## Entertainment by Neighbourhood

➡ **Downtown Kyoto** Good for cinemas. (p64)

➡ **Southern Higashiyama** Home to Gion, come here for geisha entertainment and kabuki. (p88)

➡ **Northern Higashiyama** This district is your best bet for performances of *nō*. (p100)

# Lonely Planet's Top Choices

**Miyako Odori** (p88) Kyoto's most dazzling geisha dance.

**Minami-za** (p88) The most mesmerising kabuki performances in the city.

**Kyoto Cinema** (p64) The best indie films from round the world.

**Kyoto Cuisine & Maiko Evening** (p90) One of the best ways to actually meet a geisha is at Gion Hatanaka.

**Camellia Tea Experience** (p90) A refreshing cuppa and a window into the culture.

## Best Geisha Dances

**Kyō Odori** (p88) Held between the first and third Sunday in April.

**Miyako Odori** (p88) Held throughout April.

**Kitano Odori** Held between 15 and 25 April at Kamishichiken Kaburen-jō Theatre, east of Kitano-Tenman-gū.

**Kamogawa Odori** (p64) Held between 1 and 24 May.

**Gion Odori** (p90) Held between 1 and 10 November.

## Best Arthouse Cinemas

**Kyoto Cinema** (p64) Cosy downtown cinema that screens a truly eclectic variety of domestic and international films.

**Kyoto Minami Kaikan** (p77) The best spot in town to see international art-house offerings.

# Best Classical Music Venues

**Kyoto Concert Hall** (p77) Kyoto's premier classical music venue.

**ALTI** (p77) Another great classical music spot located alongside the Kyoto Gosho.

## Best Live Music Venues

**Taku-Taku** (p64) A downtown 'live house' with a storied history.

**Jittoku** (p107) An atmospheric 'live house' in an old sake warehouse.

## Best Tea Ceremony Experiences

**Club Ōkitsu Kyoto** (p77) Sublime tea ceremonies in an exquisite setting.

**Camellia Tea Experience** (p90) A perfect introduction to 'The Way of Tea'.

**En** (p90) Approachable, fun and right near the main tourist trail.

## NEED TO KNOW

### Get the Scoop

**Kansai Scene** (www.kansaiscene.com) This magazine has listings of foreigner-friendly bars as well as detailed event listings. It's available at major bookshops and foreigner-friendly businesses. See the website for places where you can grab a copy.

**Deep Kyoto** (www.deepkyoto.com) This website has listings on little-known Kyoto bars, cafes and restaurants, as well as some event information.

### Dress Code

➡ Classical music halls: smart casual.

➡ Geisha dances: smart casual.

➡ Private geisha entertainment: smart casual or semi-formal.

➡ Kabuki and nō (a stylised dance-drama performed on a bare stage): smart casual.

PLAN YOUR TRIP ENTERTAINMENT

# Shopping

*Kyoto has a fantastic variety of both traditional and modern shops. Most of these are located in the Downtown Kyoto area, making the city a very convenient place to shop. Whether you're looking for fans and kimono or the latest electronics and cameras, Kyoto has plenty to offer.*

## Shopping in Kyoto

Kyoto has a long history as Japan's artistic and cultural workshop: it's the place where the country's finest artisans used their skills to produce the goods used in tea ceremonies, calligraphy, flower arrangement and religious ceremonies, as well as in kimono fabrics and other textiles. Indeed, Kyoto is the best place to find traditional arts and crafts in all of Japan.

Of course, Kyoto has far more to offer than just traditional items. You will also find the latest fashions in the Shijō-Kawaramachi shopping district, the latest electronics on Teramachi-dōri and a wondrous assortment of food products in markets such as Nishiki. And if you're lucky enough to be in town on the 21st or the 25th of the month, you should make every effort to visit one of the city's excellent flea markets.

## Shopping Strips

Shopping neighbourhoods in Kyoto tend to be organised by specialities, which makes things easier if you're after specific items. Following are some of Kyoto's most important shopping streets and what you'll find there:

➡ **Teramachi-dōri, north of Oike-dōri** Traditional Japanese crafts, tea-ceremony goods, green tea and antiques.

➡ **Teramachi-dōri, south of Shijō-dōri** Electronics and computers.

➡ **Shijō-dōri, between Kawaramachi-dōri and Karasuma-dōri** Department stores, fashion boutiques and traditional arts and crafts.

➡ **Shinmonzen-dōri** Antiques.

➡ **Gojō-zaka** Pottery.

## Shopping by Neighbourhood

➡ **Downtown Kyoto** The entire downtown area is one giant shopping district. (p65)

➡ **Kyoto Station Area** Big electronics and camera shops surround the station. (p51)

➡ **Southern Higashiyama** Ceramics and traditional crafts. (p90)

➡ **Northern Higashiyama** Great traditional craft shops. (p100)

---

### MUST-SEE FLEA MARKETS

Many travellers plan their trips around the cherry blossoms or one of Kyoto's great festivals. Few, however, plan their trips around Kyoto's brilliant markets. This is a shame because Kyoto's two monthly markets are among the best flea markets in all of Asia. The dates to keep in mind are the 21st of the month for the Kōbō-san Market at Tō-ji, and the 25th of the month for the Tenjin-san Market at Kitano Tenman-gū. Note that these markets are close enough together to hit on one slightly extended stay in Kyoto.

# Lonely Planet's Top Choices

**Ippo-dō Tea** (p65) This is *the* place to buy green tea, both *matcha* (powdered) and leaf.

**Kyoto Handicraft Center** (p100) For one-stop souvenir shopping, this place can't be beaten.

**Kyūkyō-dō** (p65) A convenient downtown all-round traditional souvenir shop.

**Wagami no Mise** (p65) The selection of *washi* (Japanese handmade paper) is just mind-boggling here.

**Takashimaya** (p65) Our favourite department store in Kyoto.

## Best for Electronics

**Bic Camera** (p51) A mammoth retailer of electronics, computers, cameras and much more.

**Yodobashi Camera** (p52) All the gizmos you could ever want, and a great restaurant floor.

## Best for Foodie Gifts

**Nishiki Market** (p55) Head here for traditional food-related gifts, including cooking implements, tea, sweets and sake.

**Takashimaya** (p65) The food floor here is superb and the selection of kitchenware and dining ware on the 6th floor is not to be missed.

## Best Department Stores

**Takashimaya** (p65) An elegant and rich assortment of shops, along with great restaurants and a food floor to boggle the mind.

**Daimaru** (p65) A sumptuous selection at this vast downtown store.

## Best for Fashion

**OPA** (p66) Youth fashions and kitschy knick-knacks galore.

**Mina** (p65) Uniclo leads the way at this downtown fashion hub.

**Kyoto Marui** (p65) A new department store with a dedicated fashionista following.

## Best for Traditional Japanese Items

**Wagami no Mise** (p65) There's a huge selection of *washi* at this downtown shop.

**Zōhiko** (p65) A wonderland for the lover of lacquerware.

**Nijūsan-ya** (p66) Boxwood combs and other geisha accoutrements.

**Kamiji Kakimoto** (p66) Another great *washi* shop with things such as washi computer printer paper.

**Takashimaya** (p65) The 6th floor of this department store has great lacquerware, pottery, wood crafts and so on.

**Kyoto Handicraft Center** (p100) The quality of goods at this one-stop handicraft shop is excellent and the English-speaking salespeople make shopping a breeze.

## Best Markets

**Kōbō-san Market** (p77) From used kimonos to ceramics to antiques, this market has it all.

**Tenjin-san Market** (p107) You'll find everything from junk to treasures at this monthly market.

**Chion-ji Tezukuri-ichi** (p100) If you like handmade crafts, don't miss this monthly temple fair.

**Nishiki Market** (p55) Food is only the start of the offerings at Kyoto's most famous market.

## NEED TO KNOW

### Opening Hours

➡ Department stores: 10am to 7pm, closed one or two days a month

➡ Smaller shops: 9am to 5pm, may be closed Sunday

### Bargaining

Bargaining in Japan is just not done. Possible exceptions are antique shops, flea markets, camera and electronics stores (especially second-hand shops). The word 'discount' is usually understood by shop assistants. If they are willing to drop the price, accept the first offer – don't haggle further as it will make things very awkward for the staff.

### Payment

Departments stores, modern stores, boutiques etc accept credit cards. Some small traditional shops only accept cash.

# ◉ Temples & Shrines

*Kyoto's temples and shrines are the main draw for many visitors to the city, and for good reason: they are among the best examples of religious architecture on earth. Moreover, temples are where you will find Japan's most superb gardens. With over 1000 Buddhist temples and more than 400 Shintō shrines, exploring these wonders is the work of a lifetime.*

## What to Do at a Temple

There are no steadfast rituals you must follow when visiting a Buddhist temple. Many temples require that you remove your shoes before climbing the steps into the main hall (wearing a pair of slip-on shoes will make this a lot easier). If there is a low slatted board *(sunoko)* on the ground, step out of your shoes onto this.

At many temples, you can pay a small fee (usually ¥500) for a cup of *matcha* (powdered green tea) and a Japanese sweet, which you can enjoy while looking over the garden. Few foreigners take advantage of this wonderful way to enjoy a temple.

## What to Do at a Shrine

There is a distinct ritual to visiting a shrine, but as long as you behave in a respectful manner, you do not have to follow it closely. If you want to do as the locals do, here is the basic drill: rinse your mouth and hands with pure water at a *temizuya* (small pavilion), using the stone ablution *chōzuya* (basin) and *hishaku* (bamboo ladle) provided for this purpose. Rinse both hands before pouring water into a cupped hand to rinse the mouth. Do not spit the water into the basin; rather, spit it onto the gravel that surrounds the basin.

Next, proceed to the *haiden* (worshippers' hall), which stands before the main hall of the shrine. Here, you will find an offering box over which a bell hangs with a long rope attached. Visitors toss a coin into the box, then grab and shake the rope to 'wake the gods', bow twice, clap loudly twice, bow again twice (once deeply, once lightly), and then step back and to the side.

Amulets are popular at shrines. *Omamori* (special talismans) are purchased to ensure good luck or ward off evil. *Omikuji* (fortunes) are chosen by drawing a numbered rod from a box and taking the corresponding fortune slip.

## Temples & Shrines by Neighbourhood

➡ **Kyoto Station Area** Two of Kyoto's biggest temples are found here: Nishi Hongan-ji and Higashi Hongan-ji. (p50)

➡ **Southern Higashiyama** Superb temples are thick on the ground, including Kiyomizu-dera, Chion-in and Shōren-in, and colourful Yasaka-jinja. (p80)

➡ **Northern Higashiyama** A green area rich in temples and shrines, including Nanzen-ji, Ginkaku-ji and Heian-jingū. (p93)

➡ **Northwest Kyoto** Three Unesco World Heritage sites head the list: Kinkaku-ji, Ryōan-ji and Ninna-ji. (p103)

➡ **Arashiyama & Sagano** Tenryū-ji leads the procession of fine temples here. (p110)

➡ **Kitayama Area & North Kyoto** There are interesting temples and shrines here, including Kurama-dera, Sanzen-in and Jingo-ji. (p119)

## Lonely Planet's Top Choices

**Nanzen-ji** (p93) This is a world of Zen temples and sub-temples scattered amid trees.

**Ginkaku-ji** (p94) The famed 'Silver Pavilion' boasts one of Kyoto's finest gardens.

**Kinkaku-ji** (p103) A golden apparition rises above a tranquil reflecting pond; it's arguably Kyoto's most impressive single sight.

**Tenryū-ji** (p110) This temple takes *shakkei* (borrowed scenery) to a new level: it borrows the entire sweep of Arashi-yama's beautiful mountains.

**Daitoku-ji** (p72) Each subtemple at this Zen complex contains a sublime garden – a must for garden lovers with an aversion to crowds.

**Chion-in** (p81) A vast Pure Land Buddhist temple – the Vatican of Japanese Buddhism.

## Best for Quiet Contemplation

**Shōren-in** (p85) An often overlooked beauty in Southern Higashiyama.

**Hōnen-in** (p96) Peace and quiet just a stone's throw from the Path of Philosophy.

**Tōfuku-ji** (p75) Outside of autumn foliage season, you might have the place to yourself.

**Manshu-in** (p118) Head north to enjoy the serenity at this quaint retreat.

## Best Temple Gardens

**Ryōan-ji** (p105) Fifteen mystical rocks against a sea of white gravel – what could it all mean?

**Tōfuku-ji** (p75) A modern masterpiece in moss, gravel and stone.

**Saihō-ji** (p112) They don't call it Moss Temple (Koke-dera) for nothing – it's a green wonderland.

## Best Shrines & Temples for Children

**Kiyomizu-dera** (p80) There's a lot to do at this 'interactive temple'.

**Chion-in** (p81) Children are captivated by the grand spaces of this bustling temple.

**Fushimi Inari-Taisha** (p70) Your children will be mesmerised by the shrine gates here.

**Kurama-dera** (p120) Older children will enjoy the climb up to this mountain temple.

## Best Shrines

**Fushimi Inari-Taisha** (p70) Not just the best shrine in Kyoto, but the best in all Japan.

**Heian-jingū** (p98) A shrine modelled on the former Imperial Palace.

**Shimogamo-jinja** (p73) A green corridor through the forest leads to a vermillion sanctuary.

## Best Temples for Views

**Tenryū-ji** (p110) The view of the Arashiyama mountains over the pond here is sublime.

**Ginkaku-ji** (p94) Climb the path behind the garden for a classic view over the city.

**Kiyomizu-dera** (p80) The view across the Kyoto basin here is worth the walk up the hill.

## NEED TO KNOW

### Temple or Shrine?

Buddhist temples and Shintō shrines were historically intertwined, until they were separated by government decree in 1868. But centuries of coexistence means the two resemble each other architecturally. The easiest way to tell the two apart is to check the gate. The main entrance of a shrine is a *torii* (gate) – usually two upright pillars joined at the top by two horizontal crossbars. *Torii* are often painted bright vermilion. In contrast, the *mon* (main entrance gate) of a temple is constructed of several upright pillars or casements, joined at the top by a multitiered roof. *Mon* often contain guardian figures, usually Niō (deva kings).

### Temple Entry Fees

You can enter the grounds of many temples for free, especially larger ones. Others charge an admission fee of about ¥400. Many temples have gardens or special halls that require an admission charge, also of about ¥400.

### Shrine Entry Fees

You can enter most shrines for free. Some shrines have treasure houses or other special buildings that require an admission fee of about ¥400.

### Temple & Shrine Opening Hours

You can enter many shrines 24 hours a day. The same goes for some larger temples. Otherwise, most temples are open 9am to 5pm, seven days a week.

# Explore Kyoto

# Neighbourhoods at a Glance

## ❶ Kyoto Station Area p48

Dominated by the eponymous Kyoto Station, this neighbourhood serves as the gateway to Kyoto. Apart from the impressive station building itself, this area is not particularly attractive. That said, there are a few worthwhile sights here: Higashi Hongan-ji and Nishi Hongan-ji are two vast temples within walking distance of the station.

## ❷ Downtown Kyoto p53

If you don't give a hoot about temples, shrines and gardens, you might never leave Downtown Kyoto. It has just about everything you need: an incredible variety of accommodation, restaurants, nightlife, shopping and entertainment options. And, yes, there are even a few

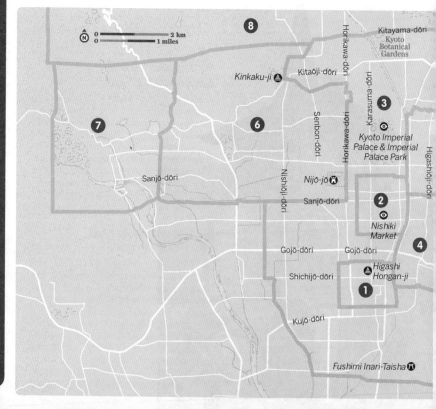

small temples, shrines and museums, plus the famed Nishiki Market.

### ❸ Central Kyoto p68

Central Kyoto comprises the entire middle of the city (except Downtown Kyoto and the Kyoto Station area). It includes the Kyoto Imperial Palace and its lovely park. To the north is Shimogamo-jinja, a shrine in a forest setting, and to the south Tō-ji, one of Kyoto's oldest temples.

### ❹ Southern Higashiyama p78

Southern Higashiyama, at the base of the Higashiyama (Eastern Mountains), is Kyoto's richest area for sightseeing. Thick with temples, shrines, museums and traditional shops, it's great to explore on foot, with some pedestrian-only walkways plus parks and expansive temple grounds. It's also

home to the Gion entertainment district and some of the city's finest ryokan (traditional Japanese inns).

### ❺ Northern Higashiyama p91

At the northern end of the Higashiyama mountains, this area is packed with first-rate attractions and soothing greenery, making it one of the best parts of the city for relaxed sightseeing. It stretches from Nanzen-ji in the south to Ginkaku-ji in the north, two temples linked by the lovely Path of Philosophy (Tetsugaku-no-Michi). Other attractions include Hōnen-in, a quiet temple overlooked by the crowds, and the museums around Okazaki-kōen.

### ❻ Northwest Kyoto p101

Northwest Kyoto contains two of Kyoto's most important temples: Kinkaku-ji, also known as the Golden Pavilion, and Ryōan-ji, home of Japan's most famous Zen garden. Other sights include the Shogun's castle of Nijō-jō and the enclosed world of Myōshin-ji.

### ❼ Arashiyama & Sagano p108

Arashiyama and Sagano, two adjoining neighbourhoods at the base of Kyoto's western mountains, form the city's second-most-popular sightseeing district. Foreign and domestic tourists flock here to see Tenryū-ji, a temple with a stunning mountain backdrop, and the famous Arashiyama Bamboo Grove. There are also several small temples and a fine hilltop villa: Ōkōchi-Sansō.

### ❽ Kitayama Area & North Kyoto p116

North Kyoto includes several important sites in the far northern Higashiyama area and other areas of northern Kyoto. Still further north, the Kitayama (Northern Mountains) area contains several quaint villages that make great day trips out of the city: Kurama, Kibune, Ōhara and Takao. Kurama and Kibune are usually visited together via a hiking trail that connects them. Ōhara and Takao, usually visited separately, contain superb temples and pleasant rural scenery.

NEIGHBOURHOODS AT A GLANCE

# Kyoto Station Area

## Neighbourhood Top Five

❶ Feeling the power of Japanese Buddhism expressed in the soaring main halls and their glittering interiors at **Higashi Hongan-ji** (p50). Its recently refurbished main hall is one of the largest wooden buildings on earth.

❷ Climbing to the roof of **Kyoto Station** (p50).

❸ Savouring the views from the top of **Kyoto Tower** (p50).

❹ Immersing yourself in the grandeur of **Nishi Hongan-ji** (p50).

❺ Escaping the concrete jungle and taking a breather in **Shōsei-en** (p50).

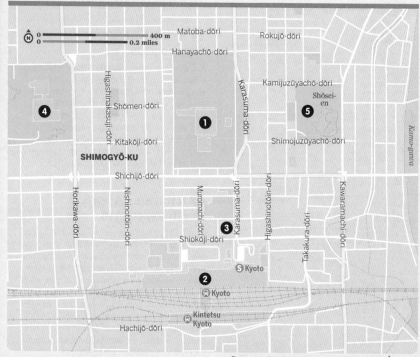

For more detail of this area, see Map p212 ➡

# Explore: Kyoto Station Area

For most travellers to Kyoto, the Kyoto Station area serves as the entry point to the city. Odds are, your first step in Kyoto will be onto one of the train platforms in Kyoto Station. This being the case, we should warn you that your first glimpse of the city is likely to be an anticlimax at best, a rude shock at worst: the area around the station is a sea of concrete, neon and billboards. But, rest assured, there is good stuff in every direction.

Like the areas around most train stations in Japan, the Kyoto Station area is chock-a-block with hotels. However, many people choose to stay in other parts of the city, so they usually hightail it to their digs and skip sightseeing in the Kyoto Station area entirely. This is a shame, since there are some worthwhile sights here, including two of Kyoto's largest and most impressive temples: Higashi Hongan-ji and Nishi Hongan-ji.

Of course, this being the city's main transport hub, the focus here is less on sightseeing and more on meeting your basic needs. The station building itself is packed with restaurants and shops, as are the streets surrounding the buildings. There's a lot of good food here, but few people would head to this area just to eat, given the offerings in other parts of the city.

## Local Life

→ **Hang-out** The steps leading up to the roof of the station on the west side of the main concourse of Kyoto Station are where local youths congregate.

→ **Shopping in a hurry** Bic Camera (p51), one of the city's largest and cheapest electronics and camera shops, is connected directly to Kyoto Station by the Nishinotō-in gate.

→ **Food for the trip** Porta (p52), the shopping mall underneath the north side of the station, is crammed with shops that sell takeaway food.

## Getting There & Away

→ **Train** The JR lines, including the *shinkansen* (bullet train), and the private Kintetsu line operate to/from Kyoto Station.

→ **Bus** Many city buses, JR buses and other bus lines operate to/from the Kyoto Station Bus Terminal (on the north side of the station).

→ **Subway** The Karasuma subway line stops directly underneath Kyoto Station (the Kyoto Station stop is called simply 'Kyoto').

## Lonely Planet's Top Tip

During high seasons for tourism (cherry-blossom season in April and foliage season in November), the taxi ranks on the south and north side of Kyoto Station can be very long. If you're in a hurry, walk a few blocks north of the station and hail a cab off the street.

 **KYOTO STATION AREA**

 **Best Things to See**

→ Higashi Hongan-ji (p50)
→ Nishi Hongan-ji (p50)
→ Shōsei-en (p50)

For reviews, see p50. →

 **Best Places to Eat**

→ Cube (p51)
→ Eat Paradise (p51)
→ Kyoto Rāmen Kōji (p51)

For reviews, see p51. →

**Best Places to Shop**

→ Bic Camera (p51)
→ Yodobashi Camera (p52)
→ Isetan Department Store (p52)

For reviews, see p51. →

# ⊙ SIGHTS

### HIGASHI HONGAN-JI BUDDHIST TEMPLE

Map p212 (東本願寺; Karasuma-dōri, Shichijō-agaru, Shimogyō-ku; ⊘5.50am-5.30pm Mar-Oct, 6.20am-4.30pm Nov-Feb; ⊠Kyoto Station) FREE A short walk north of Kyoto Station, Higashi Hongan-ji (Eastern Temple of the True Vow) is the last word in all things grand and gaudy. Considering its proximity to the station, the free admission, the awesome structures and the dazzling interiors, this temple is the obvious spot to visit when near the station. The temple is dominated by the vast **Goei-dō** (main hall), said to be the second-largest wooden structure in Japan, standing 38m high, 76m long and 58m wide.

The recently refurbished hall contains an image of Shinran, the founder of the sect, although the image is often hidden behind sumptuous gilded doors. The adjoining **Amida-dō** hall is presently under restoration. This restoration is expected to be completed in December 2015, but the hall is not slated to open until the spring of 2016.

There's a tremendous **coil of rope** made from human hair on display in the passageway. Following the destruction of the temple in the 1880s, a group of female temple devotees donated their locks to make the ropes that hauled the massive timbers used for reconstruction.

Higashi Hongan-ji was established in 1602 by Shogun Tokugawa Ieyasu in a 'divide and conquer' attempt to weaken the power of the enormously popular Jōdo Shin-shū (True Pure Land) school. The temple is now the headquarters of the Ōtani branch of Jōdo Shin-shū.

### SHŌSEI-EN GARDENS

Map p212 (渉成園; ☑371-9210; Karasuma-dōri, Shichijō-agaru, Shimogyō-ku; admission ¥500; ⊘9am-3.30pm; ⊠Kyoto Station) About five minutes' walk east of Higashi Hongan-ji, this garden is a nice green island in a vast expanse of concrete. While it's not on par with many other gardens in Kyoto, it's worth a visit if you find yourself in need of something to do near Kyoto Station, perhaps paired with a visit to the temple. The lovely grounds, incorporating the **Kikoku-tei** villa, were completed in 1657.

### NISHI HONGAN-JI BUDDHIST TEMPLE

Map p212 (本本願寺; Horikawa-dōri, Hanayachō-sagaru, Shimogyō-ku; ⊘6am-5pm Nov-Feb, 5.30am-5.30pm Mar, Apr, Sep & Oct, to 6pm May-Aug; ⊠Kyoto Station) FREE A vast temple complex about 15 minutes' walk northwest of Kyoto Station, Nishi Hongan-ji comprises five buildings that feature some of the finest examples of architecture and artistic achievement from the Azuchi-Momoyama period (1568–1600). The **Goei-dō** (main hall) is a marvellous sight. Another must-see building is the **Daisho-in** hall, which has sumptuous paintings, carvings and metal ornamentation. A small garden and two *nō* (stylised Japanese dance-drama) stages are connected with the hall. The dazzling **Kara-mon** has intricate ornamental carvings.

In 1591 Toyotomi Hideyoshi ordered the building of this temple to serve as the new headquarters for the Jōdo Shin-shū (True Pure Land) school of Buddhism. It was originally called simple Hongan-ji (Temple of the True Vow). Later Tokugawa Ieyasu saw the power of this sect as a threat to his power and sought to weaken it by encouraging a breakaway faction of this sect to found Higashi Hongan-ji (*higashi* means 'east') in 1602. This temple, the original Hongan-ji, then became known as Nishi Hongan-ji (*nishi* means 'west').

Nishi Hongan-ji now functions as the headquarters of the Hongan-ji branch of the Jōdo Shin-shū school, with over 10,000 temples and 12 million followers worldwide.

### KYOTO STATION NOTABLE BUILDING

Map p212 (京都駅; Karasuma-dōri, Higashishiokōji-chō, Shiokōji-sagaru, Shimogyō-ku; ⊠Kyoto Station) The Kyoto Station building is a striking steel-and-glass structure, a kind of futuristic cathedral for the transport age. You are sure to be impressed by the tremendous space that arches above you as you enter the main concourse. Moreover, you will probably enjoy a brief exploration of the many levels of the station, all the way up to the 15th-floor observation level.

The station building contains several food courts, as well as the Isetan Department Store (p52) and the Kyoto Tourist Information Center (TIC; p188). Be sure to take the escalator from the 7th floor on the east side of the building up to the 11th-floor glass corridor that runs high above the main concourse of the station.

### KYOTO TOWER NOTABLE BUILDING

Map p212 (京都タワー; Karasuma-dōri, Shichijō-sagaru, Shimogyō-ku; admission ¥770; ⊘9am-

9pm, last entry 8.40pm; ⊞Kyoto Station) Located right outside the Karasuma (north) gate of Kyoto Station, this retro tower looks like a rocket perched atop the Kyoto Tower Hotel. The tower provides excellent views in all directions and you can really get a sense for the Kyoto *bonchi* (flat basin). It's a great place to get orientated to the city upon arrival. There are free mounted binoculars to use, and these allow ripping views over to Kiyomizu-dera and as far south as Osaka.

#  EATING

### EAT PARADISE                        JAPANESE ¥

Map p212 (イートパラダイス; ☑352-1111; 11F Kyoto Station Bldg, Karasuma-dōri, Shiokōji-sagaru, Shimogyō-ku; ⊙11am-10pm; ⊞Kyoto Station) Up on the 11th floor of the Kyoto Station building, you'll find this collection of decent restaurants. Among the choices here are **Tonkatsu Wako** for *tonkatsu* (deep-fried breaded pork cutlets), **Ten-ichi** for sublime tempura, and **Wakuden** for approachable *kaiseki* (Japanese haute cuisine).

Take the west escalators from the main concourse to get here – Eat Paradise is in front of you when you get to the 11th floor. Note that the restaurants here can be crowded, especially at lunchtimes on weekends.

---

### FIRST IMPRESSIONS

Your first impression of Kyoto will probably be a bit of a letdown. While Kyoto Station itself is an impressive building, when you see the sea of drab buildings that surround the station, you'll probably wonder if you've gotten off at the right stop. Don't despair: Kyoto *is* a beautiful city, it's just that its beauty is hidden away in corners and pockets of the city, often behind walls. As soon as you get into the sightseeing districts of Southern Higashiyama, Northern Higashiyama and Arashiyama, you'll see what we mean. Even near Kyoto Station, you'll see the lovely pagoda at Tō-ji, which will give you faith that there is plenty of beauty to be found in the 'Old Capital'.

---

### CUBE                                JAPANESE ¥

Map p212 (ザ キューブ; ☑371-2134; 11F Kyoto Station Bldg, Karasuma-dōri, Shiokōji-sagaru, Shimogyō-ku; ⊙11am-10pm; ⊞ Kyoto Station) This is a great collection of restaurants located on the 11th floor of the Kyoto Station building. Most of the restaurants here serve Japanese food. You'll see it on your left as you arrive by escalator on the 11th floor.

### KYOTO RĀMEN KŌJI                    RĀMEN ¥

Map p212 (京都拉麺小路; ☑361-4401; 10F Kyoto Station Bldg, Karasuma-dōri, Shiokōji-sagaru, Shimogyō-ku; rāmen ¥700-1000; ⊙11am-10pm; ⊞Kyoto Station) If you love noodles, do not miss this collection of seven *rāmen* restaurants on the 10th floor of the Kyoto Station building (on the west end, take the escalators that start in the main concourse). Buy tickets from the machines, which have pictures but no English writing.

In addition to *rāmen*, you can get green-tea ice cream and other Japanese desserts at **Chasen**, and *tako-yaki* (battered octopus pieces) at **Miyako**.

### CAFFE VELOCÉ                        CAFE ¥

Map p212 (カフェ・ベローチェ; ☑342-5165; 843-2 Higashishiokoji-chō, Shiokoji-dōri-Nshinotōin higashi-iru, Shimogyō-ku; sandwiches from ¥250; ⊙6.30am-11pm; ◙; ⊞Kyoto Station) This casual cafe is a great place to kill some time while waiting for a train. All the usual coffee and tea drinks are available, along with some pastries and sandwiches.

### SHUSAI JŌJŌ                         IZAKAYA ¥¥

Map p212 (酒采乗々; ☑371-2010; Nishino-toin, Shichijō-sagaru, Shimogyō-ku; dinner from ¥2500; ⊙5.30pm-2am; ⑤Karasuma line to Kyoto, ⊞JR Tōkaidō Main line to Kyoto) Shusai Jōjō is a funky modern *izakaya* (Japanese pub-eatery) within walking distance of Kyoto Station. Sit at the counter or at one of the tables. There's an excellent variety of sake to choose from and a wide variety of dishes to go with it.

#  SHOPPING

### BIC CAMERA                          ELECTRONICS

Map p212 (ビックカメラ; ☑353-1111; 927 Higashi Shiokōji-chō, Shimogyō-ku; ⊙10am-9pm; ⊞Kyoto Station) This vast new shop is directly connected to Kyoto Station via the Nishinotō-in gate; otherwise, it's accessed by leaving the north (Karasuma) gate and walking west. You will be amazed by the sheer amount of goods this store has on display.

Just be sure that an English-operating manual is available for your purchases. For computer peripherals and software, keep in mind that not all items on offer will work with English-operating systems.

### YODOBASHI CAMERA
ELECTRONICS

Map p212 (ヨドバシカメラ; ✆351-1010; 590-2 Higashi Shiokōji-chō, Shimogyō-ku; ⊙9.30am-10pm; ⧖Kyoto Station) This mammoth shop sells a range of electronics, camera and computer goods, and also has a restaurant floor, supermarket, bookshop, cafe and, well, the list goes on. It's a few minutes' walk north of Kyoto Station.

### PORTA SHOPPING MALL
SHOPPING CENTRE

Map p212 (ポルタ; ✆365-7528; B1 fl, Kyoto Station Bldg, Karasuma-dōri, Shiokōji-sagaru, Shimogyō-ku; ⊙10am-8pm; ⧖Kyoto Station) Located under the front (north side) of Kyoto Station (take the escalators down from just outside the central gate), you'll find this utilitarian shopping mall that's crammed with restaurants, cafes, clothing stores and electronics/camera shops. It's good for a quick bite before a long trip.

### ISETAN DEPARTMENT STORE
DEPARTMENT STORE

Map p212 (ジェイアール京都伊勢丹; ✆352-1111; Kyoto Station Bldg, Karasuma-dōri, Shiokōji-sagaru, Shimogyō-ku; ⊙10am-8pm, closed irregularly; ⧖Kyoto Station) This large, elegant department store is located inside the Kyoto Station building, making it perfect for a last-minute spot of shopping before hopping on the train to the airport. Don't miss the B1 and B2 food floors.

### KUNGYOKU-DŌ
CRAFTS

Map p212 (薫玉堂; ✆371-0162; Horikawa-dōri, Nishihonganji-mae, Shimogyō-ku; ⊙9am-5.30pm, closed 1st & 3rd Sun each month; ⧖Kyoto Station) A haven for the olfactory sense, this shop has sold incense and aromatic woods (for burning, similar to incense) for four centuries. This is a great place to pick up some distinctively Japanese souvenirs and gifts which are easy to carry home.

### KŌJITSU SANSŌ
OUTDOOR GEAR

Map p212 (好日山荘; ✆708-5178; 5th fl, Kyoto Yodobashi Camera, Karasuma-dōri, Shichijō-sagaru, Shimogyō-ku; ⊙9.30am-10pm; ⧖Kyoto Station) On the 5th floor of the Yodobashi Camera building, this is one of Kyoto's biggest outdoor goods shops. If you're heading up to the Japan Alps to do some hiking, you might want to stop here before getting on the train.

### KYŌSEN-DŌ
CRAFTS

Map p212 (京扇堂; ✆371-4151; www.kyosendo.co.jp; Tsutsugane-chō 46, Higashinotōin-dōri, Shōmen-agaru, Shimogyō-ku; ⊙9am-5pm Mon-Sat, 10am-6pm Sun & public holidays; ⧖Kyoto Station) Kyōsen-dō sells a colourful variety of paper fans; here you can see the process of assembling the fans and even paint your own.

### ÆON MALL KYOTO
SHOPPING CENTRE

Map p212 (イオンモール; 1 Nishikujō Toriiguchi-chō, Minami-ku; ⊙10am-9pm, food floor until 10pm; ⧖Kyoto Station) A five-minute walk southwest of Kyoto Station (exit Hachijō-guchi), this huge shopping mall is a good place to kill some time, grab a meal and do some shopping before getting on a train.

You'll find branches of most of the big Japanese retailers here, including Muji, Uniqlo, Montbell, Daiso and Sofmap (computers etc). The 4th floor is the food floor and is home to the usual Japanese and international chains.

### POPONDETTA ÆON MALL KYOTO SHOP
TOYS

Map p212 (ポポンデッタ イオンモールKYOTO店; ✆644-9220; 4th fl, Æon Mall Kyoto, 1 Nishikujō, Toriiguchi-chō, Minami-ku; ⊙10am-9pm; ⧖Kyoto Station) If you've got a child who likes trains, don't miss this excellent toy train shop. In addition to a wide range of toy trains, you'll find a great model railroad layout to keep the kids entertained.

### AVANTI
DEPARTMENT STORE

Map p212 (アバンティ; ✆682-5031; Higashikujō Nishisannō-chō 31, Minami-ku; ⊙10am-9pm; ⧖Kyoto Station) This department store has a decent bookshop on its 6th floor, and a food court and supermarket on its B1 floor. It's geared mostly to younger Kyoto shoppers but it's good for browsing if you have time to kill while waiting for a train. Take the underground passage from Kyoto Station.

# Downtown Kyoto

## Neighbourhood Top Five

❶ Walking through **Nishiki Market** (p55), marvelling at all the weird and wonderful ingredients that go into Kyoto cuisine. Nishiki is the perfect way to spend a rainy day in Kyoto, and it's a good antidote to an overdose of temples.

❷ Taking an evening stroll along **Ponto-chō** (p56).

❸ Delving into the wonderful world of manga at the **Kyoto International Manga Museum** (p56).

❹ Getting lost in the department-store food floors at **Takashimaya** (p65) or **Daimaru** (p65).

❺ Shopping for the perfect gift in the shopping district around **Shijō and Kawaramachi streets**.

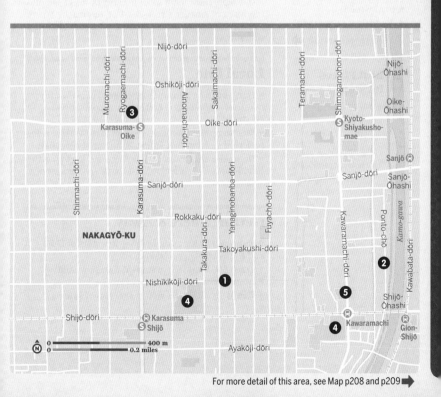

For more detail of this area, see Map p208 and p209 ➡

## Lonely Planet's Top Tip

Finding a good place to eat in Downtown Kyoto can be confusing (there are almost *too many* places to choose from). If you want a lot of choice in a small area, hit one of the *resutoran-gai* (restaurant floors) at Takashimaya or Daimaru.

###  Best Places to Eat

➡ Ippūdō (p57)

➡ Kyōgoku Kane-yo (p60)

➡ Yoshikawa (p62)

For reviews, see p57. ➡

###  Best Places to Drink

➡ Bar Bunkyu (p64)

➡ Bar K6 (p63)

➡ World Peace Love (p64)

For reviews, see p62. ➡

###  Best Places to Shop

➡ Wagami no Mise (p65)

➡ Aritsugu (p65)

➡ Takashimaya (p65)

➡ Daimaru (p65)

For reviews, see p65. ➡

# Explore: Downtown Kyoto

Downtown Kyoto is not really a place you go for sightseeing. Rather, it's where you go to do everything else: eat, drink, shop and sleep. That said, it does contain a handful of first-rate sights, but sightseeing here is more about soaking up the vibe than checking out individual places.

Downtown Kyoto is easily reached from almost anywhere in town: the city's two subway lines serve the area, as does the private Hankyū line, and the private Keihan line, which stops just across the river. You could even walk from Kyoto Station to Downtown Kyoto in about half an hour. Downtown Kyoto is bounded by the Kamo-gawa (the river) to the east, Karasuma-dōri to the west, Oike-dōri to the north and Shijō-dōri to the south. In this relatively small square area, you will find the thickest selection of restaurants, shops, hotels and businesses in all of Kyoto.

The main streets of Shijō and Kawaramachi hold some of the biggest shops, but you'll also find a huge selection of shops in the area's four covered shopping streets (known as *shōtengai*): Sanjō (good for restaurants), Teramachi (a mix of art, religious items and tat), Shinkyōgoku (mostly tacky souvenirs for children) and Nishiki Market (the city's main food market). But don't just explore these main shopping streets: also head into the maze of smaller streets west of Teramachi, where you'll find a great array of interesting boutiques and restaurants.

## Local Life

➡ **Hang-out** The Mina (p65) shopping complex, with branches of Uniqlo and Loft stores, is popular with everyone.

➡ **Meeting point** Starbucks (p63) at Sanjō-Ōhashi is the preferred meeting spot for locals and foreigners alike.

➡ **Romantic spot** Paris has the Seine and Kyoto has the Kamo-gawa. This is where local couples go for a bit of 'quality time'.

## Getting There & Away

➡ **Subway** The Karasuma subway line stops at Shijō and Karasuma-Oike stations.

➡ **Train** The Hankyū line stops at Karasuma and Kawaramachi.

➡ **Bus** Many city buses stop in Downtown Kyoto.

JAMIE MARSHALL / TRIBALEYE IMAGES / GETTY IMAGES ©

## TOP SIGHT
# NISHIKI MARKET

**Nishiki Market (Nishiki-kōji Ichiba) is one of Kyoto's real highlights, especially if you have an interest in cooking and eating. Commonly known as Kyoto no daidokoro (Kyoto's Kitchen) by locals, Nishiki is where a lot of Kyoto's high-end restaurateurs and wealthy individuals do their food shopping. If you want to see all the weird and wonderful foods that go into Kyoto cuisine, this is the place.**

Nishiki Market is right smack in the centre of town, one block north of Shijō-dōri, running from Teramachi *shōtengai* to Takakura-dōri (ending almost behind Daimaru department store). Covered for its entire length, this pedestrian-only market is home to 126 shops (at last count). It's said that there were stores here as early as the 14th century, and it's known for sure that the street was a wholesale fish market in the Edo Period (1603–1868). After the end of Edo, as Japan entered the modern era, the market became a retail market, which it remains today.

The emphasis is on locally produced Japanese food items like *tsukemono* (Japanese pickles), tea, beans, rice, seaweed and fish (if you know how to read Japanese or know what to look for, you'll even see the odd bit of whale meat). In recent years the market has been evolving from a strictly local food market into a tourist attraction, and you'll now find several souvenir shops selling Kyoto-style souvenirs mixed in among the food stalls.

The Aritsugu knife shop turns out some of the most exquisite knives on earth. Take time to pick the perfect one for your needs, then watch as the craftsmen carefully put a final edge on the knife with the giant round sharpening stone – the end product will be so sharp it will scare you.

### DON'T MISS...
➡ Iketsuru Kajitsu (p62)
➡ Aritsugu (p65)

### PRACTICALITIES
➡ 錦市場
➡ Map p208
➡ Nishikikōji-dōri, btwn Teramachi & Takakura, Nakagyō-ku
➡ ⏰9am-5pm
➡ Ⓢ Karasuma line to Shijō, Ⓗ Hankyū line to Karasuma or Kawaramachi

# ◉ SIGHTS

**NISHIKI MARKET**                    MARKET
See p55.

**PONTO-CHŌ**                    NEIGHBOURHOOD
Map p208 (先斗町; Ponto-chō, Nakagyō-ku;
Ⓢ Tōzai line to Sanjo-Keihan or Kyoto-Shiyakusho-
mae, Ⓡ Keihan line to Sanjo, Hankyū line to Kawaramachi) There are few streets in Asia that rival
this narrow pedestrian-only walkway for
atmosphere. Not much to look at by day, the
street comes alive by night, with wonderful
lanterns, traditional wooden exteriors, and
elegant Kyotoites disappearing into the
doorways of elite old restaurants and bars.

Ponto-chō is a great place to spot *geiko*
(geisha) and *maiko* (apprentice geisha) making their way between appointments, especially on weekend evenings at the Shijō-dōri
end of the street. Many of the restaurants
and teahouses can be difficult to enter, but
several reasonably priced, accessible places
can be found. Even if you have no intention
of patronising the businesses here, it makes a
nice stroll in the evening, perhaps combined
with a walk in nearby Gion (see p89).

**KYOTO INTERNATIONAL
MANGA MUSEUM**                    MUSEUM
Map p208 (京都国際マンガミュージアム;
www.kyotomm.jp; Karasuma-dōri, Oike-agaru,
Nakagyō-ku; adult/child ¥800/300; ⊙10am-
6pm, closed Wed; Ⓢ Karasuma or Tōzai lines to
Karasuma-Oike) This fine museum has a collection of some 300,000 manga (Japanese
comic books). Located in an old elementary
school building, the museum is the perfect
introduction to the art of manga. While
most of the manga and displays are in Japanese, the collection of translated works is
growing. In addition to the galleries that
show both the historical development of
manga and original artwork done in manga
style, there are beginners' workshops and
portrait drawings on weekends.

Visitors with children will appreciate
the children's library and the occasional
performances of *kami-shibai* (humorous
traditional Japanese sliding-picture shows),
not to mention the artificial lawn where the
kids can run free. The museum hosts six-
month-long special exhibits yearly: check
the website for details.

**MUSEUM OF KYOTO**                    MUSEUM
Map p208 (京都文化博物館; Takakura-dōri,
Sanjō-agaru, Nakagyō-ku; admission ¥500, extra
for special exhibitions; ⊙10am-7.30pm, closed
Mon; Ⓢ Tōzai lines to Karasuma-
Oike) This museum is worth visiting if a special exhibition is on (the regular exhibits
are not particularly interesting and don't
have much in the way of English explanations). On the 1st floor, the Roji Tempō is a
reconstruction of a typical merchant area
in Kyoto during the Edo period (this section
can be entered free; some of the shops sell
souvenirs and serve local dishes). Check the
*Kyoto Visitor's Guide* for upcoming special
exhibitions.

**KALEIDOSCOPE MUSEUM
OF KYOTO**                    MUSEUM
Map p208 (京都万華鏡ミュージアム; 📞254-
7902; 706-3 Dongeinmae-chō, Aneykōji-dōri,

---

## ROMANTIC WALKS IN KYOTO

Kyoto is one of the world's great walking cities, especially after dark. If you fancy an
evening stroll with someone special, here are a few romantic routes:

**Ponto-chō** Take a short but sweet stroll through one of the most atmospheric lanes
in Asia. Expect crowds in the evening.

**Kiyamachi** The section of Kiyamachi-dōri between Oike and Gojō is incredibly beautiful after dark, especially during cherry-blossom season. Only the busy section between Sanjō and Shijō is a little gaudy for our taste.

**Kiyomizu to Yasaka** While it's clogged with tourists during the day, the main tourist
route from Kiyomizu-dera down to Yasaka-jinja (p83) is usually almost deserted after
dark. It's truly magical at this time.

**Path of Philosophy** The crowds are usually gone by 5pm here, leaving this scenic
pathway (p96) to locals and savvy travellers.

**Gion** A brief stroll along Hanami-kōji, across Shijō, and over to Shimbashi (p82) is
sure to seal the deal on any budding romance.

Higashinotōin higashi-iru, Nakagyō-ku; adult/child ¥300/200, special exhibits extra; ⏱10am-6pm, closed Mon or following day if Mon is a holiday; ⓈKarasuma or Tōzai lines to Karasuma-Oike) This one-room museum is filled with unexpected wonders. Frankly, we had no idea of the variety and complexity in the field of kaleidoscopes. We don't know who will enjoy this more, children or the adults trying to keep them entertained. It's right behind the Museum of Kyoto.

### SHIORI-AN
MUSEUM

Map p208 (紫織庵; ☏241-0215; Aneyakōji-dōri, Takakura, Nakagyō-ku; admission ¥500; ⏱10am-5pm; ⓈKarasuma or Tōzai lines to Karasuma-Oike) Set in a large traditional merchant's house, this kimono shop/museum is a great place to learn about kimonos and the history of kimonos. You can also see the way part of the traditional building was converted into a Western-style building around the turn of last century (when Japan became fascinated with all things Western). There is an English brochure available.

 **EATING**

### ★ IPPŪDŌ
RĀMEN ¥

Map p208 (一風堂; ☏213-8800; Higashinotō-in, Nishikikōji higashi-iru, Nakagyō-ku; rāmen ¥750-950; ⏱11am-2am; ◨; ⓈKarasuma line to Shijō) There's a reason that there's usually a line outside this *rāmen* joint at lunchtime: the *rāmen* is awesome and the bite-sized *gyōza* (dumplings) are to die for. We recommend the *gyōza* set meal (¥750 or ¥850 depending on your choice of *rāmen*). It's on Nishiki-dōri, next to a post office and diagonally across from a Starbucks.

### CAFÉ BIBLIOTEC HELLO!
CAFE ¥

Map p208 (カフェビブリオティックハロー!; ☏231-8625; 650 Seimei-chō, Nijō-dōri, Yanaginobanba higashi-iru, Nakagyō-ku; meals from ¥1000, coffee ¥450; ⏱11.30am-midnight; ◨; ⓈTōzai line to Kyoto-Shiyakusho-mae) As the name suggests, books line the walls of this cool cafe located in a converted *machiya* (traditional Japanese townhouse). You can get the usual range of coffee and tea drinks here, as well as light cafe lunches. It's popular with young ladies who work nearby and it's a great place to relax with a book or magazine. Look for the plants out the front.

### TSUKIMOCHIYA NAOMASA
SWEETS ¥

Map p208 (月餅家　直正; ☏231-0175; 530 Kamiōsaka-chō, Kiyamachi-dōri, Sanjō-agaru, Nakagyō-ku; tsukimochi ¥150; ⏱9.30am-7pm, closed Thu & 3rd Wed of month; ⓇKeihan line to Sanjō) This classic old sweet shop, about 50m north of Sanjō-dōri on Kiyamachi-dōri, is a great place to get acquainted with traditional Kyoto sweets. Just point at what looks good and staff will wrap it up nicely for you. There's no English sign; look for the traditional Kyoto exterior and the sweets in the window.

### BIOTEI
VEGETARIAN ¥

Map p208 (びお亭; ☏255-0086; 2nd fl, M&I Bldg, 28 Umetada-chō, Sanjō-dōri, Higashinotōin nishi-iru, Nakagyō-ku; lunch from ¥860; ⏱lunch & dinner; closed Sun, Mon, dinner Thu & lunch Sat; ✒◨; ⓈTōzai or Karasuma lines to Karasuma-Oike) Located diagonally across from the Nakagyō post office, this is a favourite of Kyoto vegetarians and has an English menu. It serves daily sets of Japanese vegetarian food (the occasional bit of meat is offered as an option, but you'll be asked your preference). The seating is rather cramped but the food is very good and carefully made from quality ingredients.

It's on the corner. Go up the metal spiral staircase.

### NISHIKI WARAI
OKONOMIYAKI ¥

Map p208 (錦わらい; ☏257-5966; 1st fl, Mizukōto Bldg, 597 Nishiuoya-chō, Nishikikōji-dōri, Takakura nishi-iru, Nakagyō-ku; okonomiyaki from ¥680; ⏱11.30am-midnight; ◨; ⓈKarasuma line to Shijō, ⓇHankyū line to Karasuma) This Nishiki-dōri restaurant is a great place to try *okonomiyaki* (savoury pancakes) in casual surroundings. It can get a little smoky, but it's a fun spot to eat. It serves sets from as little as ¥680 at lunch.

It's about 20m west of the west end of Nishiki Market; look for the English sign in the window.

### RĀMEN KAIRIKIYA
RĀMEN ¥

Map p208 (ラーメン魁力屋; ☏251-0303; 1st fl, Hijikata Bldg, 435-2 Ebisu-chō, Kawaramachi-dōri, Sanjō-agaru, Nakagyō-ku; rāmen from ¥650; ⏱11am-3am; ◨; ⓈTōzai line to Kyoto-Shiyakusho-mae) Not far from the Sanjō–Kawaramachi intersection, this popular *rāmen* specialist welcomes foreigners with an English menu and friendly staff. It's got several types of *rāmen* to choose from and tasty sets that include items like fried rice, fried chicken or *gyōza*, all for about ¥950.

It's pretty easy to spot: look for the red-and-white signage.

### KERALA
INDIAN ¥

Map p208 (ケララ; ☎251-0141; 2nd fl, KUS Bldg, Kawaramachi-dōri, Sanjō-agaru, Nakagyō-ku; lunch/dinner from ¥850/2600; ⏱11.30am-2pm & 5-9pm; ✍◎; ⓢTōzai line to Kyoto-Shiyakusho-mae) This narrow restaurant upstairs on Kawaramachi-dōri is Kyoto's best Indian restaurant. The ¥850 lunch set menu is an excellent deal, as is the vegetarian lunch, and the English menu is a bonus. Dinners run closer to ¥2500 per head and are of very high quality. Finish off the meal with the incredibly rich and creamy coconut ice cream.

Kerala is located on the 2nd floor; look for the steet-level food display.

### MUSASHI SUSHI
SUSHI ¥

Map p208 (寿しのむさし; ☎222-0634; Kawaramachi-dōri, Sanjō-agaru, Nakagyō-ku; all plates ¥140; ⏱11am-10pm; ◎; ⓢTōzai line to Kyoto-Shiyakusho-mae, ⒭Keihan line to Sanjō) If you've never tried a *kaiten-zushi* (conveyor-belt sushi restaurant), don't miss this place – all the dishes are a mere ¥140. It's not the best sushi in the world, but it's cheap, reliable and fun. Needless to say, it's easy to eat here: you just grab what you want off the conveyor belt.

If you can't find what you want on the belt, there's also an English menu. Musashi is just outside the entrance to the Sanjō covered arcade; look for the miniature sushi conveyor belt in the window.

### OOTOYA
SHOKUDŌ ¥

Map p208 (大戸屋; ☎255-4811; 2nd fl, Goshoame Bldg, Sanjō-dōri, Kawaramachi higashi-iru, Nakagyō-ku; meals from ¥480; ⏱11am-11pm; ⓢTōzai line to Kyoto-Shiyakusho-mae, ⒭Keihan line to Sanjō) Ootoya is a clean, modern Japanese restaurant that serves a range of standard dishes at bargain-basement prices. It's popular with Kyoto students and young office workers. The large picture menu makes ordering a breeze. Look for the English sign, then climb a flight of steps.

### LUGOL
CAFE ¥

Map p208 (ルゴール; ☎213-2888; 50-1 Nakano-chō, Shinmachi-dōri, Oike-agaru, Nakagyō-ku; lunch sets ¥880; ⏱11.30am-11pm, closed 3rd Wed

of month; ⓢKarasuma or Tōzai lines to Karasuma-Oike) For a quick snack or cuppa in groovy surroundings, this cosy coffee shop on the west side of Downtown Kyoto is a very nice choice. We go there for decorating ideas as much as for the drinks.

### MEW'Z CAFE
ASIAN FUSION ¥

Map p208 (ミューズカフェ; ☎212-2911; 717-1 Yōhōjimae-chō, Teramachi-dōri, Nijō-agaru, Nakagyō-ku; lunch/dinner sets from ¥750/1160; ⏱11.30am-10pm Thu, Fri & Sun-Tue, noon-11pm Sat; ☎; ⓢTōzai line to Kyoto-Shiyakusho-mae) This pan-Asian cafe-restaurant on Teramachi-dōri is a great place to relax between bouts of antique hunting in the nearby shops. The place is pleasantly spacious, the music is usually good and the food is generally tasty.

### KŌSENDŌ-SUMI
JAPANESE ¥

Map p208 (光泉洞寿み; ☎241-7377; Aneyakōji-dōri, Sakaimachi higashi-iru, Nakagyō-ku; daily lunch ¥980; ⏱11.30am-3.30pm Mon-Sat; ⓢKarasuma or Tōzai lines to Karasuma-Oike) For a pleasant lunch downtown, try this unpretentious little restaurant located in an old Japanese house. The daily lunch special, which is usually simple and healthy Japanese fare, is always displayed out the front for your inspection. It's near the Museum of Kyoto, next to a small car park.

### KARAFUNEYA COFFEE SANJŌ HONTEN
CAFE ¥

Map p208 (からふねや珈琲三条本店; ☎254-8774; 39 Daikoku-chō, Kawaramachi-dōri, Sanjō-sagaru, Nakagyō-ku; simple meals around ¥900; ⏱9am-1am; ◎; ⓢTōzai line to Kyoto-Shiyakusho-mae, ⒭Keihan line to Sanjō) This casual coffee and dessert shop, right downtown on Kawaramachi-dōri, is smack in the middle of Kyoto's main shopping district. It's a great spot for a pick-me-up during a day of retail therapy.

Japan is famous for its plastic food models, but this place takes them to a whole new level – it's like some futuristic dessert museum. We like the centrepiece of the display: the mother of all sundaes that goes for ¥10,000 to ¥18,000 and requires advance reservation to order. Lesser mortals can try the tasty *matcha* (powdered green tea) parfait for ¥780 or any of the cafe drinks and light meals on offer.

## ℹ️ KYOTO COMMON SENSE

Common sense varies from place to place. In New York, you take the subway. In Kathmandu, you avoid drinking the tap water. In Russia, you don't challenge the locals to drinking contests. In Kyoto, even if you dispense with common sense, you don't run the risk of serious trouble, but there are a few things to keep in mind that will make everything easier and perhaps a little safer:

➡ Look both ways when exiting a shop or hotel onto a pavement – there is almost always someone on a bicycle coming tearing your way. This is especially important if you have young ones in tow.

➡ Don't take a taxi in the main Higashiyama sightseeing district during cherry blossom season – the streets will be so crowded that it will be faster to walk or cycle.

➡ Never wait in line for food even in the busy season. There are so many restaurants in Kyoto that it doesn't makes sense to wait to get into a crowded restaurant (you'll see local tourists queuing at popular spots, but there's no need to follow their example).

### CAFÉ INDEPENDANTS                      CAFE ¥

Map p208 (カフェ　アンデパンダン; 📞255-4312; Basement, 1928 Bldg, Sanjō-Gokomachi kado, Nakagyō-ku; salads/sandwiches from ¥400/800; ⏰11.30am-midnight; ⓈTōzai line to Kyoto-Shiyakusho-mae) Located beneath a gallery, this cool subterranean cafe offers a range of light meals and cafe drinks in a bohemian atmosphere (after you eat, check out the gallery space upstairs). A lot of the food offerings are displayed for you to choose from. The emphasis is on healthy sandwiches and salads.

Take the stairs on your left before the gallery.

### LIBERTE                                      FRENCH ¥

Map p208 (リベルテ; 📞253-0600; 65-2 Tokiwagi-chō, Teramachi-dōri, Nijō-agaru, Nakagyō-ku; dishes from ¥600, lunch sets ¥1000, drinks from ¥320; ⏰8am-9pm Tue-Sun; ⓈTōzai line to Kyoto-Shiyakusho-mae) With a bakery downstairs and a simple bistro-style restaurant upstairs, this charming French spot is a great place to stop for lunch while perusing the shops on Teramachi-dōri. The daily lunch specials are simple but sufficient and the clean, well-lit space is very relaxing.

### CAPRICCIOSA                              ITALIAN ¥

Map p208 (カプリチョーザ; 📞221-7496; Kawaramachi-dōri, Sanjō-sagaru, Nakagyō-ku; lunch/dinner from ¥1000/1500; ⏰11.30am-11pm; 🚻; 🚈Keihan line to Sanjō) For heaped portions of pasta at rock-bottom prices you won't do much better than this long-time student favourite. Pasta dishes start at around ¥800 and you can try pizzas, salads, and various

meat and fish dishes. It will not be the best Italian you've ever had, but you'll probably leave full and happy.

It's near the Sanjō-Kawaramachi crossing; look for the red-brick steps and the green awning. There's an English menu and an English sign.

### SARYO ZEN CAFE                            CAFE ¥

Map p208 (茶寮「然」カフェ; Zenkashoin Kyoto Muromachi Store, 271-1 Takoyakushi-chō, Muromachi-dōri, Nijō-sagaru, Nakagyō-ku; drinks from ¥1000; ⏰10am-7pm, closed 2nd & 4th Mon of month; 🚻; ⓈKarasuma or Tōzai line to Karasuma-Oike) This brilliant modern tea room is a great place for a break – a break from sightseeing and a break from the ubiquitous international coffee chains that are taking over the city. You can enjoy a cup of *matcha* tea served with a delicious Kyoto sweet, all in extremely comfortable surroundings.

### YAK & YETI                               NEPALESE ¥

Map p208 (ヤック&イェティ; 📞213-7919; Gokomachi-dōri, Nishikikōji-sagaru, Nakagyō-ku; curry lunch sets from ¥750; ⏰11.30am-3pm & 5-11pm Tue-Sun; 🚻; ⓈKarasuma line to Shijō) This tiny joint serves more than just the *dal bhaat* (rice and lentil curry) that most people associate with Nepalese cuisine. In fact, the fare (good curries and tasty nan bread) is probably closer to Indian. There is counter seating, but we like to sit on the comfortable cushions. English menus available.

The staff is pretty chuffed about being listed in Lonely Planet guidebooks and has posted a picture of an old edition out the front – should be no trouble finding it.

★**KYŌGOKU KANE-YO**      UNAGI ¥¥

Map p208 (京極かねよ; ☎221-0669; 456 Matsugaechō, Rokkaku, Shinkyōgoku higashi-iru, Nakagyō-ku; unagi over rice from ¥1200; ⏰11.30am-9pm; 🚇; ⓢTōzai line to Kyoto-Shiyakusho-mae) This is a good place to try *unagi* (eel), that most sublime of Japanese dishes. You can choose to either sit downstairs with a nice view of the waterfall, or upstairs on the tatami. The *kane-yo donburi* (eel over rice; ¥1200) set is excellent value. Look for the barrels of live eels outside and the wooden facade.

**TSUKIJI SUSHISEI**      SUSHI ¥¥

Map p208 (築地寿司清; ☎252-1537; 581 Obiya-chō, Takakura-dōri, Nishikikōji-sagaru, Nakagyō-ku; sushi sets ¥1296-3150; ⏰11.30am-3pm & 5-10pm Mon-Fri, 11.30am-10pm Sat, Sun & holidays; 🚇; ⓢKarasuma line to Shijō) On the basement floor, next to Daimaru department store, this simple restaurant serves excellent sushi. You can order a set or just point at what looks good. You can see inside the restaurant from street level, so it should be easy to spot.

**UOSUE**      JAPANESE ¥¥

Map p208 (うをすえ; ☎351-1437; 724 Shinmei-chō, Ayakōji-dōri, Higashinotōin higashi-iru, Shimogyō-ku; lunch/bentō ¥1080, dinner from ¥3990; ⏰11am-2pm & 5-10pm, closed Sun & lunch Sat; ⓢKarasuma line to Karasuma) Uosue is one of the best-value Japanese places in town. It's a traditional Kyoto-style restaurant with a clean interior and friendly proprietors. For lunch, try the wonderful *nijū bentō* for ¥1080. At dinner the *omakase ryōri kōsu* is a great way to sample *kaiseki ryōri* (Japanese haute cuisine) without breaking the bank: it costs just ¥3990.

---

## JAPANESE-STYLE CAFES

If you'd like a change from the international coffee chains you're used to back home, why not try a uniquely Japanese cafe or teahouse? These places usually serve a variety of drinks based on green tea, including *matcha* (powdered green tea), along with a variety of interesting Japanese sweets. Here are a few places we recommend:

➡ Saryo Zen Cafe (p59)

➡ Toraya Karyō Kyoto Ichijō (p76)

➡ Kasagi-ya (p86)

➡ Kagizen Yoshifusa (p86)

---

It's next to a tiny shrine – keep an eye out for the sake barrels out the front.

**TŌSUIRŌ**      TOFU ¥¥

Map p208 (豆水楼; ☎251-1600; Kiyamachi-dōri, Sanjō-agaru, Nakagyō-ku; lunch/dinner ¥2000/5000; ⏰11.30am-2pm & 5-9.30pm Mon-Sat, noon-8.30pm Sun; ⓢTōzai line to Kyoto-Shiyakusho-mae) We really like this specialist tofu restaurant. It's got great traditional Japanese decor and in summer you can sit on the *yuka* (dining platform) outside and take in a view of the Kamo-gawa. You will be amazed by the incredible variety of dishes that can be created with tofu.

At lunch the *machiya-zen* (tofu set; ¥2205) is highly recommended. At dinner we suggest the Higashiyama tofu set (¥3858). Tōsuirō is at the end of an alley on the north side.

**DIN TAI FUNG**      TAIWANESE ¥¥

Map p208 (鼎泰豐; ☎221-8811; 3rd fl, Kyoto Takashimaya Department Store, Shijo-Kawara-machi, Shimogyō-ku; lunch & dinner sets from ¥2000; ⏰10.30am-8pm Mon-Sat; 🚊Hankyū line to Kawaramachi) If you're downtown and you feel like a break from Japanese food, head to this popular Taiwanese place on the 3rd flood of Takashimaya. You have to drop about ¥2000 to get full here, but it's worth it: the dumplings are superb!

**HONKE TAGOTO**      NOODLES ¥¥

Map p208 (本家 田毎; ☎221-3030; Sanjō-dōri, Teramachi higashi-iru, Nakagyō-ku; dishes ¥1000, courses ¥3000-6000; ⏰11am-9pm; 🚇; ⓢTōzai line to Kyoto-Shiyakusho-mae, 🚊Keihan line to Sanjō) This casual restaurant in the Sanjō covered arcade serves a variety of *soba* (thin brown buckwheat noodles) and *udon* (thick white wheat noodles) dishes. It can get crowded at lunchtime and the service can be rather brusque, but the noodles are very good and the English/picture menu helps with ordering. The tempura *teishoku* (set-course meal) makes a great lunch.

**LE BOUCHON**      FRENCH ¥¥

Map p208 (ブション; ☎211-5220; 71 Enoki-chō, Nijō-dōri, Teramachi higashi-iru, Nakagyo-ku; set meals from about ¥1500; ⏰11.30am-2.30pm & 5.30-9.30pm; 🚇; ⓢTōzai line to Kyoto-Shiyakusho-mae) For casual French fare at reasonable prices, Le Bouchon is a great choice. Like a good Parisian bistro, it tends to be boisterous, crowded and approachable. The set meals are the way to go and the fish dishes usually outshine the meat dishes.

**MUKADE-YA**  JAPANESE ¥¥

Map p208 (百足屋; ☑256-7039; Shinmachi-dōri, Nishikikōji-agaru, Nakagyō-ku; lunch/dinner from ¥1640/5400; ⊙11am-2pm & 5-9pm, closed Wed; Ⓢ Karasuma line to Shijō) Mukade-ya is an atmospheric restaurant located in an exquisite *machiya* west of Karasuma-dōri. For lunch try the special *bentō*: two rounds (five small dishes each) of delectable *obanzai* (Kyoto-style home cooking) fare. *Kaiseki* (Japanese haute cuisine) courses start at ¥5400.

**GANKO**  SUSHI ¥¥

Map p208 (がんこ; ☑255-1128; 101 Nakajima-chō, Sanjō-dōri, Kawaramachi higashi-iru, Nakagyō-ku; lunch ¥1000-2500, dinner around ¥5000; ⊙11am-11pm; 🖼; Ⓢ Tōzai line to Kyoto-Shiyakusho-mae or Sanjō Keihan, Ⓡ Keihan line to Sanjō) This giant four-storey dining hall is part of Kansai's biggest sushi chain. The ground floor is the sushi area (you can order non-sushi dishes here as well); it has a long sushi counter and plenty of tables (and room for a stroller if you have tots in tow). It's very popular with both tourists and locals.

There's an extensive English/picture menu and the set meals are good value. Downstairs is an *izakaya* (pub-eatery) and upstairs has rooms for parties. This place may have the most plastic-looking food models of any restaurant window in Kyoto. It's near the Sanjō-Ōhashi bridge.

**MUMOKUTEKI CAFE**  VEGETARIAN ¥¥

Map p208 (ムモクテキカフェ; www.mumokuteki.com; 2nd fl, Human Forum Bldg, 351 Iseya-chō, Gokomachi-dōri, Rokkaku-sagaru, Nakagyō-ku; meals from ¥1500; ⊙11.30am-10pm; 😊🍴🖼; Ⓡ Hankyū line to Kawaramachi) This vegetarian cafe hidden above a shop in the Teramachi shopping arcade is a lifesaver for many Kyoto vegetarians. The food is tasty, varied and served in casual surroundings. Most of it is vegan, but non-vegan options are clearly marked on the menu. It's hidden up a flight of steps above a clothing shop called Spinns; the steps are located inside the shop.

**ZU ZU**  IZAKAYA ¥¥

Map p208 (厨厨; ☑231-0736; Ponto-chō, Takoyakushi-agaru, Nishi-gawa, Nakagyō-ku; dinner ¥3000-4000; ⊙6pm-2am, to midnight Sun, closed Tue; Ⓡ Hankyū line to Kawaramachi) This Ponto-chō *izakaya* is a fun place to eat. The

best bet when ordering is to ask the waiter for a recommendation. The fare is sort of nouveau Japanese, with menu items such as shrimp with tofu and chicken with plum sauce. Look for the white stucco exterior and black bars on the windows.

**GANKO NIJŌ-EN**  JAPANESE ¥¥

Map p208 (がんこ二条苑; ☑223-3456; Kiyamachi-dōri, Nijō-sagaru, Nakagyō-ku; lunch & dinner course from ¥3000; ⊙11am-10pm; Ⓢ Tōzai line to Kyoto-Shiyakusho-mae) This is an upmarket branch of the Ganko chain that serves sushi and simple *kaiseki* sets. There's a picture menu and you can stroll in the stunning garden before or after your meal. It's near the Nijō-Kiyamachi crossing; you can't miss the grand entrance or the food models in the glass window.

**OMEN NIPPON**  NOODLES ¥¥

Map p208 (おめんNippon; ☑253-0377; 171 Kashiwaya-chō, Shijō-dōri, Ponto-chō nishi-iru, Nakagyo-ku; udon ¥1150; ⊙11.30am-3pm & 5-10pm, closed Thu; 🖼; Ⓡ Hankyū line to Kawaramachi) This is one of two downtown branches of the famous Ginkaku-ji noodle restaurant. It serves a variety of healthy set meals, such as a good ¥1980 lunch set that includes noodles and a few sides.

It's a small, calm place that's a nice oasis amid the downtown mayhem, good for a light lunch while out shopping, and it has an English menu to boot. Look for the word 'Nippon' on the sign.

**TAGOTO HONTEN**  KAISEKI ¥¥

Map p208 (田ごと本店; ☑221-1811; 34 Otabi-chō, Shijō-dōri, Kawaramachi nishi-iru, Nakagyō-ku; lunch/dinner from ¥1600/3400; ⊙lunch 11am-3pm, dinner 4.30-9pm; 🖼; Ⓡ Keihan line to Shijō, Hankyū line to Kawaramachi) Across the street from Takashimaya department store, this longstanding Kyoto restaurant serves approachable *kaiseki* fare in a variety of rooms, both private and common. Its *kiku* set (¥2000) includes some sashimi, a bit of tempura and a variety of other nibblies. *Kaiseki* dinner courses start at ¥6480 and you must make reservations in advance.

This is a good spot for those who want a civilised meal downtown in relaxing surroundings. There's an English sign.

**SHI-SHIN SAMURAI CAFE AND BAR**  CAFE ¥¥

Map p208 (士心; ☑231-5155; 230-1 Kamimyōkakuji-chō,  Koromonotana-dōri,

Oshikōji-agaru, Nakagyō-ku; lunch/dinner from ¥1000/2500; ⏰noon-11pm, closed Tue; 📷; 🄢Karasuma or Tōzai lines to Karasuma-Oike) 🔖 We're not entirely sure about the connection between samurai and world peace, but there's no doubting the young owner's wish to improve the world through interesting food, drinks and atmosphere. The food is quite good, including some of the best *edamame* (soybeans in the pod) and garlic fried noodles in Kyoto.

The 1st floor has latticed windows and an English sign and menu out the front.

### FUJINO-YA
JAPANESE ¥¥

Map p208 (藤の家; ☎221-2446; Ponto-chō, Shijō-agaru, Nakagyō-ku; tempura sets ¥2700; ⏰4.30-11pm, closed Wed; 🚃Hankyū line to Kawaramachi) This is one of the easiest places for non-Japanese to enter on Ponto-chō, a street where many of the other restaurants turn down even unfamiliar Japanese diners. Here you can feast on tempura, *okonomiyaki, yaki-soba* (fried noodles) and *kushikatsu* (deep-fried skewers of meat, seafood and vegetables) in tatami rooms overlooking the Kamo-gawa.

### ⭐ROAN KIKUNOI
KAISEKI ¥¥¥

Map p208 (露庵菊乃井; ☎361-5580; www.kikunoi.jp; 118 Saito-chō, Kiyamachi-dōri, Shijō-sagaru, Shimogyō-ku; lunch/dinner from ¥4000/10,000; ⏰11.30am-1.30pm & 5-8.30pm; ⏰📷; 🚃Hankyū line to Kawaramachi, Keihan line to Gion-Shijō) Roan Kikunoi is a fantastic place to experience the wonders of *kaiseki* cuisine. It's a clean, intimate space located right downtown. The chef takes an experimental and creative approach to *kaiseki* and the results are a wonder for the eyes and palate. It's highly recommended. Reserve through your hotel or ryokan concierge.

### ⭐YOSHIKAWA
TEMPURA ¥¥¥

Map p208 (吉川; ☎221-5544; www.kyoto-yoshikawa.co.jp; Tominokōji, Oike-sagaru, Nakagyō-ku; lunch ¥3000-25,000, dinner ¥6000-25,000; ⏰11am-2pm & 5-8.30pm; 📷; 🄢Tōzai line to Karasuma-Oike or Kyoto-Shiyakusho-mae) This is the place to go for delectable tempura. It offers table seating, but it's much more interesting to sit and eat around the small counter and observe the chefs at work. It's near Oike-dōri in a traditional Japanese-style building. Reservation required for tatami room; counter and table seating unavailable on Sunday.

### KIYAMACHI SAKURAGAWA
KAISEKI ¥¥¥

Map p208 (木屋町 櫻川; ☎255-4477; Kiyamachi-dōri, Nijō-sagaru, Nakagyō-ku; lunch/dinner sets from ¥5000/10,000; ⏰11.30am-2pm & 5-9pm, closed Sun; 🄢Tōzai line to Kyoto-Shiyakusho-mae) This elegant restaurant on a scenic stretch of Kiyamachi-dōri is an excellent place to try *kaiseki*. The modest but fully satisfying food is beautifully presented and it's a joy to watch the chef in action. The warmth of the reception adds to the quality of the food. Reservations are recommended and smart casual is the way to go here.

### SHUNSAI TEMPURA ARIMA
TEMPURA ¥¥¥

Map p208 (旬菜天ぷら 有馬; ☎344-0111; 572 Sanno-chō, Muromachi-dōri, Takatsuji-agaru, Simogyō-ku; meals from ¥5000; ⏰11.30am-2pm & 5.30-10.30pm, closed Thu; 📷; 🄢Karasuma line to Shijō) Tempura is one of Japan's most divine dishes and this friendly downtown restaurant is a great place to try it. It's a tiny family-run joint that is at home with foreign guests. The English-language menus and set meals make ordering a breeze. It's on a corner with a small English sign.

### MISHIMA-TEI
JAPANESE ¥¥¥

Map p208 (三嶋亭; ☎221-0003; 405 Sakuranochō, Teramachi-dōri, Sanjō-sagaru, Nakagyō-ku; sukiyaki lunch/dinner from ¥9500/12,700; ⏰11.30am-10pm, closed Wed; 📷; 🄢Tōzai line to Kyoto-Shiyakusho-mae) This is a good place to sample sukiyaki (thin slices of beef cooked in a sake, soy and vinegar broth). The quality of the meat here is very high, which is hardly surprising when you consider there is a butcher right downstairs. There is an English menu and a discount for foreign travellers! It's in the intersection of the Sanjō and Teramachi covered arcades.

# DRINKING & NIGHTLIFE

### IKETSURU KAJITSU
JUICE BAR

Map p208 (池鶴果実; ☎221-3368; Nishikikōji-dōri, Yanaginobanba higashi-iru, Nakagyō-ku; juice ¥450; ⏰9am-6.30pm, closed Wed; 🄢Karasuma line to Shijō, 🚃Hankyū line to Karasuma) We love this fruit-juice specialist in Nishiki Market. In addition to all the usual favourites, it sometimes has durian on hand and can whip up a very unusual durian juice. Look for the fruit on display – it's on the south side of the market, a little east of Yanaginobanba-dōri.

### INODA COFFEE CAFE
Map p208 (イノダコーヒー; ☎221-0507; Sakaimachi-dōri, Sanjō-sagaru, Nakagyō-ku; coffee from ¥500; ◷7am-8pm; ⑤Karasuma or Tōzai lines to Karasuma-Oike) This chain is a Kyoto institution and has branches across the city. Though slightly expensive, the 'old Japan' atmosphere makes it worth a try, especially if you want to try a Japanese, rather than international, coffee chain.

### PARK CAFÉ CAFE
Map p208 (パークカフェ; ☎211-8954; 1st fl, Gion Bldg, 340-1 Aneyakō-ji kado, Gokomachi-dōri, Nakagyō-ku; drinks from ¥450; ◷noon-11pm; ⑤Tōzai line to Kyoto-Shiyakusho-mae) This cool little cafe always reminds us of a Melbourne coffee shop. It's on the edge of the Downtown Kyoto shopping district and is a convenient place to take a break. The comfy seats invite a nice long linger over a cuppa and the owner has an interesting music collection.

### SOMUSHI KOCHAYA KOREAN TEAHOUSE
Map p208 (素夢子古茶家; ☎253-1456; Karasuma, Sanjō nishi-iru, Nakagyō-ku; tea/meals from ¥500/1000; ◷11am-9pm, closed Wed; ⑤Karasuma or Tōzai lines to Karasuma-Oike) This is the only Korean teahouse we've ever seen in Japan. It's a good place to go when you need a change from the creeping monoculture of coffee chain stores. It's a dark, woodsy and atmospheric spot with a variety of herbal teas (the menu details what they're good for). The teahouse also serves a few light meals.

### STARBUCKS KYOTO SANJŌ-ŌHASHI CAFE
Map p208 (スターバックス京都三条大橋店; ☎213-2326; 113 Nakajima-chō, Sanjō-dōri, Kawaramachi higashi-iru, Nakagyō-ku; coffee drinks from ¥300; ◷8am-11pm; 🍴🛜) This Starbucks branch makes a great meeting point when exploring Downtown Kyoto. The free wi-fi is also super convenient (just make sure you register in advance online).

### BAR K6 BAR
Map p208 (バーK6; ☎255-5009; 2nd fl, Le Valls Bldg, Nijō-dōri, Kiyamachi higashi-iru, Nakagyō-ku; drinks from ¥600; ◷6pm-3am, until 5am Fri & Sat; ⑤Tōzai line to Kyoto-Shiyakusho-mae, 🚃Keihan line to Jingu-Marutamachi) Overlooking one of the prettiest stretches of Kiyamachi-dōri, this upscale modern Japanese bar has a great selection of single malts and some of the best cocktails in town. There's even a local craft brew on offer. It's popular with well-heeled locals and travellers staying at some of the top-flight hotels nearby.

### TADG'S GASTRO PUB PUB
Map p208 (ダイグ ガストロ パブ; ☎213-0214; www.tadgs.com; 1st fl, 498 Kamikoriki-chō, Nakagyō-ku; drinks from ¥500; ◷lunch & dinner until late, closed Wed; ⑤Tōzai line to Kyoto-Shiyakusho-mae) Looking out on a particularly scenic stretch of Kiyamachi-dōri, Tadg's is a great place for a drink or two in the evening and you can choose from an extensive selection of craft beers, along with a variety of wines, sake and spirits. Seating is available, including an enclosed garden out the back for smokers.

It's also a good place to grab a meal (from around ¥600); menu items include pizza, salads and some Irish dishes.

### SAKE BAR YORAMU BAR
Map p208 (酒バー よらむ; ☎213-1512; www.sakebar-yoramu.com; 35-1 Matsuya-chō, Nijō-dōri, Higashinotoin higashi-iru, Nakagyō-ku; sake tasting sets from ¥1200; ◷6pm-midnight, closed Sun-Tue; ⑤Karasuma or Tōzai lines to Karasuma-Oike) Named for Yoramu, the Israeli sake expert who runs Sake Bar Yoramu, this bar is highly recommended for anyone after an education in sake. It's very small and can only accommodate a handful of people. By day, it's a *soba* restaurant.

### ROCKING BAR ING BAR
Map p208 (ロック居酒屋ING; ☎255-5087; www.kyotoingbar.com; 2nd fl, Royal Bldg, 288 Minamikurayama-chō, Nishikiyamachi-dōri, Takoyakushi-agaru, Nakagyō-ku; drinks from ¥550; ◷6pm-2am Sun-Thu, to 5am Fri & Sat; 🚃Hankyū line to Kawaramachi) This *izakaya*-cum-bar on Kiyamachi is one of our favourite spots for a drink in Kyoto. It offers cheap bar snacks (¥350 to ¥750) and drinks, good music and friendly staff. It's in the Royal building; you'll know you're getting close when you see all the hostesses out trawling for customers on the streets nearby.

### A BAR IZAKAYA
Map p208 (居酒屋A (あ; ☎213-2129; www.a-bar.net; 2nd fl, Reiho Kaikan, 366 Kamiya-chō, Nishikiyamachi-dōri, Shijō-agaru, Nakagyō-ku; drinks from ¥350; ◷6pm-1am; 🚃Keihan line to Gion-Shijō, Hankyū line to Kawaramachi) This is a raucous student *izakaya* with a log-cabin interior located in the Kiyamachi area. There's a big menu to choose from and everything's cheap (dishes ¥160 to ¥680). The best part

comes when staff add up the bill – you'll swear they've undercharged you by half!

It's a bit tough to find – look for the small black-and-white sign at the top of a flight of concrete steps above a place called Reims.

### SAMA SAMA
BAR

Map p208 (サマサマ; ☎241-4100; 532-16 Kamiōsaka-chō, Kiyamachi, Sanjō-agaru, Nakagyō-ku; drinks ¥600-700; ◷8pm-2am, closed Mon; ⓢTōzai line to Kyoto-Shiyakusho-mae) This place seems like a very comfortable cave somewhere near the Mediterranean. Scoot up to the counter or make yourself at home on the floor cushions and enjoy a wide variety of drinks, some of them from Indonesia (like the owner). It's down an alley just north of Sanjō; the alley has a sign for Sukiyaki Komai Tei.

### ATLANTIS
BAR

Map p208 (アトランティス; ☎241-1621; 161 Matsumoto-chō, Ponto-chō-Shijō-agaru, Nakagyō-ku; ◷6pm-2am, to 1am Sun; ⓡHankyū line to Kawaramachi) This is one of the few bars on Ponto-chō that foreigners can walk into without a Japanese friend. It's a slick, trendy place that draws a fair smattering of Kyoto's beautiful people, and wannabe beautiful people. In summer you can sit outside on a platform looking over the Kamo-gawa. It's often crowded so you may have to wait a bit to get in, especially if you want to sit outside.

### RUB-A-DUB
BAR

Map p208 (ラブアダブ; ☎256-3122; Kiyamachi-dōri, Sanjō-sagaru, Nakagyō-ku; ◷7pm-2am, to 5am Sat; ⓡKeihan line to Sanjō) At the northern end of Kiyamachi-dōri, this is a funky little reggae bar with a shabby tropical look. It's a good place for a quiet drink on weekdays, but on Friday and Saturday nights you'll have no choice but to bop along with the crowd. Look for the stairs heading down to the basement next to a *rāmen* shop.

### ★WORLD PEACE LOVE
CLUB

Map p208 (ワールドピースラブ; ☎213-4119; http://world-kyoto.com; Basement, Imagium Bldg, 97 Shin-chō, Nishikiyamachi, Shijō-agaru, Shimogyō-ku; admission ¥2500-3000, drinks from ¥500; ◷8pm-1am, closed irregularly but usually Mon, Tue & Thu; ⓡHankyū line to Kawaramachi) World is Kyoto's largest club and it naturally hosts some of the biggest events. It has two floors, a dance floor and lockers where you can leave your stuff while you dance the night away. Events include everything from deep soul to reggae and techno to salsa.

### BAR BUNKYU
BAR

Map p208 (バー 文久; ☎211-1982; www.barbunkyu.jimdo.com; 534 Ebisu-chō, Kawaramachi, Sanjō-sagaru, Futasujime higashi-iru, Nakagyō-ku; drinks from ¥1000; ◷6pm until late, closed Thu; ⓢTōzai line to Kyoto-Shiyakusho-mae) This intimate and uber-cool whisky bar is a great place to go for a quiet drink when downtown. It can only seat a handful of guests around the small wooden counter. The friendly bartender will be happy to help you choose a tipple. If you're coming from Kawaramachi, turn at the Catholic church and look for it on your right.

 **ENTERTAINMENT**

### KAMOGAWA ODORI
DANCE

Map p208 (鴨川をどり; ☎221-2025; Ponto-chō, Sanjō-sagaru, Nakagyō-ku; normal/special seat/ special seat incl tea ¥2000/4000/4500; ◷shows 12.30pm, 2.20pm & 4.10pm; ⓢTōzai line to Kyoto-Shiyakusho-mae) Geisha dances from 1 to 24 May at Ponto-chō Kaburen-jō Theatre in Ponto-chō.

### TAKU-TAKU
LIVE MUSIC

Map p208 (磔磔; ☎351-1321; www.geisya.or.jp/~takutaku/; Tominokōji-dōri-Bukkōji, Shimogyō-ku; admission ¥1500-3500; ◷7-9pm; ⓡHankyū line to Kawaramachi) This is one of Kyoto's most atmospheric live music clubs, with a long history of hosting some great local and international acts. Check the *Kyoto Visitor's Guide* and flyers in local coffee shops for details on upcoming events. It's rather hard to spot: the sign is only in Japanese. Look for the wooden sign with black *kanji* on it and go through the gate.

### KYOTO CINEMA
CINEMA

Map p208 (京都シネマ; ☎353-4723; 3rd fl, Cocon Karasuma, 620 Suiginya-chō, Karasuma-dōri, Shijō-sagaru, Shimogyō-ku; ◷10am-9pm; ⓢKarasuma line to Shijō) This is one of Kyoto's only art-house cinemas. Movies are almost always screened in their original language, with Japanese subtitles. It's in the Cocon Karasuma building, directly connected to Shijō Station; take exit 2.

# 🛍 SHOPPING

★ **WAGAMI NO MISE** HANDICRAFTS

Map p208 (倭紙の店; ☑341-1419; 1st fl, Kajinoha Bldg, 298 Ōgisakaya-chō, Higashinotōin-dōri, Bukkōji-agaru, Shimogyō-ku; ⏰9.30am-5.30pm Mon-Fri, to 4.30pm Sat; ⑤Karasuma line to Shijō) A short walk from the Shijō-Karasuma crossing, this place sells a fabulous variety of handmade *washi* (Japanese handmade paper) for reasonable prices. It's one of our favourite shops in Kyoto for souvenirs.

★ **ARITSUGU** KNIVES

Map p208 (有次; ☑221-1091; 219 Kajiya-chō, Nishikikōji-dōri, Gokomachi nishi-iru, Nakagyō-ku; ⏰9am-5.30pm; Ⓡ Hankyū line to Kawaramachi) While you're in Nishiki Market, have a look at this store – it's where you can find some of the best kitchen knives in the world. It also carries a selection of excellent and unique Japanese kitchenware.

★ **ZŌHIKO** LACQUERWARE

Map p208 (象彦; ☑229-6625; www.zohiko.co.jp; 719-1 Yohojimae-chō, Teramachi-dōri, Nijō-agaru, Nakagyō-ku; ⏰10am-6pm; ⑤Tōzai line to Kyoto-Shiyakusho-mae) Zōhiko is the best place in Kyoto to buy one of Japan's most beguiling art/craft forms: lacquerware. If you aren't familiar with just how beautiful these products can be, you owe it to yourself to make the pilgrimage to Zōhiko. You'll find a great selection of cups, bowls, trays and various kinds of boxes.

If you want a gift or souvenir that really makes an impression, this is a great choice!

★ **TAKASHIMAYA** DEPARTMENT STORE

Map p208 (高島屋; ☑221-8811; Shijō-Kawaramachi Kado, Shimogyō-ku; ⏰10am-8pm, restaurants to 9.30pm; Ⓡ Hankyū line to Kawaramachi) The *grande dame* of Kyoto department stores, Takashimaya is almost a tourist attraction in its own right, from the mind-boggling riches of the basement food floor to the wonderful selection of lacquerware and ceramics on the 6th floor. And don't miss the kimonos!

★ **MINA** SHOPPING CENTRE

Map p208 (ミーナ京都; ☑222-8470; Kawaramachi-dōri, Shijō-agaru, Nakagyō-ku; ⏰restaurants 11am-midnight; Ⓡ Keihan line to Gion-Shijō, Hankyū line to Kawaramachi) One of Kyoto's trendiest shopping malls, Mina has branches of two of Japan's most interesting chains: Uniqlo, a budget clothing brand that has spread overseas, and Loft, a fashionable department store that stocks all manner of curios and gift items.

★ **KYŪKYO-DŌ** HANDICRAFTS

Map p208 (鳩居堂; ☑231-0510; 520 Shimohonnōjimae-chō, Teramachi-dōri, Aneyakōji-agaru, Nakagyō-ku; ⏰10am-6pm Mon-Sat, closed Sun; ⑤Tōzai line to Kyoto-Shiyakusho-mae) This old shop in the Teramachi covered arcade sells a selection of incense, *shodō* (calligraphy) goods, tea-ceremony supplies and *washi*. Prices are on the high side but the quality is good. Overall, this is your best one-stop shop for distinctively Japanese souvenirs.

**IPPŌDŌ TEA** TEA

Map p208 (一保堂茶舖; ☑211-3421; www.ippodo-tea.co.jp; Teramachi-dōri, Nijō-agaru, Nakagyō-ku; ⏰9am-7pm Mon-Sat, to 6pm Sun & holidays; ⑤Tōzai line to Kyoto-Shiyakusho-mae) This old-style tea shop sells the best Japanese tea in Kyoto. Its *matcha* makes an excellent and lightweight souvenir. Try a 40g container of *wa-no-mukashi* (meaning 'old-time Japan') for ¥1600, which makes 25 cups of excellent green tea. Ippōdō is north of the city hall, on Teramachi-dōri. It has an adjoining teahouse (open 11am to 5.30pm).

**DAIMARU** DEPARTMENT STORE

Map p208 (大丸; ☑211-8111; Tachiuri Nishi-machi 79, Shijō-dōri, Takakura nishi-iru, Shimogyō-ku; ⏰10am-8pm, restaurants 10am-9pm; ⑤Karasuma line to Shijō, Ⓡ Hankyū line to Karasuma) Daimaru has fantastic service, a brilliant selection of goods and a basement food floor that will make you want to move to Kyoto.

**FUJII DAIMARU**
**DEPARTMENT STORE** DEPARTMENT STORE

Map p208 (フジイダイマル; ☑221-8181; Shijō-dōri, Teramachi nishi-iru; ⏰10.30am-8pm; ⑤Hankyū line to Kawaramachi) This smallish department store on Shijō-dōri is very popular with local young ladies who flock here to peruse the interesting selection of up-to-the-minute fashions and jewellery. Older Kyotoites head to the basement food floor to snag great bargains on a wide selection of food, including great takeaway sushi and tropical fruit.

**KYOTO MARUI** DEPARTMENT STORE

Map p208 (丸井; ☑257-0101; 68 Shin-chō, Shijō-dōri, Kawaramachi higashi-iru, Shimogyō-ku;

**DOWNTOWN KYOTO** SHOPPING

## BOOKSTORES IN KYOTO

At present Kyoto's main source of English-language books, the Junkudō store in the BAL building on Kawaramachi-dōri is closed while the BAL building is being rebuilt. While it's closed, a much smaller Junkudō with a limited selection of English-language books is operating in the Asahi Kaikan building on the east side of Kawaramachi-dōri, just north of Sanjō-dōri. The BAL building with the new full-size Junkudō is expected to open in August 2015. When it does, it will offer a great selection of English-language books. The BAL building can be found on the east side of Kawaramachi-dōri, about midway between Sanjō and Shijō.

⊘10.30am-8.30pm, restaurants to 10pm; 🚊Hankyū line to Kawaramachi) This new youth-oriented department store hails from Tokyo and brings some of that fashion sense with it. It's a good place to see what's hot with the local fashionistas.

### NIJŪSAN-YA ACCESSORIES
Map p208 (二十三や; ☑221-2371; Shijō-dōri, Kawaramachi higashi-iru, Shimogyō-ku; ⊘10am-8pm; 🚊Hankyū line to Kawaramachi) Boxwood combs and hair clips are one of Kyoto's most famous traditional crafts, and they are still used in the elaborate hairstyles of the city's geisha and *maiko*. This tiny hole-in-the-wall shop has a fine selection for you to choose from (and if you don't like what's on view, you can ask if it has other choices in stock – it usually does).

### TANAKAYA HANDICRAFTS
Map p208 (田中彌; ☑221-1959; Shijō-dōri, Yanaginobanba higashi-iru, Shimogyō-ku; ⊘10am-6pm, closed Wed; Ⓢation Karasuma line to Shijō) Tanakaya is one of the best places in Kyoto to buy *kyō-ningyō* (Kyoto dolls). In addition to the full range of *kyō-ningyō*, the shop sells display stands and screens, Japanese traditional shell game pieces and miniature Gion Matsuri floats. It's easy to spot by its dolls in the window.

### MEIDI-YA FOOD
Map p208 (明治屋; ☑221-7661; Sanjō-dōri, Kawaramachi higashi-iru, Nakagyō-ku; ⊘10am-9pm; 🚊Keihan line to Sanjō) This famous Sanjō-dōri gourmet supermarket has an outstanding selection of imported food and an excellent selection of wine.

### KAMIJI KAKIMOTO HANDICRAFTS
Map p208 (紙司柿本; ☑211-3481; 54 Tokiwagi-chō, Teramachi-dōri, Nijō-agaru, Nakagyō-ku; ⊘9am-6pm; 🚊Keihan line to Jingū-Marutamachi) This is one of our favourite places to buy *washi* in Kyoto. It's got such unusual items as *washi* computer printer paper and *washi* wallpaper, along with great letter writing and wrapping paper.

### RAKUSHIKAN HANDICRAFTS
Map p208 (楽紙館; ☑221-1070; Takoyakushi-dōri, Takakura nishi-iru, Nakagyō-ku; ⊘10.30am-6pm, closed Mon; Ⓢation Karasuma line to Shijō) This *washi* specialist is a true wonderland for artists, creative types and anyone who knows just how beautiful this paper can be. There are three floors to explore and occasional *washi*-making demonstrations.

### TOKYU HANDS DEPARTMENT STORE
Map p208 (東急ハンズ京都店; ☑254-3109; http://kyoto.tokyu-hands.co.jp; Shijō-dōri, Karasuma higashi-iru, Shimogyō-ku; ⊘10am-10.30pm; Ⓢation Karasuma line to Shijō) While the Kyoto branch of Tokyu Hands doesn't have the selection of bigger branches in places like Tokyo, it's still well worth a browse for fans of gadgets and interesting housewares. It's a good place for an interesting gift or souvenir.

### MINAKUCHI-YA TEXTILES
Map p208 (水口弥; ☑221-3076; Takakura-dōri, Nishikikōji-aguru, Nakagyō-ku; ⊘10am-6pm Tue-Sat, 11am-5pm Sun; Ⓢation Karasuma line to Shijō) This shop sells *noren* (curtains that hang in the entry of Japanese restaurants) and a wide variety of other fabric goods such as placemats, *tenugui* (small hand towels), handkerchiefs and bedding.

### OPA SHOPPING CENTRE
Map p208 (河原町オーパ; ☑255-8111; Kawaramachi-dōri, Shijō-agaru, Nakagyō-ku; ⊘11am-9pm; 🚊Hankyū line to Kawaramachi) This youth-oriented shopping centre is the place to go to see swarms of *ko-gyaru* (brightly clad Japanese girls) and their friends. It's also a decent spot for those who want to check out a wide variety of fashion boutiques and other hip shops.

## SHIN-PUH-KAN    SHOPPING CENTRE

Map p208 (新風館; ☎213-6688; Karasuma-dōri, Aneyakōji-kudaru, Nakagyō-ku; ☺shops 11am-8pm Sun-Thu, to 9pm Fri & Sat, restaurants 11am-11pm, closed irregularly; ⓈKarasuma line to Karasuma-Oike) This interesting shopping complex has a variety of boutiques and restaurants clustered around a huge open-air atrium. The offerings run to the cutting-edge and ephemeral, which attracts the young kids who congregate here. Occasional art and music performances are held in the atrium.

## ERIZEN    TEXTILES

Map p208 (ゑり善; ☎221-1618; Shijō-Kawaramachi, Otabi-chō, Shimogyō-ku; ☺10am-7pm Tue-Sun; ⓇHankyū line to Kawaramachi) Roughly opposite Takashimaya department store, Erizen is one of the best places in Kyoto to buy a kimono or kimono fabric. It has a great selection of *kyō-yūzen* (Kyoto dyed fabrics) and other kimono fabrics. Prices are not cheap but the service is of a high level. Staff can measure you for a kimono and are happy to post it to your home later.

## TSUJIKURA    CRAFTS

Map p208 (辻倉; ☎221-4396; 7th fl, Tsujikura Bldg, Kawaramachi-dōri, Shijō-agaru higashi-gawa, Nakagyō-ku; ☺11am-8pm, closed Wed; ⓇHankyū line to Kawaramachi) A short walk north of the Shijō-Kawaramachi crossing, Tsujikura has a good selection of waxed-paper umbrellas and paper lanterns with traditional and modern designs.

## NISHIHARU    CRAFTS

Map p208 (西春; ☎211-2849; Teramachj-Sanjō Kado, Nakagyō-ku; ☺2-6.30pm; ⓈTōzai line to Kyoto-Shiyakusho-mae, ⓇKeihan line to Sanjō) This is an attractive shop dealing in wood-block prints. All prints are accompanied by English explanations and the owner is happy to take the time to find something you really like.

## ART FACTORY    CLOTHING

Map p208 (アートファクトリー; ☎213-3131; 498 Higashigawa-chō, Teramachi-dōri, Takoyakushi-agaru, Nakagyō-ku; ☺11am-8pm; ⓈKarasuma line to Shijō, ⓇHankyū line to Kawaramachi) A T-shirt with your name written in kanji, *katakana* or *hiragana* across the chest is a great souvenir, and this place can make them in just a few minutes. Look for the T-shirts displayed outside (strangely, there is no sign in English or Japanese, but it calls itself 'Art Factory').

## COCON KARASUMA    SHOPPING CENTRE

Map p208 (古今烏丸; ☎352-3800; 620 Suiginya-chō, Karasuma-dōri, Shijō-sagaru, Shimogyō-ku; ☺10am-midnight; ⓈKarasuma line to Shijō) In the midst of Kyoto's banking district, this new shopping, dining and entertainment complex is always worth a look. The offerings range from books to furniture, with an art-house cinema and several restaurants in-between.

## TANIYAMA MUSEN    ELECTRONICS

Map p208 (タニヤマムセン; ☎343-0221; Teramachi-dōri, Shijō-sagaru, Shimogyō-ku; ☺10am-9pm; ⓇHankyū line to Kawaramachi) Taniyama Musen (*musen* is the old Japanese word for 'radio') is one of the few old-school retailers to survive in Kyoto's old electronics district of Teramachi. Its prices are often just as good as the bigger places near Kyoto Station and you can actually speak to the clerks here (well, that is, if you can muster a bit of Japanese).

## KYOTO ANTIQUE CENTER    ANTIQUES

Map p208 (京都アンティークセンター; ☎222-0793; Teramachi-dōri, Nijō-agaru, Nakagyō-ku; ☺10.30am-7pm, closed Tue; ⓈTōzai line to Kyoto-Shiyakusho-mae) A collection of semi-independent antique shops under one roof, this Teramachi-dōri emporium has oddities, curios and treasures to make those yen burn a hole in your pocket. If you're in the market for an interesting (and possibly pricey) gift for the folks back home, you might find it here.

# Central Kyoto

KYOTO GOSHO (IMPERIAL PALACE) AREA | NORTH-CENTRAL KYOTO | SOUTH-CENTRAL KYOTO | SOUTHEAST KYOTO
NORTHEAST KYOTO | WEST KYOTO

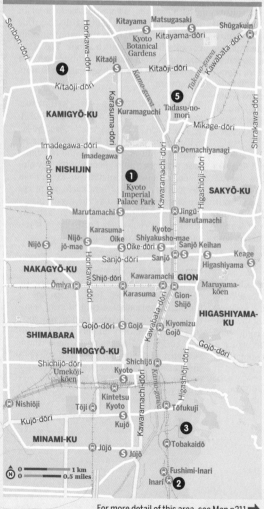

## Neighbourhood Top Five

**1** Entering the hidden world of the **Kyoto Imperial Palace** (p71) and marvelling at the splendour of the Japanese court. In addition to the stunning buildings and interiors, the gardens are lovely and make for pleasant strolling.

**2** Wandering through the hypnotic arcades of *torii* (Shintō shrine gates) at **Fushimi Inari-Taisha** (p70).

**3** Strolling through the expansive grounds of **Tōfuku-ji** (p75).

**4** Visiting the many subtemples at **Daitoku-ji** (p72).

**5** Taking a stroll through the long and tree-lined approach to **Shimogamo-jinja** (p73).

For more detail of this area, see Map p211 ➡

# Explore: Central Kyoto

The area we refer to as Central Kyoto is not so much a distinct neighbourhood as it is a vast swathe of the city that surrounds the better-known sightseeing districts of Downtown Kyoto, the Kyoto Station Area, Southern Higashiyama and Northern Higashiyama. Central Kyoto runs from the hills that form the northern border of the city proper to the flat suburbs south of Kyoto Station. As such, it is not an area that one would attempt to explore in one day.

The best way to enjoy Central Kyoto is to choose one or two sights that are relatively close to each other and focus on them. You can often link sights in Central Kyoto with sights in other nearby sightseeing districts, like Downtown Kyoto or the Southern Higashiyama area.

There are many possible routes that take advantage of the offerings here. For example, you could start in the southeast region of the area with a visit to Fushimi Inari-Taisha and Tōfuku-ji, then head north into the Southern Higashiyama area.

Likewise, you might pay a visit to the walled-in Zen world of Daitoku-ji, with its wonderful subtemples, and then continue into Northwest Kyoto to visit the shining apparition of Kinkaku-ji – the famed 'Golden Pavilion'.

Needless to say, because of its size, this area lends itself to being explored by bicycle.

## Local Life

➡ **Hang-out** Kyoto families with children gather on sunny weekends along the banks of the Kamo-gawa, just north of Kamo-Ōhashi.

➡ **Jogging route** Local runners favour the many paths of the Kyoto Imperial Palace Park (p71).

➡ **Picnic spot** Spread a blanket and eat alfresco in the expansive fields of the Kyoto Botanical Gardens (p73).

## Getting There & Away

➡ **Train** Take the JR or Keihan lines to sights in the southeast.

➡ **Bus** Take buses to sights in the northeast.

➡ **Subway** Take the Karasuma subway line to sights in the north and city centre. Take the Tōzai subway line to Nijō-jō.

## Lonely Planet's Top Tip

During cherry-blossom season (early April), the city's main tourist sites will be mobbed. If you want to enjoy the blossoms without the crowds, head to the banks of the Kamo-gawa or Takano-gawa, north of Imadegawa-dōri.

###  Best Places to Eat

➡ Papa Jon's (p75)
➡ Toraya Karyō Kyoto Ichijō (p76)
➡ Hiragana-kan (p76)

For reviews, see p75. ➡

###  Best Places for a Stroll

➡ Kyoto Imperial Palace Park (p71)
➡ Shimogamo-jinja (p73)
➡ Fushimi Inari-Taisha (p70)

For reviews, see p70. ➡

###  Best Places for Kids

➡ Umekōji Steam Locomotive Museum (p74)
➡ Fushimi Inari-Taisha (p70)
➡ Kyoto Botanical Gardens (p73)

For reviews, see p70. ➡

**CENTRAL KYOTO**

## TOP SIGHT
# FUSHIMI INARI-TAISHA

**With seemingly endless arcades of vermilion *torii* (shrine gates) spread across a thickly wooded mountain, this vast shrine complex is a world unto its own. It is, quite simply, one of the most impressive and memorable sights in all of Kyoto. A pathway wanders 4km up the mountain and is lined with dozens of atmospheric sub-shrines.**

Fushimi Inari was dedicated to the gods of rice and sake by the Hata family in the 8th century. As the role of agriculture diminished, deities were enrolled to ensure prosperity in business. Nowadays the shrine is one of Japan's most popular, and is the head shrine for some 40,000 Inari shrines scattered the length and breadth of the country.

As you explore the shrine, you will come across hundreds of stone foxes. The fox is considered the messenger of Inari, the god of cereals, and the stone foxes, too, are often referred to as Inari. The key often seen in the fox's mouth is for the rice granary. On an incidental note, the Japanese traditionally see the fox as a sacred, somewhat mysterious figure capable of 'possessing' humans – the favoured point of entry is under the fingernails.

The walk around the upper precincts of the shrine is a pleasant day hike. It also makes for a very eerie stroll in the late afternoon and early evening, when the various graveyards and miniature shrines along the path take on a mysterious air. It's best to go with a friend at this time.

On 8 April there's a Sangyō-sai festival with offerings and dances to ensure prosperity for national industry. During the first few days in January, thousands of believers visit this shrine as their *hatsu-mōde* (first shrine visit of the New Year) to pray for good fortune.

### DON'T MISS...

➡ View of Kyoto from the upper trails

➡ The fox-shaped prayer plaques hanging everywhere (pictured above)

### PRACTICALITIES

➡ 伏見稲荷大社

➡ 68 Yabunouchi-chō, Fukakusa, Fushimi-ku

➡ ⊙dawn-dusk

➡ Ⓡ JR Nara line to Inari, Keihan line to Fushimi-Inari

#  SIGHTS

**FUSHIMI INARI-TAISHA**     SHINTO SHRINE
See p70.

---

##  Kyoto Gosho (Imperial Palace) Area

**KYOTO IMPERIAL PALACE PARK**     PARK
Map p211 (京都御苑; Kyoto Gyōen; Nakagyō-ku; ☉dawn-dusk; ⑤Karasuma line to Marutamachi or Imadegawa) FREE The Kyoto Imperial Palace (Kyoto Gosho) and Sentō Gosho are surrounded by the spacious Kyoto Imperial Palace Park, which is planted with a huge variety of flowering trees and open fields. It's perfect for picnics, strolls and just about any sport you can think of. Take some time to visit the pond at the park's southern end, which contains gorgeous carp. The park is most beautiful in the plum- and cherry-blossom seasons (late February and late March, respectively).

The plum arbour is located about midway along the park on the west side. There are several large *shidareze-zakura* (weeping cherry trees) at the north end of the park, making it a great cherry-blossom destina-tion. The park is between Teramachi-dōri and Karasuma-dōri (to the east and west) and Imadegawa-dōri and Marutamachi-dōri (to the north and south).

**SENTŌ GOSHO PALACE**     HISTORIC BUILDING
Map p211 (仙洞御所; ☎211-1215; Kyoto Gyōen, Nakagyō-ku; ⑤Karasuma line to Marutamachi or Imadegawa) The Sentō Gosho is the second imperial property located within the Kyoto Imperial Palace Park (the other one is the Kyoto Gosho, which is located about 100m northwest). The structures within this walled compound are not particularly grand, but the magnificent gardens, laid out in 1630 by renowned landscape design-er Kobori Enshū, are excellent.

It was originally constructed in 1630 during the reign of Emperor Go-Mizunō as a residence for retired emperors. The palace was repeatedly destroyed by fire and reconstructed; it continued to serve its purpose until a final blaze in 1854, after which it was never rebuilt. Today only two structures, the **Seika-tei** and **Yūshin-tei** teahouses, remain.

Visitors must obtain advance permis-sion from the Imperial Household Agency (see p72) and be more than 20 years old.

CENTRAL KYOTO SIGHTS

---

## ◉ TOP SIGHT
## KYOTO IMPERIAL PALACE

The Kyoto Imperial Palace (Kyoto Gosho) served as the official residence of the emperor of Japan from the late 12th century until the 19th century and the palace remains an imperial household property. The Kyoto Imperial Palace and its surrounding park is the heart of Kyoto, both spatially and metaphorically. It occupies a huge expanse of Central Kyoto – a green haven amid a sea of concrete. The palace recalls the city's proud heritage as the capital of the country and seat of the imperial court for over 1000 years.

While the palace is indeed important from a historical perspective, the application requirement and need to tour the grounds as part of a guided tour (see p72) detract somewhat from the overall experience. For this reason, many visitors choose to admire the grounds from the outside.

In spring and autumn, it is possible to enter the palace without reservation. Otherwise, you can visit the palace as part of a guided tour. The tour takes about an hour and covers the various halls inside the palace, including the Shishin-den (Ceremonial Hall), Ko Gosho (Small Palace), Tsune Gosho (Regular Palace) and Oike-niwa (Pond Gar-den). Regrettably, it is forbidden to enter any of these.

**DON'T MISS...**
➡ Cherry trees
➡ Shishin-den (Ceremonial Hall)

**PRACTICALITIES**
➡ 京都御所
➡ Map p211
➡ Kyoto Gosho, Nakagyō-ku
➡ ⑤Karasuma line to Marutamachi or Imadegawa

**ℹ RESERVATION & ADMISSION TO KYOTO'S IMPERIAL PROPERTIES**

Permission to visit the Kyoto Gosho, Sentō Gosho, Katsura Rikyū and Shūgaku-in Rikyū is granted by the Kunaichō, the **Imperial Household Agency** (宮内庁京都事務所; Map p211; ☑211-1215; ◷8.45am-noon & 1-5pm Mon-Fri; ⑤Karasuma line to Imadegawa), which is inside the Imperial Palace Park (Kyoto Gyōen), the park that surrounds the Kyoto Imperial Palace (Kyoto Gosho). You have to fill out an application form and show your passport. Children can visit if accompanied by adults over 20 years of age (but are forbidden entry to the other three imperial properties of Katsura Rikyū, Sentō Gosho and Shūgaku-in Rikyū). Permission to tour the palace is usually granted the same day (try to arrive at the office at least 30 minutes before the start of the tour you'd like to join). Guided tours, sometimes in English, are given at 10am and 2pm Monday to Friday. The tour lasts about 50 minutes.

The Gosho can be visited without reservation during two periods each year, once in the spring and once in autumn. The dates vary each year, but as a general guide, the spring opening is around the last week of April and the autumn opening is in the middle of November. Check with the Tourist Information Center (p188) for exact dates.

One-hour tours (in Japanese) start daily at 11am and 1.30pm. The route takes you past lovely ponds and pathways and, in many ways, a visit here is more enjoyable than a visit to the Gosho, especially if you are a fan of Japanese gardens.

## ◉ North-Central Kyoto

★**DAITOKU-JI**   BUDDHIST TEMPLE
Map p211 (大徳寺; 53 Daitokuji-chō, Murasakino, Kita-ku; ◷dawn-dusk; ⑤Karasuma line to Kitaōji) **FREE** Daitoku-ji is a separate world within Kyoto – a world of Zen temples, perfectly raked gardens and wandering lanes. It's one of the most rewarding destinations in this part of the city, particularly for those with an interest in Japanese gardens. The temple serves as the headquarters of the Rinzai Daitoku-ji school of Zen Buddhism. The highlights among the 24 subtemples include **Daisen-in**, **Kōtō-in**, **Ōbai-in**, **Ryōgen-in** and **Zuihō-in**.

The eponymous **Daitoku-ji** is on the eastern side of the grounds. It was founded in 1319, burnt down in the next century and rebuilt in the 16th century. The **San-mon** gate (1589) has a self-carved statue of its erector, the famous tea-master Sen no Rikyū, on its 2nd storey.

The Karasuma subway line is the best way to get here. From the station, walk west along Kitaōji-dōri for about 15 minutes. You'll see the temple complex on your right. The main entrance is bit north of Kitaōji. If you enter from the main gate, which is

on the east side of the complex, you'll soon after find Daitoku-ji on your right.

**DAISEN-IN**   BUDDHIST TEMPLE
Map p211 (大仙院; 54-1 Daitokuji-chō, Murasakino, Kita-ku; admission ¥400; ◷9am-5pm Mar-Nov, to 4.30pm Dec-Feb; ⑤Karasuma line to Kitaōji) The two small Zen gardens in this subtemple of Daitoku-ji are elegant examples of 17th-century *kare-sansui* (dry landscape) style. Here the trees, rocks and sand are said to represent and express various spectacles of nature, from waterfalls and valleys to mountain lakes. It's one of the more popular subtemples here.

**KŌTŌ-IN**   BUDDHIST TEMPLE
Map p211 (高桐院; 73-1 Daitokuji-chō, Murasakino, Kita-ku; admission ¥400; ◷9am-4.30pm; ⑤Karasuma line to Kitaōji) On the far western edge of the Daitoku-ji complex, this sublime garden is one of the best in all of Kyoto and it's worth a special trip. It's located within a fine bamboo grove that you traverse via a moss-lined path. Once inside there is a small stroll garden which leads to the centrepiece: a rectangle of moss and maple trees, backed by bamboo. Take some time on the verandah here to soak it all up.

**ZUIHŌ-IN**   BUDDHIST TEMPLE
Map p211 (瑞峯院; ☑491-1454; 81 Daitokuji-chō, Murasakino, Kita-ku; admission ¥400; ◷9am-5pm; ⑤Karasuma line to Kitaōji) A subtemple of Daitoku-ji, Zuihō-in enshrines the 16th-century Christian *daimyō* (domain lord) Ōtomo Sōrin. In the early 1960s, a landscape architect named Shigemori Misuzu

rearranged the stones in the back rock garden into the shape of a crucifix! More interesting is the main rock garden, which is raked into appealing patterns reminiscent of water ripples. It's roughly in the middle of the complex; you may have to ask for directions.

### ŌBAI-IN
BUDDHIST TEMPLE

Map p211 (黄梅院; ☑231-7015; 83-1 Daitokuji-chō, Murasakino, Kita-ku; admission ¥600; ⊙end Mar-early May & early Oct-early Dec; Ⓢ Karasuma line to Kitaōji) If you are lucky enough to be in Kyoto during autumn when this subtemple of Daitoku-ji is opened to the public, you should make an effort to visit. It is a world of interlinked gardens, including an incredibly rich moss garden and a starkly simple *kare-sansui*. We rank this as one of the finest gardens in Kyoto. When you enter the Daitoku-ji complex via the east (main) gate, it's on the left.

### RYŌGEN-IN
BUDDHIST TEMPLE

Map p211 (龍源院; ☑491-7635; 82-1 Daitokuji-chō, Murasakino, Kita-ku; admission ¥350; ⊙9am-4.30pm; Ⓢ Karasuma line to Kitaōji) Ryōgen-in is a fine subtemple in the Daitoku-ji complex. It has two pleasing gardens, one moss and one *kare-sansui*. The *kare-sansui* has an interesting island in its midst that invites lazy contemplation. When you enter the Daitoku-ji complex via the east (main) gate, it's on the left, just before Ōbai-in.

### SHIMOGAMO-JINJA
SHINTO SHRINE

Map p211 (下鴨神社; 59 Izumigawa-chō, Shimogamo, Sakyō-ku; ⊙6.30am-5pm; ☐ Kyoto City bus 205 to Shimogamo-jinja-mae, ☐ Keihan line to Demachiyanagi) **FREE** This shrine, dating from the 8th century, is a Unesco World Heritage site. It is nestled in the fork of the Kamo-gawa and Takano-gawa rivers, and is approached along a shady path through the lovely Tadasu-no-mori. This wooded area is said to be a place where lies cannot be concealed and is considered a prime location to sort out disputes. The trees here are mostly broadleaf (a rarity in Kyoto) and they are gorgeous in the springtime.

The shrine is dedicated to the god of harvest. Traditionally, pure water was drawn from the nearby rivers for purification and agricultural ceremonies. The **Hondō** (Main Hall) dates from 1863 and, like the **Haiden** hall at its sister shrine, Kamigamo-jinja, is an excellent example of *nagare*-style shrine architecture. The annual *yabusame* (horseback archery) event here is spectacular. It happens on 3 May in Tadasu-no-mori.

### KYOTO BOTANICAL GARDENS
PARK

Map p211 (京都府立植物園; Shimogamohangi-chō, Sakyō-ku; gardens adult ¥200, child ¥0-150, greenhouse adult ¥200, child ¥0-150; ⊙9am-5pm, greenhouse 10am-4pm, closed 28 Dec-4 Jan; Ⓢ Karasuma line to Kitayama) The Kyoto Botanical Gardens occupy 240,000 sq metres and feature 12,000 plants, flowers and trees. It is pleasant to stroll through the rose, cherry and herb gardens or see the rows of camphor trees and the large tropical **greenhouse**. This is a good spot for a picnic. It's also a great spot for a *hanami* (cherry-blossom viewing) party, and the blossoms here tend to hold on a little longer than those elsewhere in the city.

---

## ⊙ South-Central Kyoto

### TŌ-JI
BUDDHIST TEMPLE

(東寺; 1 Kujō-chō, Minami-ku; admission to Kondō, Kōdō & Treasure Hall ¥500 each, pagoda, Kondō & Kōdō ¥800, grounds free; ⊙8.30am-5.30pm, to 4.30pm Sep-Mar; Ⓢ Karasuma line to Kyoto, ☐ Kintetsu Kyoto line to Toji) One of the main sights south of Kyoto Station, Tō-ji is an appealing complex of halls and a fantastic pagoda that makes a fine backdrop for the monthly flea market held on the grounds. The temple was established in 794 by imperial decree to protect the city. In 823 the emperor handed it over to Kūkai (known posthumously as Kōbō Daishi), the founder of the Shingon school of Buddhism.

Many of the temple buildings were destroyed by fire or fighting during the 15th century, and most of the remaining buildings were destroyed in the Momoyama period.

The **Nandai-mon** (Main Gate) was transported here in 1894 from Sanjūsangen-dō in Southern Higashiyama. The **Kōdō** (Lecture Hall) dates from the 1600s and contains 21 images representing a Mikkyō (esoteric Buddhist) mandala. The **Kondō** (Main Hall), which was rebuilt in 1606, combines Chinese, Indian and Japanese architectural styles and contains statues depicting the Yakushi (Healing Buddha) trinity.

In the southern part of the garden stands the **Gojū-no-tō**, a five-storey pagoda that, despite having burnt down five times, was doggedly rebuilt in 1643. Standing at 57m, it is now the highest pagoda in Japan.

**WORTH A DETOUR**

## A BUDDHIST PARADISE: DAIGO-JI

**Daigo-ji** (醍醐寺; 22 Higashiōji-chō, Daigo, Fushimi-ku; admission Sampō-in ¥600, Kondō Hall & Pagoda ¥600, grounds free; ⊙9am-5pm Mar-Nov, to 4pm Dec-Feb; §Tōzai line to Daigo) is a sprawling temple complex located in the Daigo district of Kyoto, which lies on the east side of the Higashiyama mountains, accessible by the Tōzai subway line. Outside of the cherry-blossom season (early April), it's not a high-priority destination, but it makes a good half-day trip for those who like hiking and want a break from the more famous temples in the city centre.

Daigo-ji was founded in 874 by Shobo, who gave it the name Daigo (meaning 'the ultimate essence of milk'). This refers to the five periods of Buddha's teaching, which were compared to the five forms of milk prepared in India; the highest form is called *daigo* in Japanese.

The temple was expanded into a vast complex on two levels, **Shimo Daigo** (lower) and **Kami Daigo** (upper). Kami Daigo is atop **Daigo-yama**, behind the temple. During the 15th century those buildings on the lower level were destroyed, with the sole exception of the five-storey pagoda. Built in 951, this pagoda is treasured as the oldest of its kind in Japan and is the oldest existing building in Kyoto.

In the late 16th century, Hideyoshi took a fancy to Daigo-ji and ordered extensive rebuilding. It is now one of the Shingon school's main temples. To explore Daigo-ji thoroughly and at a leisurely pace, mixing some hiking with your temple-viewing, you will need at least half a day.

The subtemple **Sampō-in** is a fine example of the amazing opulence of that period. The Kanō paintings and the garden are special features.

From Sampō-in it's a steep and tiring 50-minute climb up to Kami Daigo. To get here, walk up the large avenue of cherry trees, through the Niō-mon gate, out the back gate of the lower temple, up a concrete incline and into the forest, past the pagoda.

To get to Daigo-ji, take the Tōzai line subway east from central Kyoto to the Daigo stop, and walk east (towards the mountains) for about 10 minutes. Make sure that the train you board is bound for Rokujizō, as some head to Hama-Ōtsu instead. Admission to the grounds is free most of the year but during the cherry-blossom and autumn-foliage seasons it costs ¥600.

The Kōbō-san market fair is held here on the 21st of each month. There is also a regular market that runs on the first Sunday of each month.

### UMEKŌJI STEAM LOCOMOTIVE MUSEUM
MUSEUM

(梅小路蒸気機関車館; Kankiji-chō, Shimogyō-ku; adult/child ¥400/100, train ride ¥200/100; ⊙10am-5pm, closed Mon, except during spring break (25 Mar-7 Apr) & summer break (21 Jul-7 Aug); ⊡Kyoto City bus 33, 205 or 208 from Kyoto Station to Umekō-ji Kōen-mae) A hit with steam-train buffs and kids, this excellent museum features 18 vintage steam locomotives (dating from 1914 to 1948) and related displays. It is in the former JR Nijō Station building, which was recently relocated here and thoughtfully reconstructed. You can take a 10-minute ride on one of the smoke-spewing choo-choos (departures at 11am, 1.30pm and 3.30pm).

### SUMIYA PLEASURE HOUSE
NOTABLE BUILDING

(角屋もてなしの文化美術館; ☎351-0024; Nishishinyashikiageya-chō 32, Shimogyō-ku; adult ¥1000, child ¥500-800; ⊙10am-4pm Tue-Sun; ⊡Kyoto City bus 205 from Kyoto Station, ®JR line to Tanbaguchi) Sumiya Pleasure House is the last remaining *ageya* (pleasure house) in the old Shimabara pleasure quarter. Built in 1641, this stately two-storey, 20-room structure allows a rare glimpse into Edo-era nirvana. With its delicate latticework exterior, Sumiya has a huge open kitchen and an extensive series of rooms (including one extravagantly decorated with mother-of-pearl inlay). Special tours in Japanese (requiring advance reservations by phone in Japanese) allow access to the 2nd storey and are conducted daily.

Shimabara, a district northwest of Kyoto Station, was Kyoto's original pleasure quarters. At its peak during the Edo period (1603–1868) the area flourished, with more than 20 enormous *ageya* – magnificent banquet halls where artists, writers and statesmen gathered in a 'floating world' ambience of conversation, art and fornication. Geisha were often sent from their *okiya* (living quarters) to entertain patrons at these restaurant-cum-brothels. By the start of the Meiji period, however, such activities had drifted north to the Gion district and Shimabara had lost its prominence.

**MIBU-DERA**     BUDDHIST TEMPLE

(壬生寺; ☏841-3381; Bōjō, Bukkō-ji kita-iru, Nakagyō-ku; ⏰8.30am-4.30pm; ☒Hankyū line to Ōmiya) FREE Mibu-dera was founded in 991 and belongs to the Risshū school. Mibu-dera houses tombs of pro-shogunate Shinsen-gumi members, who fought bloody street battles resisting the forces that succeeded in restoring the emperor in 1868. Except for an unusual stupa covered in Jizō statues, the temple is of limited interest. It is, however, definitely worth visiting during Mibu *kyōgen* (comic drama) performances in late April, or the Setsubun celebrations in early February.

## ◉ Southeast Kyoto

**★TŌFUKU-JI**     BUDDHIST TEMPLE

(東福寺; 15-778 Honmahi, Higashiyama-ku; admission garden ¥400, Tsūtenkyō bridge ¥400, grounds free; ⏰9am-4pm Apr-Oct, 8.30am-4pm Nov-early Dec, 9am-3.30pm early Dec-Mar; ☒Keihan line to Tōfukuji, JR Nara line to Tōfukuji) Home to a spectacular garden, several superb structures and beautiful precincts, Tōfuku-ji is one of the finest temples in Kyoto. It's well worth a special visit and can easily be paired with a trip to Fushimi Inari-Taisha (the two are linked by the Keihan train line).

Founded in 1236 by the priest Enni, Tōfuku-ji belongs to the Rinzai sect of Zen Buddhism. As this temple was intended to compare with Tōdai-ji and Kōfuku-ji in Nara, it was given a name combining characters from the names of each of these temples.

The present temple complex includes 24 subtemples; at one time there were 53. The huge **San-mon** is the oldest Zen main gate in Japan. The **Hōjō** (Abbot's Hall) was reconstructed in 1890. The gardens, laid out in 1938, are well worth a visit. The northern garden has stones and moss neatly arranged in a chequerboard pattern. From a viewing platform at the back of the gardens, you can observe the **Tsūten-kyō** (Bridge to Heaven), which spans a valley filled with maples.

Tōfuku-ji offers regular Zen meditation sessions for beginners, but don't expect coddling or English-language explanations: this is the real deal. Get a Japanese speaker to inquire at the temple about the next session (it holds about four a month for beginners).

Note that Tōfuku-ji is one of Kyoto's most famous autumn foliage spots, and it is invariably packed during the peak of colours in November. Otherwise, it's often very quiet.

 **EATING**

## ✗ Kyoto Gosho Area & North-Central Kyoto

**★PAPA JON'S**     CAFE ¥

Map p211 (パパジョンズカフェ 本店; ☏415-2655; 642-4 Shokokuji-chō, Karasuma-dōri, Kamidachiuri higashi-iru, Kamigyō-ku; lunch from ¥850; ⏰10am-9pm, closed irregularly; ⏰🚭; ⓈKarasuma line to Imadegawa) A three-minute walk from the north border of the Kyoto Imperial Palace Park, this clean, well-lit place serves brilliant New York cheesecake and great coffee drinks. Other menu items include pizza, homemade quiche, soup and tasty salads.

**BON BON CAFÉ**     CAFE ¥

Map p211 (ボンボンカフェ; ☏213-8686; Kawaramachi, Imadegawa, Higashi-iru, Kita-gawa, Kamigyō-ku; coffee/sandwiches from ¥350/500; ⏰11am-11pm; ☒Keihan line to Demachiyanagi) If you find yourself in need of a light meal or drink while you're in the Demachiyanagi area, this casual open-air cafe is an excellent choice. There is a variety of cakes and light meals on offer. It's on the west bank of the Kamo-gawa and outdoor seats here are very pleasant on warm evenings.

While there is no English menu, much of the ordering can be done by pointing, and the young staff can help you figure out what's not on display.

**HONYARADŌ**     JAPANESE ¥

Map p211 (ほんやら洞; ☏222-1574; Imadegawa, Teramachi nishi-iru, Kamigyō-ku; lunch ¥700; ⏰noon-10pm; ☒Keihan line to Demachiyanagi) This woodsy place overlooking the Kyoto Imperial Palace Park was something of a gathering spot for Kyoto's countercultural elite during the hippy days. It has the lived-in feeling of an eccentric friend's house,

**WORTH A DETOUR**

## FUSHIMI: KYOTO'S SAKE DISTRICT

Fushimi, home to 37 sake breweries, is one of Japan's most famous sake-producing regions. Its location on the Uji-gawa made it perfect for sake production, as fresh, high-quality rice was readily available from the fields of neighbouring Shiga-ken and the final product could be easily loaded onto boats for export downriver to Osaka.

Despite its fame, Fushimi is one of Kyoto's least-attractive areas. It's also a hard area to navigate due to a lack of English signage. It's probably only worth a visit if you have a real interest in sake and sake production.

To get to Fushimi, take a local or express train (not a limited express) from Sanjō Station on the Keihan line to Chūshojima Station (¥270, 20 minutes).

The largest of Fushimi's sake breweries is **Gekkeikan Sake Ōkura Museum** (月桂冠大倉記念館; ☑623-2056; www.gekkeikan.co.jp; Minamihama-chō 247, Fushimi-ku; adult/child ¥300/100; ⏰9.30am-4.30pm), the world's leading producer of sake. Although most of the sake is now made in Osaka, a limited amount is still handmade in a Meiji-era *sakagura* (sake brewery) here in Fushimi. The museum is home to a collection of artefacts and memorabilia tracing the 350-year history of Gekkeikan and the sake-brewing process.

**Kizakura Kappa Country** (キザクラカッパカントリー; ☑611-9919; Shioya-chō 228, Fushimi-ku; ⏰11.30am- 2pm & 5-10pm Mon-Fri, 11am-2pm & 3-10pm Sat & Sun) FREE is a short walk from Gekkeikan. The vast complex houses both sake and beer breweries, courtyard gardens and a small gallery dedicated to the mythical (and sneaky) creature Kappa. The restaurant-bar is an appealing option for a bite and a bit of fresh-brewed ale.

with stacks of books and magazines. The lunch deal (a daily stew set) is good value. Surprisingly, considering the ambience, there aren't many veggie options.

⭐**TORAYA KARYŌ KYOTO ICHIJŌ** CAFE ¥¥
Map p211 (虎屋菓寮 京都一条店; ☑441-3113; 400 Hirohashidono-chō, Ichijō-dōri, Karasuma-nishi-iru, Kamigyō-ku; tea & sweets from ¥1200; ⏰10am-6pm; ♿⭕; Ⓢ Karasuma line to Imadegawa) This gorgeous tearoom-cafe is a stone's throw from the west side of the Kyoto Imperial Palace Park. It's fantastic for a break from sightseeing in this part of town. The menu has some pictures and simple English. You can enjoy a nice cup of *matcha* (powdered green tea) and a Japanese sweet for about ¥1200.

**MANZARA HONTEN** JAPANESE ¥¥¥
Map p211 (まんざら本店; ☑253-1558; Kawaramachi-dōri, Ebisugawa-agaru, Nakagyō-ku; dinner courses from ¥5500; ⏰5pm-midnight; Ⓢ Karasuma line to Jingū-Marutamachi) Located in a converted *machiya* (traditional Japanese townhouse), Manzara represents a pleasing fusion of traditional and modern Japanese culture. The fare is creative modern Japanese and the surroundings are decidedly stylish. The *omakase* (chef's recommendation) course is good value, and à

la carte dishes are available from ¥500. Last orders are at 11.30pm.

## ✖ Northeast Kyoto

⭐**HIRAGANA-KAN** SHOKUDŌ ¥
(ひらがな館; ☑701-4164; 44 Tanaka-Nishihinokuchi-chō, Sakyō-ku; lunch & dinner from ¥750; ⏰11.30am-2.30pm & 6-10.30pm, closed Tue; Ⓡ Eizan line to Mototanaka) This place, popular with Kyoto University students, dishes up creative variations on chicken, fish and meat. The menu is in Japanese only and if you're at a loss for what to order try the tasty 'roll chicken *katsu*', a delectable and filling creation of chicken and vegetables. Look for the words 'Casual Restaurant' on the white awning.

⭐**PRINZ** CAFE ¥
(プリンツ; ☑712-3900; Tanakatakahara-chō 5, Sakyō-ku; lunch from ¥1000; ⏰11.30am-11pm; Ⓡ Eizan line to Chayama) Behind the blank white facade of Prinz, you'll find a cafe-restaurant, gallery, bookshop, garden and library – a chic island of coolness in an otherwise bland residential neighbourhood. The lunch set usually includes a light assortment of Western and Japanese dishes, generally on the healthy side.

## DIDI
INDIAN ¥¥

(ディディ; ☎791-8226; Tanaka-Ōkubo-chō 22, Sakyō-ku; lunch & dinner ¥1000-2000; ☺11am-10pm, closed Wed; ☺🍴🖿; 🚃Eizan line to Mototanaka) A cosy little spot in the north of town past Hyakumamben and Kyoto University, this friendly smoke-free restaurant serves passable Indian lunch and dinner sets. There are plenty of vegetarian choices on the menu, which is available in English.

# ✖ Southeast Kyoto

### ★ORGANIC CAFÉ COCOHANA
KOREAN ¥

(オーガニックカフェここはな; ☎525-5587; 13-243-1 Honmachi, Higashiyama-ku; lunch from ¥864; ☺10am-6pm; 🚃Keihan line to Tōfukuji) This place is one of a kind: a Korean cafe in a converted old Japanese house. Dishes include *bibimbap* (a Korean rice dish) and *kimchi* (Korean pickles). A full range of coffee and tea is also available. It's a woody, rustic place with both table and tatami seating. It makes a great stop while exploring southeastern Kyoto.

# ✖ West Kyoto

### KAZARIYA
SWEETS ¥

Map p211 (かざりや; ☎491-9402; Murasakino Imamiya-chō, Kita-ku; sweets ¥500; ☺10am-5.30pm, closed Wed; 🚃Kyoto City bus 46 to Imamiya-jinja) For more than 300 years, Kazariya has been specialising in *aburi-mochi* (grilled rice cakes coated with soya-bean flour) that are served with *miso-dare* (sweet-bean paste). It's a nice place to go for some tea and a sweet after exploring the grounds of Daitoku-ji.

### DEN SHICHI
SUSHI ¥¥

(傳七; ☎323-0700; Saiin, 4-1 Tatsumi-chō, Ukyo-ku; lunch/dinner from ¥518/2700; ☺11.30am-2pm & 5-10.30pm; 🚃Hankyū line to Saiin) This is one of the best reasonably priced sushi restaurants in Kyoto. It's a classic: long counter, bellowing sushi chefs and great fresh fish. The lunch sets are unbelievable value and the glass sushi cases make ordering a little easier than at some other places. Look for the black-and-white sign about 100m west of Saiin Station on Shijō-dōri. It's almost always hopping and doesn't take reservations, so you may have to give your name and wait – but it will definitely be worth it.

# ☆ ENTERTAINMENT

### KYOTO CONCERT HALL
CONCERT HALL

Map p211 (京都コンサートホール; ☎711-2980, ticket counter 711-3231/3090; www.kyoto-ongeibun.jp/kyotoconcerthall; Shimogamo, 1-26 Hangi-chō, Sakyō-ku; 🚇Karasuma line to Kitayama) This is Kyoto's main classical music venue. It's a lovely hall with excellent acoustics that never fails to draw an appreciative crowd of knowledgeable Kyotoites. Check *Kyoto Visitor's Guide* for upcoming concerts.

### ALTI
CONCERT HALL

Map p211 (京都府立府民ホール アルティ; ☎441-1414; Karasuma-dōri, Ichijō-sagaru, Kamigyō-ku; 🚇Karasuma line to Imadegawa) Classical music and dance performances are held at this midtown venue. Check *Kyoto Visitor's Guide* for upcoming concerts.

### CLUB ŌKITSU KYOTO
JAPANESE CULTURE

Map p211 (京都桜橘倶楽部「桜橘庵」; ☎411-8585; www.okitsu-kyoto.com; 524-1 Mototsuchimikado-chō, Kamichōjamachi-dōri, Shinmachi higashi-iru, Kamigyō-ku; 🚇Karasuma line to Imadegawa) Okitsu provides an upmarket introduction to various aspects of Japanese culture including tea ceremony and the incense ceremony. The introduction is performed in an exquisite Japanese villa near the Kyoto Imperial Palace and participants get a real sense of the elegance and refinement of traditional Japanese culture. It also offers kimono dressing upon request (note that kimono dressing is not offered alone: it must be part of a package including tea ceremony and/or incense ceremony).

### KYOTO MINAMI KAIKAN
CINEMA

(京都みなみ会館; ☎661-3993; Nishikujō, Higashihieijō-chō 79, Minami-ku; 🚃Kintetsu line to Tōji) Try this excellent little theatre for lesser-known foreign art-house and eclectic Japanese films. It's on Kujō-dōri.

# 🔒 SHOPPING

### KŌBŌ-SAN MARKET
MARKET

(弘法さん 東寺露天市; ☎691-3325; 1 Kujō-chō, Tō-ji, Minami-ku; ☺dawn-dusk 21st of each month; 🚃Kintetsu line to Tōji) This market is held at Tō-ji each month to commemorate the death of Kōbō Taishi, who in 823 was appointed abbot of the temple. If you're after used kimonos, pottery, bric-a-brac and general Japanalia, this is the place.

# Southern Higashiyama

## Neighbourhood Top Five

**1** Climbing to the top of the Southern Higashiyama district to visit one of Kyoto's most colourful temples: **Kiyomizu-dera** (p80). This temple is almost always crowded but there's plenty of room to move about and the throngs add to the energy of the place.

**2** Letting your soul be soothed by the chanting monks at **Chion-in** (p81).

**3** Sipping a cup of green tea while looking over the sublime garden at **Shōren-in** (p85).

**4** Clapping your hands to awaken the gods at **Yasaka-jinja** (p85).

**5** Taking an evening stroll through the world of geisha in **Gion** (p82).

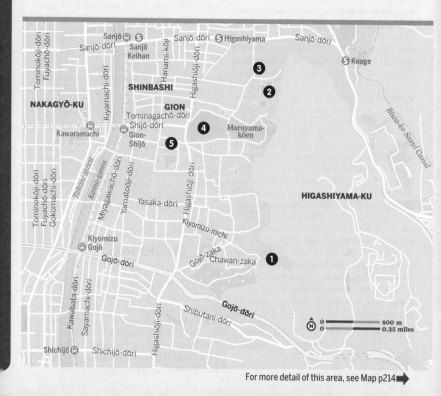

For more detail of this area, see Map p214 ➡

# Explore: Southern Higashiyama

Stretching along the base of the Higashiyama (Eastern Mountains) from the top of Shichijō-dōri to the top of Sanjō-dōri, Southern Higashiyama comprises the thickest concentration of sights in all of Kyoto. This area is home to some of Kyoto's best temples, including Kiyomizu-dera, Chion-in and Kōdai-ji, the green sanctuary of Maruyama-kōen, and several of the city's loveliest lanes: Ishibei-koji, Shimbashi and Nene-no-Michi. Needless to say, this is where you should begin your exploration of Kyoto.

There is a well-established sightseeing route through this district that starts at Kiyomizu-dera and finishes on Sanjō-dōri. It's best to walk this from south (Kiyomizu) to north (Sanjō), as you'll be going slowly downhill most of the way, but it's possible to do it from north to south. Note that this route does not cover some of the sights at the southern end of this district, like Sanjūsangen-dō, a fine temple, and the Kyoto National Museum.

A half day is usually sufficient to cover the main walking route in Southern Higashiyama, but if you eat lunch en route and take your time, you could easily spend a full day in this area. Note that this is Kyoto's most popular sightseeing district, so it will be crowded during peak seasons. Also, don't forget that the lanes here are almost deserted in the evening and a stroll through the darkened streets can be magical.

Downhill from the main sightseeing route, you'll find Gion, Kyoto's high-end entertainment and geisha district. This area is most scenic in the evening, which is also when you stand the best chance of spotting geisha.

## Local Life

→ **Hang-outs** Maruyama-kōen (p84), a green oasis in the middle of Southern Higashiyama, is popular with locals for picnics, strolls and dates.

→ **Eating** The scenic lanes of Ninen-zaka and Sannen-zaka (p84) are lined with tea shops and restaurants.

→ **Expat's favourite** Kyoto expats who crave a proper Western breakfast or a proper pizza head to the restaurants at the Hyatt Regency Kyoto (p140).

## Getting There & Away

→ **Train** The private Keihan line provides access to Southern Higashiyama. Get off at Gion-shijō or Shichijō Stations and walk uphill (east).

→ **Bus** Kyoto City buses serve various stops in the district and are a good way to access Kiyomizu-dera.

→ **Subway** The Tōzai subway line's Higashiyama Station offers easy access to the northern end of the district.

## Lonely Planet's Top Tip

During the cherry-blossom season in early April, the streets of Southern Higashiyama will be choked with traffic. *Do not* get in a taxi or bus in this area at this time unless you just want to sit there. Walking or taking the train/subway is the way to go during high season.

### ✕ Best Places to Eat

→ Rāmen Santōka (p86)
→ Omen Kodai-ji (p87)
→ Kikunoi (p87)

For reviews, see p86. ➡

### 🍸 Best Places to Drink

→ Gael Irish Pub (p88)
→ Gion Finlandia Bar (p88)
→ Bar Main Higashiyama (p88)

For reviews, see p88. ➡

### ⦿ Best Places for a Stroll

→ Gion (p82)
→ Ninen-zaka & Sannen-zaka (p84)
→ Maruyama-kōen (p84)

For reviews, see p80. ➡

SOUTHERN HIGASHIYAMA

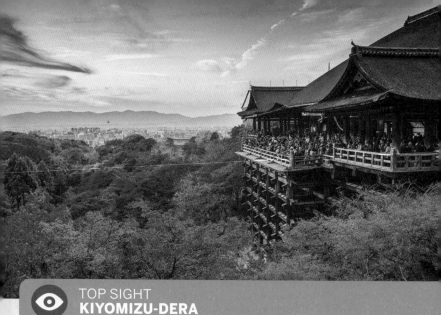

## TOP SIGHT
# KIYOMIZU-DERA

With a commanding position overlooking Kyoto, the superb Buddhist temple of Kiyomizu-dera is the city's spiritual heart and soul. Built around a holy spring (Kiyomizu means 'pure water'), the temple has been drawing pilgrims since the 8th century AD. In addition to halls holding fine Buddhist images, the complex includes a small Shintō shrine that is associated with matters of the heart – buy a prayer plaque here to assure success in romance. There's even a secret underground passage that allows you to experience symbolic rebirth by passing through the womb of a Bodhisattva.

First built in 798, Kiyomizu-dera belongs to the Hossō sect of Buddhism. The present buildings are reconstructions dating from 1633. The **Hondō** (Main Hall), which houses a Jūichi-men (11-headed) Kannon figure, features a huge verandah that juts out over the hillside, supported by 139 15m-high wooden pillars. Just below this verandah is **Otowa-no-taki** spring, where visitors drink the sacred waters believed to bestow health and long life.

After exiting the Hondō/verandah, up to your left, you will find **Jishu-jinja**, where visitors try to ensure success in love by closing their eyes and walking about 18m between a pair of 'Love Stones'.

Before you enter the actual temple precincts, visit one of the oddest sights in Japan: the **Tainai-meguri**. By entering the hall, you are figuratively entering the womb of Daizuigu Bosatsu, a female Bodhisattva who has the power to grant any human wish.

During the cherry-blossom season, autumn-foliage season and the summer O-bon season (a Buddhist observance honouring ancestral spirits), Kiyomizu-dera holds evening 'light-ups', when the trees and buildings are illuminated. Dates are: 12 to 21 March, 25 March to 10 April, 6 to 16 August and 11 November to 4 December.

### DON'T MISS...

➡ Cherry blossom, autumn and O-Bon light-ups

➡ Tainai-meguri

### PRACTICALITIES

➡ 清水寺

➡ Map p214

➡ 1-294 Kiyomizu, Higashiyama-ku

➡ admission ¥300

➡ ⏱6am-6pm

➡ 🚌Kyoto City bus 206 to Kiyōmizu-michi or Gojō-zaka, 🚃Keihan line to Kiyomizu-Gojō

## TOP SIGHT
## CHION-IN

**Called by some 'the Vatican of Pure Land Buddhism', this vast temple is one of the most impressive sights in all of Kyoto. The headquarters of one of Japan's most popular Buddhist sects, Chion-in receives millions of pilgrims annually, and it's one of the best places to see Japanese religious faith in action. Enter the enormous main hall and soak up the spiritual energy of the place: chanting monks, praying pilgrims and incense slowly spiralling to the heavens. Then set off and explore the many subtemples and halls.**

The single most impressive sight in Southern Higashiyama, Chion-in is a must-see for those with a taste for the grand and glorious. It was built by the monk Genchi in 1234 on the site where his mentor, Hōnen, had once taught and eventually fasted to death. Today it is still the headquarters of the Jōdo school, which was founded by Hōnen, and it is a hive of religious activity.

The oldest of the present buildings date from the 17th century. The two-storey **San-mon** gate at the main entrance is the largest in Japan, and prepares the visitor for the massive scale of the temple. The immense main hall (Miei-dō Hall), which measures 35m wide and 45m long, houses an image of Hōnen and is connected with the Dai Hōjō hall by a 'nightingale' floor that squeaks as one walks over it.

After visiting the main hall, with its fantastic gold altar, walk around to the back to see the temple's gardens. On the way, you'll pass a darkened hall with a small statue of Amida Buddha glowing eerily in the darkness. It's a nice contrast to the splendour of the main hall.

Chion-in's **temple bell** was cast in 1633. It is the largest temple bell in Japan. It's up a flight of steps at the southeastern corner of the temple precincts.

### DON'T MISS...

➡ The temple bell
➡ Chanting monks in the main hall

### PRACTICALITIES

➡ 知恩院
➡ Map p214
➡ 400 Rinka-chō, Higashiyama-ku
➡ admission inner buildings & garden ¥500, grounds free
➡ ⊙9am-4.30pm
➡ ⑤Tōzai line to Higashiyama

#  SIGHTS

**KIYOMIZU-DERA**     BUDDHIST TEMPLE
See p80.

**CHION-IN**     BUDDHIST TEMPLE
See p81.

**SANJŪSANGEN-DŌ TEMPLE**   BUDDHIST TEMPLE
Map p214 (三十三間堂; 657 Sanjūsangendōma wari-chō, Higashiyama-ku; admission ¥600; ⏰8am-4.30pm Apr-Oct, 9am-3.30pm Nov-Mar; 🚌Kyoto City bus 206 or 208 to Sanjūsangen-dō-mae, 🚆Keihan line to Shichijō) This superb temple's name refers to the 33 *sanjūsan* (bays) between the pillars of this long, narrow building. The building houses 1001 wooden statues of Kannon (the Buddhist goddess of mercy); the chief image, the 1000-armed Senjū-Kannon, was carved by the celebrated sculptor Tankei in 1254. It is flanked by 500 smaller Kannon images, neatly lined in rows. The visual effect is stunning, making this a must-see in Southern Higashiyama and a good starting point for exploration of the area.

The original temple, called Rengeō-in, was built in 1164 at the request of the retired emperor Go-shirakawa. After it burnt to the ground in 1249, a faithful copy was constructed in 1266.

If you look closely, you might notice that the supposedly 1000-armed statues don't have the required number. Just keep in mind that a nifty Buddhist mathematical formula holds that 40 arms are the equivalent of 1000 because each saves 25 worlds.

At the back of the hall are 28 guardian statues in a variety of expressive poses. The gallery at the western side of the hall is famous for the annual **Tōshiya festival**, held on 15 January, when archers shoot arrows along the length of the hall. The ceremony dates from the Edo period, when an annual contest was held to see how many arrows could be shot from the southern to northern end in 24 hours. The all-time record was set in 1686, when an archer successfully landed more than 8000 arrows at the northern end.

**KYOTO NATIONAL MUSEUM**     MUSEUM
Map p214 (京都国立博物館; www.kyohaku.go.jp; 527 Chaya-machi, Higashiyama-ku; adult/student ¥500/250; ⏰9.30am-6pm, to 8pm Fri, closed Mon; 🚌Kyoto City bus 206 or 208 to Sanjūsangen-dō-mae, 🚆Keihan line to Shichijō) The Kyoto National Museum is Kyoto's premier art museum and plays host to the highest level exhibitions in the city. It was founded in 1895

---

## ◉ TOP SIGHT
# GION

Gion is the famous entertainment and geisha quarter on the eastern bank of the Kamo-gawa. While Gion's true origins were in teahouses catering to weary visitors to Yasaka-jinja (a neighbourhood shrine), by the mid-18th century the area was Kyoto's largest pleasure district. Despite the looming modern architecture, there are still some places left in Gion for an enjoyable walk.

**Hanami-kōji** runs north–south and bisects Shijō-dōri. The southern section is lined with 17th-century traditional restaurants and teahouses, many of which are exclusive establishments for geisha entertainment. At the south end you reach Gion Corner (p90) and **Gion Kōbu Kaburen-jō Theatre** (祇園甲部歌舞練場).

If you walk from Shijō-dōri along the northern section of Hanami-kōji and take your third left, you will find yourself on **Shimbashi**, which is one of Kyoto's most beautiful streets and, arguably, the most beautiful street in all of Asia, especially in the evening and during cherry-blossom season. A bit further north lie **Shinmonzen-dōri** and **Furumonzen-dōri**, running east–west. Wander in either direction along these streets, which are packed with old houses, art galleries and shops specialising in antiques.

### DON'T MISS...

➡ Geisha scurrying to appointments in the early evening

➡ *Machiya* (traditional Japanese townhouses) in lanes off the main streets

### PRACTICALITIES

➡ 祇園周辺

➡ Map p214

➡ Higashiyama-ku

➡ 🚇Tōzai line to Sanjo, 🚆Keihan line to Gion-Shijō

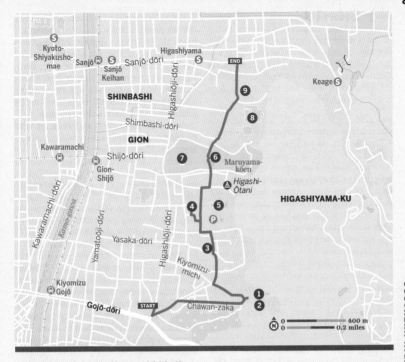

# 🚶 Neighbourhood Walk
## Southern Higashiyama Highlights

**START** GOJŌ-ZAKA BUS STOP
**FINISH** HIGASHIYAMA-SANJŌ STATION
**LENGTH** 5KM; FOUR HOURS

From Gojō-zaka bus stop on Higashiōji-dōri (bus 18, 100, 206 or 207), walk up Gojō-zaka slope. Head uphill until you reach the first fork in the road; bear right and continue up Chawan-zaka (Teapot Lane). At the top of the hill, you'll come to Kiyomizu-dera. Before you enter the temple, pay ¥100 to descend into the **❶ Tainai-meguri** (p80), the entrance to which is just to the left of the main temple entrance. Next, enter **❷ Kiyomizu-dera** (p80). After touring the temple, exit down Kiyomizu-michi. Continue down the hill and take a right at the four-way intersection down stone-paved steps. This is Sannen-zaka, where you will find tiny little **❸ Kasagi-ya** (p86), which has been serving tea and Japanese-style sweets for as long as anyone can remember. It's on the left, just below a vending machine. Halfway down Sannen-zaka, the road curves to the left. Follow it a short distance, then go right down a flight of steps into Ninen-zaka. At the end of Ninen-zaka zigzag left (at the vending machines) then right (just past the car park), and continue north. Very soon, on your left, you'll come to the entrance to **❹ Ishibei-kōji** – perhaps the most beautiful street in Kyoto. Take a detour to explore this, then retrace your steps and continue north, passing almost immediately the entrance to **❺ Kōdai-ji** (p84) on the right up a long flight of stairs.

Continue north to the T-junction; turn right, then take a quick left. You'll cross the pedestrian arcade that leads to Ōtani cemetery and then descend into **❻ Maruyama-kōen** (p84). In the centre of the park is the giant Gion *shidare-zakura*, Kyoto's most famous cherry tree. From the park, head west into the grounds of **❼ Yasaka-jinja** (p85). Then return to the park and head north to tour the grounds of the impressive **❽ Chion-in** (p81). From here it's a quick walk to **❾ Shōren-in** (p85). From Shōren-in walk down to Sanjō-dōri.

as an imperial repository for art and treasures from local temples and shrines. In the original **main hall** there are 17 rooms with displays of over 1000 artworks, historical artefacts and handicrafts. The new **Heisei Chishinkan**, designed by Taniguchi Yoshio and opened in 2014, is a brilliant modern counterpoint to the original building.

While the permanent collection is worth a visit, the special exhibitions are the real highlights. Check with the Tourist Information Center (TIC) or the *Kyoto Visitor's Guide* to see what's on while you're in town.

### KAWAI KANJIRŌ MEMORIAL HALL   MUSEUM

Map p214 (河井寛治郎記念館; 569 Kanei-chō, Gojō-zaka, Higashiyama-ku; admission ¥900; ⏰10am-5pm, closed Mon & around 11-20 Aug & 24 Dec-7 Jan, dates vary each year; 🚌Kyoto City bus 206 or 207 to Umamachi) This small memorial hall is one of Kyoto's most commonly overlooked little gems. The hall was the home and workshop of one of Japan's most famous potters, Kawai Kanjirō (1890–1966). The 1937 house is built in rural style and contains examples of Kanjirō's work, his collection of folk art and ceramics, his workshop and a fascinating *nobori-gama* (stepped kiln). The museum is near the intersection of Gojō-dōri and Higashiōji-dōri.

### ROKUHARAMITSU-JI   BUDDHIST TEMPLE

Map p214 (六波羅蜜寺; 📞561-6980; Gojō-dōri, Yamatoōji-agaru higashi, Higashiyama-ku; treasure house adult/child ¥600/400; ⏰8.30am-4.30pm; 🚌Kyoto City bus 206 to Kiyomizu-michi) An important Buddhist pilgrimage stop, this temple was founded in 963 by Kūya Shōnin, who carved an image of an 11-headed Kannon and installed it in the temple in the hope of stopping a plague that was ravaging Kyoto at the time. The temple itself is unremarkable but the treasure house at the rear contains a rare collection of 15 fantastic statues.

The most intriguing statue in the temple's collection is a standing likeness of Kūya, staff in hand and prayer gong draped around his neck, with a string of tiny figurines parading from his gums. Legend holds that while praying one day, these manifestations of the Buddha suddenly ambled out of his mouth.

### KENNIN-JI   BUDDHIST TEMPLE

Map p214 (建仁寺; 584 Komatsu-chō, Yamatoōji-dōri, Shijo-sagaru, Higashiyama-ku; admission ¥500; ⏰10am-4pm; 🚃Keihan line to Gion-Shijō) Founded in 1202 by the monk Eisai, Kennin-ji is the oldest Zen temple in Kyoto. It is an island of peace and calm on the border of the boisterous Gion nightlife district and it makes a fine counterpoint to the worldly pleasures of that area. The highlight at Kennin-ji is the fine and expansive *karesansui* (dry-landscape rock garden). The painting of the twin dragons on the roof of the **Hōdō** hall is also fantastic.

Access to the Hōdō is via two gates with rather puzzling English operating instructions (you'll see what we mean).

### NINEN-ZAKA & SANNEN-ZAKA   NEIGHBOURHOOD

Map p214 (二年坂・三年坂; Higashiyama-ku; 🚌Kyoto City bus 206 to Kiyomizu-michi or Gojō-zaka, 🚃Keihan line to Kiyomizu-Gojō) Just downhill from and slightly to the north of Kiyomizu-dera, you will find one of Kyoto's loveliest restored neighbourhoods, the Ninen-zaka–Sannen-zaka area. The name refers to the two main streets of the area: Ninen-zaka and Sannen-zaka, literally 'Two-Year Hill' and 'Three-Year Hill' (the years referring to the ancient imperial years when they were first laid out). These two charming streets are lined with old wooden houses, traditional shops and restaurants. If you fancy a break, there are many teahouses and cafes along these lanes.

### KŌDAI-JI   BUDDHIST TEMPLE

Map p214 (高台寺; 526 Shimokawara-chō, Kōdai-ji, Higashiyama-ku; admission ¥600; ⏰9am-5pm; 🚌Kyoto City bus 206 to Yasui, 🚇Tōzai line to Higashiyama) This exquisite temple was founded in 1605 by Kita-no-Mandokoro in memory of her late husband, Toyotomi Hideyoshi. The extensive grounds include gardens designed by the famed landscape architect Kobori Enshū, and teahouses designed by the renowned master of the tea ceremony, Sen no Rikyū.

The temple holds three annual special night-time illuminations, when the gardens are lit by multicoloured spotlights. The illuminations are held from mid-March to early May, 1 to 18 August and late October to early December.

### MARUYAMA-KŌEN   PARK

Map p214 (円山公園; Maruyama-chō, Higashiyama-ku; 🚇Tōzai line to Higashiyama) Maruyama-kōen is a favourite of locals and visitors alike. This park is the place to come to escape the bustle of the city centre and amble around gardens, ponds, souvenir

## DRESSING UP IN MAIKO COSTUME

If you ever wondered how *you* might look as a *maiko* (apprentice geisha), Kyoto has many organisations in town that offer the chance. **Maika** (舞香; Map p214; ☑551-1661; www.maica.tv; 297 Miyagawa suji 4-chōme, Higashiyama-ku; maiko/geisha from ¥6500/8000; ⬛Keihan line to Gion-Shijo or Kiyomizu-Gojo) is in the Gion district. Here you can be dressed up to live out your *maiko* fantasy. Prices begin at ¥6720 for the basic treatment, which includes full make-up and formal kimono (studio photos cost ¥500 per print and you can have stickers made from these). If you don't mind spending some extra yen, it's possible to head out in costume for a stroll through Gion (and be stared at like never before!). The process takes about an hour. Call to reserve at least one day in advance.

shops and restaurants. Peaceful paths meander through the trees and carp swim in a pond in the park's centre.

For two weeks in early April, when the park's cherry trees come into bloom, the calm atmosphere is shattered by hordes of drunken revellers having *hanami* (cherry-blossom viewing) parties under the trees. The centrepiece is a massive *shidare-zakura* (weeping cherry tree); this is one of the most beautiful sights in Kyoto, particularly when lit up from below at night. For those who don't mind crowds, this is a good place to see the Japanese at their most uninhibited. Arrive early and claim a spot high on the east side of the park, from where you can peer down on the mayhem below.

### YASAKA-JINJA                    SHINTO SHRINE

Map p214 (八坂神社; 625 Gion-machi, Kita-gawa, Higashiyama-ku; ⊙24hr; Ⓢ Tōzai line to Higashiyama) FREE This is considered the guardian shrine of the Gion entertainment district. It's a bustling, colourful place that is well worth a visit while exploring Southern Higashiyama; it can easily be paired with Maruyama-kōen, the park just up the hill.

The present buildings, with the exception of the older, two-storey west gate, date from 1654. The granite *torii* (shrine gate) on the south side was erected in 1666 and stands 9.5m high, making it one of the tallest in Japan. The roof of the main shrine is covered with cypress shingles. Among the treasures here are a pair of carved wooden *koma-inu* (guardian lion-dogs) attributed to the renowned sculptor Unkei.

This shrine is popular as a spot for *hatsu-mōde* (first shrine visit of the New Year). If you don't mind a stampede, come here around midnight on New Year's Eve or on any of the days following. Surviving the crush is proof that you're blessed by the gods!

### YASUI KONPIRA-GŪ                SHINTO SHRINE

Map p214 (安井金比羅宮; 70 Simobenten-chō, Higashiyama-ku; ⊙24hr; ⬛Kyoto City bus 204 to Higashiyama-Yasui) This interesting little Shintō shrine on the edge of Gion contains one of the most peculiar objects we've encountered anywhere in Japan: the **enkiri/enmusubi ishi**. This is a stone that is thought to bind good relationships tighter and sever bad relationships. To our eyes, it looks like some kind of shaggy igloo (you'll see what we mean).

If you'd like to take advantage of the stone's powers, here's the drill: purchase a special piece of paper from the counter next to the stone and write you name and wish on it. If you want to bind your love tighter (figuratively, of course), grasp the paper and crawl through the tunnel in the stone from front to back. If you want out of your present relationship, crawl through from back to front. Then, use the glue provided and stick your wishing paper to the ever-huge collection of wishes decorating the stone.

### ★SHŌREN-IN                      BUDDHIST TEMPLE

Map p214 (青蓮院; 69-1 Sanjōbō-chō, Awatagu-chi, Higashiyama-ku; admission ¥500; ⊙9am-5pm; Ⓢ Tōzai line to Higashiyama) This temple is hard to miss, with its giant camphor trees growing just outside the walls. Fortunately, most tourists march right on past, heading to the area's more famous temples. That is their loss, because this intimate little sanctuary contains a superb landscape garden that you can enjoy while drinking a cup of green tea (ask at the reception office).

Shōren-in, commonly called Awata Palace after the neighbourhood in which it is located, was originally the residence of the chief abbot of the Tendai school. Founded in 1150, the present building dates from 1895 and the main hall has sliding screens with paintings from the 16th and 17th centuries.

#  EATING

## ⭐RĀMEN SANTŌKA
RĀMEN ¥

Map p214 (らーめん山頭火; ☎532-1335; www.
santouka.co.jp; Yamatoōji-dōri, Sanjō-sagaru Higashi gawa, Higashiyama-ku; rāmen from ¥770;
⊙11am-2am Mon-Sat, 11am-midnight Sun & national holidays; ⓓ; Ⓢ Tōzai line to Sanjō-Keihan,
Ⓡ Keihan line to Sanjō) The young chefs at
this sleek restaurant dish out some seriously good Hokkaidō-style *rāmen* (noodles
in a meat broth with meat and vegetables).
You will be given a choice of three kinds of
soup when you order: *shio* (salt), *shōyu* (soy
sauce) or miso – we highly recommend you
go for the miso soup.

For something decadent, try the *tokusen
toroniku rāmen,* which is made from pork
cheeks, of which only 200g can be obtained
from one animal. The pork will come on a
separate plate from the *rāmen* – just shovel
it all into your bowl. The restaurant is on
the east side and ground floor of the new
Kyōen restaurant and shopping complex.

## ⭐KASAGI-YA
TEAHOUSE ¥

Map p214 (かさぎ屋; ☎561-9562; 349 Masuya
chō, Kōdai-ji, Higashiyama-ku; tea & sweets from
¥600; ⊙11am-6pm, closed Tue; ⓓ; Ⓑ Kyoto City
bus 206 to Higashiyama-Yasui) At Kasagi-ya, on
Sannen-zaka near Kiyomizu-dera, you can
enjoy a cup of *matcha* (powdered green tea)
and a variety of sweets. This funky old wood-
en shop has atmosphere to boot and friendly
staff – which makes it worth the wait if
there's a queue. It's hard to spot – you may
have to ask one of the local shop owners.

## KAGIZEN YOSHIFUSA
TEAHOUSE ¥

Map p214 (鍵善良房; ☎561-1818; www.kagizen.
co.jp/en/; 264 Gion machi, Kita-gawa, Higashiyama-
ku; kuzukiri ¥900; ⊙9.30am-6pm, closed Mon; ⓓ;
Ⓡ Hankyū line to Kawaramachi, Keihan line to Gion-
Shijō) This Gion institution is one of Kyoto's
oldest and best-known *okashi-ya* (sweet
shops). It sells a variety of traditional sweets
and has a lovely tea room out the back where
you can sample cold *kuzukiri* (transparent arrowroot noodles) served with a *kuro-
mitsu* (sweet black sugar) dipping sauce, or
just a nice cup of *matcha* and a sweet.

This is one of the best spots in Gion for a
rest. Look for the sweets in the window, the
wide front and the *noren* curtains.

## RAKUSHŌ
CAFE ¥

Map p214 (洛匠; ☎561-6892; 516 Washio-chō,
Kodaijikitamon-dōri, Shimogawara higashi-iru,

---

Higashiyama-ku; tea from ¥500; ⊙9am-6pm,
closed irregularly; ⓓ; Ⓑ Kyoto City bus 204 to
Higashiyama-Yasui) This casual little Japanese-style tea room on Nene-no-Michi in
the heart of the Southern Higashiyama
sightseeing district is well placed for a
break while doing the main tourist route in
this area. The real attraction is the small
koi (Japanese carp) pond adjoining the tea
room. The owner is a champion koi breeder
and his fish are superb!

## HISAGO
NOODLES ¥

Map p214 (ひさご; ☎561-2109; 484
Shimokawara-chō, Higashiyama-ku; meals from
¥900; ⊙11.30am-7.30pm, closed Mon; ⓓ;
Ⓑ Kyoto City bus 206 to Higashiyama-Yasui) If
you need a quick meal while in the main
Southern Higashiyama sightseeing district,
this simple noodle and rice restaurant is a
good bet. It's within easy walking distance
of Kiyomizu-dera and Maruyama-kōen.
*Oyako-donburi* (chicken and egg over rice;
¥980) is the speciality of the house.

There is no English sign; look for the
traditional front and the small collection of
food models on display. In the busy seasons,
there's almost always a queue outside.

## CAFÉ 3032
CAFE ¥

Map p214 (カフェ サンゼロサンニ; ☎531-8869;
102 Tatsumi-chō, Higashiōji-dōri, Matsubara-
agaru, Higashiyama-ku; light meals from ¥600;
⊙8am-10pm; ⓓ; Ⓑ Kyoto City bus 206 to Higashiyama-Yasui) This super-casual cafe on
Higashiōji, just down the hill from the main
Southern Higashiyama sightseeing district,
is a great place for a light lunch or cuppa.
Foreign visitors are welcomed. The fare includes sandwiches, curry, beer and coffee.

## OSHOKUJIDOKORO ASUKA
SHOKUDŌ ¥

Map p214 (お食事処明日香; ☎751-1941; 144
Nishi-machi, Sanjō-dōri, Jingū-michi nishi-iru,
Higashiyama-ku; meals from ¥850; ⊙11am-11pm,
closed Mon; ⓓ; Ⓢ Tōzai line to Higashiyama)
With an English menu, and a staff of friendly Kyoto *mama-sans* who are at home with
foreign customers, this is a great place for a
cheap lunch or dinner while sightseeing in
the Higashiyama area. The tempura *mori-
awase* (assorted tempura set) is a big pile
of tempura for only ¥1000. Look for the red
lantern and pictures of the set meals.

## SENMONTEN
CHINESE ¥

Map p214 (泉門天; ☎531-2733; Hanami-kōji-dōri,
Shimbashi-sagaru higashi-gawa, Higashiyama-ku;

per 10 dumplings ¥520; ☺6pm-2am Mon-Thur, until 3am Fri & Sat; **S**Keihan line to Gion-Shijō) This place serves one thing only: crisp fried *gyōza* (dumplings), which come in lots of 10 and are washed down with beer or Chinese *raoshu* (rice wine). If you can break the record for the most *gyōza* eaten in one sitting, your meal will be free and you'll receive more *gyōza* to take home. Look for the red-and-white sign and the glass door.

### ISSEN YŌSHOKU
OKONOMIYAKI ¥

Map p214 (壱銭洋食; ☎533-0001; Gion, Shijō Nawate kado, Higashiyama-ku; okonomiyaki ¥630; ☺11am-3am Mon-Sat, 10.30am-10pm Sun; **R**Keihan line to Gion-Shijō) Heaped with red ginger and green scallions, the *okonomiyaki* at this Gion institution is a garish snack – which somehow seems fitting considering the surrounding neighbourhood. It's open to the elements and you can't miss the griddles out the front.

### YAGURA
NOODLES ¥¥

Map p214 (やぐ羅; ☎561-1035; Shijō-dōri, Yamatoōji nishi-iru, Higashiyama-ku; soba ¥1150; ☺11.30am-9pm, closed irregularly; **R**Keihan line to Gion-Shijō) Across from Minami-za theatre, this noodle specialist is an unassuming and casual spot for a nice bowl of noodles while exploring Gion. We recommend the *nishin soba* (*soba* noodles topped with fish; ¥1100). Yagura is located between a *rāmen* joint and a Japanese gift shop – look for the bowls of noodles in the window.

### RYŪMON
CHINESE ¥¥

Map p214 (龍門; ☎752-8181; Sanjō-dōri, Higashiōji nishi-iru, Higashiyama-ku; dinner set from ¥3000; ☺5pm-5am; **S**Tōzai line to Higashiyama or Sanjō-Keihan, **R**Keihan line to Sanjō) This place may look like a total dive but the food is reliable and authentic, as the crowds of Kyoto's Chinese residents will attest. There's no English menu but there is a picture menu and some of the waitresses can speak English.

Look for the food pictures out the front.

### ★ OMEN KODAI-JI
NOODLES ¥¥

Map p214 (おめん 高台寺店; ☎541-5007; 358 Masuya-chō, Kodaiji-dōri, Shimokawara higashi-iru, Higashiyama-ku; noodles from ¥1150, set menu ¥1800; ☺11am-9pm, closed irregularly; **R**Kyoto City bus 206 to Higashiyama-Yasui) This branch of Kyoto's famed Omen noodle chain is the best place to stop while exploring the Southern Higashiyama district. It's in a remod-

elled Japanese building with a light, airy feeling. The signature udon (thick white wheat noodles) are delicious and there are many other à la carte offerings.

### SOBADOKORO SHIBAZAKI
NOODLES ¥¥

Map p214 (そば処柴崎; ☎525-3600; 4-190-3 Kiyomizu, Higashiyama-ku; soba from ¥1026; ☺11am-6pm, closed Tue; 🔲; **R**Kyoto City bus 206 to Kiyomizu-michi, **R**Keihan line to Kiyomizu-Gojō) For excellent *soba* noodles and well-presented tempura sets (among other things) in the area of Kiyomizu-dera, try this comfortable and spacious restaurant. After your meal, head upstairs to check out the sublime collection of Japanese lacquerware. Look for the low stone wall and the *noren* curtains hanging in the entryway.

### BAMBOO
IZAKAYA ¥¥

Map p214 (晩boo; ☎771-5559; Minami gawa, 1st fl, Higashiyama-Sanjō Keihan-iru, Higashiyama-ku; meals ¥4000-5000; ☺5.30pm-midnight; **S**Tōzai line to Higashiyama) Bamboo is one of Kyoto's more approachable *izakaya* (Japanese pub-eatery). It's on Sanjō-dōri, near the mouth of a traditional, old shopping arcade. You can sit at the counter here and order a variety of typical *izakaya* dishes, watching the chefs do their thing.

### ★ KIKUNOI
KAISEKI ¥¥¥

Map p214 (菊乃井; ☎561-0015; www.kikunoi.jp; 459 Shimokawara-chō, Yasakatoriimae-sagaru, Shimokawara-dōri, Higashiyama-ku; lunch/dinner from ¥4000/15,000; ☺noon-1pm & 5-8pm; ☺🔲; **R**Keihan line to Gion-Shijō) This is one of Kyoto's true culinary temples, serving some of the finest *kaiseki* (Japanese haute cuisine) in the city. Located in a hidden nook near Maruyama-kōen, this restaurant has everything necessary for the full over-the-top *kaiseki* experience, from setting, to service, to exquisitely executed cuisine, often with a creative twist. Reserve through your hotel or ryokan concierge.

### GION KARYŌ
KAISEKI ¥¥¥

Map p214 (祇園迦陵; ☎532-0025; 570-235 Gion-machi minamigawa, Higashiyama-ku; lunch & dinner courses from ¥3800; ☺11.30am-3.30pm & 5.30-11pm, closed Wed; 🔲; **R**Keihan line to Gion-Shijō) Take an old Kyoto house, renovate it to make it comfortable for modern diners, serve reasonably priced and excellent *kaiseki* and you have Karyō's recipe for success. The chef and servers are welcoming and an English menu makes ordering a snap. There are counter seats where you can watch the chef working and rooms with *hori-kotatsu* (sunken floors) for groups.

# DRINKING & NIGHTLIFE

## ★ BAR MAIN HIGASHIYAMA
BAR

Map p214 (バー メイン ヒガシヤマ; ☑541-3331; www.thesodoh.com; Garden Oriental Kyoto, Yasakakami-machi 366, Yasaka-dōri, Shimokawara higashi-iru, Higashiyama-ku; ⏰8pm-midnight; ☐Kyoto City bus 206 to Higashiyama-Yasui) This slick and elegant bar in the Garden Oriental complex, right in the heart of the Southern Higashiyama sightseeing district, is a real stunner. You can choose from counter or table seating and the atmosphere is completely relaxing. Smart casual is the way to go here.

## TŌZAN BAR
BAR

Map p214 (Sanjūsangendō-mawari, Hyatt Regency Kyoto; ☐5min walk from Shichijō Station, Keihan line) We love this cosy and cool underground retreat below the Hyatt Regency Kyoto, one of Kyoto's best hotels. It's worth a visit just to marvel at the design.

## GAEL IRISH PUB
BAR

Map p214 (ザガエルアイリッシュパブ; ☑525-0680; 2nd fl, Ōtō Bldg, Nijūikken-chō, Shijō-dōri, Yamatōji-agaru, Higashiyama-ku; drinks from ¥500; ⏰5pm-1am, later Thu-Sun; ☐Keihan line to Gion-Shijō) A cosy little Irish bar on the doorstep of Gion. It offers good food, excellent beer and friendly staff, as well as occasional live music. It's a great place to meet local expats and see what's going on in town. You'll find it up a flight of steps.

## GION FINLANDIA BAR
BAR

Map p214 (ぎおん フィンランディアバー; ☑541-3482; 570-123 Gion-machi minamigawa, Higashiyama-ku (Hanamikōji, Shijō-sagaru hitosuji-me nishi-iru minamigawa); admission ¥500, drinks about ¥900; ⏰6pm-3am; ☐Keihan Line to Gion-Shijō) This stylish Gion bar in an old geisha house is a great place for a civilised drink. The 1st floor is decorated with Finnish touches while the upstairs retains a Japanese feeling, with sunken floors and tatami mats.

## PIG & WHISTLE
PUB

Map p214 (ピッグ&ホイッスル; ☑761-6022; Kawabata-dōri, Sanjō higashi-iru; ⏰5pm-2am Sun-Thu, to 5am Fri & Sat; ☐Keihan line to Sanjō) The Pig is a relaxed British-style pub with darts, pint glasses, and fish and chips. The two main drawcards are Guinness on tap and friendly bilingual staff. It's on the 2nd floor of the Shobi building near the Sanjō-Kawabata crossing.

# ☆ ENTERTAINMENT

## ★ MINAMI-ZA
THEATRE

Map p214 (南座; ☑561-0160; www.kabuki-bito. jp/eng/contents/theatre/kyoto_minamiza.html; Shijō-Ōhashi, Higashiyama-ku; performances ¥4000-27,000; ☐Keihan line to Gion-Shijō) The oldest kabuki theatre in Japan is the Minami-za theatre in Gion. The major event of the year is the **Kaomise festival** (1 to 26 December), which features Japan's finest kabuki actors. Other performances take place on an irregular basis – check with the Tourist Information Centre. The most likely months for performances are May, June and September.

## ★ MIYAKO ODORI
DANCE

Map p214 (都をどり; ☑541-3391; www.miyako-odori.jp/english/; Gionkobu Kaburenjo, 570-2 Gionmachi-minamigawa, Higashiyama-ku; seat reserved/nonreserved/reserved incl tea ¥4200/2500/4800; ⏰shows 12.30pm, 2pm, 3.30pm & 4.50pm; ☐Kyoto City bus 206 to Gion, ☐Keihan line to Gion-Shijō) Presented by the Gion Kōbu geisha district, this is our favourite geisha dance in Kyoto. It's a real stunner and the colourful images will remain with you long after the curtain falls. It's held throughout April at the Gion Kōbu Kaburen-jō Theatre, on Hanami-kōji, just south of Shijō-dōri.

## ★ KYŌ ODORI
DANCE

Map p214 (京おどり; ☑561-1151; Miyagawachō Kaburenjo, 4-306 Miyagawasuji, Higashiyama-ku; seat reserved/nonreserved ¥4000/2000, plus ¥500 incl tea; ⏰shows 12.30pm, 2.30pm & 4.30pm; ☐Keihan line to Gion-Shijō) Put on by the Miyagawa-chō geisha district, this wonderful geisha dance is among the most picturesque performances of the Kyoto year. It's held from the first to the third Sunday in April at the **Miyagawa-chō Kaburen-jō Theatre** (宮川町歌舞練場), east of the Kamo-gawa between Shijō-dōri and Gojō-dōri.

SOUTHERN HIGASHIYAMA DRINKING & NIGHTLIFE

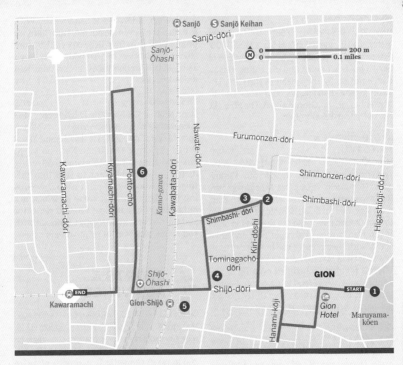

# 🏃 Neighbourhood Walk
# Night Walk Through the Floating World

**START** YASAKA-JINJA
**FINISH** KAWARAMACHI STATION
**LENGTH** 3KM; TWO HOURS

Start on the steps of **①Yasaka-jinja** (p85), at the intersection of Shijō-dōri and Higashiōji-dōri, a 10-minute walk from Shijō (Keihan line) or Kawaramachi (Hankyū line) Stations. Cross to the south side of Shijō-dōri and just after passing the Gion Hotel turn left. Walk 150m and take the second right. Another 100m brings you to Hanami-kōji, a picturesque street of *ryōtei* (traditional, high-class restaurants). Take a look then walk back north to Shijō-dōri.

Cross Shijō-dōri and go west for about 20m then turn right into Kiri-dōshi. As you continue along Kiri-dōshi, you'll cross Tominagachō-dōri, which is lined with buildings containing hundreds of hostess bars.

Kiri-dōshi crosses another street and then narrows to a tiny alley. You are about to enter Gion's most lovely area, which lies just across **②Tatsumi-bashi bridge**. This is the Shim-

bashi district, which features some of Kyoto's finest traditional architecture, most upmarket restaurants and exclusive hostess bars.

At the fork in the road you will find a small **③Tatsumi shrine**. Go left and walk west along the canal. Admire the views across the canal into some of Kyoto's finest restaurants. You will occasionally spot geisha entertaining guests in these elite places. At the end of Shimbashi, go left onto gaudy Nawate-dōri. Just before you reach Shijō-dōri, you'll pass **④Issen Yōshoku** (p87), a popular *okonomiyaki* (savoury pancake) restaurant.

Head west on Shijō-dōri, passing **⑤Minami-za** (p88), Kyoto's main kabuki theatre. Cross the Kamo-gawa on the north side of Shijō-Ōhashi and walk to the *kōban* (police box) on your right. You are now at the intersection of Shijō-dōri and **⑥Ponto-chō** (p56). Heading north brings you into a different world of upmarket restaurants, bars, clubs and cafes. At the north end of Ponto-chō at Sanjō-dōri, take a left and another left on Kiyamachi-dōri. This is a much more casual entertainment district.

★**GION ODORI** DANCE

Map p214 (祇園をどり; ☎561-0224; Gion, Higashiyama-ku; admission/incl tea ¥3500/4000; ⊙shows 1.30pm & 4pm; 🚌Kyoto City bus 206 to Gion) This is a quaint and charming geisha dance put on by the geisha of the Gion Higashi geisha district. It's held from 1 to 10 November at the **Gion Kaikan Theatre** (祇園会館), near Yasaka-jinja.

## KYOTO CUISINE & MAIKO EVENING
GEISHA DANCE

Map p214 (ぎおん畑中; ☎541-5315; www.kyoto-maiko.jp; Hatanaka Ryokan, 505 Minamigawa, Gion-machi, Yasaka-jinja Minamimon-mae, Higashiyama-ku; per person ¥18,000; ⊙6-8pm, every Mon, Wed, Fri & Sat; 🚌Kyoto City bus 206 to Gion or Chionin-mae, 🚈Keihan line to Gion-Shijō) If you want to see geisha perform and then speak with them, one of the best opportunities is at Gion Hatanaka, a Gion ryokan that offers a regularly scheduled evening of elegant Kyoto *kaiseki* food and personal entertainment by real Kyoto *geiko* (fully fledged geisha) as well as *maiko* (apprentice geisha).

**GION CORNER** THEATRE

Map p214 (ギオンコーナー; ☎561-1119; www.kyoto-gioncorner.com; Yasaka Kaikan, 570-2 Gion-machi Minamigawa, Higashiyama-ku; admission ¥3150; ⊙performances 6pm & 7pm daily mid-Mar–Nov, Fri-Sun Dec–mid-Mar; 🚈Keihan Line to Gion-Shijō) Gion Corner presents shows that include a bit of tea ceremony, koto (Japanese zither) music, ikebana (art of flower arranging), *gagaku* (court music), *kyōgen* (ancient comic plays), *kyōmai* (Kyoto-style dance) and *bunraku* (classical puppet theatre). It's geared to tourists and is fairly pricey for what you get.

# 🔒 SHOPPING

**KAGOSHIN** CRAFTS

Map p214 (籠新; ☎771-0209; 4 chō-me, Sanjō-dōri, Sanjō-Ōhashi-higashi, Higashiyama-ku; ⊙9am-6pm, closed Mon; 🚇Tōzai line to Sanjō-Keihan) Kagoshin is a small semi-open bamboo craft shop on Sanjō-dōri, only a few minutes' walk east of the Kamo-gawa. It has a good selection of baskets, chopstick holders, bamboo vases and knick-knacks.

**KYOTO SANJŌ TAKEMATSU** CRAFTS

Map p214 (京都三条 竹松; ☎751-2444; Sanjō-dōri, Sanjō-Ōhashi-higashi, Higashiyama-ku; ⊙10am-7pm; 🚇Tōzai line to Sanjō-Keihan) With a name that even residents find hard to pronounce, this fine little specialist store stocks a selection of bamboo crafts, such as baskets, bamboo vases, decorations and knick-knacks.

**TESSAI-DŌ** CRAFTS

Map p214 (てっさい堂; ☎531-9566; 463 Shimokawara-chō, Higashiyama-ku; ⊙10am-5pm; 🚌Kyoto City bus 206 to Higashiyama-Yasui) While exploring the lovely Nene-no-Michi lane in Higashiyama's main sightseeing district, you might want to step into this fine little wood-block print shop specialising in original prints, some of which are quite old. Prices average ¥10,000 per print and the owner will be happy to consult with you about what sort of print you are after.

# 🏃 SPORTS & ACTIVITIES

**CAMELLIA TEA EXPERIENCE** TEA CEREMONY

Map p214 (茶道体験カメリア; ☎525-3238; www.tea-kyoto.com; 349 Masuya-chō, Higashiyama-ku; per person ¥2000; 🚌Kyoto City bus 206 to Yasui) Camellia is a superb place to try a simple Japanese tea ceremony. It's located in a beautiful old Japanese house just off Ninen-zaka, not far from Kiyomizu-dera. The host, Atsuko, speaks fluent English and explains the ceremony simply and clearly, while managing to perform an elegant ceremony without making guests nervous. The website has an excellent map and explanation.

**EN** TEA CEREMONY

Map p214 (えん; ☎080-3782-2706; 272 Matsubara-chō, Higashiyama-ku; per person ¥2000; ⊙3-6pm, closed Wed; 🚌Kyoto City bus 206 to Gion or Chionin-mae) This is a small teahouse near Gion where you can experience the Japanese tea ceremony with a minimum of fuss or expense. English explanations are provided and tea ceremonies are held at 3pm, 4pm, 5pm or 6pm (check the website for latest times, as these may change). Reservations are recommended in high season. It's a bit tricky to find: it's down a little alley off Higashiōji-dōr. Look for the sign just south of Tenkaippin Rāmen.

# Northern Higashiyama

## Neighbourhood Top Five

❶ Immersing yourself in the green world of **Nanzen-ji** (p93). With wonderful gardens, intimate subtemples and a hidden grotto waiting in the woods, Nanzen-ji is one of Kyoto's most appealing temples.

❷ Taking the bamboo-lined path to see **Ginkaku-ji** (p94), Kyoto's famed 'Silver Pavilion'.

❸ Getting lost in thought on the flower-strewn **Path of Philosophy** (Tetsugaku-no-Michi; p96).

❹ Escaping the crowds and finding yourself at the superb Buddhist sanctuary of **Hōnen-in** (p96).

❺ Checking out the exhibits in Kyoto's museum district of **Okazaki-kōen** (p96).

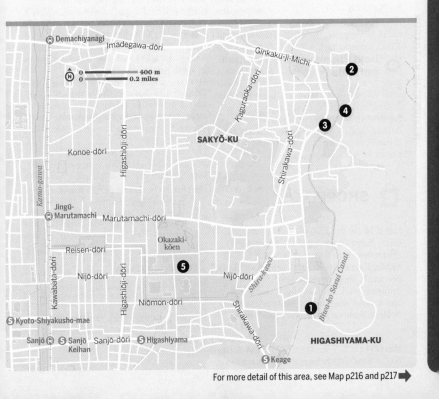

For more detail of this area, see Map p216 and p217 ➡

## Lonely Planet's Top Tip

Visit the big-name sights here (Ginkaku-ji, Eikan-dō and Nanzen-ji) early on a weekday morning to avoid the crowds. Alternatively, go right before closing.

### Best Places to Eat

→ Omen (p99)
→ Goya (p98)
→ Falafel Garden (p98)

For reviews, see p98. ➡

### Best Places to Shop

→ Chion-ji Tezukuri-ichi (p100)
→ Kyoto Handicraft Center (p100)
→ Tōzandō (p100)

For reviews, see p100. ➡

### Best Places for Kids

→ Okazaki-kōen (p96)
→ Heian-jingū (p98)
→ Path of Philosophy (p96)

For reviews, see p93. ➡

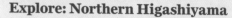
# Explore: Northern Higashiyama

Running along the base of the Higashiyama (Eastern Mountains) from Sanjō-dōri in the south to Imadegawa-dōri in the north, the Northern Higashiyama area is one of Kyoto's most important sightseeing districts. It contains a long strip of temples including Nanzen-ji, Eikan-dō, Hōnen-in and Ginkaku-ji, all connected by the lovely Path of Philosophy. It's also home to museums, parks and a few interesting Shintō shrines.

Northern Higashiyama can be divided into two main sections: the strip of temples located directly at the base of the mountains, most of which are accessible from the Path of Philosophy; and the museums/shrine district known as Okazaki-kōen (Okazaki Park), which occupies a wide swathe of the area between the mountains and the river.

It comprises a fairly large area and can be explored on foot, mostly over car-free walkways, making it one of the most pleasant areas for sightseeing in Kyoto. You can explore most of Northern Higashiyama in about half a day, but a full day allows a more leisurely pace.

Many people use Kyoto City bus 5 to access this area. This is convenient as this bus traverses the entire district, but keep in mind that this bus is often crowded and it can be slow. If coming from Kyoto Station or downtown, it's probably better to take the subway here. The Tōzai subway line will get you to Higashiyama Station, which is convenient for Okazaki-kōen, and Keage Station, which is convenient for Nanzen-ji and sights north. Unfortunately, there are no trains or subways convenient to the northern end of this district. A variety of buses will take you to downtown and Kyoto Station.

This is the best area in Kyoto for bicycling – a rental bike is one of the best ways to explore Northern Higashiyama.

## Local Life

→ **Hang-out** The pond behind the Kyoto Municipal Museum of Art (p98) is popular with local parents and couples for picnics and lazy afternoon naps.
→ **Exercise** Local fitness buffs and nature lovers make a daily pilgrimage up Daimonji-yama (p96).
→ **Freebie** The Kyoto Municipal Museum of Art (p97) hosts all kinds of special free exhibits.

## Getting There & Away

→ **Train** The Keihan line stops at stations on the west side of the district.
→ **Bus** Kyoto City bus 5 traverses the district. Several other city buses stop here as well.
→ **Subway** The Tōzai subway line is the best way to access Northern Higashiyama.

LONELY PLANET / GETTY IMAGES ©

## TOP SIGHT
# NANZEN-JI

**Nanzen-ji, a complex of Zen temples and subtemples tucked against the Higashiyama (Eastern Mountains), is the Platonic form of Japanese Buddhist temple. It's got it all: a fine little *kare-sansui* (dry landscape) garden, soaring main halls, great gardens and an incredibly scenic location. Despite its popularity it doesn't feel crowded, even during the autumn-foliage season (November), when the maples turn crimson and stand in beautiful contrast to the moss beneath their boughs.**

Nanzen-ji began its life as a retirement villa for Emperor Kameyama. Upon his passing in 1291, it was dedicated as a Zen temple. It operates now as the headquarters of the Rinzai school of Zen.

At the entrance to the temple stands the San-mon gate (1628), its ceiling adorned with Tosa and Kanō school murals of birds and angels. Beyond the San-mon is the Honden (Main Hall) with a dragon painting on the ceiling.

Beyond the Honden, the Hōjō hall contains the Leaping Tiger Garden, a classical *kare-sansui* garden. Sadly, a tape loop in Japanese detracts from the experience of the garden. You can enjoy a cup of tea (¥400) as you sit on tatami mats gazing at a small waterfall; ask at the reception desk.

After visiting the Honden and the Leaping Tiger Garden, walk under the aqueduct and take a hard left and walk up the hill. Climb the steps to Kōtoku-an, a fine subtemple nestled at the base of the mountains. It's free to enter and you will have the place to yourself about half the time.

Several fine subtemples surround the complex: Nanzen-in, Konchi-in and Tenju-an (see p95).

### DON'T MISS...

➡ Kōtoku-an
➡ Hōjō (Leaping Tiger Garden)

### PRACTICALITIES

➡ 南禅寺
➡ Map p216
➡ 86 Fukuchi-chō, Nanzen-ji, Sakyō-ku
➡ admission Hōjō garden ¥500, San-mon gate ¥400, grounds free
➡ ⓧ8.40am-5pm Mar-Nov, to 4.30pm Dec-Feb
➡ 🚌Kyoto City bus 5 to Eikandō-michi, ⓢTōzai line to Keage

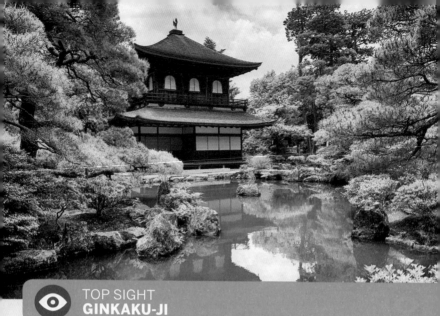

# TOP SIGHT
# GINKAKU-JI

At the northern end of the Path of Philosophy, Kyoto's famed Silver Pavilion (Ginkaku-ji) is an enclosed paradise of ponds, thick moss, classical Japanese architecture and swaying bamboo groves. It is unquestionably one of the most luxurious gardens in the city and belongs near the top of any Kyoto sightseeing itinerary. Just be sure to visit when the crowds are likely to be thin: early on a weekday morning or just before closing. Or wait for a rainy day: the moss here is superb under a light rain.

In 1482 shogun Ashikaga Yoshimasa constructed a villa at this fine mountainside location, which he used as a genteel retreat from the turmoil of civil war. Although Ginkaku-ji translates as Silver Pavilion, this is simply a nickname to distinguish it from Kinkaku-ji (p103; the Golden Pavilion on the other side of town). The main hall, which overlooks the pond, was originally covered in black lacquer. After Yoshimasa's death it was converted to a temple. The temple belongs to the Shōkoku-ji sect of the Rinzai school of Zen.

You will find walkways leading through the gardens, which were laid out by painter and garden designer Sōami. The gardens include meticulously raked cones of white sand known as *kōgetsudai*, designed to reflect moonlight and enhance the beauty of the garden at night.

In addition to the Buddha image in the main hall, the Tōgudō (residence of Yoshimasa) houses an effigy of Yoshimasa dressed in monk's garb.

Don't miss the footpath that leads to a viewpoint over Kyoto and all the way to the western mountains. The path starts at the northeast corner of the garden and can be climbed in a few minutes.

## DON'T MISS...

➡ Footpath to views over Kyoto

➡ Small waterfall at back of garden (follow the path)

## PRACTICALITIES

➡ 銀閣寺

➡ Map p216

➡ 2 Ginkaku-ji-chō, Sakyō-ku

➡ admission ¥500

➡ ⏱8.30am-5pm Mar-Nov, 9am-4.30pm Dec-Feb

➡ 🚌Kyoto City bus 5 to Ginkakuji-michi stop

# 👁 SIGHTS

**NANZEN-JI**　　　　　　BUDDHIST TEMPLE
See p93.

**GINKAKU-JI**　　　　　　BUDDHIST TEMPLE
See p94.

**NANZEN-IN**　　　　　　　GARDENS
Map p216 (南禅院; ☎771-0365; Fukuchi-chō, Nanzen-ji, Sakyō-ku; adult ¥300, child ¥150-250; ⏲8.40am-5pm; 🚌Kyoto City bus 5 to Eikandō-michi, Ⓢ Tōzai line to Keage) FREE This subtemple of Nanzen-ji is up the steps after you pass under the aqueduct. It has an attractive garden designed around a heart-shaped pond. This garden is best seen in the morning or around noon, when sunlight shines directly into the pond and illuminates the colourful carp.

**TENJU-AN**　　　　　　BUDDHIST TEMPLE
Map p216 (天授庵; 86-8 Fukuchi-chō, Nanzen-ji, Sakyō-ku; admission ¥400; ⏲9am-5pm Mar–mid-Nov, to 4.30pm mid-Nov–Feb; 🚌Kyoto City bus 5 to Eikandō-michi, Ⓢ Tōzai line to Keage) A subtemple of Nanzen-ji, Tenju-an is located on the south side of San-mon, the main gate of Nanzen-ji. Constructed in 1337, Tenju-an has a splendid garden and a great collection of carp in its pond.

**KONCHI-IN**　　　　　　BUDDHIST TEMPLE
Map p216 (金地院; 86-12 Fukuchi-chō, Nanzen-ji, Sakyō-ku; admission ¥400; ⏲8.30am-5pm Mar-Nov, to 4.30pm Dec-Feb; 🚌Kyoto City bus 5 to Eikandō-michi, Ⓢ Tōzai line to Keage) Just south-west of the main precincts of Nanzen-ji, this fine subtemple has a wonderful garden designed by Kobori Enshū. If you want to find a good example of the *shakkei* (borrowed scenery) technique, look no further.

**NANZEN-JI OKU-NO-IN**　　BUDDHIST TEMPLE
Map p216 (南禅寺奥の院; Fukuchi-chō, Nanzen-ji, Sakyō-ku; ⏲dawn-dusk; 🚌Kyoto City bus 5 to Eikandō-michi, Ⓢ Tōzai line to Keage) FREE Perhaps the best part of Nanzen-ji is overlooked by most visitors: Nanzen-ji Oku-no-in, a small shrine hidden in a forested hollow behind the main precinct. It's here that pilgrims pray while standing under the falls, sometimes in the dead of winter.

To get here, walk up to the red-brick aqueduct in front of Nanzen-in. Follow the road that runs parallel to the aqueduct up into the hills, and walk past (or through) Kōtoku-an, a small subtemple on your left.

Continue up the steps into the woods until you reach a waterfall in a beautiful mountain glen.

**NOMURA MUSEUM**　　　　MUSEUM
Map p216 (野村美術館; ☎751-0374; Nanzen-ji, Shimokawara-chō 61, Sakyō-ku; admission ¥700; ⏲10am-4.30pm Tue-Sun Mar-early Jun & Sep-early Dec; 🚌Kyoto City bus 5 to Eikandō-michi, Ⓢ Tōzai line to Keage) This museum is a 10-minute walk north of Nanzen-ji. Exhibits include scrolls, paintings, implements used in tea ceremonies and ceramics that were bequeathed by business magnate Nomura Tokushiki. If you have an abiding interest in the tea ceremony or in Japanese decorative techniques such as lacquer and *maki-e* (decorative lacquer technique using silver and gold powders), this museum makes an interesting break from temple-hopping.

**MURIN-AN**　　　　　　GARDENS
Map p216 (無鄰菴; ☎771-3909; Nanzen-ji, Kusakawa-chō, Sakyō-ku; admission ¥400; ⏲9am-4.30pm; Ⓢ Tōzai line to Keage) Often overlooked by the hordes that descend on the Higashiyama area, this elegant villa, built in 1896, was the home of prominent statesman Yamagata Aritomo (1838–1922) and the site of a pivotal 1902 political conference as Japan was heading into the Russo-Japanese War. The grounds contain well-preserved wooden buildings, including a fine Japanese tearoom. The Western-style annexe is characteristic of Meiji-period architecture and the serene garden features small streams that draw water from the Biwa-ko Sosui canal.

For ¥300 you can savour a bowl of frothy *matcha* (powdered green tea) while viewing the *shakkei* backdrop of the Higashiyama mountains. It's particularly beautiful in the maple-leaf season of November.

**EIKAN-DŌ**　　　　　　BUDDHIST TEMPLE
Map p216 (永観堂; 48 Eikandō-chō, Sakyō-ku; admission ¥600; ⏲9am-5pm; 🚌Kyoto City bus 5 to Eikandō-michi, Ⓢ Tōzai line to Keage) Perhaps Kyoto's most famous (and most crowded) autumn-foliage destination, Eikan-dō is a superb temple just a short walk south of the famous Path of Philosophy. Eikan-dō is made interesting by its varied architecture, its gardens and its works of art. It was founded as Zenrin-ji in 855 by the priest Shinshō, but the name was changed to Eikan-dō in the 11th century to honour the philanthropic priest Eikan.

In the **Amida-dō** hall at the southern end of the complex is a famous statue of Mikaeri Amida Buddha glancing backwards.

From Amida-dō, head north to the end of the curving covered **garyūrō** (walkway). Change into the sandals provided, then climb the steep steps up the mountainside to the **Tahō-tō** pagoda, from where there's a fine view across the city.

### PATH OF PHILOSOPHY
### (TETSUGAKU-NO-MICHI)     NEIGHBOURHOOD

Map p216 (哲学の道; Sakyō-ku; 🚌Kyoto City bus 5 to Eikandō-michi or Ginkakuji-michi, 🚇Tōzai line to Keage) This is one of the most pleasant walks in all of Kyoto. Lined with flowering plants, bushes and trees, it is a corridor of colour for most of the year. Follow the traffic-free route along a canal lined with cherry trees that come into spectacular bloom in early April. It only takes 30 minutes to do the walk, which starts at Nyakuōji-bashi, above Eikan-dō, and leads to Ginkaku-ji.

The path takes its name from one of its most famous strollers: 20th-century philosopher Nishida Kitarō, who is said to have meandered lost in thought along the path.

During the day, be prepared for crowds (especially in the cherry-blossom season); a night stroll will definitely be quieter.

### REIKAN-JI     BUDDHIST TEMPLE

Map p216 (霊鑑寺; ☎771-4040; 12 Shi-shigatani goshonodan-chō, Sakyō-ku; ⏰10am-4pm spring & autumn; 🚌Kyoto City bus 5 or 17 to Ginkakuji-michi) Only open to the public in spring and autumn, Reikan-ji is one of Kyoto's great lesser-visited attractions.

During the spring opening, you will find the grounds positively rioting with camellia. In autumn, the brilliant reds of the maples will dazzle the eye. The small collection of artworks in the main building is almost as good as the colours outside. Check with the Tourist Information Center for exact opening dates, as they vary by year.

### ★HŌNEN-IN     BUDDHIST TEMPLE

Map p216 (法然院; 30 Goshonodan-chō, Shishiga-tani, Sakyō-ku; ⏰6am-4pm; 🚌Kyoto City bus 5 to Ginkakuji-michi) **FREE** One of Kyoto's hidden pleasures, this temple was founded in 1680 to honour the priest Hōnen. It's a lovely, secluded temple with carefully raked gardens set back in the woods. The temple buildings include a small gallery where frequent exhibitions featuring local and international artists are held. If you need to escape the crowds that positively plague nearby Ginkaku-ji, come to this serene refuge. It's a 12-minute walk from Ginkaku-ji, on a side street above the Path of Philosophy (Tetsugaku-no-Michi); you may have to ask for directions.

### OKAZAKI-KŌEN AREA     NEIGHBOURHOOD

Map p216 (岡崎公園; Okazaki, Sakyo-ku; 🚇Tōzai line to Higashiyama) Okazaki-kōen is an expanse of parks and canals that lies between Niōmon-dōri and Heian-jingū. Two of Kyoto's significant museums can be found here, as well as two smaller museums. If you're in Kyoto on a rainy day and need to do some indoor sightseeing, this area has enough to keep you sheltered for most of the day.

---

### DAIMONJI-YAMA CLIMB

Located directly behind Ginkaku-ji, Daimonji-yama is the main site of the the Daimonji Gozan Okuribi. From almost anywhere in town the Chinese character for 'great' (大; *dai*) is visible in the middle of a bare patch on the face of this mountain. On 16 August this character is set ablaze to guide the spirits of the dead on their journey home. The view of Kyoto from the top is unparalleled.

Take Kyoto City bus 5 to the Ginkaku-ji Michi stop and walk up to Ginkaku-ji. Here, you have the option of visiting the temple or starting the hike immediately. The 5km hike takes about two hours. To find the trailhead, turn left in front of the temple and head north for about 50m towards a stone *torii* (shrine gate). Just before the *torii*, turn right up the hill.

The trail proper starts just after a small car park on the right. It's a broad avenue through the trees. A few minutes of walking brings you to a red banner hanging over the trail (warning of forest fires). Soon after this you must cross a bridge to the right, then continue up a smaller, switchback trail. When the trail reaches a saddle not far from the top, go to the left. You'll climb a long flight of steps before coming out at the top of the bald patch. The sunset from here is great, but bring a torch.

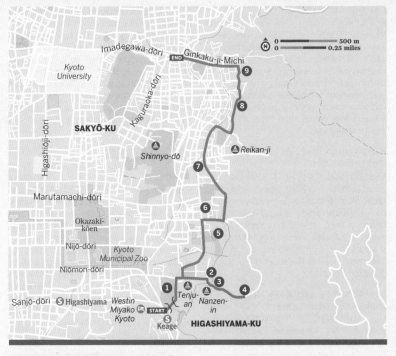

# 🏃 Neighbourhood Walk
## A Philosophical Meander

**START** KEAGE STATION
**FINISH** GINKAKU-JI-MICHI BUS STOP
**LENGTH** ABOUT 6KM; FOUR HOURS

Start at Keage Station on the Tōzai subway line, walk downhill, cross the pedestrian overpass, head back uphill and go through the tunnel under the old funicular tracks. This leads to a narrow street that winds towards **❶ Konchi-in** (p95).

Just past Konchi-in, take a right on the main road and walk up through the gate into **❷ Nanzen-ji** (p93). Continue east, up the slope and you'll soon see the brick Sōsui aqueduct on your right; cross under this, take a quick left and walk up the hill towards the mountains. You'll come first to the lovely **❸ Kōtoku-an** (p93) subtemple. Beyond this, the trail enters the woods. Follow it up to the secluded **❹ Nanzen-ji Oku-no-in** (p95), a tiny shrine built around a waterfall.

Return the way you came and exit the north side of Nanzen-ji, following the road through a gate. You'll soon see **❺ Eikan-dō** (p95), a large temple famous for its artworks and pagoda. At the corner just beyond Eikan-dō, a sign in English and Japanese points up the hill to the Path of Philosophy. If you're hungry, take a short detour north to **❻ Hinode Udon** (p99), a fine noodle restaurant. Otherwise, head up the hill to the **❼ Path of Philosophy** (Tetsugaku-no-michi; p96), which is the pedestrian path that heads north along the canal.

It's then a straight shot up the lovely tree-lined canal for about 800m until you reach a small sign in English and Japanese pointing up the hill to **❽ Hōnen-in** (p96). Follow the sign, take a left at the top of the hill, walk past a small park and you'll see the picturesque thatched gate of Hōnen-in. After checking out the temple (free), exit via the thatched gate and take a quick right downhill.

From here, follow the narrow side streets north to **❾ Ginkaku-ji** (p94), the famed Silver Pavilion. Ginkaku-ji-Michi bus stop is near the intersection of Shirakawa-dōri and Imadegawa-dōri (bus 5, 56, 100, 203 or 204 from Kyoto Station).

### NATIONAL MUSEUM OF MODERN ART
MUSEUM

Map p216 (京都国立近代美術館; www.momak.go.jp; Enshōji-chō, Okazaki, Sakyō-ku; admission ¥430; ⊙9.30am-5pm, closed Mon; ⑤Tōzai line to Higashiyama) This museum is renowned for its Japanese ceramics and paintings. There is an excellent permanent collection, which includes many pottery pieces by Kawai Kanjirō. The coffee shop here overlooks a picturesque canal.

### KYOTO MUNICIPAL MUSEUM OF ART
MUSEUM

Map p216 (京都市美術館; 124 Enshōji-chō, Okazaki, Sakyō-ku; admission varies; ⊙9am-5pm, closed Mon; ⑤Tōzai line to Higashiyama) This fine museum holds several major exhibitions a year, as well as a variety of free shows. It's always worth stopping by to see if something is on while you are in town. The pond behind the museum is a great place for a picnic.

### MIYAKO MESSE & FUREAI-KAN KYOTO MUSEUM OF TRADITIONAL CRAFTS
MUSEUM

Map p216 (みやこめっせ・京都伝統産業ふれあい館; 9-1 Seishōji-chō, Okazaki, Sakyō-ku; ⊙9am-5pm; ⑤Tōzai line to Higashiyama) **FREE** This multipurpose hall has excellent displays of Kyoto crafts. Exhibits include wood-block prints, lacquerware, bamboo goods and gold-leaf work. It's in the basement of Miyako Messe (Kyoto International Exhibition Hall).

### HEIAN-JINGŪ
SHINTO SHRINE

Map p216 (平安神宮; Nishitennō-chō, Okazaki, Sakyō-ku; admission garden ¥600; ⊙6am 5pm Nov-Feb, 6am-6pm Mar-Oct; ⑤Tōzai line to Higashiyama) One of Kyoto's more popular sights, this shrine was built in 1895 to commemorate the 1100th anniversary of the founding of Kyoto. The shrine buildings are colourful replicas, reduced to a two-thirds scale, of the Imperial Court Palace of the Heian period (794–1185). About 500m in front of the shrine is a massive steel **torii** (shrine gate). Although it appears to be entirely separate, this is actually considered the main entrance to the shrine itself.

The vast **garden** here, behind the shrine, is a fine place for a wander and particularly lovely during the cherry-blossom season. With its large pond and Chinese-inspired bridge, the garden is a tribute to the style that was popular in the Heian period.

One of Kyoto's biggest festivals, the **Jidai Matsuri** is held here on 22 October. On 2 and 3 June, **Takigi nō** is also held here. Takigi nō is a picturesque form of *nō* (stylised dance-drama performed on a bare stage) performed in the light of blazing fires. Tickets cost ¥3000 if you pay in advance (ask at the Tourist Information Center for the location of ticket agencies) or you can pay ¥4000 at the entrance gate.

## ✖ EATING

### ★GOYA
OKINAWAN ¥

Map p216 (ゴーヤ; ☑752-1158; 114-6 Nishida-chō, Jōdo-ji, Sakyō-ku; meals from ¥700; ⊙noon-5pm & 6pm-midnight, closed Wed; ⑩; ☐Kyoto City bus 5 to Ginkakuji-michi) We love this Okinawan-style restaurant for its tasty food, stylish interior and comfortable upstairs seating. It's perfect for lunch and it's just a short walk from Ginkaku-ji. At lunch it serves simple dishes like taco rice (¥880) and *gōya champurū* (bitter melon stir-fry; ¥730), while dinners comprise a wide range of *izakaya* (Japanese pub) fare.

### KARAKO
RĀMEN ¥

Map p216 (からこ; ☑752-8234; 12-3 Tokusei-chō, Okazaki, Sakyō-ku; rāmen from ¥650; ⊙11.30am-2pm & 6pm-2am, to 1am Mon, closed Tue; ⑩; ☐Kyoto City bus 206 to Higashiyama-Nijō) Karako is our favourite *rāmen* restaurant in Kyoto. While it's not much on atmosphere, the *rāmen* (noodles in a meat broth with meat and vegetables) is excellent – the soup is thick and rich and the *chashū* (pork slices) melt in your mouth. We recommend the *kotteri* (thick soup) *rāmen*. Look for the lantern outside.

### FALAFEL GARDEN
ISRAELI ¥

Map p216 (ファラフェルガーデン; ☑712-1856; www.falafelgarden.com; 15-2 Kamiyanagi-chō, Tanaka, Sakyō-ku; falafel from ¥410; ⊙11am-9.30pm; ☑⑩; ☐Keihan line to Demachiyanagi) This funky place near Demachiyanagi Station serves excellent falafel and a range of other dishes, as well as offering a set menu (from ¥1000).

### KIRAKU
OKONOMIYAKI ¥

Map p216 (きらく三条本店; ☑761-5780; 208 Nakanochō, Sanjō-Shirakawa, Higashiyama-ku; okonomiyaki from ¥1000; ⊙11.30am-2pm & 5pm-midnight, closed Mon; ⑤Tōzai line to Higashiyama or Keage) This approachable and friendly *okonomiyaki* restaurant on Sanjō, close to Nanzen-ji, is an excellent place to stop for lunch while exploring the area or for dinner after a long day of sightseeing. In addition to the *okonomiyaki* (savoury pancakes), you'll find dishes like *gyoza* (dumplings) and *yaki-soba* (fried noodles).

### HINODE UDON                                   NOODLES ¥

Map p216 (日の出うどん; ☏751-9251; 36 Kitanobō-chō, Nanzenji, Sakyō-ku; noodles from ¥450; ◷11am-3.30pm, closed Sun, 1st & 3rd Mon, except for Apr & Nov; ▣; ▣Kyoto City bus 5 to Eikandō-michi) Filling noodle and rice dishes are served at this pleasant shop with an English menu. Plain udon (thick white wheat noodles) are only ¥500, but we recommend you spring for the *nabeyaki udon* (pot-baked udon in broth) for ¥950. This is a good lunch spot when temple-hopping in the Northern Higashiyama area.

### EARTH KITCHEN COMPANY           BENTŌ ¥

Map p216 (あーすきっちんかんぱにー; ☏771-1897; 9-7 Higashi Maruta-chō, Kawabata, Marutamachi, Sakyō-ku; lunch ¥735; ◷10.30am-6.30pm Mon-Fri, closed Sat & Sun; ▣; ▣Keihan line to Jingū-Marutamachi) 🍃 Set on Marutamachi-dōri near the Kamo-gawa, this tiny spot seats just two people but does a bustling business serving tasty takeaway lunch *bentō* (boxed meals). If you fancy a picnic lunch for your temple-hopping and the ease of an English menu, this is the place.

### SHINSHINDŌ NOTRE
### PAIN QUOTIDIEN                              CAFE ¥

Map p216 (進々堂; ☏701-4121; Kitashirakawa, Oiwake-chō 88, Sakyō-ku; coffee from ¥340; ◷8am-6pm, closed Tue; ▣; ▣Kyoto City bus 206 to Hyakumamben) This atmospheric old Kyoto coffee shop is a favourite of Kyoto University students for its curry and bread lunch set (¥780), which is kind of an acquired taste. It's located near the university. Look for the glazed tile bricks and the big window out the front. There's a small English sign and English menus are available.

### ★OMEN                                    NOODLES ¥¥

Map p216 (おめん; ☏771-8994; 74 Jōdo-ji Ishibashi-chō, Sakyō-ku; noodles from ¥1150; ◷11am-9pm, closed Thu & 1 other day a month; ▣; ▣Kyoto City bus 5 to Ginkakuji-michi) This elegant noodle shop is named after the thick white noodles that are served in broth with a selection of seven fresh vegetables. Just say '*omen*' and you'll be given your choice

of hot or cold noodles, a bowl of soup to dip them in and a plate of vegetables (put these into the soup along with sesame seeds).

There's also an extensive à la carte menu. You can get a fine salad here, brilliant *tori sansho yaki* (chicken cooked with Japanese mountain spice) and good tempura. It's about five minutes' walk from Ginkaku-ji in a traditional Japanese house with a lantern outside. Highly recommended.

### AU TEMPS PERDU                        FRENCH ¥¥

Map p216 (オ・タン・ペルデュ; ☏762-1299; 64 Enshōji-chō, Okazaki, Sakyō-ku; food/drink from ¥1300/500; ◷closed Mon; ▣; ▣Tōzai line to Higashiyama) Overlooking the Shirakawa Canal, just across the street from the National Museum Modern of Art, this tiny indoor/outdoor French-style cafe offers some of the best people-watching in Northern Higashiyama. It's easy to pull a baby stroller up to these outdoor tables.

### CAFÉ DE 505                                  CAFE ¥¥

Map p216 (カフェ　ド　ゴマルゴ; ☏771-5086; Enshōji-chō, Okazaki, Sakyō-ku; dishes ¥1000-1500; ◷9.30am-4.30pm Tue-Sun; ▣Tōzai line to Higashiyama) At the National Museum of Modern Art, this is a great spot for a pick-me-up while museum-hopping in Okazaki.

### OKARIBA                                 WILD GAME ¥¥

Map p216 (お狩り場; ☏751-7790; Higashitenno-chō 43-3, Okazaki, Sakyō-ku; dinner ¥4000; ◷5pm-midnight, closed Mon; ▣Kyoto City bus 5 to Higashitenno-chō) For an experience you won't soon forget, try Okariba. If it crawls, walks or swims, it's probably on the menu. The *inoshishi* (wild boar) barbecue is a good start. Those who don't eat meat can try the fresh *ayu* (Japanese trout). Look for the sign of the hunting pig out the front.

### TORITO                                    YAKITORI ¥¥

Map p216 (とりと; ☏752-4144; Higashi Marutamachi 9-5, Marutamachi-dōri, Kawabata higashi-iru, Sakyō-ku; dinner ¥3500-4000; ◷5.30pm-midnight, closed Tue; ▣Keihan line to Jingū-Marutamachi) This is part of the new wave of *yakitori* (skewers of chicken, and other meats or vegetables) restaurants in Kyoto that are updating the old standards in interesting and tasty ways. The food is very good and will likely appeal to non-Japanese palates. Dishes include *negima* (long onions and chicken; ¥315 for two sticks) and *tsukune* (chicken meatballs; ¥462 for two sticks).

It's near the corner of Marutamachi and Kawabata-dōri; you can see inside to the counter.

**OKUTAN** TOFU ¥¥

Map p216 (奥丹; ☎771-8709; Nanzen-ji, Fukuchi-chō 86-30, Sakyō-ku; set meals ¥3150; ☺11am-4.30pm Mon-Fri, to 5pm Sat & Sun, closed Thu; Ⓟ; ⑤Tōzai line to Keage) Just outside the precincts of Nanzen-ji is Okutan, a restaurant within the luxurious garden of Chōshō-in. This is a popular place that has specialised in vegetarian temple food for hundreds of years. Try a course of *yudōfu* (tofu cooked in a pot) together with vegetable side dishes (¥3150). Be warned: it can get crowded here in the cherry-blossom and autumn-foliage seasons.

**ZAC BARAN** INTERNATIONAL ¥¥

Map p216 (ザックバラン; ☎751-9748; Shōgo-in, Sannō-chō 18, Sakyō-ku; meals ¥1500; ☺6pm-4am, closed Tue; 🚌Kyoto City bus 206 to Kumanojinja-mae) Near the Kyoto Handicraft Center, this is a good spot for a light meal or a drink. It serves a variety of spaghetti dishes as well as a good lunch special. Look for the picture of the Freak Brothers near the downstairs entrance.

**HYŌTEI** KAISEKI ¥¥¥

Map p216 (瓢亭; ☎771-4116; Nanzen-ji, Kusagawa-chō 35, Sakyō-ku; kaiseki lunch/dinner from ¥23,000/27,000, shōkadō bentō lunch ¥5000; ☺11am-7.30pm; ⑤Tōzai line to Keage) The Hyōtei is considered to be one of Kyoto's oldest and most picturesque traditional restaurants. In the main building you can sample exquisite *kaiseki* (Japanese haute cuisine) courses in private tea rooms. Set meals are available from ¥5000.

 # DRINKING & NIGHTLIFE

**METRO** CLUB

Map p216 (メトロ; ☎752-4765; www.metro.ne.jp; BF Ebisu Bldg, Kawabata-dōri, Marutamachi-sagaru, Sakyō-ku; admission ¥500-3000; ☺about 7pm-3am; 🚃Keihan line to Jingū-Marutamachi) Metro is part disco, part 'live house' (small concert hall) and it even hosts the occasional art exhibition. It attracts creative types and has a different theme nightly, so check ahead in *Kansai Scene* to see what's going on. Tourists are entitled to one free drink (bring your passport). Metro is inside exit 2 of the Jingū-Marutamachi Station on the Keihan line.

**KICK UP** BAR

Map p216 (キックアップ; ☎761-5604; Higashikomonoza-chō 331, Higashiyama-ku; drinks/food from ¥600/500; ☺7pm-midnight, closed Wed; ⑤Tōzai line to Keage) Just across the street from the Westin Miyako Kyoto, this wonderful bar attracts a regular crowd of Kyoto expats, local Japanese and guests from the Westin. It's subdued, relaxing and friendly.

 # ☆ ENTERTAINMENT

**KYOTO KANZE KAIKAN NŌ THEATRE** THEATRE

Map p216 (京都観世会館; ☎771-6114; 44 Okazaki Enshoji-chō, Sakyō-ku; admission ¥3500-13,000; ☺9.30am-5pm, closed Mon; ⑤Tōzai line to Higashiyama) This is your best bet for seeing *nō* (stylised dance-drama performed on a bare stage).

 # 🔒 SHOPPING

**KYOTO HANDICRAFT CENTER** CRAFTS

Map p216 (京都ハンディクラフトセンター; ☎761-7000; www.kyotohandicraftcenter.com; 21 Entomi-chō, Shōgoin, Sakyō-ku; ☺10am-7pm; 🚌Kyoto City bus 206 to Kumano-jinja-mae) Offers a good range of Japanese arts and crafts such as wood-block prints, Japanese dolls, damascene crafts, pearls, clothing and books. English-speaking staff are on hand and currency exchange is available. It's within walking distance of the main Higashiyama sightseeing route.

**TŌZANDŌ** SWORDS

Map p216 (東山堂; ☎762-1341; 24 Shōgoin Entomi-chō, Sakyō-ku; ☺10am-7pm; 🚌Kyoto City bus 206 to Kumano-jinja-mae) If you're a fan of Japanese swords and armour, you have to visit this wonderful shop on Marutamachi (diagonally opposite the Kyoto Handicraft Center). It has authentic swords, newly made Japanese armour, martial arts goods etc, and there's usually someone on hand who can speak English.

**CHION-JI TEZUKURI-ICHI** HANDICRAFTS

Map p216 (知恩寺手作り市; ☎781-9171; Tanaka Monzen-chō 103, Sakyō-ku; 🚌Kyoto City bus 206 to Hyakumamben) This 'handmade market' is held at Chion-ji from dawn to dusk on the 15th of the month. Wares include food and handmade clothes. This is a good chance to see Kyoto's alternative community.

# Northwest Kyoto

## Neighbourhood Top Five

**1** Being dazzled by the single most impressive sight in all of Kyoto: the gold-plated main hall of **Kinkaku-ji** (p103), the famed 'Golden Pavilion'.

**2** Feeling the power of the shogun at **Nijō-jō** (p104).

**3** Meditating on the 15 magical rocks in the Zen garden at **Ryōan-ji** (p105).

**4** Searching for 'Old Kyoto' in the weaving district of **Nishijin** (p105).

**5** Strolling through the enclosed world of Zen temples at **Myōshin-ji** (p106).

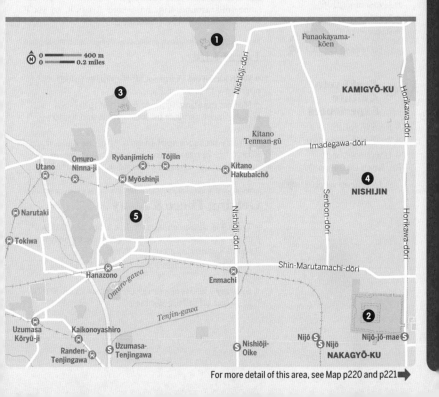

For more detail of this area, see Map p220 and p221 ➡

## Lonely Planet's Top Tip

Since Ryōan-ji and Kinkaku-ji (the two most famous sights in Northwest Kyoto) and Arashiyama are all on the west side of town, it makes sense to visit these in one day. Take a taxi between Arashiyama and Kinkaku-ji or Ryōan-ji (or vice versa).

 **Best Places to Eat**

➡ Saraca Nishijin (p107)

➡ Kanei (p107)

➡ Toyouke-jaya (p107)

For reviews, see p107. ➡

 **Best Places to Gaze on a Garden**

➡ Myōshin-ji (p106)

➡ Taizō-in (p106)

➡ Ryōan-ji (p105)

For reviews, see p103. ➡

 **Best Kyoto Culture Experiences**

➡ Nishijin (p105)

➡ Orinasu-ken (p105)

➡ Urasenke Chadō Research Center (p106)

For reviews, see p103. ➡

# Explore: Northwest Kyoto

Northwest Kyoto comprises the section of the city that runs from Kyoto's main castle, Nijō-jō, all the way to the base of the mountains in the northwest corner of the city. This large area contains some of Kyoto's most celebrated temples like Kinkaku-ji (Golden Pavilion) and Ryōan-ji (with its mystical rock garden), along with the awe-inspiring samurai castle of Nijō-jō, and the old weaving district of Nishijin.

Like the Central Kyoto area, the sights here are quite spread out and you shouldn't try to cover them all in one day. Rather, pick a few that are clustered close together and visit them in half a day, then consider spending the rest of the day in an adjoining sightseeing district. Many people visit Kinkaku-ji and Ryōan-ji in the morning, then continue by taxi down to the Arashiyama and Sagano area (p108), which is also on the west side of the city.

With the exception of sights in the inner part of this district (like Nijō-jō, which is on the Tōzai subway line), it's a bit time-consuming to see the sights in Northwest Kyoto. Most sights are best accessed by city bus. Myōshin-ji and nearby sights are also served by the Japan Railways (JR) line and by the private Randen Kitano line. If you're a keen cyclist, you can also explore the area on a bicycle, but keep in mind that there are some hills around Kinkaku-ji and Ryōan-ji, so you'll work up quite a sweat in summer.

# Local Life

➡ **With kids** Tōei Uzumasa Movie Village (p106) is popular with local families.

➡ **Market meeting** Tenjin-san Market (p107) is a popular meeting place for local expats and Kyoto residents.

➡ **Cherry blossom spot** In early April the Randen Kitano line between Narutaki and Utano Stations passes through a tunnel of blooming cherry trees.

# Getting There & Away

➡ **Train** The JR Sagano/San-in line stops near Myōshin-ji and Tōei Uzumasa Movie Village, while the private Randen Kitano line stops near Ninna-ji.

➡ **Bus** Kyoto City buses serve all the sights in this district.

➡ **Subway** The Tōzai subway line stops very close to Nijō-jō (get off at Nijō-jō-mae).

# TOP SIGHT
# KINKAKU-JI

Kyoto's famed 'Golden Pavilion', Kinkaku-ji is one of the world's most impressive religious monuments. The sight of the gold-plated pavilion rising over its reflecting pool is the kind of image that burns itself into your memory for years to come. Of course, there's more to this temple than just its shiny main hall. The grounds are spacious and include another pond, a tea arbour and some lovely greenery. Just don't expect to have the place to yourself – Kinkaku-ji is on everyone's 'must-see' list.

Originally built in 1397 as a retirement villa for shogun Ashikaga Yoshi-mitsu, Kinkaku-ji was converted into a Buddhist temple by his son, in compliance with his wishes. Also known as Rokuon-ji, Kinkaku-ji belongs to the Shōkokuji school of Buddhism.

The three-storey pavilion is covered in bright gold leaf and features a bronze phoenix on top of the roof. The mirror-like reflection of the temple in the Kyō-ko pond is very photogenic, especially when the maples are ablaze in autumn.

In 1950 a young monk consummated his obsession with the temple by burning it to the ground. The monk's story is fictionalised in Mishima Yukio's 1956 novel *The Temple of the Golden Pavilion*. In 1955 a full reconstruction was completed, following the original design exactly, but the gold-foil covering was extended to the lower floors.

After visiting the gold-plated pavilion, check out the Ryūmon-taki waterfall and Rigyoseki stone, which looks like a carp attempting to swim up the falls. Nearby, there is a small gathering of stone Jizō figures onto which people throw coins and make wishes.

The quaint teahouse **Sekka-tei** embodies the spirit of *wabi-sabi* (rustic simplicity) that defines the Japanese tea-ceremony ethic. It's at the top of the hill shortly before the exit of the temple. Because of the enormous popularity and fame of this temple, it's almost always crowded – try to visit early on a weekday morning.

## DON'T MISS

➡ Sekka-tei
➡ Ryūmon-taki waterfall and Rigyo-seki stone

## PRACTICALITIES

➡ 金閣寺
➡ Map p220
➡ 1 Kinkakuji-chō, Kita-ku
➡ admission ¥400
➡ ⊘9am-5pm
➡ 🚌Kyoto City bus 205 from Kyoto Station to Kinkakuji-michi, Kyoto City bus 59 from Sanjo-Keihan to Kinkakuji-mae

# TOP SIGHT
## NIJŌ-JŌ

Standing like a direct challenge to the might of the Emperor in the nearby Imperial Palace, the shogun castle of Nijō-jō is a stunning monument to the power of the warlords who effectively ruled Japan for centuries. For those with an interest in Japan's feudal past and an eye for magnificent interiors, Nijō-jō is a fascinating destination. It has stunning (almost rococo) interiors, and the castle grounds contain expansive gardens that are perfect for a relaxing stroll.

Nijō-jō was built in 1603 as the official residence of Tokugawa Ieyasu. The ostentatious style was intended as a demonstration of Ieyasu's prestige and to signal the demise of the emperor's power.

To safeguard against treachery, Ieyasu had the interior fitted with 'nightingale' floors (intruders were detected by the squeaking boards) and concealed chambers where bodyguards could keep watch and spring out at a moment's notice.

In 1868 the last Tokugawa shogun, Yoshinobu, surrendered his power to the newly restored Emperor Meiji inside Nijō-jō.

## DON'T MISS

➡ Seiryu-en
➡ Ōhiroma Yon-no-Ma (Fourth Chamber)

## PRACTICALITIES

➡ 二条城
➡ Map p220
➡ 541 Nijōjō-chō, Nijō-dōri, Horikawa nishi-iru, Nakagyō-ku
➡ admission ¥600
➡ ⊘8.45am-5pm, closed Tue in Dec, Jan, Jul & Aug
➡ ⑤Tōzai line to Nijō-jō-mae

Nijō-jō is built on land that was originally occupied by the 8th-century Imperial Palace, which was abandoned in 1227. The **Shinsen-en Garden**, just south of the castle, is all that remains of the original palace. This forlorn garden has small shrines and a pond.

The Momoyama-era **Kara-mon** gate, originally part of Hideyoshi's Fushimi-jō in the south of the city, features lavish, masterful woodcarving and metalwork. After passing through the gate, you enter the **Ninomaru** palace, which is divided into five buildings with numerous chambers. Access to the buildings used to depend on rank – only those of highest rank were permitted into the inner buildings. The **Ōhiroma Yon-no-Ma** (Fourth Chamber) has spectacular screen paintings.

The neighbouring **Honmaru** palace dates from the mid-19th century. After the Meiji Restoration in 1868, the castle became a detached palace of the imperial household and in 1939 it was given to Kyoto City. These days it's only open for a special autumn viewing.

Don't miss **Seiryu-en**, the garden that surrounds the inner castle buildings. This superb garden was designed by Kobori Enshū, Japan's most celebrated garden designer. This vast garden comprises three separate islets spanned by stone bridges and is meticulously maintained. The Ninomaru palace and garden take about an hour to walk through. A detailed fact sheet in English is provided.

Keep in mind that the castle is on the itinerary of every foreign and Japanese tour group and it can be packed. If you're after peace and quiet, try an early-morning or late-afternoon visit. If you must visit during the middle of the day, you might find that touring the buildings quickly and then savouring the gardens is the most relaxing way to enjoy the castle.

# ⊙ SIGHTS

**KINKAKU-JI**  BUDDHIST TEMPLE
See p103.

**NIJŌ-JŌ**  CASTLE
See p104.

**NISHIJIN**  NEIGHBOURHOOD
(西陣; Nishijin, Kamigyō-ku; ⬛Kyoto City bus 9 to Horikawa-Imadegawa) Nishijin is Kyoto's traditional textile centre, the source of all those dazzling kimono fabrics and obi (kimono sashes) that you see around town. The area is famous for Nishijin-ori (Nishijin weaving). There are quite a few *machiya* (traditional Japanese townhouses) in this district, so it's a good place simply to wander.

**NISHIJIN TEXTILE CENTER**  MUSEUM
Map p220 (西陣織会館; ☑451-9231; Horikawa-dōri, Imadegawa-sagaru, Kamigyō-ku; ⊙9am-5pm; ⬛Kyoto City bus 9 to Horikawa-Imadegawa) **FREE** In the heart of the Nishijin textile district, this is worth a peek before starting a walk around the area. There are displays of completed fabrics and kimonos, as well as weaving demonstrations and occasional kimono fashion shows. It's on the southwest corner of the Horikawa-dōri and Imadegawa-dōri intersection.

**ORINASU-KAN**  MUSEUM
Map p220 (織成館; 693 Daikoku-chō, Kamigyō-ku; adult/child ¥500/350; ⊙10am-4pm, closed Mon; ⬛Kyoto City bus 9 to Horikawa-Imadegawa) This atmospheric and usually quiet museum, housed in a Nishijin weaving factory, has impressive exhibits of Nishijin textiles. The **Susamei-sha** building across the street is also open to the public and worth a look.

**KITANO TENMAN-GŪ**  SHINTO SHRINE
Map p220 (北野天満宮; Bakuro-chō, Kamigyō-ku; ⊙5am-6pm Apr-Sep, 5.30am-5.30pm Oct-Mar; ⬛Kyoto City bus 50 from Kyoto Station to Kitano-Tenmangū-mae) **FREE** The most atmospheric Shintō shrine in Northwest Kyoto, Kitano Tenman-gū is also home to Tenjin-San Market (p107), one of Kyoto's most popular flea markets. It's a pleasant spot for a lazy stroll and the shrine buildings are beautiful. The present buildings were built in 1607 by Toyotomi Hideyori; the grounds contain an extensive grove of plum trees, which burst into bloom in early March.

Kitano Tenman-gū was established in 947 to honour Sugawara Michizane (845–903), a noted Heian-era statesman and scholar. It is

said that, having been defied by his political adversary Fujiwara Tokihira, Sugawara was exiled to Kyūshū for the rest of his life. Following his death in 903, earthquakes and storms struck Kyoto, and the Imperial Palace was repeatedly struck by lightning. Fearing that Sugawara, reincarnated as Raijin (god of thunder), had returned from beyond to avenge his rivals, locals erected and dedicated this shrine to him.

Unless you are trying to avoid crowds, the best time to visit is during the **Tenjin-san** market fair, held on the 25th of each month.

**RYŌAN-JI**  BUDDHIST TEMPLE
Map p220 (龍安寺; 13 Goryōnoshitamachi, Ryōan-ji, Ukyō-ku; admission ¥500; ⊙8am-5pm Mar-Nov, 8.30am-4.30pm Dec-Feb; ⬛Kyoto City bus 59 from Sanjō-Keihan to Ryoanji-mae) You've probably seen a picture of the rock garden here – it's one of the symbols of Kyoto and one of Japan's better-known sights. Ryōan-ji belongs to the Rinzai school and was founded in 1450. The garden, an oblong of sand with an austere collection of 15 carefully placed rocks, apparently adrift in a sea of sand, is enclosed by an earthen wall. The designer, who remains unknown to this day, provided no explanation.

Although many historians believe the garden was arranged by Sōami during the Muromachi period (1333–1576), some contend it is a much later product of the Edo period (1603–1868). It is Japan's most famous **hira-niwa** (flat garden void of hills or ponds) and reveals the stunning simplicity and harmony of the principles of Zen meditation.

There is no doubt that it's a mesmerising and attractive sight, but it's hard to enjoy amid the mobs who come to check it off their 'must-see list'. An early-morning visit on a weekday is probably your best hope of seeing the garden under contemplative conditions. If you go when it's crowded, you'll find the less-famous garden around the corner of the stone garden a nice escape.

**NINNA-JI**  BUDDHIST TEMPLE
Map p220 (仁和寺; 33 Omuroōuchi, Ukyō-ku; admission Kondō ¥500, Reihōkan ¥500, grounds free; ⊙9am-5pm Mar-Nov, 9am-4.30pm Dec-Feb; ⬛Kyoto City bus 59 from Sanjo-Keihan to Omuro Ninna-ji, Kyoto City bus 26 from Kyoto Station to Omuro Ninna-ji) Few travellers make the journey all the way out to this sprawling temple complex, but most who do find it a pleasant spot. It's a good counterpoint to the crowded temples nearby.

Originally containing more than 60 structures, Ninna-ji was built in 888 and is the head temple of the Omuro branch of the Shingon school. The present temple buildings, including a **five-storey pagoda**, date from the 17th century. On the extensive grounds is a peculiar grove of short-trunked, multi-petalled cherry trees called Omuro-no-Sakura, which draw large crowds in April.

Separate entry fees (an extra ¥500 each) are charged for both the **Kondō** (Main Hall) and **Reihōkan** (Treasure House), which are only open for the first two weeks of October.

## MYŌSHIN-JI
BUDDHIST TEMPLE

Map p220 (妙心寺; 1 Myoshin-ji-chō, Hanazono, Ukyō-ku; admission to main temple free, other areas of complex ¥500; ⊙9.10-11.50am & 1-3.40pm; 🚍Kyoto City bus 10 from Sanjo-Keihan to Myōshin-ji Kita-mon-mae) Myōshin-ji is a separate world within Kyoto, a walled-off complex of temples and subtemples that invites lazy strolling. Myōshin-ji dates from 1342 and belongs to the Rinzai school. There are 47 subtemples, but only a few are open to the public.

From the north gate, follow the stone avenue flanked by rows of temples to the southern part of the complex. The eponymous **Myōshin-ji** temple is roughly in the middle of the complex. Your entry fee entitles you to a tour of several of the buildings of the temple. The ceiling of the **Hattō** (Lecture Hall) here features Tanyū Kanō's unnerving painting *Unryūzu* (meaning 'Dragon glaring in eight directions'). Stand directly beneath the dragon; doing so makes it appear that it's spiralling up or down.

**Shunkō-in** (春光院; Map p220; ☎462-5488; www.shunkoin.com), a subtemple of Myōshin-ji, offers highly recommended *zazen* (seated Zen meditation) sessions for foreigners with English explanations for ¥1000.

## TAIZŌ-IN
BUDDHIST TEMPLE

Map p220 (退蔵院; Myoshin-ji-chō, Hanazono, Ukyō-ku; admission ¥500; ⊙9am-5pm; 🚍Kyoto City bus 10 from Sanjo-Keihan to Myōshin-ji Kita-mon-mae) This subtemple is in the southwestern corner of the grounds of Myōshin-ji. The *kare sansui* (dry-landscape rock garden) is well worth a visit.

## KŌRYŪ-JI
BUDDHIST TEMPLE

Map p220 (広隆寺; ☎861-1461; Uzumasa Hachioka-chō 32, Ukyō-ku; adult ¥700, child ¥400-500; ⊙9am-5pm Mar-Nov, to 4.30pm Dec-Feb; 🚃Keifuku line to Uzumasa) Kōryū-ji, one of the oldest temples in Japan, was founded in 622 to honour Prince Shōtoku, an enthusiastic promoter of Buddhism. It's notable mostly for its collection of Buddhist statuary and so a visit with a knowledgeable guide is a good way to learn about the different levels of beings in the Buddhist pantheon. It's a bit out of the way, but it can be paired with nearby Myōshin-ji to form a half-day tour for those with an interest in Japanese Buddhism.

The **Hattō** (Lecture Hall) to the right of the main gate houses a magnificent trio of 9th-century statues: Buddha, flanked by manifestations of Kannon. The **Reihōkan** (Treasure House) contains numerous fine Buddhist statues, including the *Naki Miroku* (Crying Miroku) and the renowned *Miroku Bosatsu* (Bodhisattva of the Future), which is extraordinarily expressive. A national upset occurred in 1960 when an enraptured university student embraced the statue in a fit of passion (at least, that was his excuse) and inadvertently snapped off its little finger.

## TŌEI UZUMASA MOVIE VILLAGE
THEME PARK

Map p220 (東映太秦映画村; Tōei Uzumasa Eiga Mura; ☎864-7716; www.toei-eigamura.com/en/; Uzumasa Higashi Hachigaoka-chō 10, Ukyō-ku; adult/child 6-18yr/under 6yr ¥2200/1300/1100; ⊙9am-5pm; 🚃JR Sagano/San-in line to Uzumasa) In the Uzumasa area, Tōei Uzumasa Movie Village is a rather touristy affair. It does, however, have some recreations of Edo-period street scenes that give a decent idea of what Kyoto must have looked like before the advent of concrete.

The main conceit of the park is that real movies are actually filmed here. While this may occasionally be the case, more often than not it's a show laid on for the tourists. Aside from this, there are displays relating to various aspects of Japanese movies and regular performances involving Japanese TV and movie characters such as the Power Rangers. This should entertain the kids – adults will probably be a little bored.

## URASENKE CHADŌ RESEARCH CENTER
TEA SCHOOL

Map p220 (茶道資料館; ☎431-6474; Horikawa-dōri, Teranouchi-agaru, Kamigyō-ku; admission ¥500; ⊙9.30am-4.30pm; 🚇Karasuma line to Kuramaguchi) Anyone interested in tea ceremony should make this their first stop. Urasenke is Japan's largest tea school and hosts hundreds of students annually who come from branch schools worldwide to further their studies in 'the way of tea'.

The gallery located on the 1st and 2nd floors holds quarterly exhibitions on tea-related arts. The entrance fee entitles you

## IN HOT WATER

After a day spent marching from temple to temple, nothing feels better than a good hot bath. Kyoto is full of *sentō* (public baths), ranging from small neighbourhood baths with one or two tubs to massive complexes offering saunas, mineral baths and even electric baths. The **Funaoka Onsen** (船岡温泉; Map p220; 82-1 Minami-Funaoka-chō-Murasakino, Kita-ku; admission ¥410; ☺3pm-1am Mon-Sat, 8am-1am Sun & holidays; 🚌Kyoto City Bus No 9 from Kyoto Station to Horikawa-Kuramaguchi) is one of the best in Kyoto. This old bath boasts outdoor bathing and a sauna, plus some museum-quality wood-carvings in the changing room (apparently carved during Japan's invasion of Manchuria). Bring your own bath supplies (soap, shampoo, a towel to dry yourself and another small towel for washing); if you forget, though, you can buy toiletries and rent towels at the front desk. Washing buckets are available free inside the bathing area.

To find it, head west from Horikawa-dōri along Kuramaguchi-dōri. It's on the left, not far past the Lawson convenience store. Look for the large rocks out the front.

to a bowl of *matcha* (powdered green tea) and a sweet.

The Konnichi-an library has more than 50,000 books (about 100 in English), plus videos on tea, which can be viewed.

If you'd like more information, contact Urasenke's Office of International Affairs.

## 🍴 EATING

### ★SARACA NISHIJIN — CAFE ¥
Map p220 (さらさ西陣; ☎432-5075; 11-1 Murasakino Higashifujinomori-chō, Kita-ku; lunch from ¥940; ☺noon-11pm, closed Wed; 🚌Kyoto City bus 206 to Daitoku-ji-mae) This is one of Kyoto's most interesting cafes – it's inside an old *sentō* (public bathhouse) and the original tiles have been preserved. Light meals and coffee (¥480) are the staples. It's near Funaoka Onsen.

### ★KANEI — NOODLES ¥
Map p220 (かね井; ☎441-8283; 11-1 Murasakino Higashifujinomori-chō, Kita-ku; noodles from ¥950; ☺11.40am-2.30pm & 5-7pm Tue-Sun; 🚌Kyoto City bus 206 to Daitoku-ji-mae) A small traditional place not far from Funaoka Onsen, Kanei is the place to go if you're a *soba* (buckwheat noodles) connoisseur – the noodles are made by hand and are delicious. The owners don't speak much English, so here's what to order: *zaru soba* (¥950) or *kake soba* (*soba* in a broth; ¥1000). Handmade *soba* quickly loses its taste and texture, so eat it quickly. Kanei is on the corner, a few metres west of Saraca Nishijin.

### ★TOYOUKE-JAYA — TOFU ¥
Map p220 (とようけ茶屋; ☎462-3662; Imadegawa-dōri-Onmae nishi-iru, Kamigyō-ku; set meals from ¥650; ☺11am-3pm, closed Thu; 🚌Kyoto City bus 101 to Kitano Tenmangū-mae) Locals line up for the tofu lunch sets at this famous restaurant across from Kitano Tenman-gū. Set meals usually include tofu, rice and miso soup. It gets very crowded, especially when a market is on at the shrine. If you can get here when there's no queue, pop in for a healthy meal.

## ☆ ENTERTAINMENT

### JITTOKU — LIVE MUSIC
Map p220 (拾得; ☎841-1691; Ōmiya-dōri-Shimotachiuri; ☺5.30pm-midnight, live music 7-9pm; 🚇Tōzai line to Nijōjō-mae) Jittoku is in an atmospheric old *sakagura* (sake brewery). It plays host to a variety of shows – check *Kansai Scene* to see what's on.

## 🛍 SHOPPING

### TENJIN-SAN MARKET — MARKET
Map p220 (天神さん 〔北野天満宮露天市〕; ☎461-0005; Kitano Tenman-gū, Bakuro-chō, Kamigyō-ku; ☺dawn to dusk, 25th of each month; 🚌Kyoto City bus 50 or 101 to Kitano Tenmangū-mae) This market is held on the 25th of each month at Kitano Tenman-gū (p105) and marks the birthday (and coincidentally the death) of the Heian-era statesman Sugawara Michizane (845–903). Explore the shrine before or after you do your shopping.

### NISHIJIN TEXTILE CENTER — KIMONO, OBI
Map p220 (西陣織会館; ☎451-9231; Horikawa-dōri, Imadegawa-sagaru, Kamigyō-ku; ☺9am-5pm; 🚌Kyoto City bus 9 to Horikawa-Imadegawa) This place sells a variety of goods fashioned from Nishijin textiles. Goods on offer range from neckties to obi (kimono sashes).

# Arashiyama & Sagano

## Neighbourhood Top Five

**1** Entering the magical green world of the **Arashi-yama Bamboo Grove** (p110). If you've seen *Crouching Tiger, Hidden Dragon,* you'll know what to expect.

**2** Meditating on the garden at **Tenryū-ji** (p110).

**3** Meandering the trails through the garden at the superb **Ōkōchi Sansō** (p110) villa.

**4** Hiking up to the moss garden at **Giō-ji** (p113).

**5** Visiting with our simian cousins at **Arashiyama Monkey Park Iwatayama** (p113).

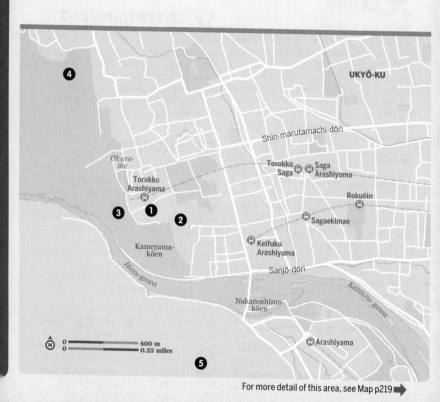

For more detail of this area, see Map p219 ➡

# Explore: Arashiyama & Sagano

Located at the base of the mountains on the west side of the city, the Arashiyama and Sagano area is Kyoto's second-most important sightseeing district after Southern Higashiyama. It's home to Kyoto's most iconic sight, the Arashiyama Bamboo Grove, along with the superb Tenryu-ji Zen temple and the expansive Ōkōchi Sansō villa.

A half day is sufficient to do the main tourist track through the area, which usually starts at Tenryū-ji and ends at Adashino Nenbutsu-ji (or whenever you get tired). Keep in mind that getting out to this area from Downtown Kyoto will take about an hour if you take public transport, and about half an hour if you go by taxi.

Since some of the best sights in Northwest Kyoto, like Kinkaku-ji and Ryōan-ji, are not far from Arashiyama and Sagano, you can make a full-day tour of western Kyoto if you are willing to travel between these two areas by taxi.

There are several ways to get to Arashiyama and Sagano from Downtown Kyoto and the Kyoto Station area. If you're coming from Downtown Kyoto, Kyoto City bus 11 will get you from Shijō-dōri to Tenryū-ji-mae (the main Arashiyama stop). Alternatively, you can take the Tōzai subway line to the westernmost stop, Uzumasa-Tenjin-gawa, and transfer to the Randen street tram, which will take you to central Arashiyama.

From Kyoto Station, you can take the JR Sagano/San-in line and get off at Saga Arashiyama Station (be careful to take only the local train, as the express does not stop in Arashiyama).

## Local Life

➡ **Hang-outs** Kameyama-kōen (p110) is popular with locals for picnics.

➡ **Romantic strolls** The Hozu-gawa riverbank is favoured for romantic strolls in the early evening.

➡ **Family favourite** Arashiyama Monkey Park Iwatayama (p113) is a favourite of Kyoto's kids.

## Getting There & Away

➡ **Train** The JR Sagano/San-in line from Kyoto Station to Saga-Arashiyama Station. The Keifuku Arashiyama, Randen, line from Ōmiya Station to Keifuku Arashiyama Station. The Hankyū Arashiyama line from downtown to Arashiyama (change en route at Katsura).

➡ **Bus** From Marutamachi-dōri, bus 93; from Shijō-dōri, bus 11; from Kyoto Station, bus 28.

➡ **Subway** The Tōzai subway line stops at Uzumasa-Tenjin-gawa, where you can transfer to the Randen street tram.

## Lonely Planet's Top Tip

The main drag of Arashiyama and Sagano is over-developed and unlovely. As soon as you can, head west into the hills to escape (via Tenryū-ji or straight through the Arashiyama Bamboo Grove).

**ARASHIYAMA & SAGANO**

 **Best Places to Eat**

➡ Hakko Shokudo Kamoshika (p114)

➡ Shigetsu (p115)

➡ Hiranoya (p115)

For reviews, see p114. ➡

 **Best Places to Enjoy Nature**

➡ Arashiyama Bamboo Grove (p110)

➡ Kameyama-kōen (p110)

➡ Ōkōchi Sansō (p110)

For reviews, see p110. ➡

 **Best Places to Gaze on a Garden**

➡ Tenryū-ji (p110)

➡ Giō-ji (p113)

➡ Takiguchi-dera (p113)

For reviews, see p110. ➡

# ⊙ SIGHTS

### TENRYŪ-JI
BUDDHIST TEMPLE

Map p219 (天龍寺; 68 Susukinobaba-chō, Saga-Tenryū-ji, Ukyō-ku; admission ¥600; ⊙8.30am-5.30pm, to 5pm 21 Oct-20 Mar; ☐Kyoto City bus 28 from Kyoto Station to Arashiyama-Tenryuji-mae, ☐JR Sagano/San-in line to Saga-Arashiyama or Hankyū line to Arashiyama, change at Katsura) This fine temple has one of the most attractive gardens in all of Kyoto, particularly during the cherry-blossom and autumn-foliage seasons. It's lovely for a stroll. The main 14th-century Zen garden, with its backdrop of the Arashiyama mountains, is a good example of *shakkei* (borrowed scenery). Unfortunately, it's no secret that the garden here is world class, so it pays to visit early in the morning or on a weekday.

Tenryū-ji is a major temple of the Rinzai school. It was built in 1339 on the old site of Go-Daigo's villa after a priest had a dream of a dragon rising from the nearby river. The dream was seen as a sign that the emperor's spirit was uneasy and so the temple was built as appeasement – hence the name *tenryū* (heavenly dragon). The present buildings date from 1900. You will find Arashiyama's famous bamboo grove situated just outside the north gate of the temple.

### ARASHIYAMA BAMBOO GROVE
PARK

Map p219 (嵐山竹林; Ogurayama, Saga, Ukyō-ku; ⊙dawn-dusk; ☐Kyoto City bus 28 from Kyoto Station to Arashiyama-Tenryuji-mae, ☐JR Sagano/San-in line to Saga-Arashiyama or Hankyū line to Arashiyama, change at Katsura) **FREE** Walking into this extensive bamboo grove is like entering another world – the thick green bamboo stalks seem to continue endlessly in every direction and there's a strange quality to the light. You'll be unable to resist trying to take a few photos, but you might be disappointed with the results: photos just can't capture the magic of this place. The grove runs from just outside the north gate of Tenryū-ji to just below Ōkōchi Sansō villa.

### ★ŌKŌCHI SANSŌ
HISTORIC BUILDING

Map p219 (大河内山荘; 8 Tabuchiyama-chō, Sagaogurayama, Ukyō-ku; admission ¥1000; ⊙9am-5pm; ☐Kyoto City bus 28 from Kyoto Station to Arashiyama-Tenryuji-mae, ☐JR Sagano/San-in line to Saga-Arashiyama or Hankyū line to Arashiyama, change at Katsura) This is the lavish estate of Ōkōchi Denjirō, an actor famous for his samurai films. The sprawling stroll gardens may well be the most lovely in all of Kyoto, particularly when you consider the brilliant views eastwards across the city. The house and teahouse are also sublime. Be sure to follow all the trails around the gardens. Hold onto the tea ticket you were given upon entry to claim the tea and cake that comes with admission.

### KAMEYAMA-KŌEN
PARK

Map p219 (亀山公園; Sagaogurayama, Ukyō-ku; ☐Kyoto City bus 28 from Kyoto Station to Arashiyama-Tenryuji-mae, ☐JR Sagano/San-in line to Saga-Arashiyama or Hankyū line to Arashiyama, change at Katsura) Just upstream from Tōgetsu-kyō and behind Tenryū-ji, this park is a nice place to escape the crowds of Arashiyama. It's laced with trails, one of which leads to a lookout over Katsura-gawa and up into the Arashiyama mountains. It's especially attractive during cherry-blossom and autumn-foliage seasons. Keep an eye out for monkeys, which occasionally descend from the nearby hills to pick fruit.

### JŌJAKKŌ-JI
BUDDHIST TEMPLE

Map p219 (常寂光寺; 3 Ogura-chō, Sagaogurayama, Ukyō-ku; admission ¥400; ⊙9am-5pm; ☐Kyoto City bus 28 from Kyoto Station to Arashiyama-Tenryuji-mae, ☐JR Sagano/San-in line to Saga-Arashiyama or Hankyū line to Arashiyama, change at Katsura) This temple is perched on top of a mossy knoll and is famed for its brilliant maple trees, which turn a lovely crimson red in November, and its thatched-roof Niō-mon gate. The Hondō was constructed in the 16th century out of wood sourced from Fushimi-jō.

### RAKUSHISHA
HISTORIC BUILDING

Map p219 (落柿舎; 20 Hinomyōjin-chō, Sagaogurayama, Ukyō-ku; admission ¥200; ⊙9am-5pm Mar-Dec, 10am-4pm Jan & Feb; ☐Kyoto City bus 28 from Kyoto Station to Arashiyama-Tenryuji-mae, ☐JR Sagano/San-in line to Saga-Arashiyama or Hankyū line to Arashiyama, change at Katsura) This building was the hut of Mukai Kyorai, the best-known disciple of the illustrious haiku poet Bashō. Legend holds that Kyorai dubbed the house Rakushisha (literally 'House of the Fallen Persimmons') after he woke one morning following a fierce storm to find the persimmons he had planned to sell were all fallen from the trees in the garden and scattered on the ground.

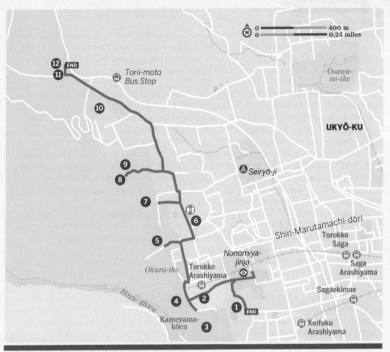

# ♣ Neighbourhood Walk
# Ambling Through Bamboo Groves & Temples

**START** TENRYŪ-JI
**FINISH** TORII-MOTO BUS STOP
**LENGTH** ABOUT 4KM; FOUR HOURS

Start at **1 Tenryū-ji** (p110), or, if you'd like to skip the temple, walk 200m north on the main road and take a left (turn at the sign that reads 'Nonomiya Shrine etc'). After checking out the temple, exit via the north gate, turn left and enter the famous **2 Arashiyama Bamboo Grove** (p110).

At the top of the hill, you can take a quick detour to sample **3 Kameyama-kōen** (p110) or enter **4 Ōkōchi Sansō** (p110), the entrance to which is almost directly in front of you.

Continuing north from Ōkōchi Sansō, head downhill and past Okura-ike pond. From here, you'll pass several smaller temples, the most appealing of which is Giō-ji.

Soon after passing the pond, you'll see the gate of **5 Jōjakkō-ji** (p110). After Jōjakkō-ji, walk straight east away from the temple gate, avoiding the temptation to take

a left out of the gate and go north. About 100m east of the Jōjakkō-ji gate, take a left (just before a cornfield) and you'll soon come to **6 Rakushisha** (p110), a charming poet's hut. After Rakushisha, continue north. About 150m further on brings you to the gate of **7 Nison-in** (p112).

Return to the main road from Nison-in and follow it gradually northwest for a few minutes. This will bring you to the turn-off for **8 Takiguchi-dera** (p113) and **9 Giō-ji** (p113), two wonderfully atmospheric little hillside temples (there is no English sign here; look for the four stone way markers). After visiting one or both of these temples, return to the main road and continue walking northwest. You'll soon see the stone steps that lead up to **10 Adashino Nem-butsu-ji** (p113) on your left. From here, it's a short walk onward to the huge orange **11 Atago Torii**. A nice place to refresh yourself is **12 Hiranoya** (p115), just north of the *torii*. You can take bus 62 or 72 from Torii-moto bus stop.

**WORTH A DETOUR**

## OUTLYING TEMPLES

There are several excellent and worthwhile temples in the southwest corner of Kyoto, lying to the south of the Arashiyama and Sagano area. Any of the three temples following could easily be tacked onto a visit to this area, particularly if you are willing to use a taxi to make the journey.

**Katsura Rikyū** (桂離宮; Katsura Detached Palace; Katsura Misono, Nishikyō-ku; ⊞Kyoto City bus 33 to Katsura Rikyū-mae, ⊞Hankyū line to Katsura), one of Kyoto's imperial properties, is widely considered to be the pinnacle of Japanese traditional architecture and garden design. Set amid an otherwise drab neighbourhood, it is (very literally) an island of incredible beauty. The villa was built in 1624 for the emperor's brother, Prince Toshihito. Every conceivable detail of the villa – the teahouses, the large pond with islets and the surrounding garden – has been given meticulous attention.

Tours (in Japanese) start at 10am, 11am, 2pm and 3pm, and last 40 minutes. Try to be there 20 minutes before the start time. An explanatory video is shown in the waiting room and a leaflet is provided in English.

You must make reservations, usually several weeks in advance, through the Imperial Household Agency (p72). There are those, however, who feel that the troublesome application process, the distance of the villa from downtown and the need to join a regimented tour detracts from the experience.

The villa is a 15-minute walk from Katsura Station, on the Hankyū line. A taxi from the station to the villa will cost around ¥700. Alternatively, Kyoto bus 33 stops at Katsura Rikyū-mae stop, which is a five-minute walk from the villa.

**Jizō-in** (☏381-3417; 23 Yamadakitano-chō, Nishikyō-ku; adult/child ¥500/300; ⊙9am-4.30pm; ⊞Kyoto bus 63 from Sanjō-Keihan to Koke-dera) is a delightful little temple that does not boast any spectacular buildings or treasures, but it has a nice moss garden and is almost completely ignored by tourists, making it a great place to sit and contemplate. From the car park near Saihō-ji (a nearby temple), there is a small stone staircase that climbs to the road leading to Jizō-in (it helps to ask someone to point the way, as it's not entirely clear).

**Saihō-ji** (西芳寺; 56 Jingatani-chō, Matsuo, Nishikyō-ku; admission ¥3000; ⊞Kyoto City bus 28 from Kyoto Station to Matsuo-taisha-mae, Kyoto bus 63 from Sanjō-Keihan to Koke-dera), one of Kyoto's best-known gardens, is famed for its superb moss garden, hence the temple's nickname: Koke-dera (Moss Temple). The heart-shaped garden, laid out in 1339 by Musō Kokushi, surrounds a tranquil pond. In order to limit the number of visitors, one must apply to visit and then copy a sutra with ink and brush before exploring the garden. While copying a sutra might seem daunting, it's actually fairly self-explanatory and if you're lost, just glance at what the Japanese visitors are doing. It's not necessary to finish the entire sutra, just do the best you can. Once in the garden, you are free to explore on your own and at your own pace.

To visit Saihō-ji you must make a reservation. Send a postcard at least one week before the date you wish to visit and include your name, number of visitors, address in Japan, occupation, age (you must be over 18) and desired date (choice of alternative dates preferred). The address: Saihō-ji, 56 Kamigaya-chō, Matsuo, Nishikyō-ku, Kyoto-shi 615-8286, JAPAN.

Enclose a stamped self-addressed postcard for a reply to your Japanese address. You might find it convenient to buy an Ōfuku-hagaki (send and return postcard set) at a Japanese post office.

### NISON-IN
BUDDHIST TEMPLE

Map p219 (二尊院; 27 Monzenchōjin-chō, Saganison-in, Ukyō-ku; admission ¥500; ⊙9am-4.30pm; ⊞Kyoto City bus 28 from Kyoto Station to Arashiyama-Tenryuji-mae, ⊞JR Sagano/San-in line to Saga-Arashiyama or Hankyū line to Arashi-yama, change at Katsura) This is a popular spot with maple-watchers. Nison-in was originally built in the 9th century by Emperor Saga. It houses two important Kamakura-era Buddha statues side by side (Shaka on the right and Amida on the left). The temple features lacquered nightingale floors.

### TAKIGUCHI-DERA  BUDDHIST TEMPLE

Map p219 (滝口寺; ☎871-3929; 10-4 Kameyama-chō, Saga, Ukyō-ku; adult/child ¥300/200; ☺9am-5pm; ᇜKyoto City bus 28 from Kyoto Station to Arashiyama-Tenryuji-mae, ᇝJR Sagano/San-in line to Saga-Arashiyama or Hankyū line to Arashiyama, change at Katsura) Takiguchi-dera was founded by Heian-era nobleman Takiguchi Nyūdō, who entered the priesthood after being forbidden by his father to marry his peasant consort Yokobue. One day, Yokobue came to the temple with her flute to serenade Takiguchi, but was again refused by him; she wrote a farewell love sonnet on a stone (in her own blood) before throwing herself into the river to perish. The stone remains at the temple.

### GIŌ-JI  BUDDHIST TEMPLE

Map p219 (祇王寺; 32 Kozaka-chō, Sagatoriimoto, Ukyō-ku; admission ¥300; ☺9am-5pm, with seasonal variations; ᇜKyoto City bus 28 from Kyoto Station to Arashiyama-Tenryuji-mae, ᇝJR Sagano/San-in line to Saga-Arashiyama or Hankyū line to Arashiyama, change at Katsura) This tiny temple near the north end of the main Arashiyama sightseeing route is one of Kyoto's hidden gems. Its main attraction is the lush moss garden outside the thatch-roofed hall of the temple.

This quiet temple was named for the Heian-era *shirabyōshi* (traditional dancer) Giō, who committed herself here as a nun at age 21 after her romance ended with Taira-no-Kiyomori, the commander of the Heike clan. She was usurped in Kiyomori's affections by a fellow entertainer, Hotoke Gozen (who later deserted Kiyomori to join Giō at the temple). Enshrined in the main hall are five wooden statues: these are Giō, Hotoke Gozen, Kiyomori, and Giō's mother and sister (who were also nuns at the temple).

### ADASHINO NENBUTSU-JI  BUDDHIST TEMPLE

Map p219 (化野念仏寺; 17 Adashino-chō, Sagatoriimoto, Ukyō-ku; admission ¥500; ☺9am-4.30pm, to 3.30pm Dec-Feb; ᇜKyoto City bus 28 from Kyoto Station to Arashiyama-Tenryuji-mae, ᇝJR Sagano/San-in line to Saga-Arashiyama or Hankyū line to Arashiyama, change at Katsura) This rather unusual temple is where the abandoned bones of paupers without kin were gathered. More than 8000 stone images are crammed into the temple grounds, dedicated to the repose of their spirits. The abandoned souls are remembered with candles each year in the Sentō Kuyō ceremony held here on the evenings of 23 and 24 Au-gust. The temple is not a must-see attraction, but it's certainly interesting and the stone images make unusual photographs.

### TOGETSU-KYŌ  BRIDGE

Map p219 (渡月橋; Saga Tenryū-ji, Susukinobaba-chō, Ukyō-ku; boat rental per hour ¥1400; ☺boat-rental stall 9am-4.30pm; ᇜKyoto City bus 28 from Kyoto Station to Arashiyama-Tenryuji-mae, ᇝJR Sagano/San-in line to Saga-Arashiyama or Hankyū line to Arashiyama, change at Katsura) This bridge is the dominant landmark in Arashiyama and is just a few minutes on foot from either the Keifuku line or Hankyū line Arashiyama stations. The original crossing, constructed in 1606, was about 100m upriver from the present bridge.

On 13 April *jūsan-mairi*, an important rite of passage for local children aged 13, takes place here. Boys and girls (many in kimono), after paying respects at Hōrin-ji (a nearby temple) and receiving a blessing for wisdom, cross the bridge under strict parental order not to look back towards the temple until they've reached the northern side of the bridge. Not heeding this instruction is believed to bring bad luck for life!

From July to mid-September, this is a good spot from which to watch *ukai* (cormorant fishing) in the evening. If you want to get close to the action, you can pay ¥1700 to join a passenger boat. The Tourist Information Center can provide more details.

You can also rent boats from the **boat-rental stall** just upstream from the bridge. It's a nice way to spend some time in Arashiyama and kids love it.

### ARASHIYAMA MONKEY PARK IWATAYAMA  PARK

Map p219 (嵐山モンキーパークいわたやま; 8 Genrokuzan-chō, Arashiyama, Ukyō-ku; adult/child ¥550/250; ☺9am-5pm mid-Mar–Oct, to 4pm Nov–mid-Mar; ᇜKyoto City bus 28 from Kyoto Station to Arashiyama-Tenryuji-mae, ᇝJR Sagano/San-in line to Saga-Arashiyama or Hankyū line to Arashiyama, change at Katsura) Though it is common to spot wild monkeys in the nearby mountains, here you can encounter them at a close distance and enjoy watching the playful creatures frolic about. It makes for an excellent photo opportunity, not only of the monkeys but also of the panoramic view over Kyoto. Refreshingly, it is the animals who are free to roam while the humans who feed them are caged in a box!

You enter the park near the south side of Tōgetsu-kyō, through the orange *torii*

## HOZU-GAWA RIVER TRIP

The **Hozu-gawa river trip** (☎0771-22-5846; Hozu-chō, Kameoka-shi; adult/child ¥3900/2500; ◷9am-3.30pm) is a great way to enjoy the beauty of Kyoto's western mountains without any strain on the legs. With long bamboo poles, boatmen steer flat-bottom boats down the Hozu-gawa from Kameoka, 30km west of Kyoto Station, through steep, forested mountain canyons, before arriving at Arashiyama.

Between 10 March and 30 November there are seven trips daily. During winter the number of trips is reduced to four per day and the boats are heated.

The ride lasts two hours and covers 16km through occasional sections of choppy water – a scenic jaunt with minimal danger. The scenery is especially breathtaking during cherry-blossom season in April and maple-foliage season in autumn.

The boats depart from a dock that is eight minutes' walk from Kameoka Station. Kameoka is accessible by rail from Kyoto Station or Nijō Station on the JR Sagano-San-in line. The Tourist Information Center provides an English-language leaflet and timetable for rail connections. The fare from Kyoto to Kameoka is ¥400 one-way by regular train (don't spend the extra for the express; it makes little difference in travel time).

(shrine gate) of Ichitani-jinja. Buy your tickets from the machine to the left of the shrine at the top of the steps. Just be warned: it's a steep climb up the hill to get to the monkeys. If it's a hot day, you're going to be drenched by the time you get to the spot where they gather.

### DAIKAKU-JI          BUDDHIST TEMPLE
Map p219 (大覚寺; ☎871-0071; 4 Osawa-chō, Saga, Ukyō-ku; adult/child ¥500/300; ◷9am-4.30pm; ⊠JR Sagano/San-in line to Saga-Arashiyama) A 25-minute walk northeast of Nison-in you will find Daikaku-ji, one of Kyoto's less-commonly visited temples. It was built in the 9th century as a palace for Emperor Saga, who then converted it into a temple. The present buildings date from the 16th century and are palatial in style; they also contain some impressive paintings. The large Osawa-no-ike pond was once used by the emperor for boating and is a popular spot for viewing the harvest moon.

## ✗ EATING

### YOSHIDA-YA          SHOKUDŌ ¥
Map p219 (よしだや; ☎861-0213; 20-24 Tsukurimichi-chō, Saga Tenryū-ji, Ukyō-ku; lunch from ¥650; ◷10.30am-5pm, closed Wed; ⊠Kyoto City bus 28 from Kyoto Station to Arashiyama-Tenryuji-mae, ⊠JR Sagano/San-in line to Saga-Arashiyama or Hankyū line to Arashiyama, change at Katsura) This quaint and friendly little *teishoku-ya* (set-meal restaurant) is the perfect place to grab a simple lunch while in Arashiyama.

All the standard *teishoku* favourites are on offer, including dishes such as *oyakodon* (egg and chicken over a bowl of rice; ¥900).

You can also cool off with a refreshing *uji kintoki* (shaved ice with sweetened green tea; ¥600). There is no English sign; the restaurant is the first place south of the station and it has a rustic front.

### HAKKO SHOKUDO KAMOSHIKA     SHOKUDŌ ¥
Map p219 (発酵食堂カモシカ; ☎862-0106; 17-1 Saga-Tenryūji-Wakamiya-chō, Ukyō-ku; meals ¥700-2000; ◷11am-3pm, closed Sun & Mon; ◐; ⊠JR Sagano/San-in line to Saga-Arashiyama) This excellent new restaurant on the north side of JR Saga-Arashiyama Station specialises in fermented Japanese foods, most of it vegetarian. The daily set, with about eight different fermented foods, is a delicious and healthy lunch option. There's an English menu and sign.

### KOMICHI          CAFE ¥
Map p219 (こみち; ☎872-5313; 23 Ōjōin-chō, Nison-in Monzen, Saga, Ukyō-ku; matcha ¥650; ◷10am-5pm, closed Wed; ⊠Kyoto City bus 28 from Kyoto Station to Arashiyama-Tenryuji-mae, ⊠JR Sagano/San-in line to Saga-Arashiyama or Hankyū line to Arashiyama, change at Katsura) This friendly little teahouse is perfectly located along the Arashiyama tourist trail. In addition to hot and cold tea and coffee, it serves *uji kintoki* (shaved ice with sweetened green tea) in summer and a variety of light noodle dishes year-round. The picture menu helps with ordering. The sign is green and black on a white background.

## MIKAZUKI JAPANESE ¥

Map p219 (三日月; ☏861-0445; Tsukurimichi-chō 35-2, Saga-Tenryū-ji, Ukyō-ku; meals ¥1000; ◷11am-4pm, closed Tue; ♨; 🚌Kyoto City bus 28 from Kyoto Station to Arashiyama-Tenryuji-mae, 🚆JR Sagano/San-in line to Saga-Arashiyama or Hankyū line to Arashiyama, change at Katsura) The thing that distinguishes this place from its neighbours on the crowded main drag is its English menu and the fact that it is a little more spacious than the others. Dishes include the typical *shokudō* (all-around inexpensive restaurant) noodle and rice classics. The tempura *teishoku* (set-course meal; ¥1600) is a good choice.

The sign is in Japanese; it's black-and-white and one of the Japanese characters looks like a bullseye.

## KAMEYAMA-YA JAPANESE ¥

Map p219 (亀山家; ☏861-0759; Kamenoo-chō, Saga, Ukyō-ku; meals ¥550-1500; ◷11am-6pm; 🚌Kyoto City bus 28 from Kyoto Station to Arashi-yama-Tenryuji-mae, 🚆JR Sagano/San-in line to Saga-Arashiyama or Hankyū line to Arashiyama, change at Katsura) We love this semi-outdoor restaurant on the banks of the Hozu-gawa. The service can be gruff, the food is only pretty good, but the location is impossible to beat. Dishes include tempura over rice and noodles. There is no English sign but there are a couple of vending machines near the entrance.

## ★SHIGETSU VEGETARIAN, JAPANESE ¥¥

Map p219 (篩月; ☏882-9725; 68 Susukinobaba-chō, Saga-Tenryū-ji, Ukyō-ku; lunch sets ¥3500, ¥5500 & ¥7500, incl temple admission; ◷11am-2pm; ♨; 🚌Kyoto City bus 28 from Kyoto Station to Arashiyama-Tenryuji-mae, 🚆JR Sagano/San-in line to Saga-Arashiyama or Hankyū line to Ar-ashiyama, change at Katsura) To sample *shōjin ryōri* (Buddhist vegetarian cuisine), try Shigetsu in the precincts of Tenryū-ji. This healthy fare has been sustaining monks for more than a thousand years in Japan, so it will probably get you through an afternoon of sightseeing. Shigetsu has beautiful garden views.

## ★HIRANOYA TEA, KAISEKI ¥¥

Map p219 (平野屋; ☏861-0359; 16 Sennō-chō, Saga-Toriimoto, Ukyō-ku; tea ¥840, dinner from ¥10,000; ◷11.30am-9pm; 🚌Kyoto City bus 72 from Kyoto Station to Otaginenbutsu-ji-mae) Lo-cated next to the Atago Torii (a large Shintō shrine gate), this thatched-roof restaurant is about as atmospheric as they get. It serves a simple cup of *matcha* (powdered green tea) for a relatively modest ¥840 (it comes with a traditional sweet). It's the per-fect way to cool off after a long slog around the temples of Arashiyama and Sagano.

You can also try full-course *kaiseki* (Japa-nese haute cuisine) meals here from ¥15,000 (by phone reservation in Japanese only).

## YUDŌFU SAGANO TOFU ¥¥

Map p219 (湯豆腐嵯峨野; ☏871-6946; 45 Susukinobaba-chō, Saga-Tenryū-ji, Ukyō-ku; lunch & dinner from ¥3800; ◷11am-7pm; 🚌Kyoto City bus 28 from Kyoto Station to Arashiyama-Tenryuji-mae, 🚆JR Sagano/San-in line to Saga-Arashiyama or Hankyū line to Arashiyama, change at Katsura) This is a popular place to sample *yudōfu* (tofu cooked in a pot). It's fairly casual, with a spacious dining room. You can usually eat here without having to wait, and there's both indoor and outdoor seating. Look for the old cartwheels outside.

## ARASHIYAMA YOSHIMURA NOODLES ¥¥

Map p219 (嵐山よしむら; ☏863-5700; Togetsu-kyō kita, Saga-Tenryū-ji, Ukyō-ku; soba dishes from ¥1080, set meals from ¥1600; ◷11am-5pm; ♨; 🚌Kyoto City bus 28 from Kyoto Station to Ar-ashiyama-Tenryuji-mae, 🚆JR Sagano/San-in line to Saga-Arashiyama or Hankyū line to Arashiyama, change at Katsura) For a tasty bowl of *soba* noodles and a million-dollar view over the Arashiyama mountains and the Togetsu-kyō bridge, head to this extremely popu-lar eatery just north of the famous bridge, overlooking the Katsura-gawa. There's an English menu but no English sign; look for the big glass windows and the stone wall.

## KITCHO ARASHIYAMA KAISEKI ¥¥¥

Map p219 (吉兆嵐山本店; ☏881-1101; www.kitcho.com/kyoto/shoplist_en/arashiyama; 58 Susukinobaba-chō, Saga-Tenryūji, Ukyō-ku; lunch/dinner from ¥36,750/42,000; ◷11.30am-3pm & 5-9pm, closed Wed; 🚆JR Sagano/San-in line to Saga-Arashiyama) Considered one of the best *kaiseki* restaurants in Kyoto (and Japan, for that matter), Kitcho Arashiyama is the place to sample the full *kaiseki* experience. Meals are served in private rooms overlooking gar-dens. The food, service, explanations and atmosphere are all first rate. We suggest having a Japanese person call to reserve, or make a booking online via its website.

ARASHIYAMA & SAGANO EATING

# Kitayama Area & North Kyoto

FAR NORTHERN HIGASHIYAMA AREA | ŌHARA | KURAMA & KIBUNE | TAKAO | NORTH & NORTHEAST KYOTO

## Neighbourhood Top Five

❶ Ascending to the mountain temple of **Kurama-dera** (p120), one of the best half-day trips in Kyoto. If you have the energy, continue over the top of the mountain and down to the village of Kibune.

❷ Escaping to the quaint rural village of Ōhara to visit the Buddhist paradise of **Sanzen-in** (p119) and then walk the rural footpaths of the village.

❸ Taking a dip on a snowy winter day in **Kurama Onsen** (p123).

❹ Eating lunch suspended over the rushing waters of the **Kibune-gawa** (p122) in the hamlet of Kibune.

❺ Climbing to **Jingo-ji** (p121), a mountain temple where you can play 'karmic frisbee'.

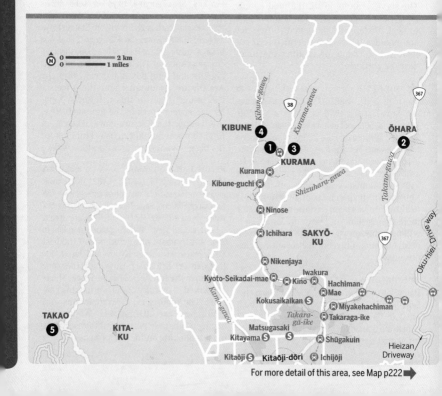

For more detail of this area, see Map p222 ➡

# Explore: Kitayama Area & North Kyoto

The Kitayama area and north Kyoto encompasses the sights at the north end of Kyoto city, including the temples of Manshu-in and Shisen-dō, the imperial villa of Shūgaku-in Rikyū, and the mountaintop temple complex of Enryaku-ji, which sits atop Hiei-zan (Mt Hiei). This section also includes four villages located in the Kitayama ('Northern Mountains') area just north of the city: Takao, Ōhara, Kurama and Kibune. All of these make interesting trips out of the city centre and are good ways to escape the crowds that plague some sights closer to downtown.

Needless to say, due to their location, most of these sights require at least half a day to visit and you shouldn't try to link any of these areas into one day trip.

All of the sights can be reached by public transport. Kurama and Kibune are a very easy 30-minute trip from Kyoto via the Eizan Dentetsu line. Likewise, Ōhara is an easy 40-minute bus trip from central Kyoto (longer in autumn-foliage season). Buses and/or funiculars will get you up Hiei-zan to visit Enryaku-ji.

## Local Life

→ **Beat the heat** Locals head to the *yuka* (dining platforms) over the river in Kibune (p120) to cool off when the Kyoto summer heat cranks up.

→ **A taste of winter** Folks who love winter scenery head up to Kurama-dera (p120) after a snowstorm hits the area.

→ **Foliage treat** The village of Ōhara (p119) is loved by locals and other Japanese for its autumn foliage.

## Getting There & Away

→ **Train** The Eizan line will get you to Kurama and Kibune.

→ **Bus** Kyoto City buses and/or Kyoto buses (they're different) serve all the destinations in these districts. JR buses also serve Takao.

→ **Car** A rental car is a good option for exploring the Kitayama area.

## Lonely Planet's Top Tip

Avoid Ōhara on busy autumn-foliage weekends in November. There's only one main road up there from Kyoto and you'll spend too much time sitting in traffic (and the temples will be crowded when you get there). Wait until Monday if you can.

### ✕ Best Places to Eat

→ Yōshūji (p123)
→ Hirobun (p123)
→ Seryō-Jaya (p122)

For reviews, see p122.

### ◉ Best Places to Hike

→ Kurama and Kibune (p120)
→ Takao (p121)
→ Hiei-zan (p121)

For reviews, see p118.

### ◉ Best Temples to Visit

→ Kurama-dera (p120)
→ Sanzen-in (p119)
→ Jingo-ji (p121)

For reviews, see p118. →

**KITAYAMA AREA & NORTH KYOTO**

# ◉ SIGHTS

## ◉ Far Northern Higashiyama Area

### SHISEN-DŌ
TEMPLE

(詩仙堂; ☎781-2954; Ichijōji, 27 Monguchi-chō, Sakyō-ku; adult ¥500, child ¥200-400; ◎9am-4.45pm; ⬛Kyoto City bus 5 from Kyoto Station to Ichijōji-kudari-matsu-machi) One of the real highlights of the far northern Higashiyama area, Shisen-dō (House of Poet-Hermits) was built in 1641 by Ishikawa Jōzan, a scholar of Chinese classics and a landscape architect who wanted a place to retire.

The hermitage is noted for its display of poems and portraits of 36 ancient Chinese poets, which can be found in the **Shisen-no-ma** room. The white-sand *kare-sansui* (dry-landscape rock garden) is lined with azaleas, which are said to represent islands in the sea. It's a tranquil place to relax.

In the garden, water flows from a small waterfall to the *shishi-odoshi*, or *sōzu*, a device designed to scare away wild boar and deer. It's made from a bamboo pipe into which water slowly trickles, fills up and swings down to empty. On the upswing to its original position the bamboo strikes a stone with a 'thwack' – just loud enough to interrupt your snooze – before starting to refill.

### MANSHU-IN
BUDDHIST TEMPLE

(曼殊院; ☎781-5010; Ichijōji, 42 Takeno uchi-chō, Sakyō-ku; adult ¥500, child ¥400-500; ◎9am-4.30pm; ⬛Eizan line to Shūgakuin) The charmingly intimate temple of Manshu-in, which served as a retreat for former emperors, is a great place to escape the crowds that descend on other Kyoto temples. The temple was originally founded by Saichō on Hiei-zan but was relocated here at the beginning of the Edo period by Ryōshōhō, the son of Prince Hachijōnomiya Tomohito (who built Katsura Rikyū).

The graceful temple architecture is often compared with Kyoto's famed Katsura Rikyū Detached Palace for its detailed woodwork and rare works of art, such as *fusuma-e* sliding doors painted by Kanō Eitoku, a famed artist of the Momoyama period. The *kare-sansui* garden by Kobori Enshū features a sea of gravel intended to symbolise the flow of a waterfall and stone islands representing cranes and turtles.

A visit to Manshu-in can be paired with a trip to nearby Shisen-dō, a charming small temple in the area.

### SHŪGAKU-IN RIKYŪ IMPERIAL VILLA
NOTABLE BUILDING

(修学院離宮; ☎211-1215; Shūgaku-in, Yabusoe, Sakyō-ku; ⬛Kyoto City bus 5 from Kyoto Station to Shūgakuinrikyū-michi) **FREE** Lying at the foot of Hiei-zan, this superb imperial villa is one of the highlights of northeast Kyoto. It was designed as a lavish summer retreat for the imperial family. The gardens here, with their views down over the city of Kyoto, are worth the trouble it takes to visit.

Construction of the villa was begun in the 1650s by Emperor Go-Mizunō, following his abdication. Work was continued by his daughter Akeno-miya after his death in 1680.

The villa grounds are divided into three enormous garden areas on a hillside – lower, middle and upper. Each has superb tea-ceremony houses: the upper, **Kami-no-chaya**, and lower, **Shimo-no-chaya**, were completed in 1659, and the middle teahouse, **Naka-no-chaya**, was completed in 1682. The gardens' reputation rests on their ponds, pathways and impressive use of *shakkei* (borrowed scenery) in the form of the surrounding hills. The view from Kami-no-chaya is particularly impressive.

One-hour tours (in Japanese) start at 9am, 10am, 11am, 1.30pm and 3pm; try to arrive early. A basic leaflet in English is provided and more detailed literature is for sale in the tour waiting room.

You must make reservations through the Imperial Household Agency (p72) – usually several weeks in advance.

### TAKARA-GA-IKE-KŌEN
PARK

(宝ヶ池公園; Iwakura, Matsugasaki, Sakyō-ku; ⬛Karasuma line to Kokusaikaikan) This expansive park is an excellent place for a stroll or picnic in natural surroundings. Far from the throngs in the city centre, it is a popular place for birdwatching and has spacious gardens. There is a 1.8km loop around the main pond, where rowboats can be hired for ¥1000 per hour.

In the northeast of the park, the **Kyoto International Conference Hall** is an unfortunate attempt at replicating Japan's traditional thatched-roof *gasshō-zukuri* style in concrete. Behind the conference hall, the **Hosho-an Teahouse** (designed by Soshitsu

Sen, Grand Tea-Master XV of the Urasenke school) is worth a look.

# ☉ Ōhara

Since ancient times Ōhara, a quiet farming town about 10km north of Kyoto, has been regarded as a holy site by followers of the Jōdo (Pure Land) school of Buddhism. The region provides a charming glimpse of rural Japan, along with the picturesque Sanzen-in, Jakkō-in and several other fine temples. It's most popular in autumn, when the maple leaves change colour and the mountain views are spectacular.

From Kyoto Station, Kyoto buses 17 and 18 run to Ōhara bus stop. The ride takes about an hour and costs ¥580. From Keihan line's Sanjō Station, take Kyoto bus 16 or 17 (¥470, 45 minutes). Be careful to board a tan-coloured Kyoto bus, not a green Kyoto City bus of the same number.

★SANZEN-IN                          BUDDHIST TEMPLE

Map p222 (三千院; 540 Raikōin-chō, Ōhara, Sakyō-ku; admission ¥700; ⊙9am-5pm Mar-Nov, to 4.30pm Dec-Feb; ☐Kyoto bus 17 or 18 from Kyoto Station to Ōhara) Famed for its autumn foliage, hydrangea garden and stunning Buddha images, this temple is deservedly popular with foreign and domestic tourists alike. The temple's garden, **Yūsei-en**, is one of the most photographed sights in Japan, and rightly so.

Take some time to sit on the steps of the **Shin-den** hall and admire the beauty of the Yūsei-en. Then head off to see **Ōjō-gokuraku-in** (Temple of Rebirth in Paradise), the hall in which stands the impressive Amitabha trinity, a large Amida image flanked by attendants Kannon and Seishi (god of wisdom). After this, walk up to the garden at the back of the temple where, in late spring and summer, you can walk among hectares of blooming hydrangeas.

Sanzen-in was founded in 784 by the priest Saichō and belongs to the Tendai school. Saichō, considered one of the great patriarchs of Buddhism in Japan, also founded Enryaku-ji.

If you're keen for a short hike after leaving the temple, continue up the hill to see the rather oddly named **Soundless Waterfall** (Oto-nashi-no-taki; 音無の滝; Map p222). Though in fact it sounds like any other waterfall, its resonance is believed to have inspired Shōmyō Buddhist chanting.

The approach to Sanzen-in is opposite the bus stop; there is no English sign but you can usually follow the Japanese tourists. The temple is located about 600m up this walk on your left as you crest the hill.

JIKKŌ-IN                            BUDDHIST TEMPLE

Map p222 (実光院; ☏744-2537; 187 Shōrinin-chō, Ōhara, Sakyō-ku; adult/child incl green tea & sweets ¥700/300; ⊙9am-4.30pm; ☐Kyoto bus 17 or 18 from Kyoto Station to Ōhara) Only about 50m north of Sanzen-in, this small temple is often praised for its lovely garden and *fudan-zakura* cherry tree, which blossoms between October and March.

SHŌRIN-IN                           BUDDHIST TEMPLE

Map p222 (勝林院; ☏744-2537; 187 Shōrinin-chō, Ōhara,Sakyō-ku; adult/child ¥300/200; ⊙9am-4.30pm; ☐Kyoto bus 17 or 18 from Kyoto Station to Ōhara) This temple is worth a look, even if only through its admission gate, to admire the thatched roof of the main hall. It's a good option if you're trying to avoid crowds. It's near Sanzen-in.

HŌSEN-IN                            BUDDHIST TEMPLE

Map p222 (宝泉院; ☏744-2409; 187 Shōrinin-chō, Ōhara, Sakyō-ku; adult ¥800, child ¥600-700; ⊙9am-5pm; ☐Kyoto bus 17 or 18 from Kyoto Station to Ōhara) A quiet option, this temple is just down the path west of the entry gate to Shōrin-in. The main tatami room offers a view of a bamboo garden and the surrounding mountains, framed like a painting by the beams and posts of the building. There is also a fantastic 700-year-old pine tree in the garden. The blood-stained Chi Tenjō ceiling boards came from Fushimi-jō castle.

JAKKŌ-IN                            BUDDHIST TEMPLE

Map p222 (寂光院; 676 Kusao-chō, Ōhara, Sakyō-ku; admission ¥600; ⊙9am-5pm Mar-Nov, to 4.30pm Dec-Feb; ☐Kyoto bus 17 or 18 from Kyoto Station to Ōhara) Jakkō-in sits on the opposite side of Ōhara from the famous Sanzen-in. It's reached by a very pleasant walk through a quaint 'old Japan' village. It's a relatively small temple and makes an interesting end point to a fine walk in the country.

The history of the temple is exceedingly tragic. The actual founding date of the temple is subject to some debate (it's thought to be somewhere between the 6th and 11th centuries), but it acquired fame as the temple that harboured Kenrei Mon-in, a lady of the Taira clan. In 1185 the Taira were soundly defeated in a sea battle against the Minamoto clan at Dan-no-ura. With the entire Taira clan slaughtered or drowned, Kenrei Mon-in threw herself into the waves with her son Antoku, the infant emperor; she was fished out – the only member of the clan to survive.

She was returned to Kyoto, where she became a nun and lived in a bare hut until it collapsed during an earthquake. Kenrei Mon-in was then accepted into Jakkō-in and stayed there, immersed in prayer and sorrowful memories, until her death 27 years later. Her tomb is located high on the hill behind the temple.

The main building of this temple burned down in May 2000 and the newly reconstructed main hall lacks some of the charm of the original. Nonetheless, it is a nice spot.

Jakkō-in is west of Ōhara. Walk out of the bus stop up the road to the traffic lights, then follow the small road to the left. You might have to ask directions on the way.

# ◉ Kurama & Kibune

Located just 30 minutes north of Kyoto, Kurama and Kibune are a pair of tranquil valleys that have been long favoured as places to escape the crowds and stresses of the city. Kurama's main attractions are its mountain temple and onsen (mineral hot spring). Kibune, an impossibly charming little hamlet just over the ridge, is a cluster of ryokan (traditional Japanese inns) overlooking a mountain river. Kibune is best in summer, when the ryokan serve dinner on platforms built over the rushing waters of Kibune-gawa, providing welcome relief from the heat.

The two valleys lend themselves to being explored together. In winter you can start from Kibune, walk 30 minutes over the ridge, visit Kurama-dera, then soak in the onsen before heading back to Kyoto. In summer the reverse route is better: start from Kurama, walk up to the temple, then down the other side to Kibune to enjoy a meal suspended above the cool river. Either way, a trip to Kurama and Kibune is probably the single best day or half-day trip possible from Kyoto city.

If you happen to be in Kyoto on the night of 22 October, be sure not to miss the **Kurama Hi Matsuri fire festival**. It's one of the most exciting festivals in the Kyoto area.

To get to Kurama and Kibune, take the Eizan line from Kyoto's Demachiyanagi Station. For Kibune, get off at the second-to-last stop, Kibune-guchi, take a right out of the station and walk about 20 minutes up the hill. For Kurama, go to the last stop, Kurama, and walk straight out of the station. Both destinations are ¥410 and take about 30 minutes to reach.

★**KURAMA-DERA**     BUDDHIST TEMPLE
Map p223 (鞍馬寺; 1074 Kurama Honmachi, Sakyō-ku; admission ¥200; ◷9am-4.30pm; ℝEiden Eizan line from Demachiyanagi to Kurama) Located high on a thickly wooded mountain, Kurama-dera is one of the few temples in modern Japan that still manages to retain an air of real spirituality. This is a magical place that gains a lot of its power from its brilliant natural setting.

The temple has a fascinating history: in 770 the monk Gantei left Nara's Toshōdai-ji in search of a wilderness sanctuary in which to meditate. Wandering in the hills north of Kyoto, he came across a white horse that led him to the valley known today as Kurama. After seeing a vision of the deity Bishamon-ten, guardian of the northern quarter of the Buddhist heaven, Gantei established Kurama-dera just below the peak of Kurama-yama. Originally belonging to the Tendai school of Buddhism, Kurama has been independent since 1949, describing its own brand of Buddhism as Kurama-kyō.

The entrance to the temple is just up the hill from Kurama Station. A tram goes to the top for ¥100 or you can hike up in about 30 minutes (follow the main path past the tram station). The trail is worth taking (if it's not too hot), since it winds through a forest of towering old-growth cryptomeria trees, passing by **Yuki-jinja** (Map p223), a small Shintō shrine, on the way. Near the peak, there is a courtyard dominated by the **Honden** (Main Hall); behind this a trail leads off to the mountain's peak.

At the top, you can take a brief detour across the ridge to **Ōsugi-gongen** (Map p223), a quiet shrine in a grove of trees. Those who want to continue to Kibune can take the trail down the other side. It's a 1.2km, 30-minute hike from the Honden to the valley floor of Kibune. On the way down are two mountain shrines, **Sōjō-ga-dani Fudō-dō** (Map p223) and **Okuno-in Maōden** (Map p223), which make pleasant rest stops.

# ⊙ Takao

The Takao area is tucked far away in the northwestern part of Kyoto. It is famed for autumn foliage and a trio of temples: Jingo-ji, Saimyō-ji and Kōzan-ji.

To reach Takao, take bus 8 from Nijō Station to the last stop, Takao (¥500, 40 minutes). From Kyoto Station, take the hourly JR bus to the Yamashiro Takao stop (¥500, 50 minutes).

**JINGO-JI**     BUDDHIST TEMPLE
(神護寺; 5 Takao-chō, Umegahata, Ukyo-ku; admission ¥500; ◷9am-4pm; ⊟JR bus from Kyoto Station to Yamashiro-Takao) This mountaintop temple is one of our favourites in all of Kyoto. It sits at the top of a long flight of stairs that stretch from the Kiyotaki-gawa to the temple's main gate. The **Kondō** (Gold Hall) is the most impressive of the temple's structures, located roughly in the middle of the grounds at the top of another flight of stairs.

After visiting the Kondō, head in the opposite direction along a wooded path to an open area overlooking the valley. Here you'll see people tossing small discs over the railing into the chasm below. These are *kawarakenage,* light clay discs that people throw in order to rid themselves of their bad karma. Be careful, it's addictive and at ¥100 for two it can get expensive (you can buy the discs at a nearby stall). The trick is to flick the discs very gently, convex side up, like a frisbee. When you get it right, they sail all the way down the valley – taking all that bad karma with them (try not to think about the hikers down below).

To get to Jingo-ji, walk down to the river from the the Yamashiro-Takao bus stop and climb the steps on the other side.

**SAIMYŌ-JI**     BUDDHIST TEMPLE
(西明寺; 2 Makino-chō, Umegahata, Ukyo-ku; admission ¥500; ◷9am-5pm; ⊟JR bus from Kyoto Station to Yamashiro-Takao) About five minutes upstream from the base of the steps that lead to Jingo-ji, this fine little temple is one of our favourite spots in Kyoto. See if you can find your way round to the small waterfall at the side of the temple. The grotto here is pure magic.

**KŌZAN-JI**     BUDDHIST TEMPLE
(高山寺; 8 Toganoo-chō, Umegahata, Ukyo-ku; admission ¥600; ◷8.30am-5pm; ⊟JR bus from

Kyoto Station to Yamashiro-Takao or Toga-no-O) Hidden amid a grove of towering cedar trees, this temple is famous for the *chuju giga* scroll in its collection. It's an ink-brush depiction of frolicking animals that is considered by many to be the precursor of today's ubiquitous manga (Japanese comics). The temple is reached by following the main road north from the Yamashiro-Takao bus stop or, more conveniently, by getting off the JR bus at the Toga-no-O bus stop, which is right outside the temple.

# ⊙ North & Northeast Kyoto

In the north of Kyoto lies Kamigamo-jinja, a fine Shintō shrine, and the imposing bulk of Hiei-zan with its mountaintop temple complex of Enryaku-ji.

**KAMIGAMO-JINJA**     SHINTO SHRINE
(上賀茂神社; 339 Motoyama, Kamigamo, Kitaku; ◷6am-5pm; ⊟Kyoto City bus 9 to Kamigamo-misonobashi) **FREE** Kamigamo-jinja is one of Japan's oldest shrines and predates the founding of Kyoto. Established in 679, it is dedicated to Raijin, the god of thunder, and is one of Kyoto's 17 Unesco World Heritage sites. The present buildings (more than 40 in all), including the impressive **Haiden** hall, are exact reproductions of the originals, dating from the 17th to 19th centuries.

The shrine is entered from a long approach through two *torii* (shrine gateways). The two large conical white-sand mounds in front of **Hosodono** hall are said to represent mountains sculpted for gods to descend upon. It's not one of Kyoto's leading sights but it's worth a look if you find yourself in the north.

**HIEI-ZAN & ENRYAKU-JI**     BUDDHIST TEMPLE
(延暦寺; 4220 Honmachi, Sakamoto, Sakyō-ku; admission ¥700; ◷8.30am-4.30pm, 9am-4pm in winter; ⊟Kyoto bus to Enryakuji Bus Center, Keihan bus to Enryakuji Bus Center) Located atop 848m-high Hiei-zan (the mountain that dominates the skyline in the northeast of the city), the Enryaku-ji temple complex is an entire world of temples and dark forests that feels a long way from the hustle and bustle of the city below. A visit to this temple is a good way to spend half a day hiking, poking around temples and enjoying the atmosphere of a key site in Japanese history.

## ℹ TRANSPORT: HIEI-ZAN & ENRYAKU-JI

You can reach Hiei-zan and Enryaku-ji by train or bus. The most interesting way is the train/cable-car/funicular route. If you're in a hurry or would like to save money, the best way is a direct bus from Sanjō Keihan or Kyoto Stations. Note that the Japanese word for funicular is *ropeway*.

**Bus/Cable Car** Take Kyoto bus (not Kyoto City bus) 17 or 18, both of which run from Kyoto Station to the Yase-eki-mae stop (¥390, about 50 minutes). From there it's a short walk to the cable-car station from where you can complete the journey.

**Direct Bus** if you want to save money (by avoiding both the cable car and funicular), there are direct Kyoto buses from Kyoto and Keihan Sanjō Stations to Enryaku-ji, which take about 70 and 50 minutes respectively (both cost ¥800).

**Train** Take the Keihan line north to the last stop, Demachiyanagi, and change to the Yase-Hienzanguchi–bound Eizan Dentetsu Eizan-line train (be careful not to board the Kurama-bound train that sometimes leaves from the same platform). Travel to the last stop, Yase-Hienzanguchi (¥260, about 15 minutes from Demachiyanagi Station), then board the cable car (¥530, nine minutes) followed by the funicular (¥310, three minutes) to the peak, from where you can walk down to the temples.

**Enryaku-ji** was founded in 788 by Saichō, also known as Dengyō-daishi, the priest who established the Tenzai school. This school did not receive imperial recognition until 823, after Saichō's death; however, from the 8th century the temple grew in power. At its height, Enryaku-ji possessed some 3000 buildings and an army of thousands of *sōhei* (warrior monks). In 1571 Oda Nobunaga saw the temple's power as a threat to his aims to unify the nation and he destroyed most of the buildings, along with the monks inside. Today only three pagodas and 120 minor temples remain.

The complex is divided into three sections: **Tōtō**, **Saitō** and **Yokawa**. The Tōtō (eastern pagoda section) contains the **Kompon Chū-dō** (Primary Central Hall), which is the most important building in the complex. The flames on the three dharma lamps in front of the altar have been kept lit for more than 1200 years. The **Daikō-dō** (Great Lecture Hall) displays life-sized wooden statues of the founders of various Buddhist schools. This part of the temple is heavily geared to group access, with large expanses of asphalt for parking.

The Saitō (western pagoda section) contains the Shaka-dō, which dates from 1595 and houses a rare Buddha sculpture of the Shaka Nyorai (Historical Buddha). The Saitō, with its stone paths winding through forests of tall trees, temples shrouded in mist and the sound of distant gongs, is the most atmospheric part of the temple. Hold

on to your ticket from the Tōtō section, as you may need to show it here.

The Yokawa is of minimal interest and a 4km bus ride away from the Saitō area. The Chū-dō here was originally built in 848. It was destroyed by fire several times and has undergone repeated reconstruction (most recently in 1971). If you plan to visit this area as well as Tōtō and Saitō, allow a full day for in-depth exploration.

# 🍴 EATING

## 🍴 Ōhara

**SERYŌ-JAYA** SHOKUDŌ ¥¥

Map p222 (芹生茶屋; ☎744-2301; 24 Shorinin-chō, Ōhara, Sakyō-ku; lunch sets from ¥1000; ⊗11am-5pm; 🚌Kyoto bus 17 or 18 from Kyoto Station to Ōhara) Just by the entry gate to Sanzen-in, Seryō-jaya serves tasty *soba* noodles and other fare. There is outdoor seating in the warmer months. Look for the food models.

## 🍴 Kurama & Kibune

Most of the restaurants in Kurama are clustered on the main road outside Kurama-dera's main gate.

Visitors to Kibune from June to September should not miss the chance to dine at one of the picturesque restaurants beside the Kibune-gawa. Known as *kawa-doko,* meals are served on platforms suspended over the river as cool water flows underneath. Most of the restaurants offer a lunch special for around ¥3000. For a *kaiseki* (Japanese haute cuisine; ¥5000 to ¥10,000) spread, have a Japanese speaker call to reserve it in advance.

### ABURAYA-SHOKUDŌ                    SHOKUDŌ ¥
Map p223 (鞍馬　油屋食堂; ☎741-2009; 252 Honmachi, Kurama, Sakyō-ku; udon & soba from ¥600; ☺10.30am-4.30pm; 🚃Eiden Eizan line from Demachiyanagi to Kurama) Just down the steps from the main gate of Kurama-dera, this classic old-style *shokudō* (all-round inexpensive restaurant) reminds us of what Japan was like before it got rich. The *sansai teishoku* (¥1750) is a delightful selection of vegetables, rice and *soba* topped with grated yam.

### KIBUNE CLUB                           CAFE ¥
Map p223 (貴船倶楽部; ☎741-3039; 76 Kibune-chō, Kurama, Sakyō-ku; coffee from ¥500; ☺11am-6pm; 📶; 🚃Eiden Eizan line from Demachiyanagi to Kibune-guchi) The exposed wooden beams and open, airy feel of this rustic cafe make it a great spot to stop for a cuppa while exploring Kibune. In winter it sometimes cranks up the wood stove, which makes the place rather cosy. It's easy to spot.

### ★YŌSHŪJI                        VEGETARIAN ¥¥
Map p223 (雍州路; ☎741-2848; 1074 Honmachi, Kurama, Sakyō-ku; meals from ¥1080; ☺10am-6pm, closed Tue; 🖉📶; 🚃Eiden Eizan line from Demachiyanagi to Kurama) Yōshūji serves superb *shōjin-ryōri* (vegetarian meals) in a delightful old Japanese farmhouse with an *irori* (open hearth). The house special, a sumptuous selection of vegetarian dishes served in red lacquered bowls, is called *kurama-yama shōjin zen* (¥2700). Or if you

just feel like a quick bite, try the *uzu-soba* (*soba* topped with mountain vegetables; ¥1080).

You'll find it halfway up the steps leading to the main gate of Kurama-dera; look for the orange lanterns out the front.

### HIROBUN                           JAPANESE ¥¥
Map p223 (ひろ文; ☎741-2147; 87 Kibune-chō, Kurama, Sakyō-ku; noodles from ¥1000, kaiseki courses from ¥8600; ☺11am-9pm; 🚃Eiden Eizan line from Demachiyanagi to Kibune-guchi) This is a good place to sample riverside or 'above-river' dining in Kibune. There's a friendly crew of ladies here who run the show and the food is quite good. Note that it does not accept solo diners for *kaiseki* courses (but you can have noodles). Look for the black-and-white sign and the lantern. Reserve for dinner.

 # SPORTS & ACTIVITIES

### KURAMA ONSEN                          ONSEN
Map p223 (鞍馬温泉; 520 Kurama Honmachi, Sakyō-ku; admission outdoor bath only ¥1000, outdoor & indoor bath ¥2500; ☺10am-9pm; 🚃Eiden Eizan line from Demachiyanagi to Kurama) One of the few onsen within easy reach of Kyoto, Kurama Onsen is a great place to relax after a hike. The outdoor bath has fine views of Kurama-yama, while the indoor bath area includes some relaxation areas in addition to the tubs. For both baths, buy a ticket from the machine outside the door of the main building.

To get to Kurama Onsen, walk straight out of Kurama Station and continue up the main street, passing the entrance to Kurama-dera on your left. The onsen is about 10 minutes' walk on the right. There's also a free shuttle bus between the station and the onsen, which meets incoming trains.

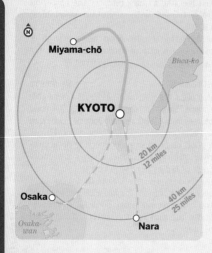

# Day Trips from Kyoto

### Nara p125
Thirty minutes away from Kyoto by express train, Nara boasts a compact collection of truly first-rate sights. If you're in Kyoto for more than four days, Nara is a must!

### Osaka p128
A short train trip from Kyoto, Osaka is a great place to see modern Japan in all its hyperkinetic intensity. If you aren't going to Tokyo, consider a trip to Osaka.

### Miyama-chō p131
If you want to see rural Japan (thatched-roof cottages etc), hire a car and head to these villages in the mountains north of the city.

# Nara

## Explore

Nara is the most rewarding day trip from Kyoto and it's very easy to reach. Indeed, by taking the Kintetsu limited express *(tokkyū)* from Kyoto Station to Kintetsu Nara Station, you're there in about 30 minutes – less time than it might take you to visit some of the more distant parts of Kyoto itself.

Whether you go by JR or Kintetsu, grab a map at the nearest tourist information centre (there's one at each station) and walk to Nara-kōen (Nara Park), which contains the thickest concentration of must-see sights in the city, including the awesome Daibutsu (Great Buddha) at Tōdai-ji. On the way, don't miss Isui-en, a compact stunner of a garden. With a 9am start, you can see the sights and be back in Kyoto in time for dinner.

## The Best...

➡ **Sight** Tōdai-ji (p125)
➡ **Place to Eat** Kameya (p127)
➡ **Place to Drink** Nara Izumi Yūsai (p128)

## Top Tip

Unless you're travelling with a Japan Rail Pass, take a comfortable *tokkyū* on the private Kintetsu line from Kyoto Station (south side of the station) to Kintetsu Nara Station.

## Getting There & Away

➡ **Kintetsu line (train)** The Kintetsu line, which runs between Kintetsu Kyoto Station (in Kyoto Station) and Kintetsu Nara Station, is the fastest and most convenient way to travel between Nara and Kyoto. There are *tokkyū* (¥1110, 33 minutes) and *kyūkō* (¥610, 40 minutes). The *tokkyū* trains run directly and are very comfortable; the *kyūkō* usually require a change at Saidai-ji.

➡ **JR line (train)** The JR Nara line also connects JR Kyoto Station with JR Nara Station (*JR Miyakoji Kaisoku*, ¥690, 41 minutes) and there are several departures an hour during the day. This is good for Japan Rail Pass holders.

## Need to Know

➡ **Area Code** ☑0742
➡ **Location** 37km south of Kyoto
➡ **Tourist Office** (☑22-9821; www.narashikanko.or.jp/en; ⊙9am-9pm)

# ◉ SIGHTS

### ★TŌDAI-JI                    BUDDHIST TEMPLE
(東大寺) Nara's star attraction is the famous Daibutsu (Great Buddha), housed in the Daibutsu-den Hall of this grand temple. Though Tōdai-ji is often packed with tour groups and schoolchildren from across the country, it's big enough to absorb huge crowds and it belongs at the top of any Nara itinerary. Except for the Daibutsu-den Hall, most of Tōdai-ji's grounds can be visited free of charge.

Before entering, check out the Nandai-mon, an enormous gate containing two fierce-looking **Niō guardians**. These recently restored wooden images, carved in the 13th century by the sculptor Unkei, are some of the finest wooden statues in all of Japan, if not the world. They are truly dramatic works of art and seem ready to spring to life at any moment. The gate is about 200m south of the temple enclosure.

### ★DAIBUTSU-DEN HALL         BUDDHIST TEMPLE
(大仏殿; Hall of the Great Buddha; 406-1 Zōshi-chō; admission ¥500, joint ticket with Tōdai-ji Museum ¥800; ⊙8am-4.30pm Nov-Feb, to 5pm Mar, 7.30am-5.30pm Apr-Sep, to 5pm Oct) Tōdai-ji's Daibutsu-den is the largest wooden building in the world. Incredibly, the present structure, rebuilt in 1709, is a mere two-thirds of the size of the original. The Daibutsu (Great Buddha) inside is one of the largest bronze figures in the world and was originally cast in 746. The present statue, recast in the Edo period, stands just over 16m high and consists of 437 tonnes of bronze and 130kg of gold.

The Daibutsu is an image of Dainichi Nyorai (also known as Vairocana Buddha), the cosmic Buddha believed to give rise to all worlds and their respective Buddhas. Historians believe that Emperor Shōmu ordered the building of the Buddha as a charm against smallpox, which ravaged Japan in preceding years. Over the centuries the statue took quite a beating from earthquakes and fires, losing its head a couple of

# Nara

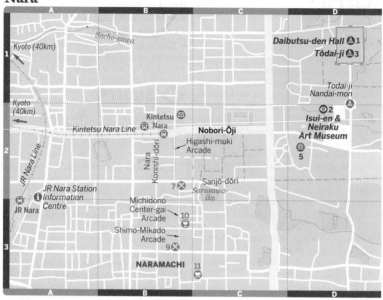

times (note the slight difference in colour between the head and the body).

As you circle the statue towards the back, you'll see a wooden column with a hole through its base. Popular belief maintains that those who can squeeze through the hole, which is exactly the same size as one of the Great Buddha's nostrils, are ensured of enlightenment. There's usually a line of children waiting to give it a try and parents waiting to snap their pictures. A hint for bigger 'kids': try going through with one or both arms above your head – someone on either end to push and pull helps, too.

### NIGATSU-DŌ & SANGATSU-DŌ
BUDDHIST TEMPLE

(二月堂、三月堂; Nigatsu-do free, Sangatsu-do ¥500; ⊘Nigatsu-do 7.30am-6pm Jun-Aug, 8am-5.45pm Apr-May & Sep-Oct, 8am-5.15pm Nov-Mar, Sangatsu-do 8am-4.30pm Nov-Feb, to 5pm Mar & Oct, 7.30am-5.30pm Apr-Sep) These subtemples of Tōdai-ji are uphill from the Daibutsu-den and far less clamorous. Climb a lantern-lined staircase to Nigatsu-dō, a national treasure from 1669 (originally built circa 750). Its verandah with sweeping views across the town (especially at dusk) may remind you of Kiyomizu-dera (p80) in Kyoto. This is where Nara's **Omizutori** Matsuri is held.

A short walk south of Nigatsu-dō is Sangatsu-dō, the oldest building in the Tōdai-ji complex and home to a small collection of fine Nara-period statues.

The halls are an easy walk east (uphill) from the Daibutsu-den. Instead of walking straight up the hill, take a hard left out of the Daibutsu-den exit, follow the enclosure past the pond and turn up the hill. This pathway is one the most scenic walks in Nara.

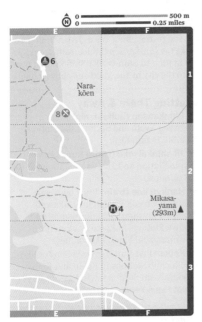

## KASUGA TAISHA    SHINTO SHRINE

(春日大社; 160 Kasugano-chō; ⊙dawn-dusk) **FREE** This sprawling shrine lies at the foot of a hill in a deeply wooded setting with herds of sacred deer awaiting handouts. Its pathways are lined with hundreds of lanterns, with many hundreds more in the shrine itself. They're illuminated in the twice-yearly **Mantōrō** lantern festivals, held in early February and mid-August.

Kasuga Taisha was founded in the 8th century by the Fujiwara family and was completely rebuilt every 20 years, according to Shintō tradition, until the end of the 19th century.

## ★ISUI-EN & NEIRAKU ART MUSEUM    GARDENS

(依水園・寧楽美術館; 74 Suimon-chō; admission museum & garden ¥650; ⊙9.30am-4.30pm, closed Tue except for Apr, May, Oct & Nov) This exquisite, contemplative Meiji-era garden features abundant greenery, ponds and walkways with stepping stones designed for you to observe each one as you walk, to appreciate their individual beauty. For ¥850 you can enjoy a cup of tea on tatami mats overlooking the garden. Admission covers the adjoining Neiraku Art Museum, displaying Chinese and Korean ceramics and bronzes in a quiet setting.

## NARA NATIONAL MUSEUM    MUSEUM

(奈良国立博物館; Nara Kokuritsu Hakubutsu-kan; ☎050-5542-8600; www.narahaku.go.jp; 50 Noborioji-chō; admission ¥520; ⊙9.30am-5pm, closed Mon) This museum is devoted to Buddhist art and is divided into two sections. Built in 1894, the **Nara Buddhist Sculpture Hall & Ritual Bronzes Gallery** contains a fine collection of *butsu-zō* (statues of Buddhas and Bodhisattvas). Buddhist images here are divided into categories, each with detailed English explanations for an excellent introduction to Mahayana Buddhist iconography. The newer **East and West wings**, a short walk away, contain the permanent collections (sculptures, paintings and calligraphy) and special exhibitions.

# ✕ EATING

## KAMEYA    OKONOMIYAKI ¥

(かめや; ☎22-2434; 9 Tarui-chō; mains ¥680-1140; ⊙11am-10pm; 🅿) A giant red lantern marks the entrance to this casual, spirited *okonomiyaki* joint, going strong since the 1960s. There's a seemingly infinite number of combinations for the savoury pancakes; the 'mix okonomiyaki' contains squid, shrimp, pork and scallops. The *yaki-soba* roll has fried noodles inside. No English spoken, but staff make it work.

## KASUGANO    SHOKUDŌ ¥

(春日野; ☎26-3311; 494 Zōshi-chō; mains ¥600-1000; ⊙8.30am-5pm; 🛜🅿) Most restaurants between Tōdai-ji and Kasuga Taisha double as souvenir shops, like this one, at the base of Wakakusa-yama and in business since 1927. Dishes span the basic – curry rice, tempura udon, *oyako-don* (chicken and egg over rice) – to diverse *gozen* set meals (¥1620). Sit in the woodsy annexe cafe rather than the shop (same menu).

## ★KURA    IZAKAYA ¥¥

(蔵; ☎22-8771; 16 Kōmyōin-chō; dishes ¥100-1000; ⊙5-10pm, closed Thu; 🅿) This friendly spot in Naramachi, styled like an old storehouse, is just 16 seats around a counter amid dark wood panels and an old beer sign. Indulge in *mini-katsu* (mini pork cutlets), *yakitori* (grilled chicken skewers) and *oden* (fish cake and veggie hot pot). Order Nara's own Kazenomori sake (¥1200), and everyone will think you're a sake sage.

# 🍷 DRINKING

**NARA IZUMI YŪSAI**      SAKE BAR
(なら泉勇斎; ☑26-6078; 22 Nishi-Terabayashi-chō; ☺11am-8pm, closed Thu) Drop in on this small standing bar in Naramachi for tastings (¥200 to ¥550) of sakes produced in Nara Prefecture (120 varieties from 29 makers, also available for purchase). There is a useful English explanation sheet. Look for the sake barrels and a sign in the window reading 'Nara's Local Sake'.

**TWO MISTLETOES**      CAFE
(トゥーミスルトゥーズ; ☑22-1139; 13 Nakashinyamachi; coffee & tea ¥360-670, lunch set menus ¥1200; ☺noon-5.30pm Wed-Sun) For a break in Naramachi, this modernist charmer feels good inside and out with spare, combed plaster walls, lots of wood, garden seating and friendly, modest staff. Teas and vegetarian home-style lunches incorporating medicinal herbs (plus coffees and cakes) may make you feel good inside and out too.

# Osaka

## Explore

Less than an hour from Kyoto by train, Osaka is the perfect way to experience the energy of a big Japanese city without going all the way to Tokyo. Unlike Kyoto, which contains dozens of discrete tourist sights, Osaka is a city that you experience in its totality. Start with a visit to the castle, Osaka-jō, then head out to Osaka Aquarium (great for kids), and be sure to finish up in Minami (the city's southern hub) to experience the full neon madness that is Osaka after dark.

One day is usually enough to experience Osaka, and trains run late enough to get you back to your lodgings in Kyoto after dinner and a few drinks. Of course, the city is packed with hotels if you are planning a big night out.

## The Best...

➡ **Sight** Osaka-jō (p128)
➡ **Place to Eat** Café Absinthe (p129)
➡ **Place to Drink** Zerro (p130)

## Top Tip

If you're travelling on a Japan Rail Pass, take the *shinkansen* (bullet train) from Kyoto Station to Shin-Osaka Station then head into the city by the Midō-suji subway line.

## Getting There & Away

➡ **Shinkansen (bullet train)** Runs between Kyoto and Shin-Osaka Stations (¥2730, 14 minutes).

➡ **JR shinkaisoku (train)** Runs between Kyoto Station and JR Osaka Station (¥540, 28 minutes).

➡ **Hankyū line (train)** Runs between Hankyū Umeda Station in Osaka and Hankyū Kawaramachi, Karasuma and Ōmiya Stations in Kyoto (*tokkyū* from Kawaramachi ¥390, 44 minutes).

➡ **Keihan line** Runs between Sanjō, Shijō or Shichijō Stations in Kyoto and Keihan Yodoyabashi Station in Osaka (*tokkyū* from Sanjō ¥400, 51 minutes).

## Getting Around

➡ **Train/Subway** The JR loop line (known as the JR *kanjō-sen*) circles the city area. There are also seven subway lines; the most useful is the Midō-suji line, which runs north to south, stopping at Shin-Osaka, Umeda (next to Osaka Station), Shinsaibashi, Namba and Tennō-ji Stations.

## Need to Know

➡ **Area Code** ☑06
➡ **Location** 45km southwest of Kyoto
➡ **Tourist Office** (大阪市ビジターズインフォメーションセンター・梅田; ☑6345-2189; www.osaka-info.jp; 1st fl, North Central Gate, JR Osaka Station; ☺8am-8pm; ℝJR lines to Osaka Station)

# 👁 SIGHTS

**OSAKA-JŌ**      CASTLE
(大阪城, Osaka Castle; www.osakacastle.net; 1-1 Osaka-jō; grounds/castle keep free/¥600, combined with Osaka Museum of History ¥900; ☺9am-5pm, to 7pm Aug; ⑤Chūō or Tanimachi line to Tanimachi 4-chōme, exit 9, ℝJR Osaka Loop line to Osaka-jō-kōen) After unifying Japan in the late 16th century, General Toyotomi Hideyoshi built this castle (1583) as a display of power, using, it's said, the labour of 100,000 workers. Although the present structure is

## HIMEJI

A visit to Himeji (姫路) is a must for any lover of castles or Japanese history. Himeji-jō, the finest castle in all of Japan, towers over this quiet, easily walkable city on the Shinkansen route between Osaka and Okayama/Hiroshima. You can visit it as a day trip from Kyoto, Nara, Osaka or Kōbe, or as a stopover en route to Hiroshima.

If you've got a Japan Rail Pass or are in a hurry, a *shinkansen* (bullet train) is the best way to reach Himeji from Kyoto (Hikari, ¥4930, 55 minutes). Note that you cannot use the Nozomi *shinkansen* if you have a Japan Rail Pass, but you can use the Sakura *shinkansen*, which run fairly frequently between Himeji and Shin-Osaka stations. If you don't have a pass, a *shinkaisoku* (special rapid train) on the JR Tōkaidō line is the best way to reach Himeji from Kyoto (¥2210, 94 minutes).

**Himeji-jō** (姫路城, Himeji Castle; 68 Honmachi; adult/child ¥1000/300; ⊙9am-5pm Sep-May, to 6pm Jun-Aug) is one of only a handful of original castles remaining (most are modern concrete reconstructions). Its nickname Shirasagi-jō (White Egret Castle) comes from its lustrous white plaster exterior and stately form on a hill above the plain. There's a five-storey main keep *(tenshū)* and three smaller keeps, and the entire structure is surrounded by moats and defensive walls punctuated with rectangular, circular and triangular openings for firing guns and shooting arrows.

a 1931 concrete reconstruction (refurbished 1997), it's nonetheless quite a sight, looming dramatically over the surrounding park and moat. Inside is an excellent collection of art, armour, and day-to-day implements related to the castle, Hideyoshi and Osaka. An 8th-floor observation deck has 360-degree views.

### OSAKA MUSEUM OF HISTORY  MUSEUM

(大阪歴史博物館, Osaka Rekishi Hakubutsukan; www.mus-his.city.osaka.jp; 4-1-32 Ōtemae; admission ¥600, combined with Osaka Castle ¥900; ⊙9.30am-5pm, to 8pm Fri, closed Tue; ⑤Tanimachi or Chūō line to Tanimachi-yonchōme, exit 9) Built above the ruins of Naniwa Palace (c 650), visible through the basement floor, this museum houses dramatically illuminated recreations of the old city and life-sized figures in the former palace court. There are interesting early-20th-century displays, and great views of Osaka-jō. English explanations are pretty sparse, so rent an English-language audio guide (¥200).

### ★OSAKA AQUARIUM KAIYŪKAN  AQUARIUM

(海遊館; www.kaiyukan.com; 1-1-10 Kaigan-dōri; adult/child ¥2300/1200; ⊙10am-8pm; ⑤Chūō line to Osakakō, exit 1) Kaiyūkan is easily one of the world's best aquariums. An 800m-plus walkway winds past displays of sea life from around the Pacific 'ring of fire': Antarctic penguins, coral-reef butterflyfish, cute Arctic otters, Monterey Bay seals and unearthly jellyfish. Most impressive is the ginormous central tank, housing a whale shark, manta and thousands of other fish

and rays. There are good English descriptions, but the audioguide (¥500) gives more detail. Expect lots of school groups.

### DŌTOMBORI STREET  STREET

(道頓堀; ⑤Midō-suji line to Namba) Just south and parallel to the canal is this pedestrianised street, where dozens of restaurants and theatres vie for attention with the flashiest of signage: giant 3-D crab, puffer fish, dragon and more.

 **EATING**

### ★CAFÉ ABSINTHE  MEDITERRANEAN ¥¥

(カフェアブサン; ☑6534-6635; www.absinthe-jp.com; 1-2-27 Kitahorie; mains lunch ¥800-1000, dinner ¥800-1600; ⊙3pm-3am, to 5am Sat & Sun, closed Tue; ⑩; ⑤Midō-suji line to Shinsaibashi, exit 7) Friendly and trendy, near the western edge of Ame-Mura, Absinthe serves fantastic cocktails, non-alcoholic drinks and juices and a rare (for Japan) Mediterranean menu (falafel, hummus and babaganoush, plus pastas and pizzas). It's a tad pricey, but you're paying for quality ingredients, stylish surrounds and the laid-back atmosphere. And, yes, it does serve absinthe.

### ★IMAI HONTEN  NOODLES ¥¥

(今井本店; ☑6211-0319; www.d-imai.com; 1-7-22 Dōtombori; dishes from ¥752; ⊙11am-10pm, closed Wed; ⑩; ⑤Midō-suji line to Namba) Step into an oasis of calm amid Dōtombori's chaos to be welcomed by kimono-clad staff

# Osaka (Minami Area)

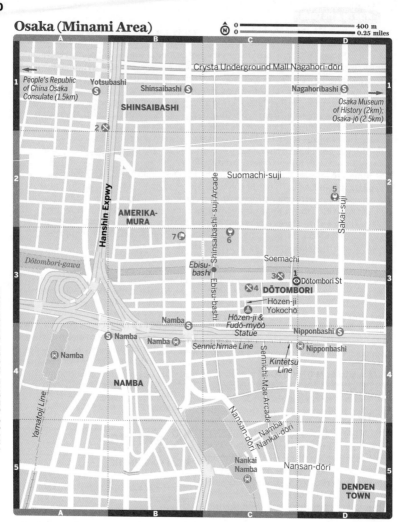

at one of the area's oldest and most revered udon specialists. Try *kitsune udon* – noodles topped with soup-soaked slices of fried tofu. Look for the traditional front, and the willow tree outside.

### ★CHIBŌ

OKONOMIYAKI ¥¥

(千房; ☎6212-2211; www.chibo.com; 1-5-5 Dōtombori; mains ¥1004-1652; ☺11am-1am Mon-Sat, to midnight Sun; 🅿; 🅂Midō-suji line to Namba) A popular place to sample Osaka's signature dish. Try the house special *Dōtombori yaki,* a toothsome treat with pork, beef, squid, shrimp and cheese. Another unique speciality: *tonpei-yaki,* an

omelette wrapped around fried pork. Some tables look out over the Dōtombori canal.

##  DRINKING

### ZERRO

BAR

(ゼロ; 2-3-2 Shinsaibashi-suji; ☺7pm-5am; 🅂Midō-suji line to Namba or Shinsaibashi) Zerro has a good range of drinks and food, energetic bilingual bartenders, and a street-level location ideal for a spot of people-watching. Come early for relaxed drinks and conversation; come late on the weekend for DJs, dancing and a lively crowd.

## Osaka (Minami Area)

CINQUECENTO                                           BAR
(チンクエチェント; 2-1-10 Higashi-Shinsaibashi;
⊙7.30pm-5am Mon-Sat, 8pm-3am Sun; ⑤Midō-
suji line to Namba or Shinsaibashi) The name is
Italian for '500', appropriate since everything at this cosy bar costs ¥500. There's
a hearty selection of food and an extensive
martini menu. It's not far from the corner
of Sakai-suji; look for the 5 in a red circle.

# Miyama-Chō

## Explore

The antidote to the urban centres of Kyoto,
Osaka and Nara is a visit to Miyama-chō, a
collection of rural hamlets in the Kitayama
(Northern Mountains) north of Kurama.
Miyama-chō has two great sights: Ashiu,
a hiker's paradise, and Kita (Kayabuki-no-
Sato), a collection of thatched-roof houses.
En route, you can stop at the temple of
Bujō-ji. While you can reach all three by
public transport, with a car you can hit
them all and even do a quick hike in Ashiu
in one long day.

## The Best...

→ **Sight** Bujō-ji (p131)
→ **Place to Eat** Morishige (p132)
→ **Place to Stay** Matabe (p132)

## Top Tip

Renting a car is easily the best way to explore
this area. Unless there's snow on the ground,
the driving is pleasant and stress free.

## Getting There & Away

→ **Train/Bus** Take a train on the JR
Sagano/San-in line from Kyoto Station to
Hiyoshi Station (¥760, 50 minutes), then
a bus from Hiyoshi to Kita (Kayabuki-no-
Sato; ¥610, 50 minutes). Note that this
bus runs only on Sundays and holidays;
on other days, it's necessary to change
midway at Miyawaki.

→ **Car** The fastest road to Miyama-chō is
Rte 162 (Shūzankaidō), but there is a lovely
but longer (two-hour) option (Rtes 38/477)
via Kurama and over Hanase-tōgei and
Sasari-tōge passes. This route is also good
for getting to Bujō-ji.

→ **Bus & Hiking** You can also get to Bujō-ji
and Ashiu (but not Kita) via Kyoto bus 32
from Demachiyanagi Station. If you're only
going to Bujō-ji, get off at Daihizan-guchi
bus stop (¥930, 95 minutes) and walk 2km
east on the narrow road. If you're going to
Ashiu, continue to Hirogawara (¥1100, 110
minutes) and hike over Sasari-tōgei pass.
From Hirogawara follow the road to the
pass and then take the trail down to Ashiu
(use Shobunsha's Yama-to-Kogen series
*Kitayama* map).

## Need to Know

→ **Area Code** ☑0771
→ **Location** 50km north of Kyoto

# ◎ SIGHTS

BUJŌ-JI                                              TEMPLE
(峰定寺; Hanase-Harachi-cho; admission ¥500,
no children under 12yr; ⊙9am-3.30pm, closed on
rainy/snowy days & Dec-Mar) Bujō-ji is a *shu-
gendo* (mountain asceticism) temple that
is also called 'the Northern Omine', a reference to Mt Omine-san in Nara Prefecture,
which is a centre for Japan's *yamabushi*
(mountain mystics). It's a 430-step climb to
the main hall.

First, you surrender your bags and cameras, and get a special pilgrim's bag and
staff, plus a printout of a mantra to chant as
you climb. Only then can you pass through
the gate and climb to the hall. Just before
the hall, ring the bell, focus your thoughts
and then climb to the verandah to soak up
the views.

It's off rte 38, 2km east of Daihizan-guchi
bus stop.

## UJI

The small city of Uji is rich in Heian-period culture. Its main claims to fame are Byōdō-in and Ujigami-jinja (both Unesco World Heritage sites) and tea cultivation. The Uji-bashi Bridge, originally all wood and the oldest of its kind in Japan (it is now constructed of concrete and wood), has been the scene of many bitter clashes in previous centuries, although traffic jams seem to predominate nowadays.

Uji can be easily reached by rail from Kyoto on the Keihan Uji line (¥320, 30 minutes) from Sanjō Station (change at Chūshojima) or the JR Nara line (¥230, 20 minutes) from Kyoto Station.

**Byōdō-in** (平等院; ☑0774-21-2861; 116 Uji-renge, Uji-shi; admission ¥600 ; ⊘8.30am-5.15pm; ⊠JR Nara line or Keihan line to Uji) is the star attraction in Uji. It's home to one of the loveliest Buddhist structures in Japan: the Hōō-dō hall, which is depicted on the back of the Japanese ¥10 coin. Perched overlooked a serene reflecting pond, this recently refurbished hall is a stunning sight. Paired with a stroll along the banks of the nearby Uji-gawa, this temple makes a good half-day trip out of Kyoto city.

### ASHIU                                                        VILLAGE

(芦生) This quiet and *tiny* village sits on the eastern edge of Miyama-chō, off rte 38 (take the turning after descending from Sasari-tōge pass). The main attraction is a 4200-hectare virgin forest to the east of the village. Administered by Kyoto University's Department of Agriculture, this is about the only remaining virgin forest in Kansai. Hiking trails enter the forest from above the stone hut at Sarari-tōge pass and from Ashiu, at the bottom of the pass (note that you should register at the office in Ashiu before entering the forest).

The most basic walk follows old train tracks along the undammed Yura-gawa river. More-involved hikes continue beyond the tracks up the river or up side valleys. If you intend to do serious hiking here, grab a copy of Shobunsha's Yama-to-Kogen *Kitayama* map at a Kyoto bookshop.

### KITA (KAYABUKI-NO-SATO)                    VILLAGE

(北村) Along rte 38, about 20 minutes' drive west of Ashiu, is Miyama-chō's star attraction: Kitamura (North Village), a hamlet with a cluster of some 50 thatched-roof farmhouses. In 1994 the village was designated a national preservation site, and since then the local government has been generously subsidising the exorbitant cost of rethatching the roofs (at an average cost of ¥6 million – around US$50,000). It's sometimes known as Kayabuki-no-Sato (the Village of Thatched-Roof Houses; かやぶきの里) and is said to contain the thickest concentration of thatched-roof houses in Japan.

Sights worth seeing include the **Minzoku Shiryokan** (Folk Museum) and the **Chisana Aibijutsukan** (Little Indigo Museum).

## ✖ EATING

### MORISHIGE                                              NOODLES ¥

(もりしげ; ☑75-1086; Miyama-chō, Uchikubo, Taninoshimo 15; noodle dishes from ¥750) A thatched-roof place that serves simple but tasty noodle dishes and *nabe* dishes.

### YURURI                                                  JAPANESE ¥¥

(厨房 ゆるり; ☑76-0741; Miyama-chō, Morisato; sets ¥3240) An elegant restaurant occupying a fine thatched-roof house. It's about half an hour north of the centre of Miyama-chō by car. Reservations are required.

## 🛏 SLEEPING

### MIYAMA HEIMAT YOUTH HOSTEL      HOSTEL ¥

(美山ハイマートユースホステル; ☑fax 75-0997; Miyama-chō, Obuchi, Nakasai 57; members/nonmembers ¥3456/4104, breakfast/dinner ¥702/1242-4644) This youth hostel is in a *kayabukiya* (thatched-roof house). It's a great place to stay while exploring Miyama-chō.

### ASIU YAMA-NO-IE                        GUESTHOUSE ¥¥

(芦生山の家; ☑77-0290; Nantan-shi, Miyama-chō, Ashiu; per person incl 2 meals ¥7560) This simple guesthouse at the entrance to the Kyoto University Research Forest is a great place to stay for hikers entering the forest. Have a Japanese speaker call to reserve.

### MATABE                                                MINSHUKU ¥¥

(またべ; ☑77-0258; Nantan-shi, Miyama-chō, Kita; per person incl 2 meals from ¥8700) For a simple *minshuku* (family-run inn), this is a great choice. Have a Japanese speaker call to reserve.

# Sleeping

*When it comes to accommodation, you're spoiled for choice in Kyoto. You can choose from traditional ryokan (Japanese-style inns), luxury hotels, 'business hotels', guesthouses, youth hostels and even capsule hotels. And this being a tourist city, you'll find that most places are perfectly at home with foreign guests.*

### Ryokan

Ryokan are traditional Japanese inns, with tatami mats on the floor and futons instead of beds. The best places serve sublime Japanese cuisine, have attentive service and beautiful rooms, often with garden views. Note that many places that call themselves ryokan are really just hotels with Japanese-style rooms. That isn't to say they aren't comfortable: they are often friendly and relaxing and may cost less than hotels. Also note that ryokan may not have private bathrooms, and at some places even toilets may be shared; enquire when you make a reservation. Finally, note that some simpler ryokan may not accept credit cards.

### Business Hotels

In Japan, 'business hotels' are budget or midrange hotels with cramped but efficient rooms and small 'unit baths' (en suite tub/shower/toilet). They usually cost ¥6000 to ¥12,000 per room and most accept credit cards. There is no room service but some of the nicer places have large shared bathrooms and saunas on their premises. The front desk staff usually speak some English. These are often your best bet in terms of price versus performance, and there is none of the formality and confusion that you might encounter at a ryokan.

### Luxury Hotels

There are several four- and five-star luxury hotels in Kyoto, including some of the top international brands. Kyoto's luxury hotels are similar to their counterparts elsewhere in the world, but some have Japanese decorative touches and attentive Japanese service.

### Youth Hostels

Kyoto's youth hostels are much like youth hostels that you'll find elsewhere in the world: not much atmosphere and a mixture of dorms and private rooms. On the plus side, Kyoto's youth hostels are accustomed to foreigners and are cleaner than many of their overseas counterparts. A room in a typical youth hostel costs about ¥3200; cash only. Membership is not necessary.

### Guesthouses

Guesthouses are similar to youth hostels, without the regimented atmosphere and with various perks thrown in, like on-site restaurants, bars etc. Guesthouses usually have both dorms, which average ¥2500 per person, and a variety of private rooms, which average ¥3500 per person.

### Capsule Hotels

Unlike most capsule hotels, which serve as refuges for sozzled salarymen who've missed the last train home, Kyoto's capsule hotels are geared to travellers, including foreign travellers. You probably already know what a capsule hotel is: a simple hotel where you sleep in a small 'capsule' and use shared bathing facilities. They're fun, but be prepared for noise.

## NEED TO KNOW

### Price Ranges

We've used the following price codes for a double room with private bathroom in high season. Ryokan often charge per person but this is noted as necessary.

| ¥ | under ¥6000 |
|---|---|
| ¥¥ | ¥6000 to ¥15,000 |
| ¥¥¥ | over ¥15,000 |

### Reservations

Making phone reservations in English is usually possible, providing you speak clearly and simply.

### Websites

**Lonely Planet** (lonely planet.com/hotels) Books accommodation.

**Japan Youth Hostels** (www.jyh.or.jp/english) Includes Kyoto's only hostel and others all across Japan.

### High & Low Seasons

Kyoto's accommodation can be booked out in the late-March/early-April cherry-blossom season and the November autumn-foliage season. It can also be hard to find rooms during Golden Week (29 April to 5 May) and O-Bon (mid-August).

### Tipping

Tipping is not usually done in Japan.

### Checking In & Out

Check-in is usually from 2pm or 3pm (sometimes later at ryokan) and is fairly rigid. However, almost all places will store your luggage for you. Check-out is generally 10am or 11am.

## Lonely Planet's Top Choices

**Hyatt Regency Kyoto** (p140) The best hotel in town – a polished operation and lovely facility.

**Tawaraya** (p138) A sublime sanctuary in the heart of the city.

**Kyoto Hotel Ōkura** (p138) Excellent value and a perfect downtown location.

## Best by Budget

### ¥

**Tour Club** (p136) Well-run and welcoming guesthouse.

**Budget Inn** (p136) A comfy little inn with everything you need.

**K's House Kyoto** (p136) An international-style backpackers favourite.

### ¥¥

**Ibis Styles Kyoto Station** (p136) Excellent-value business hotel right next to Kyoto Station.

**Hotel Sunroute Kyoto** (p139) Incredible value and a great location near Downtown Kyoto.

**Citadines Karasuma-Gojō Kyoto** (p139) Service-apartment-style hotel that manages to get it all right.

### ¥¥¥

**Tawaraya** (p138) One of the finest ryokan in Japan.

**Ritz-Carlton Kyoto** (p139) True luxury, incredible location and great views.

**Hoshinoya Kyoto** (p142) Elegant villa-style accommodation surrounded by nature in Arashiyama – accessed by private boat!

## Best Ryokan

**Tawaraya** (p138) A stay here is sure to be the memory of a lifetime.

**Hiiragiya Ryokan** (p138) A true Kyoto classic.

**Seikōrō** (p141) A lovely ryokan that combines great value and elegant rooms.

## Best Hotels

**Hyatt Regency Kyoto** (p140) The rooms, service, restaurants and amenities are all first-rate here.

**Kyoto Hotel Ōkura** (p138) An extremely comfortable and well-located hotel at a great price.

**Hotel Granvia Kyoto** (p137) Real comfort located literally on top of Kyoto Station.

## Best for Families

**Budget Inn** (p136) Perfect self-contained rooms with everything a family would need.

**Sakara Kyoto** (p140) Excellent apartment-style accommodations that are designed with families in mind.

**Westin Miyako Kyoto** (p141) An expansive hotel with all the grounds and facilities to keep everyone in the family occupied and happy.

## Best Value for Money

**Kyoto Hotel Ōkura** (p138) A first-class hotel with rates that are usually well below its nearest competitors.

**Palace Side Hotel** (p139) Great traveller's hotel with super-cheap rates.

**Tōyoko Inn Kyoto Gojō Karasuma** (p139) Business hotel at guesthouse rates.

# Where to Stay in Kyoto

| NEIGHBOURHOOD | FOR | AGAINST |
|---|---|---|
| **Kyoto Station Area** | Close to transport; plenty of dining and shopping options; good location if you intend to explore the rest of Kansai | Far from most sightseeing districts; not particularly attractive |
| **Downtown Kyoto** | In the heart of everything – shops, restaurants and nightlife; some nice strolls in the area (eg Ponto-chō) | Can feel a little busy; fairly high ambient noise on street level; crowded pavements and the odd rowdy (but harmless) reveller on the street on weekend evenings |
| **Central Kyoto** | Most parts of Central Kyoto are relatively quiet | Depending on location, can be far from sights and rather inconvenient |
| **Southern Higashiyama** | In the heart of the city's main sightseeing district; beautiful walks in every direction, including fantastic evening strolls (eg Gion/Shimbashi, Ninen-zaka) | Fewer dining options than downtown; crowded in the cherry-blossom season |
| **Nothern Higashiyama** | Lots of sights nearby; peaceful and green; nice day and evening strolls | Few negatives, unless you demand to be right in the heart of the shopping and dining district |
| **Northwest Kyoto** | Peaceful and green with some interesting sights | Inconvenient and not well served by trains or subways; few dining or shopping options |
| **Arashiyama & Sagano** | One of the main sightseeing districts; magical evening strolls along the river and among the bamboo grove | On the far west side of town, so all sights except those nearby require a long trek; few good dining or shopping options |

**SLEEPING**

## WHERE TO STAY IF KYOTO IS FULLY BOOKED

Accommodation in Kyoto can get fully booked in the spring high season (late March to late April) and autumn high season (mid-October to the end of November). If you want to visit during these times and cannot find accommodation in Kyoto, don't give up. It's perfectly possible to stay in a nearby city and 'commute' into Kyoto to do your sightseeing, especially if you're armed with a Japan Rail Pass, which allows unlimited travel on Japan's fast and comfortable *shinkansen* (bullet trains). Here are some nearby cities where you may be able to find accommodation if Kyoto is full:

**Osaka** (28 minutes by JR express train, 13 minutes by *shinkansen*) Osaka is a great Plan B if Kyoto is full. Osaka is an attraction in its own right (see p128), with plenty of good hotels, restaurants, bars and shops.

**Nara** (44 minutes by JR express train, 35 minutes by Kintetsu express train) Nara tends to book out at the same times as Kyoto, but it's worth a look. It would be a pleasant and relaxing place to stay (see p 125).

**Ōtsu** (nine minutes by JR express train) Ōtsu is a small city just over the hill from Kyoto (you could even go there by taxi if you stayed out in Kyoto until after the trains stopped). There's not too much to do here, but if you're just sleeping here, it would be fine.

**Nagoya** (36 minutes by *shinkansen*) It's a bit of a hike from Kyoto, but if you've got a Japan Rail Pass, it would be possible to stay here while exploring Kyoto. Nagoya is a big city, so there are plenty of hotels, restaurants, bars and shops.

## 🛏 Kyoto Station Area

### ★ CAPSULE RYOKAN KYOTO
CAPSULE HOTEL ¥

Map p212 (カプセル旅館京都; ☎344-1510; www.capsule-ryokan-kyoto.com; 204 Tsuchihashi-chō, Shimogyō-ku; capsule ¥3500, tw per person from ¥3990; @🛜; 🚉Kyoto Station) This unique new accommodation offers ryokan-style capsules (meaning tatami mats inside the capsules), as well as comfortable, cleverly designed private rooms. Each capsule has its own TV and cable internet access point, while the private rooms have all the amenities you might need. Free internet, wi-fi and other amenities are available in the comfortable lounge.

It's near the southeast corner of the Horikawa–Shichijo intersection.

### BUDGET INN
GUESTHOUSE ¥

Map p212 (バジェットイン; ☎344-1510; www.budgetinnjp.com; 295 Aburanokōji-chō, Aburanokōji, Shichijō-sagaru, Shimogyō-ku; tr/q/5-person r per person ¥3660/3245/2996; 😊@🛜; 🚉Kyoto Station) This well-run guesthouse is an excellent choice in this price bracket. It has eight Japanese-style private rooms, all of which are clean and well maintained. All rooms have private bathroom and toilet, and can accommodate up to five people, making it good for families. The staff is very helpful and friendly.

From Kyoto Station, walk west on Shiokōji-dōri and turn north one street before Horikawa and look for the English-language sign out the front.

### ★ TOUR CLUB
GUESTHOUSE ¥

Map p212 (ツアークラブ; ☎0353-6968; www.kyotojp.com; 362 Momiji-chō, Higashinakasuji, Shōmen-sagaru, Shimogyō-ku; d/tw/tr per person ¥3490/3885/2960; 😊@🛜; 🚉Kyoto Station) This clean, well-maintained guesthouse remains a favourite of foreign visitors to Kyoto. Facilities include internet access, a small Zen garden, laundry, wi-fi, and free tea and coffee. Most private rooms have a private bathroom and toilet, and there is a spacious quad room for families. This is probably the best choice in this price bracket.

From Kyoto Station turn north off Shichijō-dōri two blocks before Horikawa (at the faux-Greco building) and keep an eye out for the English sign.

### RYOKAN SHIMIZU
RYOKAN ¥

Map p212 (京の宿しみず; ☎371-5538; www.kyoto-shimizu.net; 644 Kagiya-chō, Shichijō-dōri, Wakamiya-agaru, Shimogyō-ku; r per person from ¥5250, Sat & nights before holidays an additional ¥1080; 😊@; 🚉Kyoto Station) A short walk north of Kyoto Station's Karasuma central gate, this friendly ryokan has a loyal following of foreign guests, and for good reason: it's clean, well run and fun. Rooms are standard ryokan style with one difference: all have private bathrooms and toilets. Bicycle rental is available.

### K'S HOUSE KYOTO
GUESTHOUSE ¥

Map p212 (ケイズハウス京都; ☎342-2444; www.kshouse.jp; 418 Naya-chō, Dotemachi-dōri, Shichijō-agaru, Shimogyō-ku; dm from ¥2400; s/d/tw per person from ¥3800/3100/3100; 😊@🛜; 🚉Kyoto Station) K's House is a large 'New Zealand–style' guesthouse that offers both private and dorm rooms. The rooms are simple but adequate and there are spacious common areas. The rooftop terrace, patio and attached bar-restaurant make this a very sociable spot and a good place to meet other travellers and share information.

### MATSUBAYA RYOKAN
RYOKAN ¥

Map p212 (松葉家旅館; ☎075-351-3727; www.matsubayainn.com; Kamijuzūyachō-dōri, Higashinotōin nishi-iru, Shimogyō-ku; r per person from ¥4400; @🛜; 🚉Kyoto Station) A short walk from Kyoto Station, this newly renovated ryokan has clean, well-kept rooms and a management that is used to foreign guests. Some rooms on the 1st floor look out on small gardens. Western (¥500 to ¥900) or Japanese breakfast (¥1000) is available.

Matsubaya also has several serviced apartments in its adjoining Bamboo House section – great for those planning a longer stay in the city.

### ★ IBIS STYLES KYOTO STATION
HOTEL ¥¥

Map p212 (イビススタイルズ 京都ステーション; ☎693-8444; www.ibis.com; 47 Higashikujō-Kamitonoda-chō, Minami-ku; r from ¥6500-10,000; 🚉Kyoto Station) Just outside the south entrance to Kyoto Station, this great new business hotel offers excellent value. The rooms are small but packed with all the features you need. The staff and management are extremely efficient. A great option for the price.

★**DORMY INN**
**PREMIUM KYOTO EKIMAE**　　　HOTEL ¥¥
Map p212　（ドーミーインPREMIUM京都駅前;
⏀371-5489;　www.hotespa.net/hotels/kyoto;
Higashishiokōji-chō 558-8, Shimogyō-ku; tw/d
from ¥12,500/11,890; @; ⏀ Kyoto Station) Almost directly across the street from Kyoto
Station, this efficient new hotel is a great
choice. Rooms are clean and well maintained and the on-site spa bath is a nice plus.

**KYŌMACHIYA RYOKAN**
**SAKURA**　　　BUSINESS HOTEL ¥¥
Map p212　（京町家旅館さくら;　⏀343-3500;
www.kyoto-ryokan-sakura.com;　Butsuguya-chō
228, Aburanokōji, Hanayachō-sagaru, Shimogyō-
ku; tw from ¥12,000; @; ⏀Kyoto Station) This
new ryokan, a relatively short walk from
Kyoto Station, has clean rooms as well as a
variety of traveller-friendly extras. Staff are
at home with foreign travellers and English
is spoken. It's a bit over to the west side of
town, but a bicycle or public transport will
get you to the sightseeing spots fairly quickly. For longer stays, ask about the serviced
apartment next door.

★**HOTEL GRANVIA KYOTO**　　　HOTEL ¥¥¥
Map p212　（ホテルグランヴィア京都;　⏀344-
8888;　www.granviakyoto.com;　Karasuma-
dōri, Shiokōji-sagaru, Shimogyō-ku; tw/d from
¥16,000/21,000;　 @ ;　⏀Kyoto Station)
Imagine being able to step out of bed and
straight into the *shinkansen* (bullet train).
This is almost possible when you stay at
the Hotel Granvia, which is located directly
above Kyoto Station. The rooms are clean,
spacious and elegant, with deep bathtubs.
This is a very professional operation with
good on-site restaurants, some of which
have views over the city.

🛏 **Downtown Kyoto**

**HOTEL UNIZO**　　　HOTEL ¥¥
Map p208　（ホテルユニゾ京都;　⏀241-3351;
www.hotelunizo.com/eng/kyoto;　Kawaramachi-
dōri, Sanjō-sagaru, Nakagyō-ku; s/d/tw from
¥10,000/17,000/19,000;　 @ ;　🚌Kyoto City
bus 5 to Kawaramachi-Sanjō, Ⓢ Tōzai line to Kyoto-Shiyakusho-mae) In the middle of Kyoto's
nightlife, shopping and dining district –
you can walk to hundreds of restaurants
and shops within five minutes – is this
standard-issue business hotel, with tiny but
adequate rooms and unit bathrooms. Noth-

ing special, but it's clean, well run and used
to foreign guests. Front rooms can be noisy,
so see if you can get something on an upper
floor or at the back.

**HOTEL VISTA PREMIO KYOTO**　　　HOTEL ¥¥
Map　p208　（ホテルビスタプレミオ京都;
⏀256-5888;　www.hotel-vista.jp;　Matsugaechō 457, Kawaramachi-dōri, Rokkaku nishi-iru,
Nakagyō-ku; s/tw from ¥6800/11,000; @ ;
Ⓢ Tōzai line to Kyoto-Shiyakusho-mae) Newly refurbished, and tucked into a lane between
two of Kyoto's main downtown shopping
streets, this is a smart, clean hotel. There
are some nice Japanese design touches in
the rooms, which are compact but adequate.
It's good value for the money and a super-
convenient location.

**HOTEL MONTEREY KYOTO**　　　HOTEL ¥¥
Map p208　（ホテルモントレ京都;　⏀251-7111;
www.hotelmonterey.co.jp/en/htl/kyoto; Manjūya-
chō 604, Karasuma-dōri, Sanjō-sagaru, Nakagyō-
ku; s/tw from ¥6500/12,000; @; Ⓢ Karasuma
or Tōzai lines to Karasuma-Oike) Within a few
minutes' walk of the Karasuma-Oike subway station (three stops north of Kyoto Station), this relatively new upmarket business
hotel is a great place to stay if you want to
be downtown: it's on the western edge of
the main shopping and dining district.

**MITSUI GARDEN HOTEL**
**KYOTO SANJŌ**　　　HOTEL ¥¥
Map p208　（三井ガーデンホテル　　京都三
条;　⏀256-3331;　www.gardenhotels.co.jp/
eng/kyoto-sanjo;　80 Mikura-chō, Sanjō-dōri,
Karasuma nishi-iru, Nakagyō-ku; s/d/tw from
¥6000/8700/9600; @; Ⓢ Tōzai or Karasuma
lines to Karasuma-Oike) Just west of the downtown dining and shopping district, this is
a clean and efficient hotel that offers good
value for the price and reasonably comfortable rooms.

**ROYAL PARK HOTEL THE KYOTO**　　　HOTEL ¥¥
Map p208　（ロイヤルパークホテル　ザ　京
都;　⏀241-1111;　www.rph-the.co.jp;　Sanjō-
dōri, Kawaramachi higashi-iru, Nakagyō-ku;
s/d from ¥10,000/12,500; 🕾; Ⓢ Tōzai line to
Kyoto-Shiyakusho-mae, 🚉Keihan line to Sanjō)
Located on Sanjō-dōri, a stone's throw from
the river and with tons of shops and restaurants within easy walking distance. The
hotel has a modern, chic feel, and rooms
are slightly larger than at standard business hotels. The French bakery downstairs
makes breakfast a breeze.

## AIRPORT HOTELS

If you find yourself in need of a bed close to your flight from Itami or Kansai airports, there are a couple of decent options:

**Green Rich Hotel Osaka Airport** (☎06-6842-1100; www.gr-osaka.com; Kūkō 1-9-6, Ikeda-shi, Osaka-fu; s/d from ¥7900/11,000; @) Right across from Osaka airport and within walking distance (10 minutes from the south terminal if you had to), this friendly little hotel is the best deal near Itami. Rooms are small but sufficient for a night before an early departure. The helpful folks at the information counter can also arrange for the hotel's shuttle bus to come and pick you up.

**Hotel Nikkō Kansai Airport** (ホテル日航関西空港; ☎072-455-1111; www.nikkokix.com; Senshū Kūkō Kita 1, Izumisano-shi, Osaka-fu; s/tw/d from ¥9500/11,000/14,500 ; @ 🛱 🖭; 🚉 JR Haruka Airport Express to Kansai Airport) This excellent hotel is the only accommodation at Kansai airport, connected to the main terminal building by a pedestrian bridge (you can even bring your luggage trolleys right to your room). Rooms are in good condition, spacious and comfortable enough for brief stays. Online reservations through hotel booking sites can result in much lower rates.

### SUPER HOTEL KYOTO SHIJŌ-KAWARAMACHI
HOTEL ¥¥

Map p208 (スーパーホテル京都・四条河原町; ☎255-9000; www.superhoteljapan.com/en/s-hotels/shijyogawara; Nakano-chō 538-1, Shinkyōgoku-dōri, Shijō-agaru, Nakagyō-ku; s/tw from ¥7180/9240; @; 🚉Hankyū line to Kawaramachi) Right in the middle of the main shopping district, a short walk from the Shinkyōgoku shopping arcade and Nishiki Market, this new business hotel is great for those who want a basic place to sleep and a convenient location. The free breakfast and large communal bathroom (rooms also have private bathrooms) are nice touches.

### ★TAWARAYA
RYOKAN ¥¥¥

Map p208 (俵屋; ☎211-5566; 278 Nakahakusan-chō, Fuyachō, Oike-sagaru, Nakagyō-ku; r per person incl 2 meals ¥55,900-74,500; 🌣@; 🚇Tōzai line to Kyoto-Shiyakusho-mae, exit 8) Tawaraya has been operating for more than three centuries and is one of the finest places to stay in the world. From the decorations to the service to the food, everything is simply the best available. It's a very intimate, warm and personal place that has many loyal guests. It's centrally located within easy walk of two subway stations and plenty of good restaurants.

### KYOTO HOTEL ŌKURA
HOTEL ¥¥¥

Map p208 (京都ホテルオークラ; ☎211-5111; http://okura.kyotohotel.co.jp; 537-4 Ichinofunairi-chō, Kawaramachi-dōri, Oike, Nakagyō-ku; s/d/tw from ¥13,600/23,000/18,400; 🌣@; 🚇Tōzai line to Kyoto-Shiyakusho-mae, exit 3) This towering hotel in the centre of town commands an impressive view of the Higashiyama mountains. Rooms are clean and spacious and many have great views, especially the excellent corner suites. You can access the Kyoto subway system directly from the hotel, which is convenient on rainy days or if you have luggage. You can often find great online rates for the Ōkura and it's one of the better value places in this price bracket.

### ★HIIRAGIYA RYOKAN
RYOKAN ¥¥¥

Map p208 (柊屋; ☎221-1136; www.hiiragiya.co.jp; Nakahakusan-chō, Fuyachō, Aneyakōji-agaru, Nakagyō-ku; r per person incl 2 meals ¥34,560-86,400; 🌣@; 🚇Tōzai line to Kyoto-Shiyakusho-mae, exit 8) This elegant ryokan has long been favoured by celebrities from around the world. Facilities and services are excellent and the location is hard to beat. Ask for one of the newly redecorated rooms if you prefer a polished sheen; alternatively, request an older room if you fancy some 'old Japan' *wabi-sabi* (imperfect beauty).

### YOSHIKAWA
RYOKAN ¥¥¥

Map p208 (吉川; ☎221-5544; www.kyoto-yoshikawa.co.jp; 135 Matsushita-chō, Tominokōji, Oike-sagaru, Nakagyō-ku; low/high season r per person incl 2 meals from ¥32,400/¥48,600; @; 🚇Tōzai or Karasuma lines to Karasuma-Oike) Located in the heart of downtown, within easy walking distance of two subway stations and the entire dining and nightlife district, this superb traditional ryokan has beautiful rooms and a stunning garden. The ryokan is famous for its tempura and its meals are of a high standard. All rooms have private bathrooms and toilets.

**RITZ-CARLTON KYOTO** HOTEL ¥¥¥

Map p208 (ザ・リッツ・カールトン京都; ☎746-5555; www.ritzcarlton.com/en/Kyoto; 543 Hokoden-chō, Nijō-Ōhashi-hotori, Nakagyō-ku; r ¥65,000-200,000; @📶; Ⓢ Tōzai line to Kyoto-Shiyakusho-mae, 🚊Keihan line to Sanjō or Jingū-Marutamachi) The brand-new Ritz-Carlton is an oasis of luxury that commands perhaps the finest views of any hotel in the city – it's on the banks of the Kamo-gawa and huge windows in the east-facing rooms take in the whole expanse of the Higashiyama mountains. The rooms are superbly designed and supremely comfortable, with plenty of Japanese touches. Common areas are elegant and the on-site restaurants and bars are excellent. Finally, there are fine spa, gym and pool facilities.

## Central Kyoto

★**HOTEL SUNROUTE KYOTO** HOTEL ¥¥

(ホテルサンルート京都; ☎371-3711; www.sunroute.jp; 406 Nanba-chō, Kawaramachi-dōri, Matsubara-sagaru, Shimogyō-ku; r from ¥6300-10,000; @📶; 🚊Hankyū line to Kawaramachi) Within easy walking distance of downtown, this brand-new hotel is a superb choice in this price bracket. As you'd expect, rooms aren't large, but they have everything you need. It's well run and comfortable with foreign travellers. In-room internet is LAN cable only, but there's free wi-fi in the 2nd-floor lobby.

**RYOKAN RAKUCHŌ** RYOKAN ¥¥

Map p211 (洛頂旅館; ☎721-2174; 67 Higashi-hangi-chō, Shimogamo, Sakyō-ku; s/tw/tr ¥5300/9240/12,600; 🚭@📶; 🚌Kyoto City bus 205 to Furitsudaigaku-mae, Ⓢ Karasuma line to Kitaōji) There is a lot to appreciate about this fine foreigner-friendly ryokan in the northern part of town: there is a nice little garden; it's entirely nonsmoking; and the rooms are clean and simple. Meals aren't served, but staff can provide you with a good map of local eateries. The downside is the somewhat out-of-the-way location.

**PALACE SIDE HOTEL** HOTEL ¥¥

Map p211 (ザ・パレスサイドホテル; ☎415-8887; www.palacesidehotel.co.jp; Okakuen-chō, Karasuma-dōri, Shimotachiuri-agaru, Kamigyō-ku; s/tw/d from ¥6300/10,200/10,200; 🚭@; Ⓢ Karasuma line to Marutamachi) Overlooking the Kyoto Imperial Palace Park, this great-value hotel has a lot going for it – friendly English-speaking staff, great service, washing machines, an on-site restaurant, well-maintained rooms and free internet terminals. Rooms are small but serviceable.

**TŌYOKO INN KYOTO GOJŌ KARASUMA** HOTEL ¥¥

(東横INN京都五条烏丸; ☎344-1045; www.toyoko-inn.com; Gojō Karasuma-chō 393, Karasuma-dōri, Matsubara-sagaru, Shimogyō-ku; s/tw incl breakfast from ¥6804/10,044; @; Ⓢ Karasuama line to Gojō) Those familiar with the Tōyoko Inn chain know that this hotel brand specialises in simple, clean, fully equipped but small rooms at the lowest price possible. There are interesting extras: free breakfast, free telephone calls inside Japan, and reduced rates on rental cars. Staff will even lend you a laptop if you need to check your email. It's a little south of the city centre, but easily accessed by subway from Kyoto Station.

**CITADINES KARASUMA-GOJŌ KYOTO** HOTEL ¥¥¥

(シタディーン京都 烏丸五条; ☎352-8900; www.citadines.jp; Matsuya-chō 432, Gojō-dōri, Karasuma higashi-iru, Shimogyō-ku; tw/d from ¥28,600/28,600; @; Ⓢ Karasuma line to Gojō) On Gojō-dōri, a bit south of the main downtown district, but within easy walking distance of the Karasuma subway line (as well as the Keihan line), this serviced apartment–hotel is a welcome addition to the Kyoto accommodation scene. The kitchens allow you to do your own cooking and other touches make you feel right at home.

## Southern Higashiyama

**GOJŌ GUEST HOUSE** GUESTHOUSE ¥

Map p214 (五条ゲストハウス; ☎525-2299; www.gojo-guest-house.com; Gojōbashi higashi 3-396-2, Higashiyama-ku; dm/s/tw ¥2600/¥3500/6600; @; 🚊Keihan line to Kiyomizu-Gojō) This is a fine guesthouse in an old wooden Japanese house, which makes the place feel more like a ryokan. It's a relaxed and friendly place at home with foreign guests. The staff speak good English and can help with travel advice. Best of all: it has *gaijin* (foreigner)-sized futons!

**JAM HOSTEL KYOTO GION** GUESTHOUSE ¥

Map p214 (JAM ジャムホステル京都祇園; ☎201-3374; www.jamhostel.com; 170 Tokiwa-chō, Higashiyama-ku; dm ¥2000-4000;

## STAYING IN A RYOKAN

Due to language difficulties and unfamiliarity, staying in a ryokan is not as straightforward as staying in a Western-style hotel. However, with a little education it can be a breeze, even if you don't speak a word of Japanese. Here's the basic drill.

When you arrive, leave your shoes in the *genkan* (entry area/foyer) and step up into the reception area. Here, you'll be asked to sign in. You'll then be shown around the place and to your room, where you will be served a cup of tea. You'll note there is no bedding to be seen in your room – your futons are in the closets and will be laid out later. Leave your luggage anywhere except the *tokonoma* (sacred alcove) that will usually contain some flowers or a hanging scroll. If it's early enough, go out to do some sightseeing.

When you return, you'll change into your *yukata* (lightweight Japanese robe) and be served dinner in your room or in a dining room. After dinner, it's time for a bath. If it's a big place, you can generally bathe anytime in the evening until around 11pm. If it's a small place, you'll be given a time slot. While you're in the bath, some mysterious elves will lay out your futon so that it will be waiting for you when you return from the bath.

In the morning, you'll be served a Japanese-style breakfast (some places these days serve a simple Western-style breakfast for those who can't stomach rice and fish in the morning). You pay at check-out, which is usually around 11am.

Keihan line to Gion Shijō) This new guesthouse boasts a convenient location on the edge of Gion and a sake bar downstairs that is a convivial place for guests to mix with local regulars. There are simple but clean dorm rooms and shared bathing facilities.

### RYOKAN UEMURA RYOKAN ¥¥
Map p214 (旅館うえむら; fax 561-0377; Ishibe-kōji, Shimogawara, Higashiyama-ku; r incl breakfast per person ¥10,000; ☻; Kyoto City bus 206 to Higashiyama-Yasui) This beautiful little ryokan is at ease with foreign guests. It's on a quaint, quiet cobblestone alley, just down the hill from some of Kyoto's most important sights. The owner prefers bookings and cancellations by fax. Book well in advance, as there are only three rooms. There's a 10pm curfew.

### GION APARTMENTS APARTMENT ¥¥
Map p214 (ザギオンアパートメンツ; www.the gionapartments.com; Yamatooji-dōri, Gōjo-agaru, Higashiyama-ku; apt from ¥12,000; ☎; Keihan line to Kiyomizu-Gōjo) This is a collection of several well-maintained apartments on the south end of Gion. Each of the apartments has a kitchenette, laundry facilities and private shower/bath. The apartments are within walking distance of Gion, Downtown Kyoto and the Southern Higashiyama tourist district.

### KYOTO YOSHIMIZU BUSINESS HOTEL ¥¥
Map p214 (京都吉水; ☑551-3995; www.yoshimi zu.com; Maruyama-kōen, Bentendō ue, Higashi-

yama-ku; r per person incl breakfast from ¥5832; ☎; Kyoto City bus 206 to Gion) This ryokan, perched at the base of the Higashiyama mountains at the top of Maruyama-kōen, is truly special. It's surrounded by greenery and it's like staying in the countryside (but only 15 minutes' walk to Gion). There is one room with Western-style beds for those uncomfortable sleeping on futons. A few rooms look out over soothing maple leaves or bamboo groves.

The only drawback is that some rooms are divided by thin walls or doors, so you can hear your neighbours talk if they are not considerate.

### SAKARA KYOTO INN ¥¥¥
Map p214 (桜香楽; www.sakarakyoto.com; 541-2 Furukawa-chō, Higashiyama-ku; r ¥11,000-25,000; ☎☻; Tōzai line to Higashiyama) This modern Japanese-style inn is conveniently located in a covered pedestrian shopping arcade just south of Sanjō-dōri, about 50m from Higashiyama subway station. It's great for couples and families, and rooms can accommodate up to five people. Each room has bath/shower, kitchenette and laundry facilities. Reservation is by email only.

### ★ HYATT REGENCY KYOTO HOTEL ¥¥¥
Map p214 (ハイアットリージェンシー京都; ☑541-1234; www.kyoto.regency.hyatt.com; 644-2 Sanjūsangendō-mawari, Higashiyama-ku; r from ¥28,500; ☻☎; Keihan line to Shichijō) The Hyatt Regency is an excellent, stylish and foreigner-friendly hotel at the southern end

of Kyoto's Southern Higashiyama sightseeing district. Many travellers consider this the best hotel in Kyoto. The staff are extremely efficient and helpful (there are even foreign staff members – something of a rarity in Japan). The on-site restaurants and bar are excellent.

The stylish rooms and bathrooms have lots of neat touches. The concierges are knowledgeable about the city and they'll even lend you a laptop to check your email if you don't have your own.

### SEIKŌRŌ                    RYOKAN ¥¥¥

Map p214 (晴鴨楼; ☑561-0771; www.ryokan. asia/seikoro; 467 Nishi Tachibana-chō, 3 chō-me, Toiyamachi-dori, Gojō-sagaru, Higashiyama-ku; r per person incl 2 meals from ¥21,600; ☯@🛜; ⓡKeihan line to Kiyomizu-Gojō) A classic ryokan with a grandly decorated lobby. It's fairly spacious, with excellent, comfortable rooms, attentive service and a fairly convenient midtown location. Several rooms look over gardens and all have private bathrooms.

### GION HOUSE              RENTAL HOUSE ¥¥¥

Map p214 (ザ祇園ハウス; ☑353-8282; www.the gionhouse.com; 563-12 Komatsu-chō, Higashiyama-ku; per night from ¥23,000; 🛜; ⓡKyoto City bus 206 to Higashiyama-Yasui, ⓡKeihan line to Gion-Shijō) This beautifully decorated traditional Japanese house stands right on the edge of Gion and would make the perfect getaway for those seeking something other than a run-of-the-mill hotel. It's spacious and comfortable, and there's everything you need to take care of yourselves for a few days in the old capital.

Step outside the door and a few minutes' walk will bring you to Gion's most atmospheric lanes. And if you can force yourself out of the comfortable futons in the morning, you can take your morning tea on a rooftop verandah.

### GION HATANAKA                RYOKAN ¥¥¥

Map p214 (祇園畑中; ☑541-5315; www.the hatanaka.co.jp; Yasaka-jinja Minami-mon mae, Higashiyama-ku; r per person incl 2 meals from ¥25,000; ☯🛜; ⓡKyoto City bus 206 to Higashiyama-Yasui) This fine ryokan is right in the heart of the Southern Higashiyama sightseeing district (less than a minute's walk from Yasaka-jinja). Despite being fairly large, it manages to retain an intimate and private feeling. In addition to bathtubs in each room, there is a huge wooden communal bath. The rooms are clean, well

designed and relaxing. The ryokan offers regularly scheduled geisha entertainment that nonguests are welcome to join.

### MOTONAGO                  RYOKAN ¥¥¥

Map p214 (旅館元奈古; ☑561-2087; www. motonago.com; 511 Washio-chō, Kōdaiji-michi, Higashiyama-ku; r per person incl 2 meals from ¥18,370; ☯@🛜; ⓡKyoto City bus 206 to Gion) This ryokan may have the best location of any in the city, and it hits all the right notes for one in this class: classic Japanese decor, friendly service, nice bathtubs and a few small Japanese gardens.

### SHIRAUME RYOKAN              RYOKAN ¥¥¥

Map p214 (白梅; ☑561-1459; www.shiraume-kyoto.jp; Gion Shimbashi, Shirakawa hotori, Shijōnawate-agaru, higashi-iru, Higashiyama-ku; r per person incl 2 meals ¥23,760-37,800, per person incl breakfast only ¥16,200-27,000; @; ⓡKeihan line to Gion-Shijō) Looking out over the Shirakawa Canal in Shimbashi, a lovely street in Gion, this ryokan offers excellent location, atmosphere and service. The decor is traditional with a small inner garden and wooden bathtubs. A great spot to sample the Japanese ryokan experience.

## 🛌 Northern Higashiyama

### KOTO INN              RENTAL HOUSE ¥¥¥

Map p216 (古都イン; ☑751-2753; koto.inn@ gmail.com; 373 Horiike-chō, Higashiyama-ku; per night from ¥15,000; ☯@🛜; ⓢTōzai line to Higashiyama) Located near the Higashiyama sightseeing district, this vacation rental is good for families, couples and groups who want a bit of privacy. It's got everything you need and is decorated with Japanese antiques. The building is traditionally Japanese, but the facilities are fully modernised.

### ★WESTIN MIYAKO KYOTO          HOTEL ¥¥¥

Map p216 (ウェスティン都ホテル京都; ☑771-7111; www.miyakohotels.ne.jp/westinkyoto; Keage, Sanjō-dōri, Higashiyama-ku; d/tw from ¥16,200/16,200, Japanese-style r from ¥18,360; ☯@🛜; ⓢTōzai line to Keage, exit 2) This *grande dame* of Kyoto hotels occupies a commanding position overlooking the Higashiyama sightseeing district (meaning it's one of the best locations for sightseeing in Kyoto). Rooms are clean and well maintained, and staff are at home with foreign guests. Rooms on the north side have great views over the city to the Kitayama mountains.

There is a fitness centre, as well as a private garden and walking trail. The hotel even has its own ryokan section for those who want to try staying in a ryokan without giving up the convenience of a hotel.

### KYOTO GARDEN RYOKAN YACHIYO
RYOKAN ¥¥¥

Map p216 (旅館八千代; ☎771-4148; www.ryokan-yachiyo.com; 34 Fukuchi-chō, Nanzen-ji, Sakyō-ku; r per person incl 2 meals ¥18,900-42,000; ❄☎; ⑤Tōzai line to Keage, exit 2) Located just down the street from Nanzen-ji, this large ryokan is at home with foreign guests. Rooms are spacious and clean, and some look out over private gardens. English-speaking staff are available.

## 🛏 Northwest Kyoto

### UTANO YOUTH HOSTEL
HOSTEL ¥

Map p220 (宇多野ユースホステル; ☎462-2288; www.yh-kyoto.or.jp/utano; Nakayama-chō 29, Uzumasa, Ukyō-ku; dm/tw per person ¥3300/4000; 🚌Kyoto City bus 26 to Yūsu-Hosuteru-mae) The best hostel in Kyoto, Utano is friendly and well organised and makes a convenient base for the sights of Northwest Kyoto (but it's a hike to reach any other part of town). There's a 10pm curfew.

### SHUNKŌ-IN
TEMPLE LODGE ¥

Map p220 (春光院; ☎462-5488; rev.taka.kawakami@gmail.com; Myōshinji-chō 42, Hanazono, Ukyō-ku; per person ¥4000-5000; 🚌; 🚃JR Sagano/San-in line to Hanazono) This is a *shukubō* (temple lodging) at a subtemple in Myōshin-ji. It's very comfortable and quiet and the main priest here speaks fluent English. For an extra ¥1000 you can try Zen meditation and go on a guided tour of the temple. Being in the temple at night is a very special experience.

## 🛏 Arashiyama & Sagano

### HOSHINOYA KYOTO
RYOKAN ¥¥¥

Map p219 (星のや京都; ☎871-0001; http://kyoto.hoshinoya.com/en/; Arashiyama Genrokuzan-chō 11-2, Nishikyō-ku; r per person incl meals from ¥70,300; 🚌Kyoto City bus 28 from Kyoto Station to Arashiyama-Tenryuji-mae, 🚃JR Sagano/San-in line to Saga-Arashiyama or Hankyū line to Arashiyama, change at Katsura) Sitting in a secluded area on the south bank of the Hozu-gawa in Arashiyama (upstream from the main

sightseeing district), this modern take on the classic Japanese inn is quickly becoming a favourite of well-heeled visitors to Kyoto in search of privacy and a unique experience. Rooms feature incredible views of the river and the surrounding mountains.

The best part is the approach: you'll be chauffeured by a private boat from a dock near Togetsu-kyō bridge to the inn (note that on days following heavy rains, you'll have to go by car instead). This is easily one of the most unique places to stay in Kyoto.

### HOTEL RAN-TEI
HOTEL ¥¥¥

Map p219 (ホテル嵐亭; ☎371-1119; hotelrantei@kyoto-centuryhotel.co.jp; Susukinobaba-chō 12, Saga-Tenryū-ji, Ukyō-ku; r per person ¥16,000-34,000; 🚇; 🚌Kyoto City bus 28 from Kyoto Station to Arashiyama-Tenryuji-mae, 🚃JR Sagano/San-in line to Arashiyama or Hankyū line to Arashiyama, change at Katsura) The excellent Ran-tei has spacious gardens and both Japanese- and Western-style accommodation. Rooms are quiet, and there's a great view from the bathroom. The Japanese-style breakfast may not suit all palates but it is filling.

### ARASHIYAMA BENKEI
RYOKAN ¥¥¥

Map p219 (嵐山辨慶旅館; ☎872-3355; www.benkei.biz; Susukinobaba-chō 34, Saga Tenryū-ji, Ukyō-ku; r per person incl meals from ¥21,000; 🚌Kyoto City Bus 28 from Kyoto Station to Arashiyama-Tenryuji-mae, 🚃JR Sagano/San-in line to Saga-Arashiyama or Hankyū line to Arashiyama, change at Katsura) This elegant ryokan has a pleasant riverside location and serves wonderful *kaiseki* (Japanese haute cuisine). The service is kind and friendly, and the river view from the spacious rooms is great.

## 🛏 Kitayama Area & North Kyoto

### RYOKAN UGENTA
RYOKAN ¥¥¥

Map p223 (旅館右源太; ☎741-2146; www.ugenta.co.jp; Kibune-chō 76, Kurama, Sakyō-ku; r per person incl meals from ¥45,150; 🚇; 🚃Eiden Eizan line to Kibune-guchi) A superb, stylish inn in the village of Kibune, about 30 minutes north of Kyoto by taxi or train. There are only two rooms – one Japanese-style and one Western-style. Both have private cypress-wood outdoor bathtubs. This would be the perfect place for a secluded getaway. The Ugenta offers a free shuttle bus to and from the station.

# Understand Kyoto

# Kyoto Today

In Kyoto today the word *enyasu* is on everybody's lips. Formed from the words *en* (the Japanese pronunciation of yen) and *yasu* (the Japanese word for cheap), *enyasu* is how Japanese speak of the yen, which has plunged in value against other world currencies in recent years. A weaker yen and a strengthening world economy have resulted in a huge influx of tourists to Kyoto. The city now finds itself trying to balance cultural preservation against economic development.

## Best on Film

**Rashomon** (1950) Kurosawa Akira's classic uses the southern gate of Kyoto as the setting for a 12th-century rape and murder story told from several perspectives.

**Sisters of Nishijin** (1952) The father of a silk-weaving family kills himself as the family is caught between the old and the new.

**Lost in Translation** (2003) Most of this film takes place in Tokyo, but there's a lovely montage of shots of the heroine's trip to Kyoto.

## Best in Print

**The Old Capital** (Kawabata Yasunari; 1962) A young woman's past is disturbed by the discovery of a twin sister in another family.

**The Temple of the Golden Pavilion** (Mishima Yukio; 1956) A fictionalised account of a young Buddhist acolyte who burned down Kyoto's famous Golden Pavilion (Kinkaku-ji) in 1950.

**Memoirs of a Geisha** (Arthur Golden; 1997) This account of the life of a Kyoto geisha was later turned into a successful movie (most of which was not filmed in Kyoto).

**The Lady and the Monk** (Pico Iyer; 1991) An account of the author's relationship with a Japanese woman against the backdrop of Kyoto.

## The Yen Drops & Kyoto Bounces Back

In December 2012 Japan's conservative Liberal Democratic Party (LDP), headed by Abe Shinzō, handily defeated the ruling Democratic Party in a general election. The party quickly implemented a raft of policy changes that become known as Abenomics. One of the main goals of the policy was to weaken the Japanese yen, in hopes that it would bring prices of Japanese exports down and stimulate the economy.

Whether due to Abenomics or world trends beyond Japan's control, one thing is clear: the yen has dropped about 25% in value against the US dollar since late 2012. It's now trading at levels not seen since before the 2008 Global Financial Crisis. And, despite some mild inflation and a tax raise that have come since the LDP took power, Japan once again seems cheap to foreign travellers.

For Kyoto, the drop in the yen could not have come at a better time. Tourists started returning in force in 2013, and in 2014 there were record numbers of arrivals in the city. The largest increase has come from other Asian countries, including China, Thailand and Taiwan.

However, the icing on the cake was the announcement by the International Olympic Committee in September 2013 that Tokyo would host the 2020 Summer Olympic Games. As Kyoto is just 2½ hours from Tokyo by *shinkansen* (bullet train), it was clear that the Tokyo Olympics would be a huge win for Kyoto as well.

## Reinventing Kyoto

The city's business and political leaders have come to realise that Kyoto's greatest potential lies in the ever-increasing numbers of tourists who visit the city, including those from nearby Asian countries. In order to meet the demand and attract even more tourists, the city has been trying to reinvent itself as a modern tourist hub and several new projects are underway.

For tourists and locals, one of the most promising is the plan to reduce vehicle traffic and widen the sidewalks along the major downtown thoroughfare of Shijo-dōri. In a further effort to make the downtown area more appealing to tourists, smoking has been banned on major streets in the area.

To make it easier for foreign tourists to enjoy a night or two in the city's plentiful ryokan (traditional Japanese inns), the city recently established a 24-hour telephone helpline that ryokan owners can call to access interpreters who speak English, Chinese, Korean, Portuguese and Spanish. While not directly accessible to the general public, the helpline is nonetheless expected to make things significantly easier for foreign tourists.

New hotels and businesses have been springing up to take advantage of the booming luxury travel market in Japan. The Ritz-Carlton Kyoto opened in February 2014 and other top-end hotels are in the works. Likewise, some of Kyoto's major retailers have been appealing to wealthy Asian guests, especially those from China.

Of course, none of this comes without controversy. As the guardian of Japan's traditional culture, Kyoto is a famously conservative city. Some Kyotoites question what will become of the city as more and more foreigners come to enjoy its rich cultural heritage. And, due to escalating tensions with China over issues such as the Senkaku (Diaoyu) Islands, there are those in Kyoto who feel ambivalent about marketing aggressively to visitors from China.

### Kyoto Is Japan in a Nutshell

With a weak yen and heightened international attention, the picture is bright for Kyoto's tourism industry. However, the city cannot escape the general demographic trends at play in Japan as a whole. Like the rest of Japan, Kyoto faces the twin problems of a declining birthrate and aging population. A decline in the population of Japan's young people hits Kyoto especially hard, because in addition to being one of Japan's tourist centres, Kyoto is also the educational capital of the country. And while the weak yen is good for hotels and ryokan that cater to foreign travellers, it's a double-edged sword for many of Kyoto's companies that have to source materials from overseas.

In some ways, the questions facing Kyoto are those that face Japan as a whole. It's likely that the way Kyoto defines itself in the coming decades will be indicative of how Japan as a nation will define itself. At present, Kyoto seems to be trending towards an open society that sees profit in active engagement with the wider world.

## population per sq km

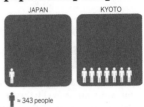

## age group
(% of population)

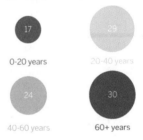

## if Kyoto were 100 people

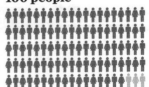

# History

From the 8th century until the late 19th century, Kyoto's history was almost synonymous with Japanese history. Kyoto was literally the stage where the great events of Japanese history unfolded. This is where emperors and shoguns vied for power. This is where the main religious sects were born and popularised. And this is where the traditional arts of Japan were polished to their present-day perfection. It is no exaggeration to say that Kyoto itself forms a vast living textbook of Japanese history: almost everywhere you step, an event took place that shaped the nation we know as Japan.

## Early History

*Jōmon* pottery vessels dating back some 15,000 years are the oldest known pottery vessels in the world.

Although the origins of the Japanese race remain unclear, anthropologists believe humans first arrived on the islands as early as 100,000 years ago via the land bridges that once connected Japan to Siberia and Korea, and by sea from the islands of the South Pacific. The first recorded evidence of civilisation in Japan are *jōmon* (pottery fragments with cord marks) produced around 10,000 BC. During the Jōmon period (10,000–300 BC), people lived a primitive existence as independent fishers, hunters and food gatherers.

This Stone Age period was gradually superseded by the Yayoi era, dating roughly from 300 BC to AD 300. The Yayoi people are considered to have had a strong connection with Korea. Their most important developments were the wet cultivation of rice and the use of bronze and iron implements, and they also introduced new practices such as weaving and shamanism. The Yayoi period witnessed the progressive development of communities represented in more than 100 independent family clusters dotting the archipelago.

As more and more of these settlements banded together to defend their land, regional groups became larger and by AD 300 the Yamato kingdom had emerged in the region of present-day Nara. Forces were loosely united around the imperial clan of the Yamato court, whose leaders claimed descent from the sun goddess, Amaterasu, and who introduced the title of *tennō* (emperor). The Yamato kingdom established Japan's first fixed capital in Nara, eventually unifying the regional

| TIMELINE | 544 | Early 7th Century | 603 |
| --- | --- | --- | --- |
| | The first Aoi (Hollyhock) Matsuri is held to pray for an end to calamitous weather that had been plaguing the city of Kyoto. The festival is still held today in May. | The vast, fertile plain of the Kyoto basin (then known as Yamashiro-no-kuni) is first settled by the Hata clan from Korea, along with another clan, the Kamo. | Kōryū-ji is established in northwest Kyoto to house a statue given to the Hata clan by Prince Shōtoku. The temple becomes the tutelary temple of the clan. |

groups into a single state. By the end of the 4th century, official relations with the Korean peninsula were established and Japan steadily began to introduce arts and industries such as shipbuilding, leather-tanning, weaving and metalwork.

During the Yamato period a highly aristocratic society with militaristic rulers developed. Its cavalry wore armour, carried swords and used advanced military techniques similar to those of northeast Asia. The Yamato government also sent envoys directly to the Chinese court, where they were exposed to philosophy and social structure.

## Buddhism & Chinese Influence

When Buddhism drifted onto the shores of Japan, Kyoto was barely more than a vast, fertile valley. First introduced from China in 538 via the Korean kingdom of Paekche, Buddhism was pivotal in the evolution of the Japanese nation. It eventually brought with it a flood of culture through literature, the arts, architecture and kanji, a system of writing in Chinese characters. However, initial uptake of Buddhism was slow until Empress Suiko (554–628) encouraged all Japanese to accept the new faith. Widespread temple construction was authorised and in 588, as recorded in the 8th-century *Nihon Shoki* (Chronicle of Japan), Japan's first great temple complex, Asuka-dera, was completed.

Gradually the wealth and power of the temples began to pose a threat to the governing Yamato court, prompting reforms from Prince Shōtoku (574–622), regent for Empress Suiko. He set up the Constitution of 17 Articles, which combined ideas from Buddhism and Confucianism to outline the acceptable behaviour of the people, and laid the guidelines for a centralised state headed by a single ruler. He also instituted Buddhism as a state religion and ordered the construction of more temples, including Nara's eminent Hōryū-ji, the world's oldest surviving wooden structure. Another significant accomplishment of Prince Shōtoku was the first compilation of Japanese history in 620; however, the book was later burned.

Reforms and bureaucratisation of government led to the establishment, in 710, of a permanent imperial capital, known as Heijō-kyō, in Nara, where it remained for 74 years.

The prosperous Nara period (710–94) saw further propagation of Buddhism and, by the end of the 8th century, the Buddhist clergy had become so meddlesome that Emperor Kammu decided to sever the ties between Buddhism and government by again moving the capital. He first moved it to Nagaoka (a suburb of Kyoto) in 784, but due to the assassination of the city's principal architect, several ominous natural disasters and superstitious beliefs regarding the location, a decade later he suddenly shifted the capital to Heian-kyō, present-day Kyoto.

SHINTŌ

The Japanese religion of Shintō is one of the few religions in the world to have a female sun deity, or a female supreme deity.

| 784 | 788 | 794 | 794 |
|---|---|---|---|
| Emperor Kammu moves the capital from Nara to Nagaoka (a suburb of Kyoto) to avoid the powerful Buddhist clergy who had previously meddled in the imperial court. | Saichō establishes a monastery atop Hiei-zan (Mt Hiei) to protect the city from the 'dangerous' northeast direction. Saichō starts a school of Buddhism known as Tendai (Tenzai). | Things go poorly in Nagaoka and Emperor Kammu searches in the Kyoto basin for another site for his capital. Late that year, he finds a suitable spot in present-day Kyoto. | A pair of temples, Tō-ji and Sai-ji, are built at the southern edge of Kyoto to protect the city and the imperial court. Tō-ji can still be visited today. |

# Establishment of Heian-Kyō

*The Tale of Genji*, written by the court-lady Murasaki Shikibu around 1004, is widely believed to be the world's first novel.

The Kyoto basin was first settled in the 7th century when the region was known as Yamashiro-no-kuni. The original inhabitants were immigrants from Korea, the Hata clan, who established Koryū-ji in 603 as their family temple in what is today the Uzumasa District. A major reason Emperor Kammu proclaimed Heian-kyō the new capital of Japan was his realisation that the city lay within a strategic natural fortress created by the rivers and mountains which surround it on three sides, fulfilling the geomantic requirements derived from proto–feng shui.

As with the previous capital in Nara, the city was laid out in accordance with Chinese geomancy in a grid pattern adopted from the Tang-dynasty capital, Chang'an (present-day Xi'an). The rectangle-shaped precincts were established west of where the Kamo-gawa flows. Originally measuring 4.5km east to west and 5.3km north to south, the city was about one-third the size of its Chinese prototype. Running through the centre was Suzaku-ōji, an 85m-wide, willow-lined thoroughfare dividing the eastern (Sakyō-ku) part of the city from the west (Ukyō-ku). The northern tip of the promenade was the site of the ornate Imperial Palace and to the far south stood the 23m-high, two-storey Rajō Gate, over 35m wide and 10m deep. However, to avoid a repeat of the power struggle between the imperial court and Buddhist clergy, only two temples, the West Temple and the East Temple (Tō-ji), were built within the city limits.

Literally, capital of peace *(hei)* and tranquillity *(an)*, the ensuing Heian period (794–1185) effectively lived up to its name. Over four centuries the city went beyond its post as a political hub to become the country's commercial and cultural centre. Towards the end of the 9th century, contact with China became increasingly sporadic, providing an opportunity for Japan to cultivate an independent heritage. This produced a great flowering in literature, the arts and religious thinking, as the Japanese adapted ideas and institutions imported from China.

The development of hiragana (Japanese characters), whose invention is attributed to the Buddhist priest Kūkai in the 9th century, led to a popular literary trend best recalled by Murasaki Shikibu's legendary saga *Genji Monogatari* (The Tale of Genji). This period in Kyoto's history conjures up romantic visions of riverside moon-gazing parties where literati drew calligraphy and composed poetry while the aristocracy frolicked in their self-imposed seclusion.

Japanese monks returning from China established two new sects, Tendai (or Tenzai, meaning Heavenly Terrace) and Shingon (True Words), that became the mainstays of Japanese Buddhism. Soon other sects were springing up and temples were being enthusiastically built.

| 798 | 869 | 10th Century | 1052 |
|---|---|---|---|
| Kiyomizu-dera is established at the foot of the Higashiyama mountains. It is said that the location was chosen by a priest from Nara who had a vision of a holy spring at the site. | The head priest of Yasaka-jinja leads a procession through the streets of Kyoto in an effort to end a series of epidemics that had plagued the city. This is the origin of today's Gion Matsuri. | Kyoto's centre gradually shifts east, closer to the Kamo-gawa and the Higashiyama. During this time imperial properties in the west are abandoned. | The Byōdō-in Buddhist temple is established. The following year, the famous Hōō-dō (Phoenix Hall) is built. The temple is one of the best examples of Heian-era architecture. |

The Heian period is considered the apogee of Japanese courtly elegance, but in the provinces a new power was on the rise – the samurai (warrior class), which built up its armed forces to defend its autonomy. Samurai families moved into Kyoto, where they muscled in on the court, and subsequent conflicts between rival military clans led to civil wars. Members of the Fujiwara, Taira and Minamoto families attacked each other, claimed control over conquered tracts of land and set up rival regimes. This was the beginning of a long period of feudal rule by successive shogunates (samurai families). This feudal system effectively lingered on for seven centuries until imperial power was restored in 1868.

## From Aristocratic to Military Rule

Although Kyoto served as home to the Japanese imperial family from 794 to 1868, it was not always the focus of Japanese political power. During the Kamakura period (1185–1333), Kamakura (near present-day Tokyo) was the national capital, while during the Edo period (1603–1868) the Tokugawa Shogunate ruled the country from Edo (present-day Tokyo). Despite the decline in influence of the imperial court, Kyoto flourished as townspeople continued developing age-old traditions.

In 1192, while the emperor remained nominal ruler in Kyoto, Minamoto Yoritomo, the first shogun of the Kamakura Shogunate, set up his headquarters in Kamakura. Yoritomo purged members of his own family who stood in his way, but after fatally falling from his horse in 1199, the Hōjō, his wife's family, eliminated all of Yoritomo's potential successors. In 1213 they became true wielders of power behind the shoguns and warrior lords.

During this era the popularity of Buddhism spread to all levels of society. From the late 12th century, Eisei (1145–1215) and other Japanese monks returning from China introduced a new sect, Zen, which encountered resistance from the established sects in Kyoto but appealed to the samurai class. Meanwhile, as the spiritual fervour grew, Japanese merchants prospered in increased trade dealings with China.

Forces beyond the sea undermined the stability of the Kamakura regime. The Mongols, under Kublai Khan, reached Korea in 1259 and sent envoys to Japan seeking Japanese submission. The envoys were expelled and the Mongols sent an invasion fleet which arrived near present-day Fukuoka in 1274. This first attack was only barely repulsed with the aid of a typhoon that destroyed up to 200 Mongol ships. Further envoys sent by Khan were beheaded in Kamakura as a sign that the government of Japan was not interested in paying homage to the Mongols.

In 1281 the Mongols dispatched an army of over 100,000 soldiers to Japan. After an initial success, the Mongol fleet was almost completely

**MONGOL INVASIONS**

It is commonly believed that the attempted Mongol invasions of Japan were deterred by typhoons before landing on Japanese soil. In fact, there was hard fighting on land (mostly in Kyūshū) in both cases before the supporting fleets were dispersed by typhoons.

| Mid-12th Century | 1168 | 1192 | 1202 |
|---|---|---|---|
| The name Kyoto (written with two Chinese characters that mean 'capital') starts to replace the original name of the city, Heian-kyo (Peaceful Capital). | The priest Eisai travels to China and observes Chang Buddhism. He later introduces this as Zen Buddhism in Japan. He also introduces the practice of tea drinking. | Minamoto Yoritomo is appointed shogun and establishes the political capital in Kamakura. While the imperial court remains in Kyoto, the real power centre of the country leaves the city. | Eisai establishes the Zen temple Kennin-ji, under sponsorship of shogun Minamoto no Yoriie. It remains one of Kyoto's most important Zen temples. |

destroyed by yet another massive typhoon that assaulted the shores of Kyushu for two days. Ever since, this lucky typhoon has been known to the Japanese as kamikaze (divine wind) – a name later given to the suicide pilots of WWII.

Although the Kamakura government emerged victorious, it was unable to pay its soldiers and lost the support of the warrior class. Emperor Go-Daigo led an unsuccessful rebellion to overthrow the shogunate and was exiled to the Oki Islands near Matsue. A year later, he escaped from the island, raised an army and toppled the government, ushering in a return of political authority to Kyoto.

## Country at War

After completing his takeover, Emperor Go-Daigo refused to reward his warriors, favouring the aristocracy and priesthood instead. In the early 14th century this led to a revolt by the warrior Ashikaga Takauji, who had previously supported Go-Daigo. When Ashikaga's army entered Kyoto, Go-Daigo fled to Mt Hiei and sent the imperial Sacred Treasures to Ashikaga in conciliation. Ashikaga installed a new emperor and appointed himself shogun, initiating the Muromachi period (1333–1568). Go-Daigo escaped from Kyoto and, the Sacred Treasures he had sent to Ashikaga being counterfeit, set up a rival court at Yoshino in a mountainous region near Nara. Rivalry between the two courts continued for 60 years until the Ashikaga made an unfulfilled promise that the imperial lines would alternate.

Kyoto gradually recovered its position of political significance and, under the control of the art-loving Ashikaga, enjoyed an epoch of cultural and artistic fruition. Talents now considered typically Japanese flourished, including such arts as landscape painting, classical *nō* drama, ikebana (flower arranging) and *chanoyu* (tea ceremony). Many of Kyoto's famous gardens date from this period, such as Saihōji's famed Koke-dera (Moss Garden) and the garden of Tenryū-ji. Kinkaku-ji (Golden Pavilion) and Ginkaku-ji (Silver Temple) were built by the Ashikaga shoguns to serve as places of rest and solitude. Eventually formal trade relations were reopened with Ming China and Korea, although Japanese piracy remained a bone of contention with both.

The Ashikaga ruled, however, with diminishing effectiveness in a land slipping steadily into civil war and chaos. By the 15th century Kyoto had become increasingly divided as *daimyō* (domain lords) and local barons fought for power in bitter territorial disputes that were to last for a century. In 1467 the matter of succession to the shogunate between two feudal lords, Yamana and Hosokawa, ignited the most devastating battle in Kyoto's history. With Yamana's army of 90,000 camped in the

The history of the struggle between the northern and southern courts of the 14th century is detailed in a Japanese historical epic known as the *Taiheiki*. Partial English translations of this work are available.

| Early 13th Century | Mid-13th Century | 1281 | 1333 |
| --- | --- | --- | --- |
| The priest Hōnen, troubled by divisions between Japan's major Buddhist sects, establishes a new populist sect known as Jōdo (Pure Land) Buddhism. He fasts to death in 1212. | The priest Shinran preaches a radical doctrine that becomes known as Jōdo-Shinshū (True Pure Land Buddhism). Followers establish the vast Higashi-Hongan-ji and Nishi-Hongan-ji. | Kublai Khan of Mongolia attempts to conquer Japan for the second time, but the invasion force is destroyed by a massive typhoon (the so-called 'kamikaze'). | The Kamakura Shogunate is defeated, Emperor Daigo II returns from exile and the political capital is re-established in Kyoto, where it remains until 1868. |

southwest and Hosokawa's force of 100,000 quartered in the north of the city, Kyoto became a battlefield. The resulting Ōnin-no-ran (Ōnin War; 1467–77) wreaked untold havoc on the city; the Imperial Palace and most of the city were destroyed by fighting and subsequent fires, and the populace was left in ruin.

The war marked the rapid decline of the Ashikaga family and the beginning of the Sengoku-jidai (Warring States) period, a protracted struggle for domination by individual *daimyō* that spread throughout Japan and lasted until the start of the Azuchi-Momoyama period in 1568.

# Return to Unity

After a succession of power struggles, the country was finally united in the late 16th century by Toyotomi Hideyoshi.

By the late 16th century, Kyoto's population had swelled to 500,000 and Toyotomi was fascinated with redesigning and rebuilding the city, which had been devastated by more than a century of war. Prior to his death in 1598 he transformed Kyoto into a castle town and greatly altered the cityscape by ordering major construction projects including bridges, gates and the Odoi, a phenomenal earthen rampart designed to isolate and fortify the perimeter of the city, and to provide a measure of flood control. He also rebuilt temples burned by Nobunaga, including the stronghold of the Ikkō sect, the great Hongan-ji.

The rebuilding of Kyoto is usually credited to the influence of the city's merchant class, which led a citizens' revival that gradually shifted power back into the hands of the townspeople. Centred on Shimogyō, the commercial and industrial district, these enterprising people founded a *machi-shū* (self-governing body) that contributed greatly to temple reconstruction. Over time temples of different sects were consolidated in one quarter of the city, creating the miniature Tera-Machi (City of Temples), which still exists.

The Azuchi-Momoyama period has been referred to as the 'Japanese Renaissance', during which the arts further prospered. Artisans of the era are noted for their boisterous use of colour and gold-leaf embellishment, which marked a new aesthetic sense in contrast to the more sombre monotones of the Muromachi period. The Zen-influenced tea ceremony was developed to perfection under Master Sen no Rikyū, who also wrote poetry and practised ikebana. The performing arts also matured, along with skill in ceramics, lacquerware and fabric-dyeing. A vogue for building castles and palaces on a flamboyant scale was also nurtured, the most impressive examples being Osaka-jō, which reputedly required three years of labour by up to 100,000 workers, and the extraordinary Ninomaru Palace in Kyoto's Nijō-jō.

The first Europeans to arrive in Japan were the Portuguese, who landed on the island of Tanegashima, south of Kyūshū, in 1543.

| 1397 | 1467 | 1482 | 1568 |
|---|---|---|---|
| Shogun Ashikaga Yoshimitsu is given a property to serve as a retirement villa. After his death, his son turns the villa into Rokuon-ji, known today as Kinkaku-ji (Golden Pavilion). | The devastating Ōnin War breaks out in Kyoto between two families competing for shogunate succession, leading to nationwide war known as the Sengoku-Jidai (Warring States) period. | Shogun Ashikaga Yoshimasa builds a retreat at the base of the Higashiyama mountains. After his death, the retreat is converted into Jishō-ji, a temple known today as Ginkaku-ji. | Oda Nobunaga, son of a *daimyō* (domain lord) in Owari Province (now known as Aichi-ken), seizes power from the imperial court in Kyoto and begins to pacify and unify central Japan. |

## Peace & Seclusion

The supporters of Toyotomi's young heir, Toyotomi Hideyori, were defeated in 1600 by his former ally, Tokugawa Ieyasu, at the decisive Battle of Sekigahara in Gifu prefecture. Tokugawa set up his *bakufu* (literally, field headquarters) at Edo, marking the start of the Edo (Tokugawa) period (1603–1868). Meanwhile the emperor and court exercised purely nominal authority in Kyoto.

There emerged a pressing fear of religious intrusion (seen as a siphoning of loyalty to the shogun) and Tokugawa set out to stabilise society and the national economy. Eager for trade, he was initially tolerant of Christian missionary activities but, fearing the Christians would support Toyotomi Hideyori's efforts to resist the *bakufu* military government, he took steps to prohibit Christianity before destroying the Toyotomi family. Japan entered a period of *sakoku* (national seclusion) during which Japanese were forbidden on pain of death to travel to (or return from) overseas or to trade abroad. As efforts to expel foreign influences spread, only Dutch, Chinese and Koreans were allowed to remain, under strict supervision, and trade was restricted to the artificial island of Dejima at Nagasaki.

The Tokugawa family retained large estates and took control of major cities, ports and mines; the remainder of the country was allocated to autonomous *daimyō*. Foreign affairs and trade were monopolised by the shogunate, which yielded great financial authority over the *daimyō*. Tokugawa society was strictly hierarchical. In descending order of importance were the nobility, who had nominal power; the *daimyō* and their samurai; farmers; and, at the bottom, artisans and merchants. Mobility from one class to another was blocked; social standing was determined by birth.

To ensure political security, the *daimyō* were required to make ceremonial visits to Edo every alternate year, while their wives and children were kept in permanent residence in Edo as virtual hostages of the government. At the lower end of society, farmers were subject to a severe system of rules that dictated in minute detail their food, clothing and housing and land surveys which were designed to extract the greatest tax yield possible.

One effect of this strict rule was to create an atmosphere of relative peace and isolation in which the arts excelled. There were great advances in haiku poetry, bunraku puppet plays and kabuki theatre. Crafts such as woodblock printing, weaving, pottery, ceramics and lacquerware became famous for their refined quality. Some of Japan's greatest expressions in architecture and painting were produced, including Katsura Rikyū in Kyoto and the paintings of Tawaraya Sōtatsu, pioneer

SAMURAI WILLIAM

*Samurai William*, by Giles Milton, is one of the most interesting accounts of the early Tokugawa period. It tells the story of William Adams, a shipwrecked English sailor, who gains the confidence of Shogun Tokugawa Ieyasu.

| 1591 | 1600 | 1603 | 1619 |
|---|---|---|---|
| The ruling shogun, Toyotomi Hideyoshi, orders the construction of a wall around the city of Kyoto. The wall extends for 23km and is traversable by seven gates. | Tokugawa Ieyasu defeats Toyotomi at the Battle of Sekigahara. The Tokugawa Shogunate government is established in Edo (present-day Tokyo), but the capital remains in Kyoto. | The castle known as Nijō-jō was built to serve as the official residence of the first Tokugawa Shogun, Ieyasu. The castle is a direct challenge to the emperor's power. | As part of the general purge of Christians ordered by the shogun, 52 Japanese Christians are burned alive on the banks of the Kamo-gawa in Kyoto. |

of the Rimpa school. Furthermore, the rigid emphasis of these times on submitting unquestioningly to rules of obedience and loyalty has lasted in the arts, and society at large, to the present day.

By the turn of the 19th century, the Tokugawa government was characterised by stagnation and corruption. Famines and poverty among the peasants and samurai further weakened the system. Foreign ships started to probe Japan's isolation with increasing insistence and the Japanese soon realised that their outmoded defences were ineffectual. Russian contacts in the north were followed by British and American visits. In 1853 Commodore Matthew Perry of the US Navy arrived with a squadron of 'black ships' to demand the opening of Japan to trade. Other countries also moved in with similar demands.

Despite being far inland, Kyoto felt the foreign pressure, which helped bring to a head the growing power struggle between the shogun and emperor, eventually pushing Japan back into a state of internal conflict. A surge of antigovernment feeling among the Japanese followed and Kyoto became a hotbed of controversy. The Tokugawa government was accused of failing to defend Japan against foreigners, and of neglecting the national reconstruction necessary for Japan to meet foreign powers on equal terms. In the autumn of 1867, forces led by Satsuma and Chōshū samurai armed with English weapons attacked the palace demanding an imperial restoration. The ruling shogun, Keiki, offered his resignation to avoid bloodshed, and Emperor Meiji resumed control of state affairs. This development has since been referred to as the Meiji Restoration.

## Emergence from Isolation

With the Meiji Restoration in 1868, the seat of Japanese national political power was restored to Kyoto, but the following year the capital was transferred to Edo along with the imperial court. Political power now resided in Edo and many great merchants and scholars of the era followed the emperor. After more than a millennium as capital, the sudden changes came as a major blow to Kyoto as the population dropped dramatically and the city entered a state of bitter depression.

Kyoto quickly set its sights on revival, taking steps to secure autonomy and rebuild its infrastructure. It again flourished as a cultural, religious and economic centre, with progressive industrial development. By the late 1800s Kyoto led the country in education reforms, establishing Japan's first kindergarten, primary and junior high schools, and a public library. In 1871 the first Kyoto Exhibition was launched, in which the Maiko and Kamogawa *odori* (dances) originated. In 1880 the nation's first public art school, the Kyoto Prefecture Art School (now

*The Coming of the Barbarians*, by Pat Barr, is perhaps the most interesting account of the opening of Japan in the mid-19th century.

| 1620 | 1646 | 1662 | 1853 |
|---|---|---|---|
| Construction starts on Katsura-Rikyū Imperial Villa. The villa was originally built to house an adopted son of Tokugawa Hideyoshi. The imperial family cooperates in the construction. | Omotesenke tea-ceremony school is founded by Sen Sosa, the great-grandson of Sen no Rikyū, Japan's great tea master. The school remains in Kyoto to this day. | The first Daimon-ji Gozan Okuribi, in which a giant Chinese character is set alight on the side of a mountain in eastern Kyoto, is held. | American Commodore Matthew Perry's 'black ships' arrive at Uraga Harbour (part of present-day Yokosuka), leading to a treaty allowing American trade with Japan. |

the Kyoto City University of Arts), was opened. In the same period the city introduced Japan's first electricity system, water system and fully functioning transport network. In 1885 work began on the monumental Lake Biwa Canal, which made Kyoto the first Japanese city to harness hydroelectric power.

In 1889 a proper city government was finally formed, which helped create an atmosphere in which industry could flourish. As traditional industry pushed on, research developed in the sciences, in particular physics and chemistry. Modern industries such as precision machinery also grew, as did the introduction of foreign technologies such as the automated weaving loom, which bolstered the struggling Nishijin textile industry. To celebrate the 1100th anniversary of the city's founding, Kyoto hosted the fourth National Industrial Exhibition Fair in 1895 and established the country's first streetcar system (fuelled by the Keage Hydroelectric Plant). The same year saw the construction of Heian-jingū (actually a 5:8 scale replica of Daigokuden, the emperor's Great Hall of State), and the birth of the Jidai Matsuri (Festival of the Ages).

Despite the apparent industrial boom, the initial stages of Kyoto's restoration were undermined by a state of virtual civil war. The abolition of the shogunate was followed by the surrender of the *daimyō*, whose lands were divided into the prefectures that exist today. With the transfer of the capital to Edo, now renamed Tokyo (Eastern Capital), the government was recentralised and European-style ministries were appointed for specific tasks. A series of revolts by the samurai against the erosion of their status culminated in the Saigō Uprising, when they were finally beaten and stripped of their power.

Despite nationalist support for the emperor under the slogan of *sonnō-jōi* (revere the emperor, repel the barbarians), the new government soon realised it would have to meet the outside world on its own terms, and the economy underwent a crash course in Westernisation and industrialisation. Foreign experts were engaged to provide assistance and Japanese students were sent abroad to acquire expertise in modern technologies. Western-style factories were established and mining was expanded under the management of *zaibatsu* (wealthy groups), such as Mitsui and Sumitomo. In 1889 Japan created a US-style constitution that gave the appearance of a democracy but preserved the authoritarian rule of the emperor and his select group of advisers.

In the 1890s Japan's growing confidence was demonstrated by the abolition of foreign treaty rights and by the ease with which it trounced China in the Sino-Japanese War (1894–95). The subsequent treaty nominally recognised Korean independence from China's sphere of influence and ceded Taiwan to Japan. Friction with Russia over control of Manchuria and Korea led to the Russo-Japanese War (1904–05), in

The salaries of the foreign specialists invited to Japan in the Meiji period are believed to have amounted to 5% of all government expenditure during the period.

| 1867 | 1869 | 1871 | 1890 |
|---|---|---|---|
| An alliance of the Chōshū and Satsuma *daimyō* (domain lords) and the titular Emperor Meiji overthrows the Tokugawa Shogunate and restores imperial rule (the so-called 'Meiji Restoration'). | The 17-year-old Emperor Meiji moves from Kyoto to Edo, renamed Tokyo the year before, where Japan's new political and economic capital is established. | Japan's first exposition is held in Kyoto. The Miyako and Kamogawa *odori* (dances performed by geisha and apprentice geisha) are first performed at the Kyoto Exhibition the following year. | The Sosui Canal, linking Biwa-ko (a lake in nearby Shiga-ken) and Kyoto is completed. The canal is still in use and can be seen running through the grounds of Nanzen-ji. |

which the Japanese navy stunned the Russians by inflicting a crushing defeat on their Baltic fleet at the Battle of Tsu-shima. For the first time, Japan commanded the respect of the Western powers.

## The Pursuit of Empire

Upon his death in 1912, Emperor Meiji was succeeded by his son, Yoshi-hito, whose period of rule was named the Taishō era. When WWI broke out, Japan sided against Germany but did not become deeply involved in the conflict. While the Allies were occupied with war, Japan took the opportunity to expand its economy at top speed.

The Shōwa period began when Emperor Hirohito ascended to the throne in 1926. A rising tide of nationalism was bolstered by the world economic depression that began in 1929. Popular unrest was marked by political assassinations and plots to overthrow the government, which led to a significant increase in the power of the militarists, who approved the invasion of Manchuria in 1931 and the installation of a Japanese puppet regime, Manchukuo. In 1933 Japan withdrew from the League of Nations and in 1937 entered into full-scale hostilities against China.

As the leader of a new order for Asia, Japan signed a tripartite pact with Germany and Italy in 1940. The Japanese military leaders viewed the USA as the main obstacle to their imperial conquest of Asia, and when diplomatic attempts to gain US neutrality failed, the Japanese drew them into WWII with a surprise attack on the US Pacific Fleet in Pearl Harbor on 7 December 1941. The intent of the strike was to neutralise the fleet, which Japan rightly viewed as its main threat in the region.

At first Japan scored rapid successes, pushing its battle fronts across to India, down to the fringes of Australia and into the mid-Pacific. But eventually the decisive Battle of Midway turned the tide of the war against Japan. Exhausted by submarine blockades and aerial bombing, by 1945 Japan had been driven back on all fronts. In August the declaration of war by the Soviet Union and the atomic bombs dropped by the USA on Hiroshima and Nagasaki were the final straws: Emperor Hirohito announced Japan's unconditional surrender.

## Postwar Reconstruction & Revival

Japan was occupied by Allied forces until 1952 under the command of General Douglas MacArthur. The chief aim was a thorough reform of Japanese government through demilitarisation, the trial of war criminals, and the weeding out of militarists and ultranationalists from the government. A new constitution was introduced which denounced war and banned a Japanese military, and also dismantled the political power

The Yamato dynasty is the longest unbroken monarchy in the world, and Hirohito's reign from 1926 to 1989 the longest of any monarch in Japan.

| 1895 | 1915 | 1941 | 1945 |
|---|---|---|---|
| Kyoto celebrates the 1100th year of its founding; a street tram service begins operation; and Hiean-jingū, one of the city's most popular Shintō shrines, is built. | The first street lamps are installed on Shijō-dōri and the accession of Emperor Taishō is celebrated throughout Japan (although he had officially become emperor three years prior). | The Imperial Japanese Navy attacks the US Pacific Fleet in Pearl Harbor, Hawaii, in a strike designed to prevent American interference in Japan's territorial expansion in Asia. | In September of this year, American occupation forces enter Kyoto for the first time. They maintain a headquarters in the city until January 1946. |

of the emperor, who stunned his subjects by publicly renouncing any claim to divine origins.

At the end of the war, the Japanese economy was in ruins and inflation was running rampant. A program of recovery provided loans, restricted imports, and encouraged capital investment and personal saving. In 1945 the Kyoto Revival Plan was drafted and, again, Kyoto was set for rebuilding. In 1949 physicist Hideki Yukawa was the first in a long line of Nobel Prize winners from Kyoto University, and the city went on to become a primary educational centre.

By the late 1950s trade was flourishing and the Japanese economy continued to experience rapid growth. From textiles and the manufacture of labour-intensive goods such as cameras, the Japanese 'economic miracle' had branched out into virtually every sector of society and Kyoto increasingly became an international hub of business and culture.

Japan was now looking seriously towards tourism as a source of income, and foreign visitors were steadily arriving on tours for both busi-

## WHO REALLY SAVED KYOTO?

Kyoto's good fortune in escaping US bombing during WWII is a well-publicised fact. Still, while it may provide patriotic colour for some Americans to hear that the city was consciously spared out of US goodwill and reverence for Kyoto's cultural heritage, not everyone agrees with the prevailing story.

The common belief is that Kyoto was rescued through the efforts of American scholar Langdon Warner (1881–1955). During the latter half of the war Warner sat on a committee that endeavoured to save artistic and historical treasures in war-torn regions. More than a half-century later, Warner is a household name in Japan and is still alluded to in discussions on the future preservation of Kyoto. He is said to have made a desperate plea to US military authorities to spare the cities of Kyoto, Nara, Kamakura and Kanazawa.

Despite this popular account, other theories have surfaced, along with documentation pointing to an elaborate conspiracy aimed at quelling anti-American sentiment in occupied Japan. The evidence has fuelled a debate as to whether or not it was in fact a well-planned public relations stunt scripted by US intelligence officials to gain the trust of a nation that had been taught to fear and hate the American enemy.

Some historians have suggested that both Kyoto and Nara were on a list of some 180 cities earmarked for air raids. Kyoto, with a population of over one million people, was a prime target (along with Hiroshima and Nagasaki) for atomic annihilation and many avow the choice could easily have been Kyoto. Nara, it has been suggested, escaped merely due to having a population under 60,000, which kept it far enough down the list not to be reached before the unconditional surrender of Japan in September 1945.

| 1964 | 1966 | 1981 | 1994 |
|---|---|---|---|
| The Tōkaidō *shinkansen* (bullet train) service opens linking Osaka and Tokyo with a station in Kyoto. | Kyoto International Conference Hall opens at Takaragaike as the first international conference hall in Japan. Takaragaike later serves as the site for the Kyoto Protocol agreement. | Karasuma subway starts between Kyoto and Kitaō-ji stations, allowing easy north–south travel through the city. The line later extends south to Takeda and north to Takaragaike. | Kyoto celebrates the 1200th anniversary of its founding and 17 Historic Monuments of Ancient Kyoto are registered as Unesco World Heritage sites, including Kinkaku-ji and Ginkaku-ji. |

ness and pleasure. By this time Kyoto had further developed as a major university centre and during the 'Woodstock era' of the late 1960s, anti-war movements and Japanese flower power mirrored those of the US and brought student activism out into the streets. The year 1966 saw the enactment of a law to preserve historical sites in the city and the opening of the Kyoto International Conference Hall, where the Kyoto Protocol was drafted in 1997.

During the 1970s Japan faced an economic recession, with inflation surfacing in 1974 and 1980, mostly due to steep price hikes for the imported oil on which Japan is still gravely dependent. By the early '80s, however, Japan had emerged as an economic superpower, and Kyoto's high-tech companies, including Kyocera, OMRON and Nintendo, were among those dominating fields such as electronics, robotics and computer technology. The notorious 'bubble economy' that followed marked an unprecedented era of free spending by Japan's nouveau riche. Shortly after the 1989 death of Emperor Shōwa and the start of the Heisei period (with the accession of Emperor Akihito), the miracle bubble burst, launching Japan into a critical economic free fall from which it has not yet fully recovered.

## Kyoto Today & Tomorrow

In 1994 Kyoto marked the 1200th anniversary of its founding. While the city celebrated its ancient heritage, however, developers celebrated this milestone by building several structures in excess of the height restrictions that had been put in place to maintain the city's traditional skyline. Fortunately, in September 2007 the Kyoto city government enacted new ordinances that restrict building heights and ban all rooftop and blinking advertisements. Meanwhile, down on street level, there was a revival of interest in the city's *machiya* (traditional wooden townhouses), and many of these fine old structures were turned into shops, restaurants and inns.

In March 2011 the Great East Japan Earthquake struck off the east coast of Japan's island of Honshū. While the quake caused no physical damage to Kyoto, it devastated the city's tourism industry. However, travellers were quick to return to Kyoto. By 2013 numbers were back to pre-quake levels, and by mid-2014 tourist arrivals were at an all-time high. In response, the city's economic and political leaders have been working hard to reinvent the city as a modern tourist destination.

As Kyoto heads into the future, the real challenge is to preserve its ancient history while meeting the desires of its citizens for economic development and modern convenience.

KYOTO PROTOCOL

In 1997 the so-called Kyoto Protocol was adopted at the Takaragaike International Conference Hall in northern Kyoto. The Kyoto Protocol is a UN program aimed at limiting greenhouse gas emissions and countering global warming.

| 1997 | 2011 | 2014 | 2014 |
|---|---|---|---|
| The futuristic Kyoto Station building, featuring a 60m-high atrium over the main concourse, opens in the same year as the Tōzai (east–west) line, Kyoto's second subway line. | On 11 March the Great East Japan Earthquake strikes off the northeast coast. While Kyoto suffers no damage, there's a massive decline in tourist numbers. | After an interval of almost 50 years, a second major parade of floats (known as the *ato matsuri*) is revived during the annual Gion Matsuri, Kyoto's biggest festival. | Due to a weak yen and reviving international economy, the number of international visitors to Kyoto reaches record levels, with huge growth in Asian travellers. |

# People & Culture

**Kyoto is the cultural heart of Japan. It is the place in which Japanese culture is at its most refined, most intense and most distinctive. Indeed, Kyoto is the place where many Japanese go to learn what it is to be Japanese. The people of Kyoto, whether they be artisans, geisha or typical office workers, bear the stamp of this rich cultural legacy in everything from their language to their manners.**

## The Culture of Kyoto

Listen carefully and you'll hear the distinctive Kyoto dialect (Kyoto-ben) all around you. *'Okini'* means 'thank you' and *'oideyasu'* means 'welcome'.

The cultural life of Kyoto was centred on the imperial court for over 1100 years. The court drew to it the finest artisans and craftspeople from across Japan, resulting in an incredibly rich cultural and artistic atmosphere. Today Kyoto is still home to many of Japan's best artists in every field, from textiles and bamboo craft to the tea ceremony. The imperial court also left its mark on the language of the city, and true Kyoto-ben (Kyoto dialect) has the lilting tones and formality of the now-departed imperial residents.

In addition to playing host to the imperial court, Kyoto has always been the headquarters of Japan's major religious sects, including Zen, Pure Land and Tendai. The astonishing preponderance of temples and shrines in the present-day city is testament to the role that Kyoto has always played in the spiritual life of the Japanese.

Kyoto's cultural life is deeply informed by the natural world. Due to its geographic location, Kyoto has always enjoyed four very distinct seasons, which are reflected in, and celebrated by, the yearly procession of Kyoto rituals and festivals. From the hanging of scrolls in people's homes and tableware in *kaiseki* (Japanese haute cuisine) restaurants, to the young ladies' *yukata* robe the night before the Gion Matsuri festival, every aspect of Kyoto is a reminder and an echo of the season. This rich and complex culture is apparent to even the most casual visitor and embodies a certain elegance, refinement and style that has few rivals elsewhere in the world.

## The People of Kyoto

Ask other Japanese about Kyotoites and they will probably say that they are cold, arrogant, conservative, haughty, indirect and two-faced. They'll tell you that Kyotoites act as though the city is still the capital and the imperial seat; that your family has to live there for three generations before it will be accepted; and that they never understand what a Kyotoite really means because they never say what they're feeling.

The good news is that most of this is exaggeration and really only applies to a small minority of older folks in traditional neighbourhoods. And, as a visitor, you'll probably never pick up on any of this. In defence of the people of Kyoto, there is a good reason for their famed indirectness: as the seat of Japan's political life for so many centuries, the residents of the city naturally learned to guard their opinions in the presence of shifting political powers. Furthermore, as the seat of Japanese cultural, artistic and spiritual life, it is hardly surprising that

Kyotoites feel a certain pride that can easily be mistaken for arrogance. The fact is that they have a lot of culture to guard, so a little conservatism is only natural.

It's difficult to talk of a Kyoto identity, of course, because it is true that there are two different cultures existing in modern-day Kyoto: that of the old and that of the young. While most older Kyotoites cling to the traditional ways of the city, the young identify with the national Japanese culture that has its epicentre somewhere in the shopping malls of Tokyo's Shibuya district. The comparison can be jarring when you see a kimono-clad older Kyoto woman sharing the pavement with a group of gaudily clad *kogals* (fashionable young things). You might conclude that you're looking at two totally different species.

## Geisha

No other aspect of Japanese culture is as misunderstood as the geisha. First – and let's get this out of the way – geisha are not prostitutes. Simply put, geisha are highly skilled entertainers who are paid to facilitate and enliven social occasions in Japan.

The origins of geisha are subject to some debate, but most historians believe that the institution started in the Edo Period (1600–1868). At this time, there were various types of prostitutes who served men in the pleasure quarters of the large cities. Eventually there arose a class of young ladies who specialised exclusively in entertainment and who did not engage in sexual relations with clients. These were the first true geisha, and over the years they became prized for their accomplishments in a wide variety of Japanese arts.

Kyoto is the capital of the geisha world. Confusingly, in Kyoto they are not called geisha; rather, they are called *maiko* or *geiko*. A *maiko* is a girl between the ages of 15 and 20 who is in the process of training to become a fully fledged *geiko* (the Kyoto word for geisha). During this five-year period, she lives in an *okiya* (geisha house) and studies traditional Japanese arts, including dance, singing, tea ceremony and *shamisen* (a three-stringed instrument resembling a lute or a banjo). During this time she will start to entertain clients, usually in the company of a *geiko*, who acts like an older sister.

Due to the extensive training she receives, a *maiko* or *geiko* is like a living museum of Japanese traditional culture. In addition to her skills, the kimono she wears and the ornaments in her hair and on her obi (kimono sash) represent the highest achievements in Japanese arts.

While young girls may have been sold into this world in times gone by, these days girls make the choice themselves. The proprietor of the *okiya* will meet the girl and her parents to determine if the girl is serious and if her parents are willing to grant her permission to enter the world of the geisha.

Once a *maiko* completes her training and becomes a *geiko*, she is able to move out of the *okiya* and live on her own. At this point, she is free to have a boyfriend, but if she gets married she has to leave the world of the geisha. It's easy to spot the difference between a *maiko* and a *geiko* – *geiko* wear wigs with minimal ornamentation (usually just a wooden comb), while *maiko* wear their own hair in an elaborate hairstyle with many bright hair ornaments called *kanzashi*. Also, *maiko* wear an elaborate long-sleeved kimono, while *geiko* wear a simpler kimono with shorter sleeves.

*Maiko* and *geiko* entertain their clients in exclusive restaurants, banquet halls, 'teahouses' (more like exclusive traditional bars) and other venues. An evening of *maiko/geiko* entertainment usually starts with a *kaiseki* meal (Japanese haute cuisine). While their customers eat, the

SEEING GEISHA

The best way to see geisha – a whole lot of geisha – is to attend one of Kyoto's spring or autumn geisha dances.

## GEISHA MANNERS

There's no doubt that catching a glimpse of a geisha is a once-in-a-lifetime Japanese experience. Unfortunately, the sport of 'geisha spotting' has really gotten out of hand in Kyoto's Gion district (the city's main geisha district). If you are on the lookout for geisha, keep in mind that the geisha you see in Gion are usually on their way to or from an appointment and can't stop for photos or conversation. If you really want to get close to a geisha, private tour agencies and high-end ryokan/hotels can arrange geisha entertainment. Also, you'll notice plenty of 'tourist geisha' in the streets of Higashiyama during the day – tourists who have paid to be made up as geisha and tend to not mind having their photo taken.

*maiko/geiko* enter the room and introduce themselves in Kyoto dialect. They proceed to pour drinks and make witty banter with the guests. Sometimes they even play drinking games. If it's a large party with a *jikata* (*shamisen* player), the girls may dance after dinner.

As you might guess, this sort of entertainment does not come cheap: a dinner with one *maiko,* one *geiko* and a *jikata* might cost about US$900, but it's definitely worth it for a once-in-a-lifetime experience.

Knowledgeable sources estimate that there are perhaps 100 *maiko* and just over 100 *geiko* in Kyoto. It's impossible to arrange private geisha entertainment without an introduction from an established patron. However, geisha entertainment can be arranged through top-end hotels, ryokan and some cultural organisations in Kyoto.

*Memoirs of a Geisha* by Arthur Golden is an entertaining fictional account of the life of a Kyoto geisha.

# Religion

Shintō and Buddhism are the main religions in Japan. Most Japanese practice some rites from both religions (though these are sometimes practised without any particular religious fervour) and are likely to pay an annual visit to a shrine and a temple, particularly during important holidays such as O-Bon and New Year's.

Shintō, or 'the way of the gods' is the indigenous religion of Japan. Shintoists believe that *kami* (gods) are present in the natural world or, at the very least, animate the natural world. Consisting of thousands of deities, the Shintō pantheon includes both local spirits and global gods and goddesses. Therefore, a devout Shintoist might worship the spirit of a nearby waterfall or that of a uniquely shaped rock, while simultaneously revering the most celebrated Shintō deity Amaterasu, the goddess of the sun. The majority of Japanese would say that their religion is Shintō, but what they would mean by this would vary widely from person to person.

Buddhism arrived from India via China and Korea sometime in the 6th century and has for the most part coexisted peacefully with Shintō. About 85 million people in Japan currently practice some form of Buddhism, though most combine their practice with the exercise of periodic Shintō rites. Japanese Buddhism is mostly Mahayana Buddhism, which is notable for its belief in bodhisattva, beings who put off entry into nirvana in order to save all beings stuck in the corrupt world of time.

Japanese Buddhists often call on the assistance of these bodhisattva, usually by chanting mantras or otherwise invoking their names rather than meditating. Zen Buddhism, however, although being a Mayahana sect, places great emphasis on meditation.

# Arts & Crafts

**Rightly described as Japan's cultural heart and soul, Kyoto is famous for keeping alive the flame of Japanese tradition. Almost all of Japan's traditional arts and crafts reached their peak of sophistication and elegance here. From kabuki to textiles, Kyoto's traditional arts and crafts reflect centuries of polishing and refinement in a city that was home to Japan's most discerning citizens for well over 1000 years.**

## A Tradition of Varied Influences

While Kyoto is rightly viewed as Japan's cultural storehouse and the capital of its traditional arts, it also boasts a long history of eagerly embracing the new, the exotic and the experimental. A case in point are the Persian carpets and Flemish tapestries which decorate the Gion Festival floats. Kyoto's savvy silk merchants managed to obtain these Silk Road products even after the Tokugawa Shogunate clamped its lid

Above: A potter making a bowl

on the country in the mid-17th century. When the Meiji Restoration of 1868 once again opened Japan to the world, Kyoto's culturally astute citizens quickly demonstrated as much enthusiasm for European classical music and painting as they did for Western science and technology. The present moment finds Kyoto, along with the rest of Japan, showing a renewed interest in the arts and crafts of its Asian neighbours.

The current artistic scene, for example, shows a new willingness to combine elements previously considered incompatible. In one of the city-sponsored art festivals, for instance, a Brahms quintet might take place on the *nō* (stylised dance-drama) stage of a Shintō shrine, or an Edo-period Buddhist temple might host a performance of *butō* (a form of Japanese modern dance).

Unfortunately, most of Kyoto's craft traditions are in crisis. The silk-weaving industry, which for centuries supported the city's economy and gave work to countless artisans, is in decline as fewer and fewer Japanese wear kimonos. In fact, all crafts tied to the traditional Japanese lifestyle are in similar danger of disappearing.

Whatever the future holds, the legacy of Kyoto's glorious past – its temples, shrines and gardens – will remain to delight the visitor. And, in spite of *pachinko* (vertical pinball-style game) parlours, car parks and other forms of urban ugliness, such things as the maple leaf garnish on your lunch-set tofu or the Nishijin-obi (decorative belt) of your waitress's kimono prove that an artistic sensibility shaped by 1200 years of tradition is still alive.

# Performing Arts

*Nō* and kabuki, Japan's best known theatrical traditions, can both be viewed in Kyoto. The city is home to several schools of *nō* and performances are frequent. *Kyōgen* (ancient comic plays, which are an offspring of *nō*) are also occasionally performed in Kyoto.

## Nō

*Nō* seems to have originated from the happy combination of indigenous Shintō-related dance and mime traditions, and dance forms that originated elsewhere in Asia. It owes its form and its repertory to the artistic dynasty of Kannami Kiyotsugu, which flourished in Kyoto between 1350 and 1450. Rather than a drama in the usual sense, a *nō* play seeks to express a poetic moment by symbolic and almost abstract means. The actors wear masks and perform before an unchanging set design, which features a painting of a large pine tree. The language used is the elegant language of Kyoto's 14th-century court. Obviously, *nō's* rather esoteric qualities make having some previous understanding of the play to be performed especially helpful. An exception to this might be the open-air Takigi Nō, performed on the evenings of 1 and 2 June in the precincts of Heian-jingū. Here, the play of firelight on brocade costumes will captivate even the most jaded viewer.

## NŌ MASKS

Despite the fact that *nō* masks are carved of wood and are therefore immovable, they are often designed so that tilting the masks at various angles can change the expression of the mask, an effect heightened by the lighting of the stage (which is often firelight).

## Kabuki

While *nō* was patronised by the Ashikaga shoguns who created the Ginkaku-ji and Kinkaku-ji, kabuki, which developed much later, was a plebeian form of entertainment supported by the merchant class which came to prominence during the long and peaceful Edo period. It is as vibrant and brash as the former is austere and refined.

Kabuki evolved mainly in Edo (present-day Tokyo), but Kyoto played a big part in its beginnings. It was here, around 1600, that an Izumo shrine priestess and her troupe of dancers started entertaining crowds on the banks of the Kamo-gawa with a new type of dance people dubbed kabuki, a slang expression that meant 'cool' or 'in vogue'. Okuni, the priestess, was the Madonna of her day and knew how to please a crowd. At a time when 'Southern Barbarian' (ie European) fashion was all the rage, she is reported to have sometimes danced in Portuguese garb with a crucifix around her neck.

Okuni's dancers were not above prostituting their talents, and when fights for the ladies' affections became a bit too frequent, the order-obsessed Tokugawa officials declared the entertainment a threat to public morality. When women's kabuki was banned, troupes of adolescent men with unshorn forelocks took over, a development that only fed the flames of samurai ardour. Finally, in 1653, the authorities mandated that only adult men with shorn forelocks could perform kabuki, a development that gave rise to one of kabuki's most fascinating and artistic elements, the *onnagata* (an actor who specialises in portraying women).

Other ingenious features of kabuki include the revolving stage (a kabuki invention), the *hanamichi* (a raised walkway connecting the stage to the back of the theatre and used for dramatic entrances and exits), on-stage assistants *(koken)* and on-stage costume changes *(hiki-nuki)*.

Unlike Western theatre, kabuki is an actor-centred, actor-driven drama. It is essentially the preserve of a small number of acting families, and the Japanese audience takes great enjoyment in watching how different generations of one family perform the same part.

A kabuki program is generally five hours long and is made up of sections of four or five different works. One of the pieces is often a dance-drama. Only the most diehard fans sit through an entire program. Many spectators slip out to enjoy a *bentō* (lunchbox) or a smoke, returning to their seats to catch the scenes they like best.

Kyoto boasted seven kabuki theatres in the Edo period. Now only one, the Minami-za, remains. Completely renovated in 1990, it stands just east of Shijō-Ōhashi, the same site it occupied back in 1615. Every December (and sometimes also November) it hosts Kaomise, during which Tokyo's most famous kabuki actors come to Kyoto to show *(mise)* their faces *(kao)*.

A statue of Okuni, fan in hand and with a samurai sword slung over one shoulder, stands at the east end of Shijō-Ōhashi, diagonally across from the Minami-za.

## Kyōgen

Designed to provide comic relief during a program of *nō* plays, *kyōgen* is farce that takes the spectator from the sublime realm of *nō* into the ridiculous world of the everyday. Using the colloquial language of the time, *kyōgen* pokes fun at such subjects as samurai, depraved priests and faithless women. Masks are not worn, and costumes tend to feature bold, colourful patterns.

The recent years have witnessed a boom in *kyōgen's* popularity, largely thanks to the influence of the mass media and the appearance of

During kabuki performances, diehard kabuki fans may ritually shout out the names of the acting houses to which their favourite performers belong. These shouts are known as *kakegoe*. The men who deliver these *kakegoe* usually lurk in the upper reaches of the theatre.

ARTS & CRAFTS PERFORMING ARTS

---

### TOP FIVE KYOTO MUSEUMS

➡ Kyoto National Museum (p82)

➡ National Museum of Modern Art (p98)

➡ Kyoto Municipal Museum of Art (p98)

➡ Kawai Kanjirō Memorial Hall (p84)

➡ Miyako Messe & Fureai-Kan Kyoto Museum of Traditional Crafts (p98)

a new generation of photogenic young actors. In Kyoto the Shigeyama family is the foremost practitioner of the art. To see *kyōgen* in its original folk-art form, try to catch a performance of Mibu *kyōgen*. These mimed Buddhist morality plays are performed today at Mibu-dera just as they were in Kyoto's early medieval period.

## Kyoto Crafts

One of the best sources of information on upcoming cultural events in Kyoto and Kansai is the magazine *Kansai Scene* (www.kansai scene.com).

After becoming capital of Japan in 784, Kyoto attracted the leading craftspeople from all over the country. They have traditionally come to the city to service the needs of Japan's imperial court, which was based in Kyoto for over 1100 years. In addition to the imperial court, Kyoto was home to the headquarters of Japan's main Buddhist sects, the *kizoku* (noble class), the main tea schools, wealthy merchants and cultured samurai. The result was a city of small workshops filled with busy artisans, all competing with each other to tempt the demanding clientele of the city.

It's hardly surprising, then, that the Kyoto 'brand' symbolises elegance, refinement and excellence. Items bearing the prefix *kyo*, as in *kyo-yūzen* (Kyoto dyed kimono fabric), are revered in Japan as the apogee of sophistication.

There are many ways for the visitor to experience Kyoto's rich craft heritage. To get a full overview of the range of Kyoto crafts, we recommend a visit to the Miyako Messe & Fureai-Kan Kyoto Museum of Traditional Crafts. A short walk away you will find the Kyoto Handicraft Center. Next, we recommend an aimless wander through the heart of Downtown Kyoto, in the region between Oike-dōri and Shijō-dōri (to the north and south) and Kawaramachi-dōri and Karasuma-dōri (to the east and west). Here, you will find dozens of shops selling traditional

---

### GEISHA CRAFTS

Kyoto's geisha, properly known in Kyoto as *geiko* or *maiko* (fully fledged and apprentice geisha, respectively), are walking museums of traditional crafts. In fact, if you want to see several of Kyoto's traditional crafts in one quick glance, the best place to look is at a *geiko* or *maiko* shuffling by on her way to an appointment. Some things to look out for include the following:

**Kimono** The kimono worn by *geiko* and *maiko* are likely to have been made right here in Kyoto, most probably in the workshops in and around the Nishijin textile district. Kimonos are the visible capital in the geisha world; they are worth thousands or even hundreds of thousands of dollars and are loaned to *maiko* by the 'mama-san' (manager) of her house.

**Obi** The obi (kimono sash) worn by *geiko* and *maiko* is where the weaving skills of Kyoto's silk weavers are given their freest rein. They are often wild and almost psychedelic explosions of colour.

**Flower hairpins** Known in Japanese as *hana-kanzashi*, these delicate hairpins are made from silk and light metal, usually with seasonal motifs. *Maiko* wear different *hana-kanzashi* each month.

**Boxwood combs** Handmade boxwood combs (*kushi* in Japanese) are indispensable for creating the wonderful hairstyles of the *maiko*. One reason for using these combs, apart from their incredibly pleasing appearance, is the fact that they don't produce static electricity.

**Umbrellas** On a rainy day, *maiko* and *geiko* are sheltered from the rain by *wagasa* (traditional Japanese umbrellas). With bamboo frames and paper or silk coverings, these umbrellas are perfectly suited to the geisha wardrobe.

Kyoto crafts interspersed with some of Kyoto's cutting-edge modern shops.

## Pottery & Ceramics

Evidence of the first Kyoto wares (*kyō-yaki*, the *yaki* meaning, in this case, 'ware') dates from the reign of Emperor Shōmu in the early 8th century. By the mid-1600s there were more than 10 different kilns active in and around the city. Of these, however, only Kiyomizu-yaki remains today. This kiln first gained prominence through the workmanship of potter Nonomura Ninsei (1596–1660), who developed an innovative method of applying enamel overglaze to porcelain. This technique was further embellished by adding decorative features such as transparent glaze *(sometsuke)*, as well as incorporating designs in red paint *(aka-e)* and celadon *(seiji)*. Kiyomizu-yaki is still actively produced in Kyoto and remains popular with devotees of the tea ceremony.

During the Edo period, many *daimyō* (domain lords) encouraged the founding of kilns and the production of superbly designed ceramic articles. The climbing kiln *(noborigama)* was widely used, and a fine example can be seen at the home of famed Kyoto potter Kawai Kanjirō. Constructed on a slope, the climbing kiln had as many as 20 chambers and could reach temperatures as high as 1400°C.

During the Meiji period, ceramics waned in popularity, but were later part of a general revival in *mingei-hin* (folk arts). This movement was led by Yanagi Sōetsu, who encouraged famous potters such as Kawai, Tomimoto Kenkichi and Hamada Shōji. The English potter Bernard Leach studied in Japan under Hamada and contributed to the folk-art revival. On his return to England, Leach promoted the appreciation of Japanese ceramics in the West.

Those with an interest in Kyoto wares – and Kiyomizu-yaki in particular – should check out the streets below Kiyomizu-dera in Southern Higashiyama. You'll find all manner of shops here selling Kiyomizu-yaki and other types of Japanese pottery. Nearby, on Gojō-dōri, between Higashiōji-dōri and Kawabata-dōri, the Tōki Matsuri (Ceramics Fair) is held on 18 to 20 July. You can also find a wide variety of ceramics in the shops on Teramachi-dōri, between Marutamachi-dōri and Oike-dōri. Finally, the 6th floor of Takashimaya department store has a great selection of pottery.

## Lacquerware

Lacquerware *(shikki* or *nurimono)* is made using the sap from the lacquer tree *(urushi)*. Once lacquer hardens it becomes inert and extraordinarily durable. The most common colour of lacquer is an amber or brown, but additives are used to produce black, violet, blue, yellow and even white. In the better pieces, multiple layers of lacquer are painstakingly applied and left to dry, and finally polished to a luxurious shine.

Japanese artisans have devised various ways to further enhance the beauty of lacquer. The most common method is *maki-e*, which involves the sprinkling of silver and gold powders onto liquid lacquer to form a picture. After the lacquer dries, another coat seals the picture. The final effect is often dazzling and some of the better pieces of *maki-e* lacquerware are now National Treasures.

There are several places in Kyoto where you can see some stunning examples of lacquerware, including *maki-e* lacquerware. The Nomura Museum has a fine collection of lacquerware utensils used in the tea ceremony. Those looking to take a bit of lacquerware home will find an excellent selection at Zōhiko.

Real Japanese lacquerware is covered with a varnish made from the *Toxicodendron vernicifluum* plant, which is known colloquially as 'the lacquer tree'. The resin from these trees produces a strong allergic rash in most people, but lifetime lacquer workers usually develop immunity.

## Textiles

Kyoto is famous for its *kyō-yūzen* textiles. *Yūzen* is a method of silk-dyeing *(senshoku)* developed to perfection in the 17th century by fan painter Miyazaki Yūzen. *Kyō-yūzen* designs typically feature simple circular flowers *(maru-tsukushi)*, birds and landscapes, and stand out for their use of bright-coloured dyes. The technique demands great dexterity in tracing designs by hand *(tegaki)* before rice paste is applied to fabric like a stencil to prevent colours from bleeding into other areas of the fabric. By repeatedly changing the pattern of the rice paste, very complex designs can be achieved.

Traditionally, when the dyeing process was complete, the material was rinsed in the Kamo-gawa and Katsura-gawa rivers (believed to be particularly effective in fixing the colours) before being hung out to dry. Every year in mid-August this ritual is re-enacted and the fabrics flap in the wind like rows of vibrant banners.

During the turbulent civil wars of the 15th century, Kyoto's weavers congregated into a textiles quarter near Kitano-Tenman-gū Shrine called Nishijin (literally, Western Camp). The industry was revamped during the Edo period and the popularity of Nishijin workmanship endured through the Meiji Restoration.

Kyoto is also famed for techniques in stencil-dyeing *(kyō-komon)* and tie-dyeing *(kyō-kanoko shibori)*. *Kyō-komon* (*komon* means 'small crest') gained notoriety in the 16th and 17th centuries, particularly among warriors who ordered the adornment of both their armour and kimono, through the stencilling of highly geometric designs onto fine silk with vibrant colours. Typically the patterns incorporate flowers, leaves and other flora.

At the other end of the refined, courtly spectrum, *aizome* (the technique of dyeing fabrics in vats of fermented indigo plants) gave Japan one of its most distinctive colours. Used traditionally in making hardy work clothes for the fields, Japan's beautiful indigo-blue can still be seen in many modern-day textile goods.

Together with Kyoto-dyed fabrics *(kyō-zome)*, Nishijin weaving (Nishijin-ori) is internationally renowned and dates to the founding of the city. Nishijin techniques were originally developed to satisfy the demands of the nobility who favoured the quality of illustrious silk fabrics. Over time new methods were adopted by the Kyoto weavers and they began to experiment with materials such as gauze, brocade, damask, satin and crepe. The best known Nishijin style is the exquisite *tsuzure* – a tightly woven tapestry cloth produced with a hand loom *(tebata)* – on which detailed patterns are preset.

In 1915 the Orinasu-kan textile museum was established to display Nishijin's fine silk fabrics and embroidery. The museum has two halls which display some stunning examples of Nishijin-ori. Nearby, the Nishijin Textile Center has decent, if touristy, displays on Nishijin-ori, including a demonstration loom, a shop selling Nishijin items and occasional kimono fashion shows.

If you'd like to purchase a kimono or an obi (kimono sash), you will find the best prices on used items at either the Kōbō-san or the Tenjin-san markets. If you're after a new kimono, try Erizen or Takashimaya.

## WABI-SABI

One of the aesthetic principles of traditional Japanese art is known as *wabi-sabi*, which is usually translated as spare, rustic, simple beauty. Many scholars trace the origins of this aesthetic to the tea ceremony, in which rough, irregular tea bowls were sometimes prized more highly than perfectly finished pieces.

## Fans

As with many of Japan's traditional crafts, fans were first made in Kyoto and continue to be prolifically produced here today. *Kyō-sensu* (Kyoto fans) first found popularity among the early aristocracy, but by the late 12th century their popularity had spread to the general populace. Though fans were originally a practical and fashionable tool to keep oneself cool in Japan's sweltering summers, they gradually took on more aesthetic purposes as Japan's arts flourished from the 15th century onwards, from plain fans used in the tea ceremony and incense smelling, to elaborate ones used in *nō* drama and traditional dance. Fans are still commonly used as decorative items and for ceremonial purposes.

Originally made from the leaves of the cypress tree, fans are now primarily made with elaborately painted Japanese paper fixed onto a skeleton of delicate bamboo ribs. The paper can feature decorations from simple geometric designs to courtly scenes from the Heian period and are often sprinkled with gold or silver leaf powder.

Fans make a lightweight and excellent souvenir of Kyoto and can be purchased at major department stores and at speciality shops such as Kyōsen-dō. The latter shop sometimes has fan-making demonstrations.

Like the practice of drinking tea, it is though that the art of paper-making was brought to Japan by Buddhist monks. It is said that the art was introduced into Japan in the early 7th century by monks who used the paper for copying sutras.

**ARTS & CRAFTS IKEBANA**

### Washi

The art of making paper by hand was introduced to Japan from China in the 5th century and it reached its golden age in the Heian era, when it was highly prized by members of the Kyoto court for their poetry and diaries. *Washi* (traditional Japanese paper) is normally produced using mulberry, but it can also be made from mountain shrubs and other plants. One distinctive type of *washi* found in Kyoto is *kyō-chiyogami,* which has traditionally been used by Japanese to wrap special gifts.

*Washi* was made in large quantities in Japan until the introduction of Western paper in the 1870s. After that time, the number of families involved in the craft plummeted. However, there are still a number of traditional papermakers active in Kyoto city and in country areas north of the city. Recently, *washi* has enjoyed something of a revival (there's even *washi* for computer printers!). There are several fine *washi* shops in Kyoto, including Wagami no Mise and Kamiji Kakimoto.

## Ikebana

Ikebana – the art of flower arranging – was developed in the 15th century and can be grouped into three main styles: *rikka* (standing flowers), *shōka* (living flowers), and free-style techniques such as *nageire* (throwing-in) and *moribana* (heaped flowers). There are several thousand different schools, the top three being Ikenobō, Ōhara and Sōgetsu, but they share one aim: to arrange flowers to represent heaven, earth and humanity. Ikebana displays were originally used as part of the tea ceremony, but can now be found in private homes – in the *tokonoma* (sacred alcove) – and even in large hotels.

Apart from its cultural associations, ikebana is also a lucrative business. Its schools have millions of students, including many young women who view proficiency in the art as a means to improve their marriage prospects.

# Architecture & Gardens

**Hidden amid a sea of concrete and neon that looks disappointingly like any other Japanese city, you will find countless pockets of astonishing beauty in Kyoto: ancient temples with graceful wooden halls, traditional townhouses clustered together along narrow streets, colourful Shintō shrines and, best of all, a profusion of gardens unlike anything else in Japan. Indeed, one of the best reasons to come to Kyoto is to immerse yourself in the city's almost limitless collection of gardens and traditional structures.**

## Architecture

### Temples

Despite the frequent earthquakes in Japan, the pagodas at Buddhist temples almost never fall down. They are designed so that each floor moves in opposition to the others in a movement known as 'the snake dance'.

Temples (*tera* or *ji*) vary widely in their construction, depending on the type of school and historical era of construction. From the introduction of Buddhism in the 6th century until the Middle Ages, temples were the most important architectural works in Japan, and hence exerted a strong stylistic influence on all other types of building.

### Evolution of Temple Design

There were three main styles of early temple architecture: *tenjikuyō* (Indian), *karayō* (Chinese) and *wayō* (Japanese). All three styles were in fact introduced to Japan via China. *Wayō* arrived in the 7th century and gradually acquired local character, becoming the basis of much Japanese wooden architecture. It was named so as to distinguish it from *karayō* (also known as Zen style), which arrived in the 12th century. A mixture of *wayō* and *karayō* (known as *setchuyō*) eventually came to dominate, and *tenjikuyō* disappeared altogether.

With their origins in Chinese architecture and with an emphasis on otherworldly perfection, early temples were monumental and symmetrical in layout. A good example of the Chinese influence can be seen in the famous Hōō-dō (Phoenix Hall) at Byōdō-in in Uji, a Tang-style pavilion.

The Japanese affinity for asymmetry eventually affected temple design, leading to the more organic – although equally controlled – planning of later temple complexes. An excellent example in Kyoto is Daitoku-ji, a Rinzai Zen monastery (a large complex containing a myriad of subtemples and gardens).

### Architectural Components

Temples generally have four gates, oriented to the north, south, east and west. The *nandai-mon* (southern gate) is usually the largest one. There is also a *chū-mon* (central gate), which is sometimes incorporated into the cloister. The *niō-mon* (guardian gate) houses frightful-looking statues of gods such as Raijin (the god of thunder) and Fū-jin (the god of wind).

The *Gojū-no-tō* (five-storey pagoda) is a major component of temple design. These are elegant wooden towers, symbolising Shaka, the Historical Buddha. Their design is a variation of the Indian stupa, a structure originally intended to hold the remains of Shaka (sometimes with an actual tooth or chip of bone, but more often represented by crystal or amber). The spire on top usually has nine tiers, representing the nine spheres of heaven.

Kyoto contains a number of excellent examples of five-storey pagodas, including the pagoda at Tō-ji, the best known and the tallest in Japan.

## Shrines

Shrines can be called *jinja, jingū, gū* or *taisha*. The original Shintō shrine is Izumo Taisha in Shimane Prefecture, which has the largest shrine hall in Japan. It is said to have been modelled on the Emperor's residence, and its style, known as *taisha-zukuri*, was extremely influential on later shrine design. Shrines tend to use simple, unadorned wood construction and are built raised above the ground on posts. The roof is gabled, not hipped as with temple architecture. The entrance is generally from the end, not the side, again distinguishing it from temple design. The distinctive roof line of shrine architecture is due to an elaboration of the structural elements of the roof. The criss-cross elements are called *chigi* and the horizontal elements are called *katsuogi*.

### Nagare Style

As Buddhism increased its influence over Shintō, it also affected the architecture. The clean lines of the early shrines were replaced with curving eaves and other ornamental details. Worshippers were provided with shelter by extending the roof or even building a separate worship hall. This led to the *nagare* style, the most common type of shrine architecture. Excellent examples in Kyoto can be found at Shimogamo-jinja and Kamigamo-jinja.

The word for the Shintō shrine gate *(torii)* is written with the kanji for 'bird' and 'be', forming a compound that means something like 'the place where the bird is'. Scholars have noted that several shamanistic traditions in mainland Asia use bird perches in a ceremonial manner.

---

### BUDDHIST IMAGES

There are dozens of images in the Japanese Buddhist pantheon, varying from temple to temple, depending on the religious school or period of construction. As you explore the temples of Kyoto, keep your eyes peeled for the following figures:

**Nyorai (Buddhas)** At the top of the Buddhist cosmic hierarchy, you will find *nyorai* (Buddhas). The four most common images are those of Shaka (Sanskrit: Sakyamuni), the Historical Buddha; Amida (Sanskrit: Amitabha), the Buddha of the Western Paradise; Miroku (Sanskrit: Maitreya), the Buddha of the Future; and Dainichi, the Cosmic Buddha.

**Bosatsu (Bodhisattva)** A *bosatsu* is a Bodhisattva, a being who puts off entry into nirvana in order to help all the beings stuck in the corrupt world of time. The most common *bosatsu* are Kannon (the god – or goddess – of mercy) and Jizō (the protector of travellers and children). Kannon is often depicted as standing in graceful flowing robes or with 1000 arms (the better to help all sentient beings). Jizō is often depicted as a monk with a staff in one hand and a jewel in the other. Other Jizō are barely distinguishable from stones with faintly carved faces or bodies. You might see these wearing red bibs, which reflects Jizō's role as protector of children.

**Myōō (Kings of Light)** These fierce-looking deities entered the Buddhist pantheon from Hinduism. You might see them arranged beside *nyorai* and *bosatsu* in Buddhist temples. The most common figure is Fudō Myōō, the Immovable God of Light. These figures act as protectors and their wrathful forms are thought to snap people out of wrongful thinking.

**Tenbu** Usually directly translated as *'ten'* or *'tenbu'*, these are a group of guardian figures inherited from Indian and Chinese cosmologies. A common example is the four heavenly kings, who guard the Buddha by surrounding him in the four directions.

## Gongen Style

The *gongen* style employs a H-shaped plan, connecting two halls with an intersecting gabled roof and hallway called an *ishi no ma*. This element symbolises the connection between the divine and the ordinary worlds. The best example of this architectural style in Kyoto is at Kitano Tenman-gū.

### Architectural Components

At the entrance to the shrine is the *torii* (gateway) marking the boundary of the sacred precinct. The most dominant *torii* in Kyoto is in front of Heian-jingū, a massive concrete structure a considerable distance south of the shrine. Fushimi Inari-Taisha in southern Kyoto has thousands of bright vermilion gates lining paths up the mountain to the shrine itself.

## Neighbourhood Shrines

Every neighbourhood in every Japanese town or city has its own tiny shrine to Jizō. Pieces of clothing or red bibs draped around Jizō figures are an attempt to cover the souls of dead children. An annual August children's festival (Jizō-bon) features two days of praying and playing around the Jizō shrine by the local children dressed in *yukata* (a light kimono for summer or for bathing in a ryokan).

The shrines are located by *fū-sui* (known in Chinese as feng shui), a specifically Asian form of geomancy. It is impossible (or bad luck) to move them, so they are found almost everywhere, often notched into concrete walls or telephone poles.

These shrines are maintained by the local community, with each person contributing a regular small sum of money. The person responsible

---

### MACHIYA: KYOTO'S TRADITIONAL TOWNHOUSE

One of the city's most notable architectural features are its *machiya*, long and narrow wooden row houses that functioned as both homes and workplaces. The shop area was located in the front of the house, while the rooms lined up behind it formed the family's private living quarters. Nicknamed 'unagi no nedoko' (eel bedrooms), the *machiya*'s elongated shape came about because homes were once taxed according to the amount of their street frontage.

A *machiya* is a self-contained world, complete with private well, store house, Buddhist altar, clay ovens outfitted with huge iron rice cauldrons, shrines for the hearth god and other deities, and interior mini-gardens.

Although well suited to Kyoto's humid, mildew-prone summers, a wooden *machiya* has a limited lifespan of about 50 years. Thus, as the cost of traditional materials and workmanship rose, and as people's desire for a more Western-style lifestyle increased, fewer and fewer people felt the urge to rebuild the old family home, as had been the custom in the past. Those considerations, plus the city's high inheritance tax, convinced many owners to tear down their *machiya*, build a seven-storey apartment building, occupy the ground floor, and live off the rent of their tenants.

The result is that Kyoto's urban landscape – once a harmonious sea of clay-tiled two-storey wooden townhouses – is now a jumble of ferro-concrete offices and apartment buildings.

Ironically, however, *machiya* are making a comeback. After their numbers drastically declined, the old townhouses began to acquire an almost exotic appeal. Astute developers began to convert them into restaurants, clothing boutiques and even hair salons. Today such shops are a major draw for the city's tourist trade, and not only foreign visitors – the Japanese themselves (especially Tokyoites) – love their old-fashioned charm.

A central Kyoto restaurant housed in a *machiya*

for the shrine changes on a yearly basis, but everyone in the area will leave offerings for Jizō, usually something they themselves have excess of, such as fruit, chocolate or sake.

# Gardens

Many of Japan's most famous gardens are in Kyoto. Most of the well-known ones are connected to temples or imperial villas. In addition to these, Kyoto's traditional dwellings and shops feature another type of garden called *tsubo-niwa* – tiny inner gardens that bring light into the building and provide its inhabitants with a sense of the seasons.

Japanese gardens make use of various ingenious devices to achieve their effect. *Shakkei* (borrowed scenery) is one such clever design ploy, by which a distant object, such as a mountain or volcano cone, is incorporated into the garden's design, adding depth and impact. Kyoto's garden designers obviously never anticipated urban sprawl. A good example of *shakkei* is the garden at Tenryū-ji, which incorporates the Arashiyama mountains into the garden design.

## History of Japanese Gardens

As with most elements of Japanese culture, the Japanese garden has its roots in China. There are reports of specially designed gardens around imperial dwellings as early as the Yamato period (300–710 AD), prior to the establishment of the first permanent capital in Nara (710). Around the time Buddhism was first brought to Japan (6th century), imperial missions to China were returning with reports on Chinese culture, including detailed descriptions of fantastic gardens there. Thus, early Japanese gardens were rich in Chinese motifs, patterns and themes from Chinese mythology.

During Japan's classical Heian Period (794–1185), when the country was ruled by emperors rather than warlords, the most important gardens were built on imperial properties. These expansive gardens usually incorporated large water features such as ponds and were designed according to Chinese principles of geomancy. Such gardens featured prominently in court life, as settings for moon-viewing parties, boating, poetry writing and, of course, romantic meetings, all of which are detailed in the classic *Tale of the Genji* (c 1021). Gardens based on Heian-era imperial gardens can be seen in the Kyoto Gosho and Heian-jingū.

The garden at the Zuihō-in subtemple at Daitoku-ji contains stones laid out in the form of the Christian cross. This subtemple was established to honour the Christian Daimyō Ōtomo Sōrin. The stones were arranged in a cross pattern in the 1960s.

Zen Buddhism became popular in Japan during the Kamakura and Muromachi Periods (1185–1568), when the distinctive form of the *kare-sansui* (dry landscape garden; Zen garden) was developed and popularised. Several of Kyoto's famous Zen gardens were laid out during this period, including the world's most famous *kare-sansui* garden: Ryōan-ji's mystical composition of 15 stones floating in a white gravel sea.

The Edo Period (1600–1868) was a time of stability and wealth for Japan. The typical garden from this era is the stroll garden, which recalls earlier imperial gardens in both expanse and detail. The best example of a garden from this period is the classic stroll garden at Katsura Rikyū imperial villa, in southwest Kyoto.

The modern period brought with it an influx of foreign influences and a freedom from classical conventions, resulting in some truly unique garden designs. The best known and most interesting modern Japanese garden designer was Shigemori Mirei (1896–1975). His pleasing abstract design on the north side of the Hōjō Garden at Tōfuku-ji is a must-see for all Japanese-garden lovers.

## Types of Japanese Gardens

Japanese gardens fall into four basic types: *funa asobi* (pleasure boat), *shūyū* (stroll), *kanshō* (contemplative) and *kaiyū* (varied pleasures).

### Funa Asobi

Popular in the Heian period, *funa asobi* gardens featured a pond used for pleasure boating. Such gardens were often built around noble mansions. The garden which surrounds Byōdō-in in Uji is a vestige of this style.

### Shūyū

The *shūyū* garden is intended to be viewed from a winding path, allowing the garden to unfold and reveal itself in stages and from different vantages. Popular during the Heian, Kamakura and Muromachi periods, *shūyū* gardens can be found around many noble mansions and temples from those eras. A celebrated example is Ginkaku-ji.

### Kanshō

The *kanshō* garden is intended to be viewed from one place. Zen rock gardens, also known as *kare-sansui* gardens, are an example of this type, which were designed to aid contemplation. Ryōan-ji is perhaps the most famous example of this type of garden. Although various interpretations of the garden have been put forth (the rocks 'represent a tiger and her cubs', for example), the garden's ultimate meaning, like that of Zen itself, cannot be expressed in words.

### Kaiyū

The *kaiyū* garden features many small gardens with one or more teahouses surrounding a central pond. Like the stroll garden, it is meant to be explored on foot and provides the viewer with a variety of changing scenes, many with literary allusions. The Katsura Rikyū imperial villa is the classic example of this type of garden.

# The Tea Ceremony

Despite all the mystery surrounding it, the tea ceremony is, at heart, simply a way of welcoming a guest with a cup of tea. In Japan, this ritual has been developed and practised for almost 500 years and is properly known as *chadō* (literally, 'the way of tea'). Of course, as with most *dō* (ways) in Japan, the practice has been ritualised and formalised to an almost unimaginable degree. In a typical tea ceremony, both the host and the guests follow a strict set of rules that vary according to the particular school of tea to which the host belongs.

## A History of Tea in Japan

Tea came to Japan from China as part of a cultural package that included kanji and Buddhism, but the beverage did not become popular until the medieval period. Buddhist monks drank tea for its medicinal and stimulatory properties, a practice that gradually spread to warrior

Above: Tea ceremony at Club Ōkitsu Kyoto (p77)

## MATCHA

The tea used in the tea ceremony is called *matcha*. *Matcha* is powdered green tea made from the best parts of the tea leaf. The tea is hand-picked, steamed, then dried and ground into powder. Most teas are infusions; that is, you put the leaves in the hot water and then take them out before drinking. When you drink *matcha*, however, you actually drink the ground tea. This is one reason it contains so many nutrients and is thought by many to be anti-carcinogenic.

society and then to commoners. By the 16th century elite urban commoners such as the merchant and tea master Sen no Rikyū (1522–91) had elevated the preparation, serving and consumption of *matcha* (powdered green tea) to an elaborate ritual. In the 17th century tea masters established their own schools of tea, and these institutions codified, spread and protected the practice over subsequent centuries.

## The Ins & Outs of Tea Ceremonies

The stepping stones that lead to the tea room are intentionally placed unevenly: they force you to empty your mind and concentrate on each step: a very Zen idea.

By this point, you're probably wondering what happens in an actual tea ceremony. First, it must be noted that tea ceremonies can be short and spontaneous or long and extremely formal. They might be held to mark an anniversary, the changing of the seasons or just as an opportunity to see old friends.

In a proper full-length tea ceremony, a group of guests arrive at the location of the gathering, perhaps a home or a temple with its own teahouse, and wait in the outer garden, a peaceful and meditative space. Upon entering the teahouse, they observe while the host arranges the charcoal and serves a special meal of *kaiseki* (Japanese haute cuisine). After the meal, guests are served some simple sweets, take a brief intermission, then return for a serving of viscous *koicha* (thick tea), followed in many cases by a round of *usucha* (thin tea). At certain moments during the gathering, the guests have the chance to admire the hanging scroll, the flower arrangement and the host's careful selection of *chadōgu* (tea utensils).

These days few people have the time or energy to produce or participate in the full-length version, and abbreviated tea ceremonies are often held. These often include just the consumption of one traditional Japanese sweet and a bowl of *usucha,* and the enjoyment of the flowers, scroll and utensils. This is the type of ceremony that most visitors to Kyoto are likely to participate in.

## Experiencing a Tea Ceremony

There are many places in Kyoto that offer tea ceremonies to foreign guests. It's important to note that, as with many things in life, you get what you pay for when it comes to tea ceremonies. The quality of the tea, the utensils, the sweets, the decorations, the setting, the skill of the host and the depth of his/her explanations vary enormously, usually in direct proportion to price. If you would like to participate in a tea ceremony, there are many options. We recommend En (p90), Club Ōkitsu Kyoto (p77) and Camellia Tea Experience (p90).

# Survival Guide

# Transport

## ARRIVING IN KYOTO

Most foreign visitors arrive in Kyoto via Kansai International Airport (KIX; Kyoto's main international entry point) or Kyoto Station by train from other cities in Japan. Kyoto is also within reach of two other airports and it's sometimes cheaper to fly into Tokyo than into KIX.

Flights, cars and tours can be booked online at lonely planet.com.

## Kansai International Airport

Built on an artificial island in Osaka Bay, Kansai International Airport (KIX) is about 75 minutes away from Kyoto by direct express trains.

At KIX, there is a tourist information counter operated by the Osaka prefectural government. It's located roughly in the centre of the international arrivals hall. It can supply maps and answer questions.

If you'd prefer not to lug your bags into Kyoto, there are several luggage delivery services that are located in the arrivals hall.

When it comes time to depart, those travelling on Japanese airlines (JAL and ANA) can make use of an advance check-in counter inside the Japan Railways

(JR) ticket office in Kyoto Station. This service allows you to check-in with your luggage at the station, which is a real bonus for those with heavy bags.

## Train

The fastest and most convenient way to move between KIX and Kyoto is the special JR *Haruka* airport express (reserved/ unreserved ¥3370/2850, 75 minutes). First and last departures from KIX to Kyoto are at 6.30am and 10.16pm Monday to Friday (6.40am on weekends); first and last departures from Kyoto to KIX are at 5.46am and 8.15pm.

If you have time to spare, you can save money by taking the *kankū kaisoku* (Kansai airport express) between the airport and Osaka Station, and then taking a regular *shinkaisoku* (special rapid train) to Kyoto. The total journey by this route takes about 95 minutes with good connections, and costs ¥1750.

## Bus

**Osaka Airport Transport** (☑06-6844-1124; www.okkbus. co.jp/en) runs frequent buses between Kyoto and KIX (¥2550, about 90 minutes). In Kyoto, the buses depart from opposite the south side of Kyoto Station, in front of Avanti department store.

## Taxi

Perhaps the most convenient option is the **MK Taxi Sky Gate Shuttle** (☑778-5489; www.mktaxi-japan.com) limousine van service, which will drop you off anywhere in Kyoto for ¥3600 – simply go to the staff counter at the south end of the KIX arrivals hall and they will do the rest. From Kyoto to the airport it is necessary to make reservations two days in advance and staff will pick you up anywhere in Kyoto and take you to the airport.

A similar service is offered by **Yasaka Taxi** (☑803-4800). Keep in mind these are shared taxis (actually vans), so you may be delayed by the driver picking up or dropping off other passengers.

## Kyoto Station

Kyoto Station is linked to nearby cities by several excellent train lines, including Japan Railways (JR). JR also has links to cities further afield, many of which are served by super-fast *shinkansen* (bullet trains). If you plan to do a lot of train travel around the rest of Japan, consider buying a Japan Rail Pass.

Private lines connect Kyoto Station with Nagoya, Nara, Osaka and Kōbe. Where they exist, private lines are always cheaper than JR. In particular, if you're travelling between Kyoto Station and Nara, you'll probably find a *tokkyū* (limited express) on the Kintetsu line to be faster and more comfortable than JR.

Kyoto Station is in the south of the city, just below Shichijō-dōri. The easiest way to get downtown from this station is to hop on the Karasuma subway line. There is a bus terminal on the north side of the station from where you can catch buses to all parts of town.

## Osaka International Airport

Osaka International Airport, commonly known as Itami (ITM), is closer to Kyoto than KIX, but it handles mostly domestic traffic. Still, you might get lucky and find that your international carrier will tack on a domestic leg from Tokyo to Itami.

You'll find an information counter with English-speaking staff in the main arrivals hall. There are several luggage delivery services in the arrivals hall if you don't want to carry your bags to Kyoto.

### Bus

**Osaka Airport Transport**
(☑06-6844-1124; www.okk bus.co.jp/en) runs frequent airport limousine buses between Itami and Kyoto Station (¥1310, 55 minutes). There are less frequent pick ups and drop offs at some

of Kyoto's main hotels. The Itami stop is outside the arrivals hall – buy your ticket from the machine near the bus stop and ask one of the attendants which stand is for Kyoto. The Kyoto Station stop is in front of Avanti department store, which is opposite the south side of the station.

### Taxi

**MK Taxi Sky Gate Shuttle**
(☑778-5489; www.mktaxi-japan. com) offers limousine van service to/from the airport for ¥2400. Call at least two days in advance to reserve, or ask at the information counter in the arrivals hall.

## Nagoya (Central Japan International Airport)

Nagoya's new Central Japan International Airport (NGO), commonly known as Centrair, may seem like a long way from Kyoto, but if you're travelling with a Japan Rail Pass, you'll find that it can be a good option, especially if you get a good deal on your flight.

### Train

The Meitetsu Tokoname Railroad line connects Centrair with Nagoya Station (¥870, 30 minutes), which connects to the Tōkaidō *shinkansen* (bullet train) line. It is therefore possible to use Centrair as your gateway to Kyoto.

The *shinkansen* (¥5800, 36 minutes) goes to/from Nagoya Station. You can save around half the cost by taking regular express trains, but you will need to change trains at least once and can expect the trip to take about three hours.

## Tokyo (Narita & Haneda International Airports)

### Air

It's perfectly possible to fly to/from Tokyo via either Narita International Airport (NRT) or Haneda International Airport (HND) when visiting Kyoto. You can catch domestic flights from either airport on to Kansai International Airport (KIX) or Osaka International Airport (ITM).

### Train

You can go by train from Narita or Haneda to Kyoto. From Narita, take the *Narita Airport Express* (N'Ex) to Tokyo Station and then switch to a *shinkansen* to Kyoto. The total journey will take about four hours and cost ¥15,860. From Haneda, take airport transport (there are several options) between the airport and either Tokyo Station or Shinagawa Station and switch to a *shinkansen*. The total journey will take about three hours and cost ¥13,490.

---

### CLIMATE CHANGE & TRAVEL

Every form of transport that relies on carbon-based fuel generates $CO_2$, the main cause of human-induced climate change. Modern travel is dependent on aeroplanes, which might use less fuel per kilometre per person than most cars but travel much greater distances. The altitude at which aircraft emit gases (including $CO_2$) and particles also contributes to their climate change impact. Many websites offer 'carbon calculators' that allow people to estimate the carbon emissions generated by their journey and, for those who wish to do so, to offset the impact of the greenhouse gases emitted with contributions to portfolios of climate-friendly initiatives throughout the world. Lonely Planet offsets the carbon footprint of all staff and author travel.

## NEGOTIATING JAPAN'S RAIL SYSTEM – PASSES & PHRASES

### Japan Rail Pass

The Japan Rail Pass is a must if you're planning extensive train travel within Japan. It will save you both money and the need to carry change each time you board a train (though with a Green Car Pass for 1st-class travel, you have to make reservations at a ticket office). The most important thing to note about the pass is that Japan Rail Passes *must be purchased outside Japan.* They are only available to foreign tourists and Japanese overseas residents. The pass cannot be used for the super express *nozomi shinkansen* service, but is OK for everything else (including other *shinkansen* services). Children between the ages of six and 11 qualify for child passes, while those below six years ride for free.

As a one-way reserved-seat Kyoto–Tokyo *shinkansen* ticket costs ¥13,520, travelling Kyoto–Tokyo–Kyoto will make a seven-day pass come close to paying off. Note that the pass is valid only on Japan Railways (JR) services (ie you still have to pay for private train services).

In order to get a pass, you must first purchase an 'exchange order' outside Japan at JAL and ANA offices or major travel agencies. Once you arrive in Japan, you must bring this order to a JR Travel Service Centre (found in most major JR stations and at Narita and Kansai international airports). You'll need to show your passport when you validate your pass. Choose the date on which your pass becomes valid carefully: if you plan to spend several days in Tokyo or Kyoto before setting off to explore Japan, set your pass to become active on the morning you leave those cities.

For more information on the pass and overseas purchase locations, visit the Japan Rail Pass website (www.japanrailpass.net).

| DURATION (DAYS) | REGULAR ADULT (¥) | REGULAR CHILD (¥) | GREEN ADULT (¥) | GREEN CHILD (¥) |
|---|---|---|---|---|
| 7 | 28,300 | 14,150 | 37,800 | 18,900 |
| 14 | 45,100 | 22,550 | 61,200 | 30,600 |
| 21 | 57,700 | 28,850 | 79,600 | 39,800 |

### Useful Words & Phrases

**TRAIN TYPES**

| | | |
|---|---|---|
| *shinkansen* | 新幹線 | bullet train |
| *tokkyū* | 特急 | limited express |
| *shinkaisoku* | 新快速 | JR special rapid train |
| *kyūkō* | 急行 | express |
| *kaisoku* | 快速 | JR rapid or express |
| *futsū* | 普通 | local |
| *kaku-eki-teisha* | 各駅停車 | local |

**OTHER USEFUL WORDS**

| | | |
|---|---|---|
| *jiyū-seki* | 自由席 | unreserved seat |
| *shitei-seki* | 指定席 | reserved seat |
| *green-sha* | グリーン車 | 1st-class car |
| *ōfuku* | 往復 | return trip |
| *katamichi* | 片道 | one way |
| *kin'en-sha* | 禁煙車 | nonsmoking car |
| *kitsuen-sha* | 喫煙車 | smoking car |

# GETTING AROUND KYOTO

Kyoto has an excellent public transport system. There is a comprehensive bus network, two subway lines, six train lines (two of which can be used like subways for trips around Kyoto) and a huge fleet of taxis.

Furthermore, being largely flat, Kyoto is a great city for cycling – it's perfectly feasible to rent or buy a bicycle on your first day in the city and never have to use the public transport system.

Note that Kyoto was not designed with motor vehicles in mind. There's no need to hire a car; in fact, it's far more trouble than it's worth.

## Bus

Kyoto has an intricate network of bus routes providing an efficient way of getting around at moderate cost. Many of the routes used by visitors have announcements in English. Most buses run between 7am and 9pm, though a few run earlier or later.

### Bus Terminals & Stops

Kyoto's main bus terminals are also train stations: Kyoto Station, Sanjō Station, Karasuma-Shijō Station and Kitaōji Station. The bus terminal at Kyoto Station is on the north side and has three main departure bays (departure points are indicated by the letter of the bay and number of the stop within that bay).

Bus stops usually have a map of destinations from that stop and a timetable for the buses serving that stop. Unfortunately, all of this information is in Japanese, so nonspeakers will simply have to ask locals for help.

## Riding Buses

Three-digit numbers written against a red background denote loop lines: bus 204 runs around the northern part of the city, and buses 205 and 206 circle the city via Kyoto Station. Buses with route numbers on a blue background take other routes.

When heading for locations outside the city centre, be careful which bus you board. Kyoto City buses are green, Kyoto buses are tan, and Keihan buses are red and white.

Bus entry is usually through the back door and exit is via the front door. Inner-city buses charge a flat fare (¥230 for adults, ¥120 for children ages six to 12, free for those younger), which you drop into the clear plastic receptacle on top of the machine next to the driver on your way out. A separate machine gives change for ¥100 and ¥500 coins or ¥1000 notes.

On buses serving the outer areas, take a *seiri-ken* (numbered ticket) on boarding. When alighting, an electronic board above the driver displays the fare corresponding to your ticket number (drop the *seiri-ken* into the ticket box with your fare).

## Bus Maps & Information

The main bus information centre is located in front of Kyoto Station. Here you can pick up bus maps, purchase bus tickets and passes (on all lines, including highway buses), and get additional information.

The Kyoto Tourist Information Center (TIC) stocks the *Bus Navi: Kyoto City Bus Sightseeing Map*, which shows the city's main bus lines. But this map is not exhaustive. If you can read a little Japanese, pick up a copy of the regular (and more detailed) Japanese bus map available at major bus terminals throughout the city, including the main bus information centre.

## Bicycle

Kyoto is a great city to explore on a bicycle. With the exception of the outlying areas, it is mostly flat and there is a useful bike path running the length of the Kamo-gawa.

Many guesthouses rent or lend bicycles to their guests and there are also rental shops around Kyoto Station, in Arashiyama and in Downtown Kyoto. With a decent bicycle and a good map, you can easily make your way all around the city.

---

### KYOTO BUS & SUBWAY PASSES

To save time and money you can buy a *kaisū-ken* (book of five tickets) for ¥1000. There's also a *shi-basu Kyoto-bus ichinichi jōshaken kādo* (one-day card) valid for unlimited travel on Kyoto City buses and Kyoto buses (these are different companies) that costs ¥500. A similar pass *(Kyoto kankō ichinichi jōsha-ken)* that allows unlimited use of the bus and subway costs ¥1200. A *Kyoto kankō futsuka jōsha-ken* (two-day bus/subway pass) costs ¥2000. *Kaisū-ken* can be purchased directly from bus drivers. The other passes and cards can be purchased at major bus terminals and at the bus information centre. Also, be sure to refer to the Kansai Thru Pass boxed text (p181).

Dedicated bicycle tours are also available.

Unfortunately, Kyoto's bike parking facilities must be among the worst in the world – hence the number of bikes you see haphazardly locked up around the city. Many bikes end up stolen or impounded during regular sweeps of the city (particularly those near entrances to train/subway stations). If your bike does disappear, check for a poster (in both Japanese and English) in the vicinity indicating the time of seizure and the inconvenient place you'll have to go to pay the ¥2000 fine and retrieve your bike.

The city *usually* does not impound bikes on Sundays or holidays, so you can park pretty much wherever you wish on those days.

If you don't want to worry about your bike being stolen or impounded, we recommend using one of the city-operated bicycle and motorcycle parking lots. There is one downtown on Kiyamachi-dōri midway between Sanjō-dōri and Shijō-dōri, another near Kyoto Station, and another in the north of town near the Eizan Densha Station at Demachi-yanagi. These places charge ¥150 per day (buy a ticket from the machine on your way in or out).

**ONLINE TRANSPORT INFORMATION**

**HyperDia** (www.hyper dia.com/en) The most useful English-language site for planning train travel around Japan.

**Kyoto-Navi** (www. kics-cn.com/kyoto-navi) A handy website for figuring out transport around Kyoto.

## Hire

A great place to rent a bicycle is the **Kyoto Cycling Tour Project** (京都サイクリングツアープロジェクト; KCTP; Map p212; ☑354-3636; www.kctp.net/en; 552-13 Higashi-Aburanokoji-chō, Aburanokōji-dōri, Shiokōji-sagaru, Shimogyō-ku; ⏰9am-7pm; ⓢKarasuma line to Kyoto, ⓡJR line to Kyoto) ✐. It rents out mountain bikes (¥1500 per day), which are perfect for getting around Kyoto. You can rent them at its main shop near Kyoto Station or four other 'cycling terminals' around town (see its website for locations). KCTP also conducts a variety of bicycle city tours, which are an excellent way to see the city.

The **B.B House Maruni** (B.B House マルニ; ☑771-6644; ⏰9am-8pm Mon-Sat) bicycle shop is a good place to rent a bicycle to explore the Northern Higashiyama area. It's within walking distance of Ginkaku-ji, but the closest bus stop is Kinrin-shako-mae. Look for it just south of a Fresco supermarket.

Most rental outfits require you to leave ID such as a passport.

## Subway

Kyoto has two efficient subway lines, operating from 5.30am to 11.30pm. Minimum adult fare is ¥210 (children ¥110).

The quickest way to travel between the north and south of the city is the Karasuma subway line. The line has 15 stops and runs from Takeda in the far south, via Kyoto Station, to the Kyoto International Conference Hall (Kokusaikaikan Station) in the north.

The east–west Tōzai subway line traverses Kyoto from Uzumasa-Tenjingawa Station in the west, meeting the Karasuma subway line at Karasuma-Oike Sta-

tion, and continuing east to Sanjō-Keihan, Yamashina and Rokujizō in the east and southeast.

## Train

The main train station in Kyoto is Kyoto Station, which is actually two stations under one roof: JR Kyoto Station and Kintetsu Kyoto Station.

In addition to the private Kintetsu line that operates from Kyoto Station, there are two other private train lines in Kyoto: the Hankyū line that operates from Downtown Kyoto along Shijō-dōri and the Keihan line that operates from stops along the Kamo-gawa.

### Buying a Ticket

All stations are equipped with automatic ticket machines, which are simple to operate. Destinations and fares are all posted above the machines in both Japanese and English – once you've figured out the fare to your destination, just insert your money and press the yen amount. Most of these machines accept paper currency in addition to coins (usually just ¥1000 notes). If you've made a mistake, press the red *tori-keshi* (cancel) button. There's also a help button to summon assistance.

### Discount Ticket Shops

Known as *kakuyasu-kippu-uriba*, these stores deal in discounted tickets for trains, buses, domestic flights, ferries, and a host of other things such as cut-rate stamps and phone cards. Typical savings on *shinkansen* tickets are between 5% and 10%, which is good news for long-term residents who are not eligible for Japan Rail Passes. Discount ticket agencies are found around train stations in medium and

## KANSAI THRU PASS

This pass is a real bonus to travellers who plan to do a fair bit of exploration in the Kansai area. It enables you to ride on city subways, private railways and city buses in Kyoto, Nara, Osaka, Kōbe and Wakayama. It also entitles you to discounts at many attractions in the Kansai area. A two-day pass costs ¥4000 and a three-day pass costs ¥5200. It is available at the Kansai International Airport travel counter on the 1st floor of the arrivals hall and at the main bus information centre in front of Kyoto Station, among other places. For more information, visit www.surutto.com/tickets/kansai_thru_english.html.

large cities. The best way to find one is to ask at the *kōban* (police box) outside the station.

Around Kyoto Station, you'll find **Tōkai Discount Ticket Shop** (Map p212; ☑north side 344-0330, south side 662-6640; ☑north side 9.30am-7.30pm Mon-Fri, 9am-7pm Sat, Sun & holidays, south side 10am-8pm).

## Taxi

Taxis are a convenient, but expensive, way of getting from place to place about town. A taxi can usually be flagged down in most parts of the city at any time. There are also a large number of *takushī noriba* (taxi stands) in town, outside most train/subway stations, department stores etc.

There is no need to touch the back doors of the cars at all – the opening/closing mechanism is controlled by the driver.

Fares generally start at ¥640 for the first 2km. The exception is **MK Taxi** (☑778-4141; www.mktaxi-japan.com), where fares start at ¥600. Regardless of which taxi company you go for, there's a 20% surcharge for rides between midnight and 6am. MK Taxi also provides tours of the city with English-speaking drivers. For a group of up to four people, prices

start at ¥22,300 for three hours.

## Car & Motorcycle

Kyoto's heavy traffic and narrow roads make driving in the city difficult and stressful. You will almost always do better riding a bicycle or catching public transport. Unless you have specific needs, do not even entertain the idea of renting a car to tour the city – it's far more cost and headache than any traveller needs (plus parking fines start at ¥15,000).

However, it makes sense to rent a car if you plan to explore certain rural areas that aren't serviced by train lines (such as Miyama-chō). Driving is on the left-hand side in Japan. A litre of petrol costs around ¥157.

### Driving Licence & Permits

Travellers from most nations are able to drive in Japan with an International Driving Permit (IDP) backed up by their own regular driving licence. The IDP is issued by your national automobile association and costs around US$5 in most countries. Make sure it's endorsed for cars and motorcycles if you're licensed for both.

Travellers from Switzerland, France and Germany (and others whose countries

are not signatories to the Geneva Convention of 1949 concerning international driving licences) are not allowed to drive in Japan on a regular international licence. Rather, travellers from these countries must have their own licence backed by an authorised translation of the same licence. These translations can be made by their country's embassy or consulate in Japan, or by the **Japan Automobile Federation** (JAF; ☑0570-00-2811, 03-6833-9000; www.jaf.or.jp; 2-2-17 Shiba, Minato-ku, Tokyo 105-0014).

### Car Hire

There are several car-hire agencies in Kyoto. **Toyota Rentacar Kyoto Eki Shinkansen-guchi Branch** (Map p212; ☑03-5954-8020, toll-free within Japan 0800-7000-815; https://rent.toyota.co.jp/en; Kamitonoda-chō 31-1, Higashi-Kujō, Minami-ku) is about a 200m walk from the south (Hachijō) exit of Kyoto Station. The **Toyota Rentacar Hyakumamben Branch** (Map p216; ☑03-5954-8020, toll-free within Japan 0800-7000-815; https://rent.toyota.co.jp/en; Tanakamonzen-chō 103-31, Sakyō-ku) at the Hyakumamben intersection in Northern Higashiyama is good for those heading north into the Kitayama area. You'll need to show an IDP to rent a car.

Typical hire rates for a small car are about ¥5000 to ¥7000 for the first day, with reductions for rentals of more than one day. Move up a bracket and you're looking at about ¥9000 to ¥14,000 for the first day, with reductions for rentals of more than one day. On top of the hire charge, there's a ¥1000 per day insurance cost.

Some car-hire agencies, including Toyota, have *some* cars with English GPS systems (called 'car navi' in Japanese). Be sure to ask when making reservations.

# Directory A–Z

## Customs Regulations

| Alcohol | up to 3 760ml bottles |
|---|---|
| Gifts/ souvenirs | up to ¥200,000 in total value |
| Perfume | 60ml (2 ounces) |
| Tobacco products | 100 cigars/ 400 cigarettes/ 500g loose |

## Electricity

100V/50Hz/60Hz

The Japanese electric current is 100V AC. Tokyo and eastern Japan are on 50Hz, and western Japan – including Nagoya, Kyoto and Osaka – is on 60Hz.

Most electrical items from elsewhere in the world will function on Japanese current.

Both transformers and plug adaptors are readily available in Kyoto's Teramachi-dōri electronics district, running south of Shijō-dōri or at Bic Camera.

## Embassies

Many countries maintain consulates in Osaka in addition to their embassies in Tokyo. Since Osaka is close to Kyoto by train, it's usually easy to visit these consulates. A few countries don't have proper consulates in Osaka or Kyoto. For these, you need to travel to the embassy in Tokyo to receive consular and citizen services.

**Australian Consulate** (☑06-6941-9271; www.australia.or.jp/en/consular/osaka; 16th fl, Twin 21 MID Tower, 2-1-61 Shiromi, Chūō-ku, Osaka)

**Canadian Embassy** (カナダ大使館; ☑03-5412-6200; www.canadainternational.gc.ca/japan-japon/index.aspx?lang=eng; 7-3-38 Akasaka, Minato-ku, Tokyo; ⑤Ginza line to Aoyama-itchōme, exit 4)

**French Consulate** (Map p216; www.consulfrance-kyoto.org; 8 Izumidono-chô, Yoshida, Sakyô-ku, Kyoto)

**German Consulate** (☑06-6440-5070; www.japan.diplo.de; 35th fl, Umeda Sky Bldg Tower East, 1-1-88-3501 Ōyodonaka, Kita-ku, Osaka)

**Irish Embassy** (☑03-3263-0695; www.irishembassy.jp; Ireland House, 2-10-7 Kōjimachi, Chiyoda-ku, Tokyo)

**Netherlands Consulate** (☑06-6944-7272; http://japan.nlembassy.org; 33rd fl, Twin 21 MID Tower, 2-1-61 Shiromi, Chūō-ku, Osaka)

**New Zealand Consulate** (☑06-6373-4583; Umeda Centre Bldg, 2-4-12 Nakazaki-nishi, Kita-ku, Osaka)

**People's Republic of China Osaka Consulate** (中華人民共和国駐大阪総領事館; ☑06-6445-9481; http://osaka.china-consulate.org/jpn/; 3-9-2 Utsubo Honmachi, Nishi-ku, Osaka)

**South Korean Consulate** (駐大阪大韓民国総領事館; Map p130; ☑06-6213-1401; http://jpn-osaka.mofa.go.kr/worldlanguage/asia/osa/main; 2-3-4 Shinsaibashi, Chūō-ku, Osaka)

**UK Consulate** (☑06-6120-5600; www.gov.uk/government/world/organisations/british-embassy-tokyo/office/british-consulate-general-osaka.ja; 19th fl, Epson Osaka Bldg, 3-5-1 Bakurōmachi, Chūō-ku, Osaka)

**US Consulate** (☎06-6315-5900; http://osaka.usconsulate.gov; 2-11-5 Nishitenma, Kita-ku, Osaka)

## Emergencies

Although most emergency operators in Kyoto don't speak English, they can usually refer you to someone who does. Have your address handy when calling for assistance. Speak slowly and clearly. Words such as 'fire', 'police' and 'ambulance' should be understood.

*Kōban* (police boxes) are small police stations typically found at city intersections. Most can be recognised by the small, round red lamp outside. They are a logical place to head to in an emergency, but remember that the police may not always speak English.

**Ambulance** (☎119)
**Fire** (☎119)
**Police** (☎110)

## Gay & Lesbian Travellers

With the possible exception of Thailand, Japan is Asia's most enlightened nation with regard to the sexual preferences of foreigners. Some travellers have reported problems when checking into love hotels with a partner of the same sex, and it does pay to be discreet in rural areas. Apart from this, same-sex couples are unlikely to encounter too many problems.

While there is a sizable gay community in Kyoto, and a number of establishments where gay men congregate, they will take a fair amount of digging to discover. There's a more active scene in Osaka and many of Kyoto's gay resi-

dents make the trip there. Lesbians are poorly served in Kyoto and Osaka and it's difficult to find specifically lesbian-friendly venues.

**Utopia** (www.utopia-asia.com) is the site most commonly frequented by English-speaking gay and lesbian people.

## Health

Japan is an advanced country with high standards of hygiene and few endemic diseases. There are no special immunisations needed to visit Japan and, other than bringing prescription medications from home, no special preparations need to be made.

## Internet Access

You'll find internet cafes and other access points in most major Japanese cities. Expect to pay from ¥200 to ¥700 per hour at an internet cafe. As a rule, internet connections are both fast (using DSL or ADSL) and reliable in Japan.

Most hotels and hostels offer free wi-fi for their guests. At most places it's free, but some places charge for it. Some places have no in-room wi-fi at all (this is particularly true of smaller older hotels and ryokan). Some hotels have LAN cable internet access points in hotel rooms instead of wi-fi (the hotels can usually provide LAN cables, but it's more convenient to bring your own to avoid having to get hold of one in each place you stay). These LAN connections usually work fine, but you may occasionally find it hard to log on due to software or hardware compatibility issues or configuration problems – in these cases the front desk staff *may* be able to help.

We use an internet symbol (@) for accommodation

---

**ADDRESSES IN KYOTO**

In Japan, finding a place from its address can be difficult, even for locals. The problem is twofold: first, the address is given by an area rather than a street; and second, the numbers are not necessarily consecutive. To find an address, the usual process is to ask directions. Officers at the numerous local police boxes (*kōban*) can give directions.

We use a simplified system for addresses. We either give the area (eg Higashiyama-ku, Nanzen-ji) or we give the street on which the place is located, followed by the nearest cross street (eg Karasuma-dōri-Imadegawa). In some cases, we also give additional information to show where the place lies in relation to the intersection of the two streets mentioned. In Kyoto, the land usually slopes gently to the south; thus, an address might indicate whether a place lies above or north of (*agaru*) or below or south of (*sagaru* or *kudaru*) a particular east–west road. An address might also indicate whether a place lies east (*higashi*) or west (*nishi*) of the north–south road. Thus, 'Karasuma-dōri-Imadegawa' simply means the place is near the intersection of Karasuma-dōri and Imadegawa-dōri; 'Karasuma-dōri-Imadegawa-sagaru' indicates that it's south of that intersection. Likewise, 'Sanjō-dōri, Karasuma nishi-iru' means that the place is on Sanjō-dōri, just west of Karasuma-dōri.

## GETTING ONLINE IN KYOTO

Wi-fi or internet is everywhere, but it is often available only to subscribers of various Japanese services, many of which are not easy for travellers to join (especially those who don't speak and read Japanese). There are a number of ways to get online, though, and Japan has been trying to improve the options for travellers.

**Freespot Map** (www.freespot.com/users/map_e.html) Has a list of internet hotspots. It's not exhaustive and the maps are in Japanese, but it's still quite useful.

**Starbucks** Virtually all Starbucks in Japan offer free wi-fi to their customers, but you must register (go to http://starbucks.wi2.co.jp).

**Kyoto City Free Wi-fi Service** The city of Kyoto has recently launched a free wi-fi access program for foreign travellers, with hotspots across the city. You must email to get the access code. Go to http://kanko.city.kyoto.lg.jp/wifi/en/ to find a map of hotspots and sign up. Note that access is limited to three hours, but you can get another access code for additional hours.

**Iijmio Japan Travel SIM** (https://t.iijmio.jp/en) You can buy these SIM cards from major electronics shops in Kyoto. Your device must be unlocked and you must be able to input the APN settings to use these. They are good for three months and offer 2GB of data. The company is tied in with Brastel and you can make (but not receive) voice calls with these. For incoming and outgoing calls, you can also use Skype. Unlike some other SIM cards, no telephone call is required to activate these cards, making them a great choice for travellers.

**B-Mobile SIM cards** (www.bmobile.ne.jp/english) You can buy B-Mobile Visitor SIM cards from major electronics shops in Kyoto. You can also order them online and have them delivered to your first night's lodgings or even to the post office at your arrival airport to hold for you. These will usually allow internet use for a specific length of time (a month is common). Note that the amount of data you can download is limited, and your device must be unlocked and you must be able to input the APN settings. These are data-only (ie no voice) but you can use Skype with them. A call is required to activate these cards (usually, but not always, someone at the shop can make the call).

**Boingo** (www.boingo.com) Subscribers to the Boingo global plan can use BB Mobile-point wi-fi at McDonald's restaurants and some other spots.

**Portable internet connections** You can rent data cards, USB dongles or pocket wi-fi devices from various phone-rental companies in Japan. The most user-friendly option with English-language service is provided by **Rentafone Japan** (☎0120-74-6487; www.rentafonejapan.com), which offers two types of pocket wi-fi from ¥3900 per week with unlimited usage.

options that have at least one computer with internet access for guests' use. We also indicate where wi-fi (🛜) is available.

## Internet Terminals

**Kinko's** (キンコーズ; Map p208; ☎213-6802; 651-1 Tearaimizu-chō, Karasuma-dōri, Takoyakushi-sagaru, Nakagyō-ku; 1st 10min ¥270, then every 10min ¥216; ⏰24hr; 🚊Karasuma line to Shijō or Karasuma-Oike) This copy shop has several terminals where

you can log on to the internet. It's expensive but conveniently located.

**Kyoto Prefectural International Center** (Map p212; ☎342-5000; 9th fl, Kyoto Station Bldg; per 15min ¥100; ⏰10am-6pm, closed 2nd & 4th Tue, public holidays; 🚊Karasuma line to Kyoto) There's no wi-fi here, so you must use the machines provided.

**Tops Café** (トップスカフェ; Map p212; ☎681-9270; www.topsnet.co.jp/5/; 2F

Daiichi Doboku Bldg, 53-1 Higashikujo-Kamitonoda-chō, Minami-ku; per 15min ¥129, plus ¥200 registration fee; ⏰24hr; 🚊Karasuma line to Kyoto, 🚉JR Tōkaidō main line, JR Tōkaidō shinkansen line to Kyoto) This is an all-night manga/internet cafe where you can actually spend the night in the booths if you want. It's just outside the south (Hachijō) exit of Kyoto Station.

## Maps

Available free at the **Kyoto Tourist Information Center** (京都総合観光案内所; TIC; Map p212; 📞343-0548; 2F Kyoto Station Bldg, Shimogyō-ku; ⏱8.30am-7pm; ⑤Karasuma line to Kyoto), the *Kyoto City Map* is a decent map of the city with several detailed insets of the major sightseeing districts. Also available is the *Bus Navi: Kyoto City Bus Sightseeing Map*, which has detailed information on bus routes in the city and some of the major stops written in both English and Japanese.

There are many other useful maps for sale at local English-language bookshops, some of which are practical for excursions outside Kyoto. Shōbunsha's *Tourist Map of Kyoto, Nara, Osaka and Kōbe* is the best privately produced map of these cities.

## Medical Services

Medical care in Japan is reasonably priced, particularly in comparison to costs in the USA. The quality of care varies enormously, from completely competent to dangerously incompetent. You'll usually find the best doctors in large teaching hospitals, such as Kyoto University Hospital. Small local clinics should be avoided unless there are no other choices.

Many hospitals and clinics will be wary of treating foreigners because they don't know how payment will be made (most Japanese belong to the national health system). Where necessary, show proof of your travel insurance or cash. If treatment is absolutely necessary, demanding firmly but politely to be treated is the best approach.

**Kyoto University Hospital** (京都大学医学部附属病院; Map p216; 📞751-3111; 54 Shōgoinkawahara-chō, Sakyō-ku; ⏱8.30am-11am; 🚃Keihan line to Jingū-Marutamachi) is the best hospital in Kyoto. There is an information counter near the entrance on the ground floor that can point you in the right direction. Patients without appointments are seen in the morning. Go at 8.30am to reduce your wait (they start seeing patients at 9am).

## Money

The currency in Japan is the yen (¥). The Japanese pronounce yen as 'en', with no 'y' sound. The kanji for yen is: 円.

Yen coins come in the following denominations:

➡ ¥1 lightweight, silver colour

➡ ¥5 bronze colour, hole in the middle, value in Chinese character

➡ ¥10 copper colour

➡ ¥50 silver colour, hole in the middle

➡ ¥100 silver colour

➡ ¥500 large with silver colour

Yen banknotes come in the following denominations:

➡ ¥1000

➡ ¥2000 (rare)

➡ ¥5000

➡ ¥10,000

### ATMs

ATMs are almost as common as vending machines in Japan. Unfortunately, most of these do not accept foreign-issued cards. Even if they display Visa and Master Card logos, most accept only Japan-issued versions of these cards.

Fortunately, Japanese postal ATMs accept cards that belong to the following international networks: Visa, Plus, MasterCard, Maestro, Cirrus, American Express, JCB, Union Pay, Discover and Diners Club. You'll find postal ATMs in almost all post offices, and you'll find post offices in even the smallest Japanese village. These ATMs have instructions in English.

Note that postal ATMs work with bank or cash cards – you cannot use credit cards, even with a PIN number, in postal ATMs. That is to say, you cannot use postal ATMs to perform a cash advance.

Most postal ATMs are open 9am to 5pm on weekdays, 9am to noon on Saturday, and are closed on Sunday and holidays. Some postal ATMs in very large central post offices are open longer hours. If you need cash outside these hours, try the **Kyoto central post office** (京都中央郵便局; Map p212; 📞365-2471; 843-12 Higashishiokōji-chō, Shimogyō-ku; ⏱9am-9pm Mon-Fri, to 7pm Sat & Sun, ATMs 12.05am-11.55pm Mon-Sat, to 9pm Sun & holidays; ⑤Karasuma line to Kyoto), next to Kyoto Station.

**Citibank** (シティバンク; Map p208; 📞212-5387; ⏱office 9am-3pm Mon-Fri, ATM 24hr; ⑤Karasuma line to Shijō) has a 24-hour ATM in its lobby that accepts most foreign-issued cards. Note that only holders of Japan-issued Citibank cards can

### USING A JAPANESE POSTAL ATM

Postal ATMs are relatively easy to use. Here's the drill: press 'English Guide', select 'Withdrawal', then insert your card, press 'Visitor Withdrawal/Card Issued Overseas', hit 'Enter' (acknowledging that a commission will be charged), input your pin number, then hit the button marked 'Kakunin' (確認), then enter the amount, hit 'Yen' and 'Confirm' and you should hear the delightful sound of banknotes being dispensed.

---

### WARNING: JAPAN IS A CASH SOCIETY!

Be warned that cold hard yen (¥) is the way to pay in Japan. While credit cards are becoming more common, cash is still much more widely used, and travellers cheques are rarely accepted. Do not assume that you can pay with a credit card; always carry sufficient cash. The only places where you can count on paying with plastic are department stores and large hotels.

For those without credit cards, it would be a good idea to bring some travellers cheques as a back-up. As in most other countries, the US dollar is still the currency of choice in terms of exchanging cash and cashing travellers cheques.

---

access the ATM after hours. To get there, start at the Shijō-Karasumaa intersection and walk west on the south side of Karasuma-dōri. You'll see it on the left after about 100m.

Finally, 7-Eleven convenience stores across Japan have linked their ATMs to international cash networks, and these often seem to accept cards that for one reason or other will not work with postal ATMs. They are open 24 hours. So, if you can't find an open post office or your card won't work with postal ATMs, don't give up: ask around for a 7-Eleven (pronounced like 'sebun erebun' in Japanese).

### Changing Money

You can change cash or travellers cheques at most banks, major post offices, discount ticket shops, some travel agents, some large hotels and most big department stores. Note that discount ticket shops (known as *kakuyasu kippu uriba* in Japanese) often have the best rates. These can be found around Kyoto Station. However, only the US dollar and euro fetch decent exchange rates.

Most major banks are located near the Shijō-Karasuma intersection, two stops north of Kyoto Station on the Karasuma subway line. Of these, **Bank of Tokyo-Mitsubishi UFJ** (三菱東京ＵＦＪ銀行; Map p208; ☑211-4583; ⑤Karasuma line to Shijō) is the most convenient for changing money and buying travellers cheques.

### Credit Cards

You can get cash advances on Visa cards at the 1st-floor Kyoto Marui Department Store branch of **Mitsui Sumitomo Bank** (三井住友銀行 四条外貨両替コーナー; Map p208; ☑223-2821; 68 Higashi-Shinchō, Shijō-dōri, Kawaramachi higashi-iru, Shimogyō-ku).

Currently there is no representation for international cardholders in Kyoto. For inquiries and emergency services, call the international numbers on the back of your card (note these down in advance in case the cards are stolen or lost).

Note that credit cards are not as widely accepted in Japan as they are in other places – so always ask in advance!

---

# Opening Hours

Following are typical business hours in Japan. Restaurants and shops sometimes close irregularly.

**Banks** 9am to 3pm Monday to Friday.

**Bars** 7pm to late, closed one day per week.

**Companies** 9am to 5pm or 6pm Monday to Friday.

**Department stores** 10am to 7pm, closed one or two days/month.

**Post offices** Local 9am to 5pm Monday to Friday; central post offices 9am to 7pm Monday to Friday and 9am to 3pm Saturday.

**Restaurants** 11am to 2pm and 6pm to 11pm, closed one day per week (often Monday or Tuesday).

**Shops** 9am to 5pm, may be closed Sunday.

---

# Post
## Branches

The **Kyoto central post office** (京都中央郵便局; Map p212; ☑365-2471; 843-12 Higashishiokōji-chō, Shimogyō-ku; ⊙9am-9pm Mon-Fri, to 7pm Sat & Sun, ATMs 12.05am-11.55pm Mon-Sat, to 9pm Sun & holidays; ⑤Karasuma line to Kyoto) is on the north side of Kyoto Station. There's a service counter on the south side of the building open 24 hours a day for airmail, small packages and special express mail services.

**Nakagyō post office** (Map p208; ☑255-1112; cnr Sanjō & Higashinotoin; ⊙9am-7pm Mon-Fri, 9am-3pm Sat, closed Sun & holidays; ⑤Karasuma line to Karasuma-Oike), at the Nishinotōin-Sanjō crossing, has a 24-hour service window on the west side of the building.

### Postal Rates

The airmail rate for postcards is ¥70 to any overseas destination; aerograms cost ¥90. Letters weighing less than 25g are ¥90 to other countries within Asia, ¥110 to North America, Europe or Oceania (including Australia and New Zealand), and ¥130 to Africa and South America. One peculiarity of the Japanese postal system is that you will be charged extra if your writing runs over onto the address side (the right side) of a postcard. All post offices provide a reliable international Express Mail Service (EMS), which is as good or better than private express shipping services.

## Sending & Receiving Mail

The symbol for post offices is a red T with a bar across the top on a white background (〒). Mail can be sent to, from or within Japan when addressed in English (Roman script).

# Public Holidays

Japan has 15 national holidays. When a public holiday falls on a Sunday, the following Monday is taken as a holiday. If that Monday is already a holiday, the following day becomes a holiday as well. And, if two weekdays (say, Tuesday and Thursday) are holidays, the day in between (Wednesday) will also become a holiday.

**Ganjitsu** (New Year's Day) 1 January

**Seijin-no-hi** (Coming-of-Age Day) Second Monday in January

**Kenkoku Kinem-bi** (National Foundation Day) 11 February

**Shumbun-no-hi** (Spring Equinox) 20 or 21 March

**Shōwa-no-hi** (Shōwa Emperor's Day) 29 April

**Kempō Kinem-bi** (Constitution Day) 3 May

**Midori-no-hi** (Green Day) 4 May

**Kodomo-no-hi** (Children's Day) 5 May

**Umi-no-hi** (Marine Day) Third Monday in July

**Yama-no-hi** (Mountain Day) 11 August (starting 2016)

**Keirō-no-hi** (Respect-for-the-Aged Day) Third Monday in September

**Shūbun-no-hi** (Autumn Equinox) 22 or 23 September

**Taiiku-no-hi** (Health-Sports Day) Second Monday in October

**Bunka-no-hi** (Culture Day) 3 November

**Kinrō Kansha-no-hi** (Labour Thanksgiving Day) 23 November

**Tennō Tanjōbi** (Emperor's Birthday) 23 December

# Taxes & Refunds

There is a 8% consumption tax on retail purchases in Japan (this is slated to increase to 10% in October 2015). Visitors on a short-stay visa can, however, avoid this tax on certain types of purchases made at major department stores and other shops that have been designated as 'Japan Tax-Free Shops' (look for a sticker in the window). Ask at the store about the specific procedure to follow. In all cases, you must show your passport to prove that you have a short-stay visa. In some cases, you'll have to fill out some paperwork or receive a tax refund at a specific counter.

If you eat at expensive restaurants and stay at 1st-class accommodation, you will encounter a service charge, which varies from 10% to 15%. A tax of 5% is added to restaurant bills exceeding ¥5000 or for hotel bills exceeding ¥10,000.

# Telephone

The area code for greater Kyoto is ☑075; unless otherwise indicated, all numbers we provide fall into this area. Japanese telephone codes consist of an area code plus a local code and number. You do not dial the area code when making a call in that area. When dialling Japan from abroad, the country code is ☑81, followed by the area code (drop the 0) and the number.

## Directory Assistance

**Local directory assistance** ☑104 (¥60 to ¥150 per call)

**Local directory assistance in English** ☑0120-36-4463 (9am to 5pm Monday to Friday)

**International directory assistance** ☑0057

## Useful International Numbers

Direct-dial international numbers include the following. There's very little difference in their rates. Dial one of the numbers, then the international country code, the local code and the number.

➠ ☑001-010 (KDDI)

➠ ☑0033-010 (NTT)

➠ ☑0041-010 (SoftBank Telecom)

For international operator-assisted calls dial ☑0051 (KDDI; operators speak English).

## Prepaid International Phone Cards

Because of the lack of pay phones from which you can make international phone calls in Japan, the easiest way to make an international

---

**CURRENCY WARNING**

Exchange rates for the US dollar and the euro are reasonable in Japan. All other currencies, including the Australian dollar and the currencies of countries near to Japan, fetch very poor exchange rates. If you want to bring cash to Japan, we suggest US dollars or euros. Or, if you must change other currencies into yen, we suggest doing so in your home country.

## PRACTICALITIES

→ **Newspapers & Magazines** There are three main English-language newspapers in Japan: the *Japan Times*, *Daily Yomiuri* and *Asahi Shimbun/International Herald Tribune*. The *Kyoto Visitor's Guide* is a good source of information on cultural and tourist events. You'll find these in large bookshops and international hotels. Some convenience stores carry English-language newspapers.

→ **Smoking** Kyoto has banned outdoor smoking downtown, around Kyoto Station and in the Kiyomizu/Sannen-zaka/Ninen-zaka sightseeing areas.

→ **Weights & Measures** Japan uses the international metric system.

call is to buy a prepaid international phone card. Most convenience stores carry at least one of the following types of phone cards. These cards can be used with any regular pay phone in Japan.

→ KDDI Superworld Card

→ NTT Communications World Card

→ SoftBank Telecom Comica Card

### Local Calls

The Japanese public telephone system is extremely reliable and efficient. Unfortunately, the number of pay phones is decreasing fast as more Japanese buy mobile phones. Local calls from pay phones cost ¥10 per minute; unused ¥10 coins are returned after the call is completed but no change is given on ¥100 coins.

In general it's much easier to buy a telephone card (*terehon kādo*) when you arrive rather than worry about always having coins on hand. Phone cards are sold in ¥500 and ¥1000 denominations (the latter earns you an extra ¥50 in calls) and can be used in most green or grey pay phones. They are available from vending machines (some of which can be found in public phone booths) and convenience stores. They come in a myriad of designs

and are also a collectable item.

### Mobile Phones

Japan's mobile-phone networks use 3G technology on a variety of frequencies. Thus, non-3G mobile phones cannot be used in Japan and most foreign mobile phones *will not work* in Japan. Furthermore, SIM cards are not commonly available in Japan. For most people who want to use a mobile phone while in Japan, the only solution is to rent one.

Several telecommunications companies in Japan specialise in short-term mobile-phone rentals, which is a good option for travellers whose own phones won't work in Japan, or whose own phones would be prohibitively expensive to use here.

**Rentafone Japan** (☑0120-74-6487; www.rentafonejapan.com) This company rents mobile phones for ¥3900 per week and offers free delivery of the phone to your accommodation. Domestic rates are from ¥35 per minute and overseas calls are ¥45 per minute.

## Time

Kyoto local time is nine hours ahead of GMT/UTC. There is no daylight-saving time.

# Tourist Information

### Kansai International Airport Tourist Information Counter (関西国際空港関西観光情報センター; ☑0724-56-6025; ☺7am-8.30pm) This counter is on the 1st floor of the international arrivals hall. Staff can provide information on Kyoto, Kansai and Japan.

### Kyoto International Community House (京都国際交流開会; KICH; Map p216; ☑752-3010; 2-1 Torii-chō, Awataguchi, Sakyō-ku; ☺9am-9pm, closed Mon; ⑤Tōzai line to Keage, exit 2) An essential stop for those planning a long-term stay in Kyoto, KICH can also be quite useful for short-term visitors. It has a library with maps, books, newspapers and magazines from around the world, and a board displaying messages regarding work, accommodation, rummage sales etc. You can send and receive faxes, and use the internet (register at the information counter). You can also pick up a copy of its excellent *Guide to Kyoto* map and its *Easy Living in Kyoto* book (note that both of these are intended for residents). You can also chill out in the lobby and watch CNN.

### Kyoto Tourist Information Center (京都総合観光案内所; TIC; Map p212; ☑343-0548; 2F Kyoto Station Bldg, Shimogyō-ku; ☺8.30am-7pm; ⑤Karasuma line to Kyoto) Located in the main concourse on the 2nd floor of the Kyoto Station building that runs between the *shinkansen* (bullet train) station and the front of the station (near Isetan department store), this is the main tourist information centre in Kyoto. English speakers are always on hand and, occasionally, speakers of other Euro-

pean and Asian languages are available.

It stocks useful maps of the city, as well as bus maps, and can answer most of your questions. Note that it's called 'Kyo Navi' in Japanese (in case you have to ask someone).

## Travel Agencies

You can find ads for travel agencies that deal with foreigners in *Kansai Scene* magazine, which is available at English-language bookshops and some guesthouses and hotels. The following agency is a good place for domestic (within Japan) travel tickets and arrangements.

**KNT** (近畿日本ツーリスト; Map p208; ☑255-0489; 437 Ebisu-chō, Kawaramachi-dōri, Sanjo-agaru, Nakagyō-ku; ☉10.30am-7pm Mon-Fri, to 6.30pm Sat & Sun)

## Travellers with Disabilities

Although Kyoto has made some attempts at making public facilities more accessible, its narrow streets and the terrain of sights such as temples and shrines make it a challenging city for people with disabilities, especially for those in wheelchairs.

If you are going to travel by train and need assistance, ask one of the station workers as you enter the station.

There are carriages on most lines that have areas set aside for those in wheelchairs. Those with other physical disabilities can use one of the seats set aside near the train exits; these are called *yūsen-zaseki* and are usually a different colour from the other seats in the carriage, making them easy to spot. You'll also find these seats near the front of buses; usually they're a different colour from the regular seats.

**MK Taxi** (☑778-4141; www.mktaxi-japan.com) can accommodate wheelchairs in many of its cars and is an attractive possibility for anyone interested in touring the city by cab.

Facilities for the visually impaired include musical pedestrian lights at many city intersections and raised bumps on railway platforms for guidance.

AD-Brain (the same outfit that publishes the monthly *Kyoto Visitor's Guide*) has produced a basic city map for people with disabilities and senior citizens. It shows wheelchair-access points in town and gives information on public transport access etc. The map is available at the **TIC** (京都総合観光案内所; Map p212; ☑343-0548; 2F Kyoto Station Bldg, Shimogyō-ku; ☉8.30am-7pm; ⓢKarasuma line to Kyoto).

The most useful information for disabled visitors to Japan is provided by the **Japanese Red Cross Language Service Volunteers** (http://www.tok-lanserv.jp/eng/; c/o Volunteers Division, Japanese Red Cross Society, 1-1-3 Shiba Daimon, Minato-ku, Tokyo 105-8521, Japan).

## Visas

Generally, visitors who are not planning to engage in income-producing activities while in Japan are exempt from obtaining visas and will be issued a *tanki-taizai* (temporary visitor) visa on arrival. Nationals of Australia, Canada, France, Ireland, Italy, the Netherlands, New Zealand, Spain, the UK and the USA are eligible for this visa.

Stays of up to six months are permitted for citizens of Austria, Germany, Ireland, Mexico, Switzerland and the UK. Citizens of these countries will almost always be given a 90-day temporary visitor visa upon arrival, which can usually be extended for another 90

days at immigration bureaux inside Japan.

Japanese law requires that visitors to the country entering on a temporary visitor visa possess an ongoing air or sea ticket or evidence thereof. In practice, few travellers are asked to produce such documents, but to avoid surprises it pays to be on the safe side.

Note that upon entering Japan, all short-term foreign visitors are required to be photographed and fingerprinted. This happens when you show your passport on arrival.

## Women Travellers

Japan is a relatively safe country for women travellers, though perhaps not as safe as some might think. Women travellers are occasionally subjected to some form of verbal harassment or prying questions. Physical attacks are very rare, but have occurred.

The best advice is to avoid being lulled into a false sense of security by Japan's image as one of the world's safest countries and to take the normal precautions you would in your home country. If a neighbourhood or establishment looks unsafe, then treat it that way. As long as you use your common sense, you will most likely find that Japan is a pleasant and rewarding place to travel.

Several train companies in Japan have recently introduced women-only cars to protect female passengers from *chikan* (men who grope women and girls on packed trains). These cars are usually available during rush-hour periods on weekdays on busy urban lines. There are signs (usually pink in colour) on the platform indicating where to board these cars, and the cars themselves are usually labelled in both Japanese and English (again, these are often marked in pink).

# Language

Japanese is spoken by more than 125 million people. While it bears some resemblance to Altaic languages such as Mongolian and Turkish and has grammatical similarities to Korean, its origins are unclear. Chinese is responsible for the existence of many Sino-Japanese words in Japanese, and for the originally Chinese kanji characters which the Japanese use in combination with the homegrown hiragana and katakana scripts.

Japanese pronunciation is easy to master for English speakers, as most of its sounds are also found in English. If you read our coloured pronunciation guides as if they were English, you'll be understood. In Japanese, it's important to make the distinction between short and long vowels, as vowel length can change the meaning of a word. The long vowels, shown in our pronunciation guides with a horizontal line on top of them (ā, ē, ī, ō, ū), should be held twice as long as the short ones. It's also important to make the distinction between single and double consonants, as this can produce a difference in meaning. Pronounce the double consonants with a slight pause between them, eg sak·ka (writer).

Note also that the vowel sound ai is pronounced as in 'aisle', air as in 'pair' and ow as in 'how'. As for the consonants, ts is pronounced as in 'hats', f sounds almost like 'fw' (with rounded lips), and r is halfway between 'r' and 'l'. All syllables in a word are pronounced fairly evenly in Japanese.

## WANT MORE?

For in-depth language information and handy phrases, check out Lonely Planet's *Japanese phrasebook*. You'll find it at **shop.lonelyplanet.com**, or you can buy Lonely Planet's iPhone phrasebooks at the Apple App Store.

## BASICS

Japanese uses an array of registers of speech to reflect social and contextual hierarchy, but these can be simplified to the form most appropriate for the situation, which is what we've done in this language guide too.

| | | |
|---|---|---|
| **Hello.** | こんにちは。 | kon·ni·chi·wa |
| **Goodbye.** | さようなら。 | sa·yō·na·ra |
| **Yes.** | はい。 | hai |
| **No.** | いいえ。 | ī·e |
| **Please.** (when asking) | ください。 | ku·da·sai |
| **Please.** (when offering) | どうぞ。 | dō·zo |
| **Thank you.** | ありがとう。 | a·ri·ga·tō |
| **Excuse me.** (to get attention) | すみません。 | su·mi·ma·sen |
| **Sorry.** | ごめんなさい。 | go·men·na·sai |

**You're welcome.**
どういたしまして。 dō i·ta·shi·mash·te

**How are you?**
お元気ですか? o·gen·ki des ka

**Fine. And you?**
はい、元気です。 hai, gen·ki des
あなたは? a·na·ta wa

**What's your name?**
お名前は何ですか? o·na·ma·e wa nan des ka

**My name is ...**
私の名前は wa·ta·shi no na·ma·e wa
…です。 ... des

**Do you speak English?**
英語が話せますか? ē·go ga ha·na·se·mas ka

**I don't understand.**
わかりません。 wa·ka·ri·ma·sen

**Does anyone speak English?**
どなたか英語を do·na·ta ka ē·go o
話せますか? ha·na·se·mas ka

## ACCOMMODATION

| Where's a ...? | …が ありますか? | ... ga a·ri·mas ka |
|---|---|---|
| campsite | キャンプ場 | kyam·pu·jō |
| guesthouse | 民宿 | min·shu·ku |
| hotel | ホテル | ho·te·ru |
| inn | 旅館 | ryo·kan |
| youth hostel | ユース ホステル | yū·su· ho·su·te·ru |

| Do you have a ... room? | …ルームは ありますか? | ...rū·mu wa a·ri·mas ka |
|---|---|---|
| single | シングル | shin·gu·ru |
| double | ダブル | da·bu·ru |

| How much is it per ...? | …いくら ですか? | ... i·ku·ra des ka |
|---|---|---|
| night | 1泊 | ip·pa·ku |
| person | 1人 | hi·to·ri |

| air-con | エアコン | air·kon |
|---|---|---|
| bathroom | 風呂場 | fu·ro·ba |
| window | 窓 | ma·do |

## DIRECTIONS

**Where's the ...?**
…はどこですか? ... wa do·ko des ka

**Can you show me (on the map)?**
(地図で)教えて (chi·zu de) o·shi·e·te
くれませんか? ku·re·ma·sen ka

**What's the address?**
住所は何ですか? jū·sho wa nan des ka

**Could you please write it down?**
書いてくれませんか? kai·te ku·re·ma·sen ka

| behind ... | …の後ろ | ... no u·shi·ro |
|---|---|---|
| in front of ... | …の前 | ... no ma·e |
| near ... | …の近く | ... no chi·ka·ku |
| next to ... | …のとなり | ... no to·na·ri |
| opposite ... | …の 向かい側 | ... no mu·kai·ga·wa |
| straight ahead | この先 | ko·no sa·ki |

| Turn ... | …まがって ください。 | ... ma·gat·te ku·da·sai |
|---|---|---|
| at the corner | その角を | so·no ka·do o |
| at the traffic lights | その信号を | so·no shin·gō o |
| left | 左へ | hi·da·ri e |
| right | 右へ | mi·gi e |

### KEY PATTERNS

To get by in Japanese, mix and match these simple patterns with words of your choice:

**When's (the next bus)?**
(次のバスは) (tsu·gi no bas wa)
何時ですか? nan·ji des ka

**Where's (the station)?**
(駅は)どこですか? (e·ki wa) do·ko des ka

**Do you have (a map)?**
(地図) (chi·zu)
がありますか? ga a·ri·mas ka

**Is there (a toilet)?**
(トイレ) (toy·re)
がありますか? ga a·ri·mas ka

**I'd like (the menu).**
(メニュー) (me·nyū)
をお願いします。 o o·ne·gai shi·mas

**Can I (sit here)?**
(ここに座って) (ko·ko ni su·wat·te)
もいいですか? mo ī des ka

**I need (a can opener).**
(缶切り) (kan·ki·ri)
が必要です。 ga hi·tsu·yō des

**Do I need (a visa)?**
(ビザ) (bi·za)
が必要ですか? ga hi·tsu·yō des ka

**I have (a reservation).**
(予約)があります。 (yo·ya·ku) ga a·ri·mas

**I'm (a teacher).**
私は(教師) wa·ta·shi wa (kyō·shi)
です。 des

## EATING & DRINKING

**I'd like to reserve a table for (two people).**
(2人)の予約を (fu·ta·ri) no yo·ya·ku o
お願いします。 o·ne·gai shi·mas

**What would you recommend?**
なにが na·ni ga
おすすめですか? o·su·su·me des ka

**What's in that dish?**
あの料理に何 a·no ryō·ri ni na·ni
が入っていますか? ga hait·te i·mas ka

**Do you have any vegetarian dishes?**
ベジタリアン料理 be·ji·ta·ri·an ryō·ri
がありますか? ga a·ri·mas ka

**I'm a vegetarian.**
私は wa·ta·shi wa
ベジタリアンです。 be·ji·ta·ri·an des

**I'm a vegan.**
私は厳格な wa·ta·shi wa gen·ka·ku na
菜食主義者 sai·sho·ku·shu·gi·sha
です。 des

## Signs

| 入口 | Entrance |
|---|---|
| 出口 | Exit |
| 営業中/開館 | Open |
| 閉店/閉館 | Closed |
| インフォメーション | Information |
| 危険 | Danger |
| トイレ | Toilets |
| 男 | Men |
| 女 | Women |

| I don't eat ... | …は 食べません。 | ... wa ta·be·ma·sen |
|---|---|---|
| dairy products | 乳製品 | nyū·sē·hin |
| (red) meat | （赤身の）肉 | (a·ka·mi no) ni·ku |
| meat or dairy products | 肉や 乳製品は | ni·ku ya nyū·sē·hin |
| pork | 豚肉 | bu·ta·ni·ku |
| seafood | シーフード 海産物 | shī·fū·do/ kai·sam·bu·tsu |

**Is it cooked with pork lard or chicken stock?**
これはラードか鶏の
だしを使って
いますか?
ko·re wa rā·do ka to·ri no
da·shi o tsu·kat·te
i·mas ka

**I'm allergic to (peanuts).**
私は
（ビーナッツ）に
アレルギーが
あります。
wa·ta·shi wa
(pī·nat·tsu) ni
a·re·ru·gī ga
a·ri·mas

**That was delicious!**
おいしかった!
oy·shi·kat·ta

**Cheers!**
乾杯!
kam·pai

**Please bring the bill.**
お勘定をください。
o·kan·jō o ku·da·sai

## Key Words

| appetisers | 前菜 | zen·sai |
|---|---|---|
| bottle | ビン | bin |
| bowl | ボール | bō·ru |
| breakfast | 朝食 | chō·sho·ku |
| cold | 冷たい | tsu·me·ta·i |
| dinner | 夕食 | yū·sho·ku |
| fork | フォーク | fō·ku |
| glass | グラス | gu·ra·su |
| grocery | 食料品 | sho·ku·ryō·hin |
| hot (warm) | 熱い | a·tsu·i |
| knife | ナイフ | nai·fu |
| lunch | 昼食 | chū·sho·ku |
| market | 市場 | i·chi·ba |
| menu | メニュー | me·nyū |
| plate | 皿 | sa·ra |
| spicy | スパイシー | spai·shī |
| spoon | スプーン | spūn |
| vegetarian | ベジタリアン | be·ji·ta·ri·an |
| with | いっしょに | is·sho ni |
| without | なしで | na·shi de |

## Meat & Fish

| beef | 牛肉 | gyū·ni·ku |
|---|---|---|
| chicken | 鶏肉 | to·ri·ni·ku |
| duck | アヒル | a·hi·ru |
| eel | うなぎ | u·na·gi |
| fish | 魚 | sa·ka·na |
| lamb | 子羊 | ko·hi·tsu·ji |
| lobster | ロブスター | ro·bus·tā |
| meat | 肉 | ni·ku |
| pork | 豚肉 | bu·ta·ni·ku |
| prawn | エビ | e·bi |
| salmon | サケ | sa·ke |
| seafood | シーフード 海産物 | shī·fū·do/ kai·sam·bu·tsu |
| shrimp | 小エビ | ko·e·bi |
| tuna | マグロ | ma·gu·ro |
| turkey | 七面鳥 | shi·chi·men·chō |
| veal | 子牛 | ko·u·shi |

## Fruit & Vegetables

| apple | りんご | rin·go |
|---|---|---|
| banana | バナナ | ba·na·na |
| beans | 豆 | ma·me |
| capsicum | ピーマン | pī·man |
| carrot | ニンジン | nin·jin |
| cherry | さくらんぼ | sa·ku·ram·bo |
| cucumber | キュウリ | kyū·ri |
| fruit | 果物 | ku·da·mo·no |
| grapes | ブドウ | bu·dō |
| lettuce | レタス | re·tas |
| nut | ナッツ | nat·tsu |
| orange | オレンジ | o·ren·ji |
| peach | 桃 | mo·mo |

| peas | 豆 | ma·me |
| pineapple | パイナップル | pai·nap·pu·ru |
| potato | ジャガイモ | ja·ga·i·mo |
| pumpkin | カボチャ | ka·bo·cha |
| spinach | ホウレンソウ | hō·ren·sō |
| strawberry | イチゴ | i·chi·go |
| tomato | トマト | to·ma·to |
| vegetables | 野菜 | ya·sai |
| watermelon | スイカ | su·i·ka |

## Other

| bread | パン | pan |
| butter | バター | ba·tā |
| cheese | チーズ | chī·zu |
| chilli | 唐辛子 | tō·ga·ra·shi |
| egg | 卵 | ta·ma·go |
| honey | 蜂蜜 | ha·chi·mi·tsu |
| horseradish | わさび | wa·sa·bi |
| jam | ジャム | ja·mu |
| noodles | 麺 | men |
| pepper | コショウ | koshō |
| rice (cooked) | ごはん | go·han |
| salt | 塩 | shi·o |
| seaweed | のり | no·ri |
| soy sauce | しょう油 | shō·yu |
| sugar | 砂糖 | sa·tō |

## Drinks

| beer | ビール | bī·ru |
| coffee | コーヒー | kō·hī |
| (orange) juice | (オレンジ)ジュース | (o·ren·ji·)jū·su |
| lemonade | レモネード | re·mo·nē·do |
| milk | ミルク | mi·ru·ku |
| mineral water | ミネラルウォーター | mi·ne·ra·ru·wō·tā |

### Question Words

| How? | どのように? | do·no yō ni |
| What? | なに? | na·ni |
| When? | いつ? | i·tsu |
| Where? | どこ? | do·ko |
| Which? | どちら? | do·chi·ra |
| Who? | だれ? | da·re |
| Why? | なぜ? | na·ze |

| red wine | 赤ワイン | a·ka wain |
| sake | 酒 | sa·ke |
| tea | 紅茶 | kō·cha |
| water | 水 | mi·zu |
| white wine | 白ワイン | shi·ro wain |
| yogurt | ヨーグルト | yō·gu·ru·to |

## EMERGENCIES

**Help!**
たすけて! — tas·ke·te

**Go away!**
離れろ! — ha·na·re·ro

**I'm lost.**
迷いました。 — ma·yoy·mash·ta

**Call the police.**
警察を呼んで。 — kē·sa·tsu o yon·de

**Call a doctor.**
医者を呼んで。 — i·sha o yon·de

**Where are the toilets?**
トイレはどこですか? — toy·re wa do·ko des ka

**I'm ill.**
私は病気です。 — wa·ta·shi wa byō·ki des

**It hurts here.**
ここが痛いです。 — ko·ko ga i·tai des

**I'm allergic to ...**
私は…アレルギーです。 — wa·ta·shi wa ... a·re·ru·gī des

## SHOPPING & SERVICES

**I'd like to buy ...**
…をください。 — ... o ku·da·sai

**I'm just looking.**
見ているだけです。 — mi·te i·ru da·ke des

**Can I look at it?**
それを見てもいいですか? — so·re o mi·te mo ī des ka

**How much is it?**
いくらですか? — i·ku·ra des ka

**That's too expensive.**
高すぎます。 — ta·ka·su·gi·mas

**Can you give me a discount?**
ディスカウントできますか? — dis·kown·to de·ki·mas ka

**There's a mistake in the bill.**
請求書に間違いがあります。 — sē·kyū·sho ni ma·chi·gai ga a·ri·mas

| ATM | ATM | ē·tī·e·mu |
| credit card | クレジットカード | ku·re·jit·to·kā·do |
| post office | 郵便局 | yū·bin·kyo·ku |
| public phone | 公衆電話 | kō·shū·den·wa |
| tourist office | 観光案内所 | kan·kō·an·nai·jo |

| Numbers | | |
|---|---|---|
| 1 | 一 | i·chi |
| 2 | 二 | ni |
| 3 | 三 | san |
| 4 | 四 | shi/yon |
| 5 | 五 | go |
| 6 | 六 | ro·ku |
| 7 | 七 | shi·chi/na·na |
| 8 | 八 | ha·chi |
| 9 | 九 | ku/kyū |
| 10 | 十 | jū |
| 20 | 二十 | ni·jū |
| 30 | 三十 | san·jū |
| 40 | 四十 | yon·jū |
| 50 | 五十 | go·jū |
| 60 | 六十 | ro·ku·jū |
| 70 | 七十 | na·na·jū |
| 80 | 八十 | ha·chi·jū |
| 90 | 九十 | kyū·jū |
| 100 | 百 | hya·ku |
| 1000 | 千 | sen |

## TIME & DATES

**What time is it?**
何時ですか？ nan·ji des ka

**It's (10) o'clock.**
(10)時です。 (jū)·ji des

**Half past (10).**
(10)時半です。 (jū)·ji han des

| am | 午前 | go·zen |
|---|---|---|
| pm | 午後 | go·go |

| Monday | 月曜日 | ge·tsu·yō·bi |
|---|---|---|
| Tuesday | 火曜日 | ka·yō·bi |
| Wednesday | 水曜日 | su·i·yō·bi |
| Thursday | 木曜日 | mo·ku·yō·bi |
| Friday | 金曜日 | kin·yō·bi |
| Saturday | 土曜日 | do·yō·bi |
| Sunday | 日曜日 | ni·chi·yō·bi |

| January | 1月 | i·chi·ga·tsu |
|---|---|---|
| February | 2月 | ni·ga·tsu |
| March | 3月 | san·ga·tsu |
| April | 4月 | shi·ga·tsu |
| May | 5月 | go·ga·tsu |
| June | 6月 | ro·ku·ga·tsu |
| July | 7月 | shi·chi·ga·tsu |
| August | 8月 | ha·chi·ga·tsu |
| September | 9月 | ku·ga·tsu |
| October | 10月 | jū·ga·tsu |
| November | 11月 | jū·i·chi·ga·tsu |
| December | 12月 | jū·ni·ga·tsu |

## TRANSPORT

| boat | 船 | fu·ne |
|---|---|---|
| bus | バス | bas |
| metro | 地下鉄 | chi·ka·te·tsu |
| plane | 飛行機 | hi·kō·ki |
| train | 電車 | den·sha |
| tram | 市電 | shi·den |

**What time does it leave?**
これは何時に ko·re wa nan·ji ni
出ますか？ de·mas ka

**Does it stop at (...)?**
(…)に (...) ni
停まりますか？ to·ma·ri·mas ka

**Please tell me when we get to (...).**
(…)に着いたら (...) ni tsu·i·ta·ra
教えてください。 o·shi·e·te ku·da·sai

**A one-way/return ticket (to Tokyo).**
(東京行きの) (tō·kyō·yu·ki no)
片道/往復 ka·ta·mi·chi/ō·fu·ku
切符。 kip·pu

| first | 始発の | shi·ha·tsu no |
|---|---|---|
| last | 最終の | sai·shū no |
| next | 次の | tsu·gi no |

| aisle | 通路側 | tsū·ro·ga·wa |
|---|---|---|
| bus stop | バス停 | bas·tē |
| cancelled | キャンセル | kyan·se·ru |
| delayed | 遅れ | o·ku·re |
| ticket window | 窓口 | ma·do·gu·chi |
| timetable | 時刻表 | ji·ko·ku·hyō |
| train station | 駅 | e·ki |
| window | 窓側 | ma·do·ga·wa |

| I'd like to hire a ... | …を借りたい のですが。 | ... o ka·ri·tai no des ga |
|---|---|---|
| bicycle | 自転車 | ji·ten·sha |
| car | 自動車 | ji·dō·sha |
| motorbike | オートバイ | ō·to·bai |

For additional Transport words and phrases, see p178.

# GLOSSARY

**agaru** – north of

**ageya** – traditional banquet hall used for entertainment

**bashi** – bridge (also *hashi*)

**bentō** – boxed lunch or dinner, usually containing rice, vegetables and fish or meat

**bosatsu** – a Bodhisattva, or Buddha attendant, who helps others to attain enlightenment

**bugaku** – dance pieces played by court orchestras in ancient Japan

**bunraku** – classical puppet theatre that uses life-size puppets to enact dramas similar to those of *kabuki*

**chadō** – tea ceremony, or 'The Way of Tea'

**chanoyu** – tea ceremony; see also *chadō*

**chō** – city area sized between a *ku* and a *chōme*

**chōme** – city area of a few blocks

**dai** – great; large

**daimyō** – domain lords under the *shōgun*

**dera** – temple (also *ji* or *tera*)

**dōri** – street

**futon** – cushion-like mattress that is rolled up and stored away during the day

**gagaku** – music of the imperial court

**gaijin** – foreigner; the contracted form of *gaikokujin*

**gawa** – river (also *kawa*)

**geiko** – Kyoto dialect for *geisha*

**geisha** – a woman versed in the arts and other cultivated pursuits who entertains guests

**gū** – shrine

**haiden** – hall of worship in a shrine

**haiku** – 17-syllable poem

**hanami** – cherry-blossom viewing

**hashi** – bridge (also *bashi*); chopsticks

**higashi** – east

**hiragana** – phonetic syllabary used to write Japanese words

**honden** – main building of a shrine

**hondō** – main building of a temple (also *kondō*)

**ikebana** – art of flower arrangement

**izakaya** – Japanese pub/eatery

**ji** – temple (also *tera* or *dera*)

**jingū** – shrine (also *jinja* or *gū*)

**Jizō** – Bodhisattva who watches over children

**jō** – castle (also *shiro*)

**JR** – Japan Railways

**kabuki** – form of Japanese theatre that draws on popular tales and is characterised by elaborate costumes, stylised acting and an all-male cast

**kaiseki** – Buddhist-inspired, Japanese haute cuisine; called *cha-kaiseki* when served as part of a tea ceremony

**kaisoku** – rapid train

**kaiten-zushi** – automatic, conveyor-belt sushi

**kampai** – cheers, as in a drinking toast

**kanji** – literally, 'Chinese writing'; Chinese ideographic script used for writing Japanese

**Kannon** – Buddhist goddess of mercy

**karesansui** – dry-landscaped rock garden

**kawa** – river (also *gawa*)

**kayabuki-yane** – traditional Japanese thatched-roof farmhouse

**ken** – prefecture, eg Shiga-ken

**kimono** – traditional outer garment similar to a robe

**kita** – north

**KIX** – Kansai International Airport

**Kiyomizu-yaki** – a distinctive type of local pottery

**ko** – lake

**kōen** – park

**koma-inu** – dog-like guardian stone statues found in pairs at the entrance to *Shintō* shrines

**kondō** – main building of a temple (also *hondō*)

**ku** – ward

**kudaru** – south of (also *sagaru*)

**kyōgen** – drama performed as comic relief between *nō* plays, or as separate events

**kyō-machiya** – see *machiya*

**kyō-ningyō** – Kyoto dolls

**kyō-ryōri** – Kyoto cuisine

**Kyoto-ben** – distinctive Japanese dialect spoken in Kyoto

**live house** – a small concert hall where music is performed

**machi** – city area (for large cities) sized between a *ku* and a *chōme*

**machiya** – traditional wooden townhouse, called *kyō-machiya* in Kyoto

**maiko** – apprentice *geisha*

**maki-e** – decorative lacquer technique using silver and gold powders

**mama-san** – older women who run drinking, dining and entertainment venues

**matcha** – powdered green tea served in tea ceremonies

**matsuri** – festival

**mikoshi** – portable shrine carried during festivals

**minami** – south

**minshuku** – Japanese equivalent of a B&B

**mizu shōbai** – the world of bars, entertainment and prostitution

**mon** – temple gate

**mura** – village

**ningyō** – doll (see also *kyō-ningyō*)

**niō** – temple guardians

**nishi** – west

**nō** – classical Japanese mask drama

**noren** – door curtain for restaurants, usually labelled with the name of the establishment

**obanzai** – Japanese home-style cooking (the Kyoto variant of this is sometimes called *kyō-obanzai*)

**obi** – sash or belt worn with *kimono*

**Obon** – mid-August festivals and ceremonies for deceased ancestors

**okiya** – old-style *geisha* living quarters

**okonomiyaki** – Japanese cabbage and batter dish cooked on an iron griddle with a variety of fillings

**onsen** – mineral hot spring with bathing areas and accommodation

**pachinko** – vertical pinball game that is a Japanese craze

**ryokan** – traditional inn

**ryōri** – cooking; cuisine (see also *kyō-ryōri*)

**ryōtei** – traditional-style, high-class restaurant; *kaiseki* is typical fare

**sabi** – a poetic ideal of finding beauty and pleasure in imperfection; often used in conjunction with *wabi*

**sagaru** – south of (also *kudaru*)

**sakura** – cherry trees

**sama** – a suffix even more respectful than *san*

**samurai** – Japan's traditional warrior class

**san** – a respectful suffix applied to personal names, similar to Mr, Mrs or Ms

**sen** – line, usually railway line

**sensu** – folding paper fan

**sentō** – public bath

**setto** – set meal; see also *teishoku*

**shakkei** – borrowed scenery; technique where features outside a garden are incorporated into its design

**shamisen** – three-stringed, banjo-like instrument

**shi** – city (to distinguish cities with prefectures of the same name)

**shidare-zakura** – weeping cherry tree

**shinkaisoku** – special rapid train

**shinkansen** – bullet train

**Shintō** – indigenous Japanese religion

**shōgun** – military ruler of pre-Meiji Japan

**shōjin-ryōri** – Buddhist vegetarian cuisine

**shokudō** – Japanese-style cafeteria/cheap restaurant

**soba** – thin brown buckwheat noodles

**tatami** – tightly woven floor matting on which shoes should not be worn

**teishoku** – set meal in a restaurant

**tera** – temple (also *dera* or *ji*)

**tokkyū** – limited express train

**torii** – entrance gate to a *Shintō* shrine

**tsukemono** – Japanese pickles

**udon** – thick, white wheat noodles

**wabi** – a Zen-inspired aesthetic of rustic simplicity

**wagashi** – traditional Japanese sweets served with tea

**wasabi** – spicy Japanese horseradish

**washi** – Japanese paper

**yudōfu** – bean curd cooked in an iron pot; common temple fare

**Zen** – a form of Buddhism

## MENU DECODER

### Rice Dishes

**katsu-don** (かつ丼) – rice topped with a fried pork cutlet

**niku-don** (牛丼) – rice topped with thin slices of cooked beef

**oyako-don** (親子丼) – rice topped with egg and chicken

**ten-don** (天丼) – rice topped with tempura shrimp and vegetables

### Izakaya Fare

**agedashi-dōfu** (揚げだし豆腐) – deep-fried tofu in a dashi broth

**chiizu-age** (チーズ揚げ) – deep-fried cheese

**hiya-yakko** (冷奴) – a cold block of tofu with soy sauce and spring onions

**jaga-batā** (ジャガバター) – baked potatoes with butter

**niku-jaga** (肉ジャガ) – beef and potato stew

**poteto furai** (ポテトフライ) – French fries

**shio-yaki-zakana** (塩焼魚) – a whole fish grilled with salt

**tsuna sarada** (ツナサラダ) – tuna salad over cabbage

### Sushi & Sashimi

**ama-ebi** (甘海老) – shrimp

**awabi** (あわび) – abalone

**hamachi** (はまち) – yellowtail

**ika** (いか) – squid

**ikura** (イクラ) – salmon roe

**kai-bashira** (貝柱) – scallop

**kani** (かに) – crab

**katsuo** (かつお) – bonito

**sashimi mori-awase** (刺身盛り合わせ) – a selection of sliced sashimi

**tai** (鯛) – sea bream

**toro** (とろ) – the choicest cut of fatty tuna belly

**uni** (うに) – sea urchin roe

## Yakitori

**gyū-niku** (牛肉) – pieces of beef

**hasami/negima** (はさみ/ねぎま) – pieces of white meat alternating with leek

**kawa** (皮) – chicken skin

**piiman** (ピーマン) – small green peppers

**sasami** (ささみ) – skinless chicken-breast pieces

**shiitake** (しいたけ) – Japanese mushrooms

**tama-negi** (玉ねぎ) – round white onions

**tebasaki** (手羽先) – chicken wings

**tsukune** (つくね) – chicken meat balls

**yaki-onigiri** (焼きおにぎり) – a triangle of rice grilled with *yakitori* sauce

**yakitori** (焼き鳥) – plain, grilled white meat

## Tempura

**kaki age** (かき揚げ) – tempura with shredded vegetables or fish

**shōjin age** (精進揚げ) – vegetarian tempura

**tempura moriawase** (天ぷら盛り合わせ) – a selection of tempura

## Rāmen

**chānpon-men** (ちゃんぽん麺) – Nagasaki-style *rāmen*

**chāshū-men** (チャーシュー麺) – *rāmen* topped with slices of roasted pork

**miso-rāmen** (みそラーメン) – *rāmen* with miso-flavoured broth

**rāmen** (ラーメン) – soup and noodles with a sprinkling of meat and vegetables

**wantan-men** (ワンタン麺) – *rāmen* with meat dumplings

## Soba & Udon

**kake soba/udon** (かけそば/うどん) – *soba/udon* noodles in broth

**kata yaki-soba** (固焼きそば) – crispy noodles with meat and vegetables

**kitsune soba/udon** (きつねそば/うどん) – *soba/udon* noodles with fried tofu

**soba** (そば) – thin brown buckwheat noodles

**tempura soba/udon** (天ぷらそば/うどん) – *soba/udon* noodles with tempura shrimp

**tsukimi soba/udon** (月見そば/うどん) – *soba/udon* noodles with raw egg on top

**udon** (うどん) – thick white wheat noodles

**yaki-soba** (焼きそば) – fried noodles with meat and vegetables

**zaru soba** (ざるそば) – cold noodles with seaweed strips served on a bamboo tray

## Unagi

**kabayaki** (蒲焼き) – skewers of grilled eel without rice

**una-don** (うな丼) – grilled eel over a bowl of rice

**unagi teishoku** (うなぎ定食) – full-set *unagi* meal with rice, grilled eel, eel-liver soup and pickles

**unajū** (うな重) – grilled eel over a flat tray of rice

## Kushiage & Kushikatsu

**ginnan** (銀杏) – ginkgo nuts

**gyū-niku** (牛肉) – beef pieces

**ika** (いか) – squid

**imo** (いも) – potato

**renkon** (れんこん) – lotus root

**shiitake** (しいたけ) – Japanese mushrooms

**tama-negi** (玉ねぎ) – white onion

## Okonomiyaki

**gyū okonomiyaki** (牛お好み焼き) – beef *okonomiyaki*

**ika okonomiyaki** (いかお好み焼き) – squid *okonomiyaki*

**mikkusu** (ミックスお好み焼き) – mixed fillings of seafood, meat and vegetables

**modan-yaki** (モダン焼き) – *okonomiyaki* with *yaki-soba* and a fried egg

**negi okonomiyaki** (ネギお好み焼き) – thin *okonomiyaki* with spring onions

## Kaiseki

**bentō** (弁当) – boxed lunch

**take** (竹) – special course

**matsu** (松) – extra-special course

**ume** (梅) – regular course

## Alcoholic Drinks

**chūhai** (チューハイ) – *shōchū* with soda and lemon

**mizu-wari** (水割り) – whisky, ice and water

**nama biiru** (生ビール) – draught beer

**oyu-wari** (お湯割り) – *shōchū* with hot water

**shōchū** (焼酎) – distilled grain liquor

**whisky** (ウィスキー) – whisky

## Coffee & Tea

**american kōhii** (アメリカンコーヒー) – weak coffee

**burendo kōhii** (ブレンドコーヒー) – blended coffee, fairly strong

**kafe ōre (**カフェオレ) – *café au lait*, hot or cold

**kōcha** (紅茶) – black, British-style tea

**kōhii** (コーヒー) – regular coffee

## Japanese Tea

**bancha** (番茶) – ordinary-grade green tea, brownish in colour

**matcha** (抹茶) – powdered green tea used in the tea ceremony

**mugicha** (麦茶) – roasted barley tea

**o-cha** (お茶) – green tea

**sencha** (煎茶) – medium-grade green tea

# Behind the Scenes

## SEND US YOUR FEEDBACK

We love to hear from travellers – your comments keep us on our toes and help make our books better. Our well-travelled team reads every word on what you loved or loathed about this book. Although we cannot reply individually to your submissions, we always guarantee that your feedback goes straight to the appropriate authors, in time for the next edition. Each person who sends us information is thanked in the next edition – the most useful submissions are rewarded with a selection of digital PDF chapters.

Visit **lonelyplanet.com/contact** to submit your updates and suggestions or to ask for help. Our award-winning website also features inspirational travel stories, news and discussions.

Note: We may edit, reproduce and incorporate your comments in Lonely Planet products such as guidebooks, websites and digital products, so let us know if you don't want your comments reproduced or your name acknowledged. For a copy of our privacy policy visit lonelyplanet.com/privacy.

## OUR READERS

**Many thanks to the travellers who used the last edition and wrote to us with helpful hints, useful advice and interesting anecdotes:**
Badong Abesamis, Ralph Baker, Ulrich Borgolte, Christian Cantos, Nick Carrigan, Diego Coruña, Gilles Herve, Erik Kon, Monta Lertpachin, Brittany Millman, Franziska Schwarz, Cinzia Redaelli, Sylvia Redaelli, Torben Retboll, Stefan Roesner, Sally Royse, Chihfang Tsai

## AUTHOR THANKS

### Chris Rowthorn

I would like to thank my family for their patience and support during the writing of this guide. I would also like to thank Kitayama Jun, SK, KT, HK and IK for their assistance. Thanks are also due to the people of Kyoto, who help me every day in countless ways. Finally, I would like to thank all readers of Lonely Planet for their feedback and input. And if any readers see me in Kyoto, please don't hesitate to stop me and let me know what you think!

### ACKNOWLEDGMENTS

Cover photograph: Gion, Kyoto, Tibor Bognar/ Alamy.

## THIS BOOK

This 6th edition of Lonely Planet's *Kyoto* guidebook was researched and written by Chris Rowthorn. The previous two editions were also written by Chris Rowthorn. This guidebook was produced by the following:

**Destination Editor** Laura Crawford

**Coordinating Editor** Kristin Odijk

**Product Editors** Briohny Hooper, Luna Soo

**Senior Cartographer** Diana Von Holdt

**Book Designer** Wibowo Rusli

**Assisting Editors** Kate Evans, Sally Schafer, Gabrielle Stefanos

**Cover Researcher** Naomi Parker

**Thanks to** Naoko Akamatsu, Sasha Baskett, Elin Berglund, Carolyn Boicos, Kate Chapman, Kate James, Elizabeth Jones,Wayne Murphy, Claire Naylor, Karyn Noble, Dianne Schallmeiner, Ellie Simpson, Ross Taylor, Tony Wheeler

**BEHIND THE SCENES**

See also separate subindexes for:

🍴 **EATING P202**

🍸 **DRINKING & NIGHTLIFE P203**

⭐ **ENTERTAINMENT P203**

🛍 **SHOPPING P203**

🏃 **SPORTS & ACTIVITIES P204**

🛏 **SLEEPING P204**

# Index

☆ **ENTERTAINMENT**

🛒 **SHOPPING**

🍷 **DRINKING & NIGHTLIFE**

# Kyoto Maps

## Sights

- Beach
- Bird Sanctuary
- Buddhist
- Castle/Palace
- Christian
- Confucian
- Hindu
- Islamic
- Jain
- Jewish
- Monument
- Museum/Gallery/Historic Building
- Ruin
- Shinto
- Sikh
- Taoist
- Winery/Vineyard
- Zoo/Wildlife Sanctuary
- Other Sight

## Activities, Courses & Tours

- Bodysurfing
- Diving
- Canoeing/Kayaking
- Course/Tour
- Sento Hot Baths/Onsen
- Skiing
- Snorkelling
- Surfing
- Swimming/Pool
- Walking
- Windsurfing
- Other Activity

## Sleeping

- Sleeping
- Camping

## Eating

- Eating

## Drinking & Nightlife

- Drinking & Nightlife
- Cafe

## Entertainment

- Entertainment

## Shopping

- Shopping

## Information

- Bank
- Embassy/Consulate
- Hospital/Medical
- Internet
- Police
- Post Office
- Telephone
- Toilet
- Tourist Information
- Other Information

## Geographic

- Beach
- Hut/Shelter
- Lighthouse
- Lookout
- Mountain/Volcano
- Oasis
- Park
- Pass
- Picnic Area
- Waterfall

## Population

- Capital (National)
- Capital (State/Province)
- City/Large Town
- Town/Village

## Transport

- Airport
- Border crossing
- Bus
- Cable car/Funicular
- Cycling
- Ferry
- Metro/MTR/MRT station
- Monorail
- Parking
- Petrol station
- Skytrain/Subway station
- Taxi
- Train station/Railway
- Tram
- Underground station
- Other Transport

*Note: Not all symbols displayed above appear on the maps in this book*

## Routes

- Tollway
- Freeway
- Primary
- Secondary
- Tertiary
- Lane
- Unsealed road
- Road under construction
- Plaza/Mall
- Steps
- Tunnel
- Pedestrian overpass
- Walking Tour
- Walking Tour detour
- Path/Walking Trail

## Boundaries

- International
- State/Province
- Disputed
- Regional/Suburb
- Marine Park
- Cliff
- Wall

## Hydrography

- River, Creek
- Intermittent River
- Canal
- Water
- Dry/Salt/Intermittent Lake
- Reef

## Areas

- Airport/Runway
- Beach/Desert
- Cemetery (Christian)
- Cemetery (Other)
- Glacier
- Mudflat
- Park/Forest
- Sight (Building)
- Sportsground
- Swamp/Mangrove

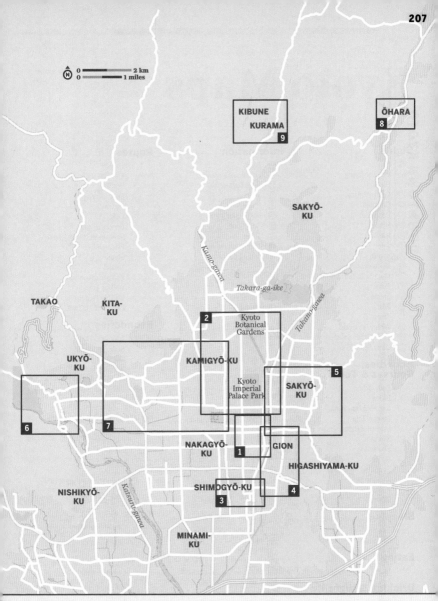

# MAP INDEX

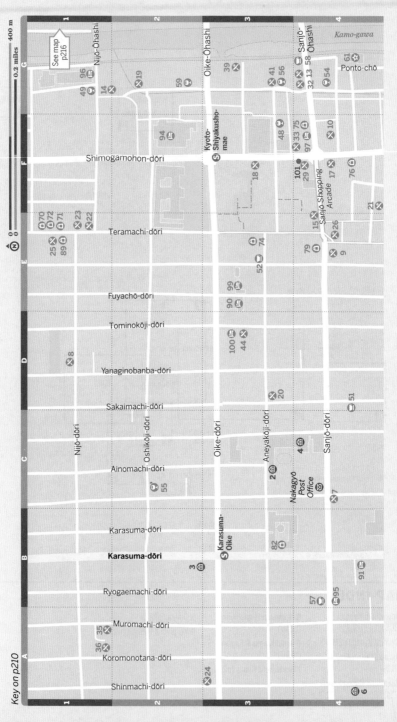

# DOWNTOWN KYOTO

Key on p210

See map p216

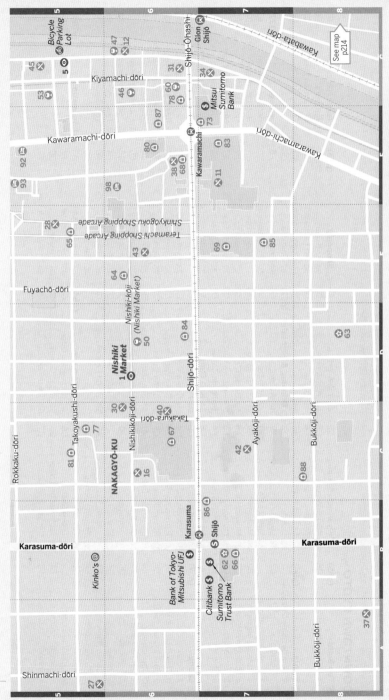

DOWNTOWN KYOTO

Bicycle Parking Lot

47
12
5
45
53
Kiyamachi-dōri
46
31
34
60
78
87
73
Mitsui Sumitomo Bank
Shijō-Ohashi
Gion Shijō
Kawabata-dōri
See map p214
Kawaramachi-dōri
80
83
Kawaramachi
38
68
11
Kawaramachi-dōri
92
93
98
28
Shinkyōgoku Shopping Arcade
Teramachi Shopping Arcade
65
43
69
85
64
Fuyachō-dōri
Nishiki-kōji (Nishiki Market)
50
84
63
Nishiki Market
1
30
40
Takakura-dōri
Nishikikōji-dōri
67
81
77
Takoyakushi-dōri
Rokkaku-dōri
NAKAGYŌ-KU
16
42
Ayakōji-dōri
Bukkōji-dōri
88
86
Karasuma
Shijō
Karasuma-dōri
Kinko's
Bank of Tokyo-Mitsubishi UFJ
Citibank
Sumitomo Trust Bank
62
66
Karasuma-dōri
37
Shinmachi-dōri
27

# KYOTO STATION AREA

See map p214

Sayamachi-dōri

Kawabata-dōri

Shichijō Shichijō

Shichijō-Ōhashi

Kamo-gawa

Shiokōji-bashi

Shichijō-dōri

**Kawaramachi-dōri**

Kawaramachi-dōri

Shimojuzuyachō-dōri

Shōsei-en

5

Takakura-dōri

24

Higashinotōin-dōri

15

26

**Karasuma-dōri**

Karasuma-dōri

21

Kyoto Station
Taxi Stand (North)

Kyoto Station
Taxi Stand (South)

10

32

13 18

3 31

33

Kyoto

22

1

Shiokōji-dōri

Muromachi-dōri

35

Kyoto Central
Post Office

29 12 30 17

Kyoto

2

Kintetsu

Kyoto

Kyoto

37

Tops
Café

23

Shōmen-dōri

Kitakōji-dōri

Shichijō-dōri

27

Bicycle
Parking
Lot

6

36

7

11

Higashinakasuji-dōri

8

34

Hachijō-dōri

25

28

16 9

20 19

14

Horikawa-dōri

**SHIMOGYŌ-KU**

4

Ōmiya-dōri

Umekōji-
kōen

Hachijō-dōri

## KYOTO STATION AREA

SOUTHERN HIGASHIYAMA

0   400 m
0   0.2 miles

**A**

Sanjō Shopping Arcade

See map p208

Magohashi-dōri

Sanjō-dōri

Sanjō

Sanjō-Ōhashi

Nawate-dōri

Ponto-chō

Kiyamachi-dōri

Furumonzen-dōri

Shinmonzen-dōri

**SHINBASHI**

Shimbashi-dōri

Kiri-dōshi

Shijō-Ōhashi

Shijō-dōri

Kawaramachi

Gion-Shijō

**GION**

Hanami-kōji

Yamatooji-dōri

Kawaramachi-dōri

Kawabata-dōri

Miyagawacho-dōri

Takase-gawa

Kamo-gawa

Ebisu-jinja

Yasaka-dōri

Kiyomizu Gojō

Gojō-Ōhashi

Gojō-dōri

Kawabata-dōri

Toiyamachi-dōri

Sayamachi-dōri

Yamatooji-dōri

Higashioji-dōri

Gojō-dōri

Shibutani-dōri

Shichijō

See map p212

Shiokōji-bashi

Shichijō-dōri

Shiokōji-dōri

**B**

**Sanjō Keihan**

Sanjō-Keihan Bus Terminal

Hanami-kōji

Higashioji-dōri

41  40 27

34

26

56  32
50  30  20
19  33
39  17  35
45  47
37  14
5
16
Ninen-zaka

10

46
48  Gojō-zaka Bus Stop
55  4

7

49
11

28
36  44
13

38
52  25
42
53
18
31  23
43  21
29

**C**

15  S  **Higashiyama**
54

See map p216

24  Sanjō-dōri

12

**Chion-in**  1

51

Maruyama-kōen

8

**HIGASHIYAMA-KU**
Higashi-Ōtani

22

**Gion** 2  6

Ishibei-kōji

9

Kiyomizu-michi

Chawan-zaka

Gojō-zaka

**Kiyomizu-dera**  3

**D**

# SOUTHERN HIGASHIYAMA

Key on p218

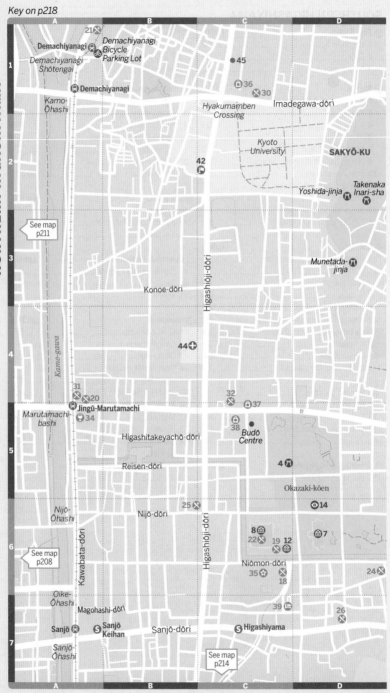

21

Demachiyanagi
Demachiyanagi
Bicycle
Parking Lot

Demachiyanagi
Shōtengai

Demachiyanagi

Kamo-
Ōhashi

45

36
30

Hyakumamben
Crossing

Imadegawa-dōri

Kyoto
University

SAKYŌ-KU

42

See map
p211

Yoshida-jinja

Takenaka
Inari-sha

Munetada-
jinja

Higashiōji-dōri

Konoe-dōri

44

31
20

Jingū-Marutamachi
34

Marutamachi-
bashi

32

37

Higashitakeyachō-dōri

38

Budō
Centre

Reisen-dōri

4

Okazaki-kōen

Nijō-
Ōhashi

25

14

Nijō-dōri

Higashiōji-dōri

See map
p208

8
22
19 12

Niōmon-dōri

35
18

7

24

Oike-
Ōhashi

Magohashi-dōri

39

26

Sanjō

Sanjō
Keihan

Sanjō-dōri

Higashiyama

Sanjō-
Ōhashi

See map
p214

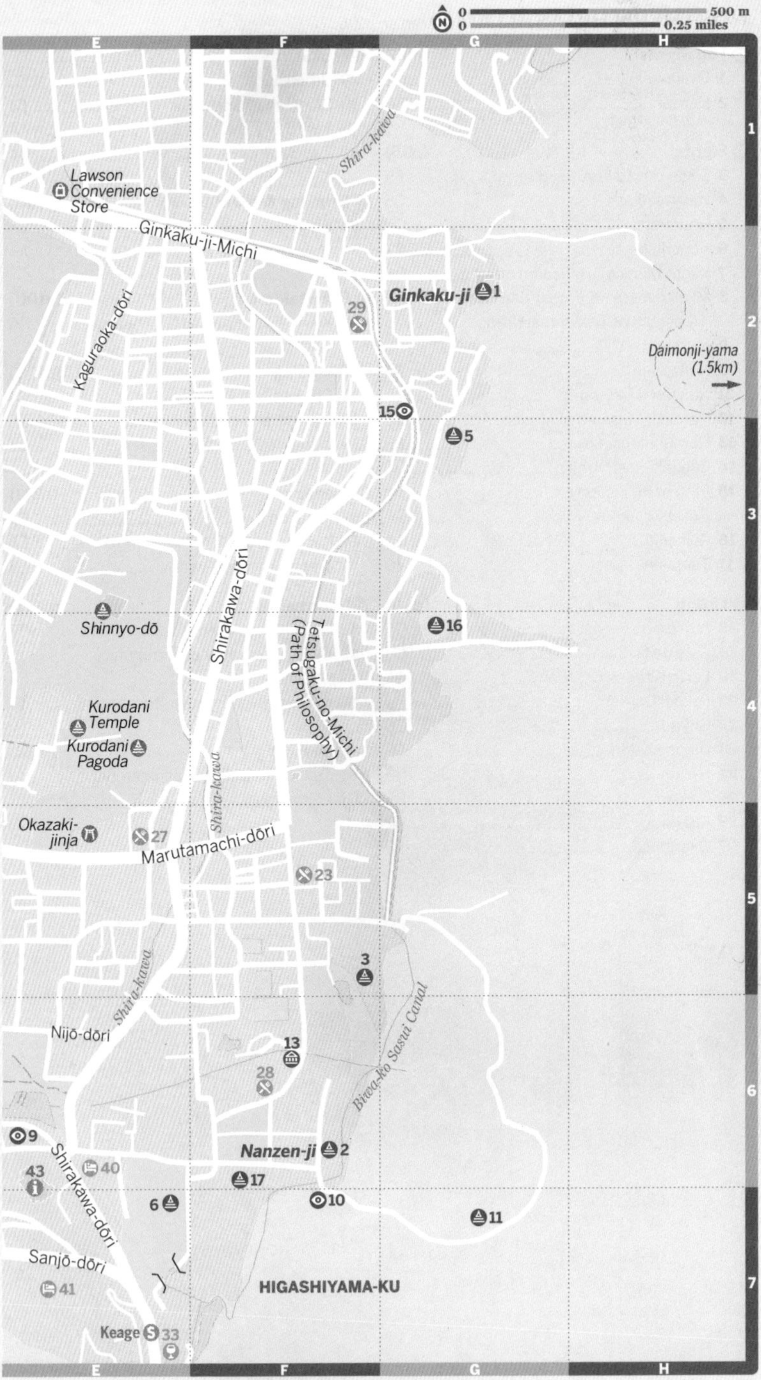
NORTHERN HIGASHIYAMA
0 500 m
0 0.25 miles
E
F
G
H
1
2
3
4
5
6
7
Lawson Convenience Store
Ginkaku-ji-Michi
Shira-kawa
Ginkaku-ji 1
29
Kaguraoka-dōri
Daimonji-yama (1.5km)
15
5
Shirakawa-dōri
Tetsugaku-no-Michi (Path of Philosophy)
Shinnyo-dō
16
Kurodani Temple
Kurodani Pagoda
Shira-kawa
Okazaki-jinja
27
Marutamachi-dōri
23
Shira-kawa
3
Nijō-dōri
13
28
Biwa-ko Sosui Canal
9
Shirakawa-dōri
40
43
Nanzen-ji 2
17
6
10
11
Sanjō-dōri
41
HIGASHIYAMA-KU
Keage
33

**ARASHIYAMA & SAGANO**

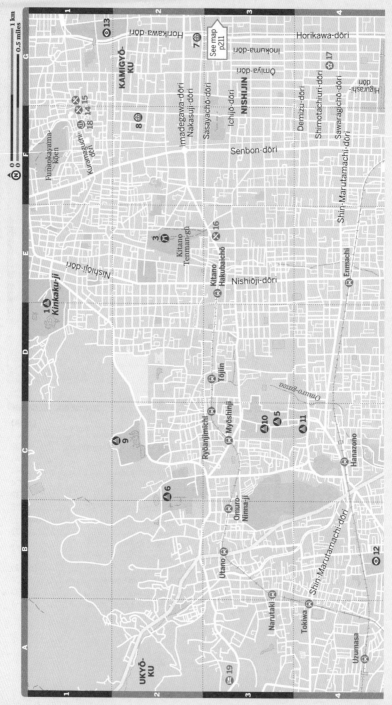

# NORTHWEST KYOTO

0.5 miles
1 km

G 1

◉ 13

Horikawa-dōri

KAMIGYŌ-KU

7 🏯

Horikawa-dōri

See map p211

Inokuma-dōri

Omiya-dōri

NISHIJIN

Ichijō-dōri

Imadegawa-dōri

Nakasuji-dōri

Sasayachō-dōri

8 🏯

Senbon-dōri

17 ✚

Demizu-dōri

Shimotachiuri-dōri

Sawaragichō-dōri

Higurashi-dōri

Shin-Marutamachi-dōri

Funaokayama-kōen

18 14 15 ✕✕✕

Kuramaguchi-dōri

F

Nishioji-dōri

3 🏯
Kitano Tenman-gū

✕ 16

E

Kitano Hakubaichō 🚉

Nishiōji-dōri

Emmachi 🚉

1 🏯 **Kinkaku-ji**

D

Tōji-in 🚉

Myōshinji 🚉

Omuro-gawa

Ryōanjimichi 🚉

9 🔺

△ 10  △ 5

△ 11

Hanazono 🚉

C

6 🔺

Omuro-Ninna-ji 🚉

Utano 🚉

12 ◉

B

Shin-Marutamachi-dōri

Narutaki 🚉

Tokiwa 🚉

Uzumasa 🚉

UKYŌ-KU

19 🔺

A

**NORTHWEST KYOTO**

# ŌHARA

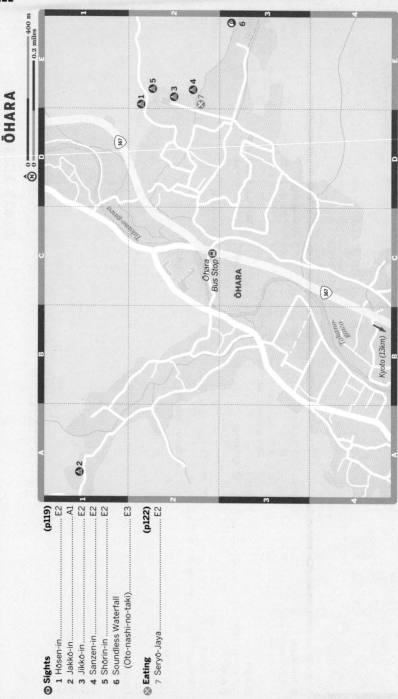

0 0.2 miles
0 400 m

# KURAMA & KIBUNE

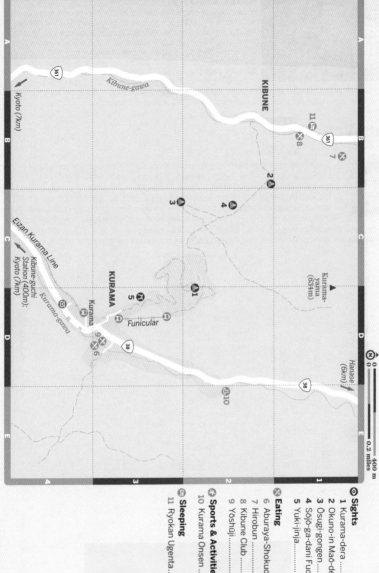

# Our Story

A beat-up old car, a few dollars in the pocket and a sense of adventure. In 1972 that's all Tony and Maureen Wheeler needed for the trip of a lifetime – across Europe and Asia overland to Australia. It took several months, and at the end – broke but inspired – they sat at their kitchen table writing and stapling together their first travel guide, *Across Asia on the Cheap*. Within a week they'd sold 1500 copies. Lonely Planet was born.

Today, Lonely Planet has offices in Franklin, London, Melbourne, Oakland, Beijing and Delhi, with more than 600 staff and writers. We share Tony's belief that 'a great guidebook should do three things: inform, educate and amuse'.

# Our Writer

## Chris Rowthorn

Chris Rowthorn has been based in Kyoto since 1992. He became a regional correspondent for *The Japan Times* in 1995 and joined Lonely Planet in 1996. He's worked on Lonely Planet's *Japan*, *Kyoto*, *Hiking in Japan* and *Tokyo* guidebooks. He speaks and reads Japanese fluently and has appeared on local TV to introduce secret temples in Kyoto. Chris's wife is from Kyoto's Arashiyama district and his two children are proudly multicultural. Chris runs Chris Rowthorn Tours (www.chrisrowthorn.com), which offers private tours and consulting about Kyoto and the rest of Japan. He also curates www.insidekyoto.com, his personal blog about the city of Kyoto.

**Published by Lonely Planet Publications Pty Ltd**
ABN 36 005 607 983
6th edition – August 2015
ISBN 978 1 74220 995 1
© Lonely Planet 2015   Photographs © as indicated 2015
10 9 8 7 6 5 4 3 2 1
Printed in China

Although the authors and Lonely Planet have taken all reasonable care in preparing this book, we make no warranty about the accuracy or completeness of its content and, to the maximum extent permitted, disclaim all liability arising from its use.